# Claude Rains

ALSO BY JOHN T. SOISTER

*Of Gods and Monsters: A Critical Guide to Universal Studios' Science Fiction, Horror and Mystery Films, 1929–1939*

McFarland, 1999

# Claude Rains

*A Comprehensive Illustrated Reference
to His Work in Film, Stage, Radio,
Television and Recordings*

*by* John T. Soister

*with* JoAnna Wioskowski
*Foreword by* Jessica Rains

McFarland & Company, Inc., Publishers
*Jefferson, North Carolina, and London*

COVER: Publicity shot of Claude Rains in *The Unsuspected* (1947)
FRONTISPIECE: Rains as Faulkland in *The Rivals* (1925). *Courtesy Jessica Rains*

**Library of Congress Cataloguing-in-Publication Data**

Soister, John T., 1950–
    Claude Rains : a comprehensive illustrated reference to his work in film, stage, radio, television and recordings / by John T. Soister with JoAnna Wioskowski ; foreword by Jessica Rains.
        p. cm.
    Dicography: p.
    Includes bibliographical references and index.
    ISBN 0-7864-0726-3 (case binding : 50# alkaline paper) ∞
    1. Rains, Claude, 1889–1967.   I. Wioskowski, JoAnna, 1971–   .
II. Title.
PN2287.R225S66   1999
791.43'028'092
[B]—DC21

99-16976
CIP

British Library Cataloguing-in-Publication data are available

Manufactured in the United States of America

*McFarland & Company, Inc., Publishers*
   *Box 611, Jefferson, North Carolina 28640*
     *www.mcfarlandpub.com*

For my sister, Cheryl, and my brother, Bill, who put up with me and my
    collection of Claude Rains stuff when we were all young;
and for Dad, who'd look at the stacks of stills, lobby cards, and pressbooks,
    and wonder when his firstborn was going to grow out of this phase;
and for Mom and Nana, who made the entire point moot by throwing
    everything out.

—JOHN T. SOISTER


Dedicated with love to the usual suspects: my parents—Frank and Joyce
    Wioskowski—the coolest parents an offspring could ask for;
my grandmas—Jennie Vasile and Carrie Wioskowski—two great ladies who
    are now real pros with Claude Rains trivia;
my mentor—Don Leifert—who encouraged me from the start;
my dear friends, a group always willing to lend a hand during this project
    and all prime examples of the true meaning of friendship.

—JOANNA WIOSKOWSKI

# Acknowledgments

While not "years in the making" or featuring "a cast of thousands," this book was a long time in coming and many people helped make it as comprehensive as it is.

Jessica Rains not only gave this volume her blessing, she trusted me with invaluable family photos, helped wash her father's mythos clean of myth, straightened out any number of iffy items in the course of the text, and then wrote a wonderful foreword. Heartfelt thanks, Jessica (and Jack, too).

Thanks are due to Mike Barson, to Philisse Barrows and James McKenzie of the Westport County Playhouse, to JoAnne Barry and the Philadelphia Orchestra, and to Frank Bresee. I'm also grateful to Louise Bowers, the librarian at Schuylkill Haven High School, who went out of her way to comb the state of Pennsylvania for the books I needed to consult in order to write this one.

Buddy Barnett, you are a gem.

Acclaimed film historian Richard Bojarski has never turned down a call for help, and this time was no exception. Thanks for the many kindnesses, Bojak.

Mary Corliss of the Museum of Modern Art must have thumbed through every Claude Rains photograph still in the place at least a dozen times. She is witty and warm and, if the speed and care with which she dealt with my requests is any indication, she does the work of three people. And her husband likes movies, too.

Many, *many* thanks to Robert G. Dickson, who again has taken a project of mine under his wing, provided loads of illustrations and information, and cheerfully offered

his very educated opinion on most of the chapters herein.

British Rains aficionado Susan Duic provided a ton of rare photographs, theater programs, and ephemera from her incredible collection, and then trundled about London and environs interviewing folk and tracking down details. There aren't enough thanks out there where Susan is concerned.

Jacqui Etheridge and Tessa Forbes of the British Film Institute are delightful and dedicated women, and some of the more insightful items herein came from their respective departments at the BFI. Thanks, too, to Bruce Hershenson and to the Morris Everett Collection, which also came up with some knockout graphics.

Rick Farmiloe is an enormously talented artist, an obsessed 16mm film collector, and a hell of a nice guy. Thanks, buddy.

Richard and Robert Frantz (and the rest of the gang) at Kinko's made the inclusion of so many rare and unique photographs in this book affordable. Thanks to them, copying and filing illustrations was a joy rather than a trial.

Diane Freiberger and Margaret Groer of Glen Mills, Pennsylvania, graciously shared facts and reminiscences about Rains with the author, and another round of thanks is due here.

Richard Gordon is a wealth of anecdotal information, and I'm indebted to him once again.

Thanks to Karen Jordan of the Westport Public Library Research Division; to John Kinsey, Co-director of Codes for Thronbury

Township; and to Cathy Zurow of the Westport News.

The LeMay Poster Company very generously loaned out photographic materials to someone they had never met—the author—merely because they were asked. That was very gracious of you, Harry LeMay; may your patronage increase.

My old friend Alan Levine did likewise, and not only is Alan one of the most honest and reasonable memorabilia dealers out there, he's one of the nicest. He's also been around forever and I hope it stays that way.

Claire Locke, the Interim Research Librarian at the Rare Book, Manuscript, and Special Collections Library of Duke University (whew!), went out of her way several times to look stuff up and fax it over in the twinkling of an eye.

The Mandelbaum brothers at Photofest are invaluable. They and their staff are unfailingly accommodating, meticulous, and patient. Thank you, Howard and Ronald.

Madeline F. Matz of the Library of Congress deserves more than just thanks for all the assistance she's given me here and elsewhere. She is one of the treasures of the Library, and I am deeply in her debt.

Thanks, too, to Jan McKee and Brian Cornell of the Recorded Music Division of the LoC; they gave structure and substance to a wearying and haphazard quest. Ditto to old time radio maven and author Martin Grams, Jr., Ike Morrison, Milt Larsen, Joyce E. Ashcroft and Jorry Fitzpatrick.

Actresses Joanna Miles and Kim Hunter set me straight on Claude's later theatrics, while Sir John Gielgud did likewise on the RADA days.

Jonathan Rosenthal of the Museum of Television and Radio must have spent days tracking down pertinent Rains credits and minutiae for this project, and the chapters on those media are as good as they are only because of his help. Thank you, Jonathan.

Blackie and Alicia Seymour of the Pentagram Library came through for me again—I wish I knew a fraction of what Blackie has forgotten about "the industry"—and not just on the Universal titles, either. What a great couple.

Susan G. Williamson (the head librarian at the Annenberg School of Communication) and Roberta Zonghi (curator and department head of the Department of Rare Books of the Boston Public Library) also unearthed some choice items, and I'd like to acknowledge their kind assistance.

Film historians Don Leifert and Bill Littman also left their tracks here; thank you, gentlemen.

To my wife, Nancy, and my kids—Jake, Katelyn, and Jeremy—who never once (to my face, at any rate) questioned my sanity when I began to wander around the house like Marley's ghost, peering intently at nothing in particular, while debating time sequences or contradictory items of information with myself; I'm b-a-a-a-a-ck.

Thanks also to Lisa Shell, Michelle Wilkinson, Christie Shell, Lawrence Guy "Bud" Hogsett III, the Welsh family (Darryl the Elder, Darryl the Younger, Donna the Only), Michael Henry, and the folks at Regester Photo.

Special thanks to Susan Armstrong (of our neighbor to the north), who conjured up several arcane references, which she zoomed (deadline, you know) cross-continent via both fax and e-mail so that they could grace the pages that follow. Above and beyond the call of duty, Susan.

Finally, to my research colleague, planning partner, and fellow Rains fanatic, JoAnna Wioskowski: your ineffable good spirits were matched only by the constant cornucopia of data and goodies which filtered through your hands and into mine. You were JoAnna on the spot with anything I needed, from tapes to stills to movie-star portraits on Dixie Cup lids, and I hope that this volume is just the first of many we work on together. Here's looking at you, kid.

To all those who egged us on, wished us well, or raised a glass to one of the finest actors ever to memorize sides, we hope you enjoy the fruits of your enthusiasm.

# Contents

# Contents

# Foreword

Claude Rains was an enigma. As a father, he was just a father—to me, he was neither an actor, nor a very complicated man; in retrospect, though, I can see that he was both. He was loving, kind, and proud. He could also be stern when he thought he ought to be stern, but he was never stern very successfully; behind the words was an odd twinkle in his eye.

He was crazy about me, and I about him.

His background belied the characters he played, who were usually haughty, elegant, debonair—and always with a stiff back and that beautiful mid–Atlantic accent. Not so, not any of it.

He was born William Claude Rains in 1889 on (in his words) "the wrong side of the river Thames" to a father who was a "jack of all trades" (and, probably, a master of none) and a mother who took in boarders to support the family. There were 12 children, nine of whom died from poverty-related illnesses. My father had had a Cockney accent so strong that I couldn't understand him when he sang his old Cockney songs to me. He also had a stutter and a further speech impediment which caused him to call himself Willie Wains.

He left school after the second grade to sell papers so he could bring the pennies and halfpennies home to his mother. Singing in the Palm Street Church choir also brought him a few pence to take home, and from there he was taken to the Haymarket Theatre, so he could run around onstage during *Sweet Nell of Old Drury*. His advancement in the theater was neither fast nor easy, but it was a linear move: from call boy ("Five

"Corn always tastes better if you steal it," said Mark Twain. "Or if you grow it yourself," said Farmer Rains. (*left to right*) Claude, Jennifer (later Jessica), and Frances Rains. *Courtesy Jessica Rains*

1

**Occasionally, an industry affair couldn't be ignored. Here, Frances is at the front, while Claude is where he's happiest—with his daughter, Jennifer. Director Michael Curtiz is on the far left.** *Courtesy Jessica Rains*

minutes, Miss Tree") to prompter, to stage manager, to understudy, and then, from small parts and good reviews to large parts. He made his film debut when he was not quite 30, and his first successful film 13 years later.

The transformation to the man I knew took place out of base necessity. When my father was in his teens, Sir Herbert Beerbohm-Tree called him into his office and told him if he was to be an actor, he needed to get rid of his Cockney accent and his speech problems. Sir Herbert gave my father money to buy elocution books. Claude went home and read and practiced. He trilled his tongue in front of the mirror; he learned to place his tongue just so to say his Rs; he listened and emulated a proper En-

glish accent; and he began to read everything he could get his hands on.

He became the man I knew. He remade himself, and, I assure you, the makeover was genuine. His past was relegated to the past, although he never forgot it. He was frugal to a fault and always managed the books for the farm I grew up on. We raised our own produce; my mother churned butter from the cream atop the milk; I gathered the eggs; and my father plowed the fields and cultivated the vegetable garden. To him, owning that farm in Pennsylvania was the most important part in his life, next to us and acting. The moment each job in Hollywood was over, the three of us boarded the Super Chief and fled back to Chester County, Pennsylvania.

Claude was not enamored of Hollywood life and was not interested in his celebrity status. He rarely attended social functions and kept me away from them to such an extent that when I went to camp at the age of ten, I told my campmates my father was a farmer. His close friends in Hollywood were few: Bette Davis, Vincent Sherman, Ronald Neame, Albert Dekker. Whenever Bette Davis would come to the farm to visit for a week, my father would tell me to keep it under my hat; he didn't want the local papers making a fuss.

He took his craft seriously. He would memorize the entire script before rehearsal started on the play or shooting commenced on the film, and he'd immerse himself in the character he was playing. As he'd drive me the ten miles from our farm to my school in Pennsylvania, I would sit with the script in my lap and feed him his lines—over and over and over again. Claude loved the process, loved the work; he rarely, however, saw one of his finished films.

When I was ten, *The Invisible Man* came to Downingtown, some 15 years after it had been made, and my father and I went off to see the movie together. Claude wrapped a scarf around his face, not only because a winter wind was blowing, but also because he didn't want anyone to recognize him. He hadn't reckoned on that famous voice of his. As soon as he opened his mouth at the ticket booth, the cashier—who was also the theater manager—realized with whom he was dealing and handed over free tickets. My father insisted on paying, but gave in when he saw that the discussion was attracting more attention than it was worth.

During the film, my father explained that they had somehow made him invisible by putting straws in his nose and mouth while they covered his face with plaster. On the way home, he told me how the process had terrified him because the sensation reminded him so of being in the trenches during World War I, when he had been gassed and had lost 90 percent of the vision in his right eye.

In 1944, my father was signed to play the part of Caesar in Gabriel Pascal's production of George Bernard Shaw's *Caesar and Cleopatra*, which was to be shot in England. Filming started less than a week after D-Day, and buzz-bombs were flying all over London. Claude had flown over from Newfoundland in a British bomber, his suitcase crammed full of nylon stockings for his friends' wives. (Whenever I find myself thinking how crazy it was—my father risking his life just to play a role—I remember how he once shrugged as he explained, simply, that "Actors are actors.") Every day he sent me a postcard, and every week a little children's book would arrive in the mail. I still have those postcards and those Mary Bear books.

For the first few days after his arrival, he was put up at London's Savoy Hotel. A little unsure of the correct procedure, he asked the clerk just exactly what he should do during an air raid; he was instructed to climb into bed and to cover his head and his vitals with pillows. On the first day of shooting, a limousine was sent to bring my father to the set from the hotel, and, stepping quickly into the car to avoid the debris that was falling everywhere from the skies, he wasn't entirely taken aback to hear the doorman—imperturbable and *veddy* British—politely call after him, "I do hope you'll have a very pleasant day."

London being too dangerous, Claude was moved shortly thereafter to "Great Fosters," an old inn outside the city. Every night, he would hear a hell of a commotion in the hallway outside his room; from the sound of it, someone was leaping wildly up and down the passageway. One night, my father opened the door and peered out. There, in the moonlight, was a man—obviously quite mad—pirouetting frantically along the length of the corridor, while dressed only in a white nightshirt. The next morning Claude broached the subject with the concierge and was told that the madman was the great Nijinsky, who, at night—when it was quiet and dark—would perform for "the ghosts."

Claude was a great storyteller. I heard these stories—and many more—often. He'd settle in a large armchair with a drink, and, once he'd get started, the tales just kept coming. He was an avid American, a faithful husband, and he drank with the best of them.

And, just like most actors, he died waiting for his agent to call.

JESSICA RAINS
*November 1998*

# Introduction

Robbin Coons—in a character study written in the mid-forties for *Motion Picture* magazine—hit the nail on the head:

The keys to male stardom are many. Van Johnson's is open, appealing boyishness. Errol Flynn's is dash and manly beauty. Charles Boyer's is urbane magnetism. Often a handsome profile and physique are sufficient to win a place among the screen's elite. But Claude Rains is different.

Coons' point, of course, was that Rains—among the greatest character actors the stage and screen have ever produced—was somewhat less than physically prepossessing. Not that this stood in his way. Albeit too short to be a conventional leading man (he traded scripted *bons mots* with numerous willowy ingenues while perched on a concealed box), he possessed an aura which sparked a half-dozen marriages and God only knows how many inter-marital dalliances. In an interview conducted with the authors of *Universal Horrors*, actress Susanna Foster remembered the middle-aged actor as having " ...a vicious little twinkle in his eye that was so cute, "while Sir John Gielgud—a student of Rains' in both men's pre-screen years—admitted enviously that "most of the girls [in his acting class at the Royal Academy of Dramatic Arts] were in love with him." Not bad for an ex–Cockney who regarded his short, stocky frame as the result of suffering from "duck's disease."

Rains' *je ne sais quoi* never had as much to do with glamour or sex appeal as with panache. Early in his film career, when the cockily insouciant actor frequently enjoyed top billing, he would easily steal the thunder from the nominal hero, when not (albeit much less frequently) handling the heroics himself. As he grew older (he was already 43 when *The Invisible Man* opened), he spent less of his time struggling to win the heroine honestly and more of it scheming to bankrupt or deflower her. Although Rains had enjoyed a splendid reputation in the legitimate theater before "appearing" as H. G. Wells' tragic, invisible protagonist, it was his burgeoning film career which made him a household name. Regular moviegoers came to discover that few featured players could cast leads into the shadows with so little effort as did Claude Rains.

According to Ira Konigsberg (*The Complete Film Dictionary*), a character actor is "A performer who specializes in secondary roles of a well-defined, often humorous nature." While there are very few who would argue Claude Rains' being considered among the premier character men of the silver screen, fewer still would regard the lion's share of the actor's roles as "humorous." Sardonic, perhaps; but humorous? Unless the role called for it, there was seldom that "vicious little twinkle" in Rains' eye on-screen. In fact, nearly all the parts he enacted between his sound film debut in 1933 and his de facto last performance in 1965 demanded that he be Machiavellian rather than mischievous, lustful rather than lusty; he was far more often headed for a jugular vein than a jocular note.

Unlike other character specialists, whose features flouted greasepaint or whose quirks

**Dapper in stripes and plaids, clutching his pipe, standing on the threshold of a life in the movies.** *The Wioskowski Collection*

defied the best screenwriting in the business (Walter Slezak's particular charm was forever remaining Walter Slezak, no matter what the charade), Claude Rains *became* John Jasper, Louis Renault, Julius Caesar, or the Devil himself. Sharp-eyed fans, ever on the lookout for the flaw in the diamond, were moved by his performances without being distracted by his technique. The actor could lay bare his soul with the twitch of an eyebrow or a casual shift in his velvet tone, undermining through nuance alone any pretense at the integrity he had so masterfully exuded up to that point. As his cads and blackguards ran the gamut from subtle malfeasance to bravura barnstorming, Rains found himself comfortably nestled in the ranks of the sundry "Men You Love to Hate."

For all this, Rains refused to be typecast as the heavy. His Adam Lemp, perennial dad to the Lane Sisters (and Gale Page), was really the prototype of the lovable but inept father figures of the fifties TV sitcoms. His Captain Renault displayed the good sense

(and belated patriotic conviction) to walk in the company of Rick Blaine, his Sir John Talbot was shaken to the core by his son's lycanthropy, and his Job Skeffington was not so much sinner as sinned against. Purely humorous roles may have eluded the suave actor, but his reading of Mr. Jordan was not without its wry moments, his Professor Challenger was bluff to the point of being bizarre, and his opening vignette in Republic's *Lisbon* must have given him and anyone ever nettled by nature's frequent intrusions a smug and hearty grin.

*Caveat lector.*

Claude Rains was an intensely private man who usually avoided the Hollywood publicity mill. Most of the interviews he gave were in support of a specific project with which he was involved and, apart from seizing every opportunity to brag about the daughter he loved so much, he usually stuck rather close to the circumstances surrounding the particular picture or play under discussion. Empirical evidence suggests that idle chatter was not the actor's style, although, pointed in the right direction—say, towards theater or farming—and allowed to build up a head of steam, he could be as expansive as anyone. Very little of his private life was fair game; to discover what lay behind the curtain, interviewers had to do their homework. Vincent Sherman, who as a young man had acted with Rains and who later came to direct him in both *Saturday's Children* (1940) and *Mr. Skeffington* (1944), admitted that this was no easy task; "Most of our conversations, then and later, were about theater and films—he was a man of mystery otherwise, who guarded his privacy even in those early years."

As he grew older, Rains showed a tendency to embellish in each retelling the stories he had already disseminated to the public. While this is hardly a weakness peculiar to thespians (or fishermen), it does make for some significant head-scratching on the part of researchers. In addition, studio puff pieces have never been trustworthy, data found in the various "profiles" published hither and thither by fan magazines are frequently at odds with bits of information put forward by Himself in the occasional interview, and newspaper articles—whether hot off the wire for national editions or painstakingly transcribed by neighborhood journalists for local publications—contain errata, typos, misspellings, misstatements, and other gaffes.

Please note that the chapter on Rains' biography is just one part of the cohesive whole and must be taken together with the entries on his work. Attempting to mention each and every item in his long and varied professional catalogue within the framework of a thumbnail biography would pay them poor tribute, while citing his various accomplishments as they occurred and then repeating them—polished, accredited, and ready for framing—in the end pages would make for appalling redundancy, an overlong appendix, and an ill-balanced book.

Essentially, this book is a celebration of the man's film mastery. JoAnna Wioskowski and I have opted to devote most of our energies to peering closely at the medium with which the actor is most closely associated by his many fans. Since Rains' motion pictures are almost always and everywhere in evidence, we thought that our efforts would be best appreciated in the area in which they could be best applied.

To all of Claude Rains' countless fans, who have marveled long and hard at the actor's larger-than-life flair for the dramatic, and plain, old-fashioned talent, we hope (with apologies to Alan Jay Lerner) that you'll enjoy this hymn to him. To all those movie lovers who are just beginning to appreciate the power of that eyebrow, the sway of that charm, or the allure of that voice: relax and enjoy yourselves. Who knows? This could be the beginning of a beautiful friendship.

JOHN T. SOISTER
*Orwigsburg, Pennsylvania*
*Summer 1999*

---

The journey into the world of Claude Rains has indeed been an interesting one and every stop that John Soister and I have made along the way has been fascinating. We have made many new friends during our sojourn and all of them share with us a great enthusiasm for the actor whom we celebrate in this volume. Each person who has given us his or her time and who has shown an interest in this project has contributed to its success. Many have been unusually generous, sharing materials and insights, and they have added to the scope of our book. To John and me, Claude Rains fans are the greatest in the world, and we thank you.

We hope our labor of love will not only stir the pot of fond memories of Claude Rains, the actor, but will move us all a step closer to appreciating Claude Rains, the man.

JOANNA WIOSKOWSKI
*Baltimore*
*Summer 1999*

# Biography

On Sunday, November 10, 1889, with Queen Victoria on the throne and the British Empire the mightiest the world had ever seen, Frederick and Emily Eliza (Cox) Rains welcomed their son, William Claude, into their midst. The latest arrival would be tallied as but one of a dozen, most of whom would perish in infancy from diseases usually associated with extreme poverty. Although folks in the Camberwell section of London didn't share in the prosperity or opportunity the times afforded to the moneyed class, the family rejoiced even as the larder shrank. With an additional mouth to feed, Fred had to expand his efforts at finding work—he had already tried his hand at everything from constructing boilers to instructing boxers—if ends were to come within distance of reaching.

As a youngster, William Claude was strangely silent; so much so, in fact, that the local doctor could only recommend that the family starve the boy in the hope that "When he's hungry, he'll ask for what he wants." Either the threat of starvation or maturity finally opened that mouth; however, Fred and Eliza were disconcerted to hear their son refer to himself as "Willie Wains." The boy's broad Cockney accent was to be expected—Camberwell was quite a distance from Oxford—but when dropped "aitches" were augmented by the substitu-

**Claude's beloved mother, Emily Eliza Cox Rains, and his father, Fred Rains, whom Claude despised.** *Courtesy Jessica Rains*

tion of "W" for "R" and worsened by a pronounced stutter, the resultant mix was very much to be deplored. Since Fred couldn't afford to do other than deplore the situation, it was left for Claude to overcome his vocal afflictions on his own as he grew older.

When he was nine, Willie was sent off to live with his grandparents. While the home life in Kent was fine, there was trouble at school; Rains' speech problems made him the subject of his schoolmates' taunting and it wasn't long before he hopped it and began to spend more time roaming the streets of London than attending to his lessons. Befriended by a boy who sang in a local church choir, Rains mustered the nerve for an audition after the choirmaster himself came to troll for talent at the school. Apparently, there was money to be had for singing, and the soprano section quickly had

9

a new addition. Fred caught up with his son after a few weeks and gave him a good tanning for his truancy, but allowed him to remain part of the church group.

From the vantage point of history, it's clear that Fred's decision was providential; the church was to serve as his son's entrée to the stage. Julia Neilson was just then preparing to open in Paul Kester's *Sweet Nell of Old Drury*, and the production required a flock of street urchins for a crowd scene. Hence, quite a few of the choirmaster's charges made their collective debut at the *Theatre Royale* in Haymarket on August 31, 1900. For young Willie Wains, there was no turning back. By the age of 11 he had quit school with his parents' consent and was taken on as call-boy and page-boy at the *Duke of York's Theatre*. Not long after, a higher salary (the equivalent of two dollars, weekly) and a more prestigious assignment (*His Majesty's Theatre*) drew the journeyman call-boy away from the *Duke of York's*.

Rains' stay at *His Majesty's Theatre* proved to be an invaluable training ground for the future actor. He found a mentor in the person of Sir Herbert Beerbohm-Tree, whose troupe regarded the theater as its home base. Tree took a liking to young Willie and introduced him to the technical aspects of the industry. The youngster still dreamt of acting, but both he and Tree knew that the deadly combination of Cockney accent and pronounced speech impediment stood in the way. The impresario's generosity and the call-boy's self-discipline gradually overcame those handicaps, though, and by his mid-teens, Rains had not only been promoted to assistant stage manager, but was made a prompter as well. Since he quickly came to know all the lines, he was soon performing bits and small parts.

As it had with Tree, the *Theatre Royale* (aka the *Haymarket Theatre*) continued to figure big in the young actor's life. Separated by a tour of Australia with Sir Harley Granville-Barker's troupe were a pair of Haymarket productions penned by Lord Dunsany: *The God of the Mountain* (wherein,

having meanwhile attained his legal majority, *Claude* Rains made his adult acting debut) in 1911, and *The Golden Doom*, in November of the following year. Maurice Maeterlinck's fantasy, *The Blue Bird*, had been the main vehicle for that Australian tour (George Bernard Shaw's *You Never Can Tell* was the alternate) and, interestingly, the *Theatre Royale* company had recorded its production of the play on film for Gaumont Pictures only the year before. As the film is apparently lost, we have no way of knowing whether the young stage manager received his first on-screen credit at this point in his career. (Tree made *his* cinematic debut in 1911, top-lining the cast list of Barker Films' *Henry VIII* as Cardinal Wolsey.)

Coincidentally, during this period Fred had tired of teaching school—the latest in his succession of vocations—and had also turned to acting. At first just another in a string of jobs undertaken to keep bread on the table, the theater—and shortly thereafter, the cinema—became a passion with the elder Rains, much as it would with his son. In a February 17, 1951, interview published in *The New Yorker* magazine, son Claude reflected that his dad was "one of the first men in England to direct silent movies and one of the first to act in talkies." Indeed, Fred was in the director's chair, as well as appearing in front of the hand-cranked camera, as early as May 1910, when he began a year's worth of one- and two-reel comedy shorts for Acme Films.

From 1913 on, other playhouses would share the Rains presence with the *Haymarket*, and in 1914, Granville-Barker again enticed his favorite actor-cum–stage manager to go on tour. This time around, the troupe favored the Americans with Euripides' *Iphigenia in Taurus*, as well as the requisite Shaw offering, *Androcles and the Lion*. Kept terribly busy with myriad duties, Rains, now 24 years old and 5'6" in height, still found time to cultivate the attention of actress Isabel Jeans. It was a veritable whirlwind romance, culminating first in marriage, then in divorce, with everything over and done with before the 1918 signing of the Armistice.

With his country mobilized for the Great War, the dutiful Rains succumbed to the invitation of Lord Kitchener and enlisted in the army. Still, as per Katharine Porter (in "The Plow and the Star," *Collier's* magazine, November 19, 1938), he wasn't all that keen on being part of a brutal war:

I didn't want to get killed or kill anyone else. And a friend over there sent word he could get me a job where I wouldn't have to do either.

That friend was nowhere to be found when the Army asked the actor to join their number, so next up was the task of finding just the "right" regiment. Rains' flair for theatricality led him instinctively to the London Scottish, whose uniform was dominated by yards of tartan and a bloody impressive-looking kilt. Despite his early reservations about the war, Rains plunged with both feet into one of Britain's roughest regiments, even then winning renown as the "Ladies from Hell."

The good luck which had been his deserted him in 1917 when, at Vimy Ridge in northern France, Rains and his mates were subjected to heavy artillery bombardment and poison gas. One horror followed another. From an infirmary bed, he discovered that the voice to which he had devoted so many hours of arduous work was gone; his vocal chords had been paralyzed. And when the bandages were removed from his face, he found that he was almost totally blind in his right eye. Little by little, his capacity for speech returned, and, years later, the actor would attribute the huskiness of his unmistakable tone to the effects of the gas. His sightlessness was yet another handicap to be overcome, and virtually no one outside of his family or the circle of his most intimate friends would be aware of it during his lifetime.

While recovering, Rains gave some thought to making the army a lifelong career; according to some accounts, he was on his way to re-enlist when an old crony from the theater made him an offer he couldn't refuse. By March 1919, the greasepaint had already supplanted the blood in his veins, and the next few years would be spent variously in the company of Henry Ainley (with whom, in 1920, Rains would make his film debut in *Build Thy House*), Norman Mac-Dermott, and the *Everyman*

**Claude of the London Scottish— decorated for valor, commissioned because of bravery, blinded and rendered mute at Vimy Ridge.** *Courtesy Jessica Rains*

*Theatre.* Whereas his previous experiences with Shaw had been few and far between— small parts in the Granville-Barker tours and a perilous moment in which, as 16-year-old assistant stage manager for *The Admirable Bashful*, he had had to fetch a doctor for the stricken GBS—he soon became a Shavian specialist.

The year 1920 also witnessed Rains' marriage to actress Marie Hemingway; a divorce followed quickly. Finding short runs in the theater infinitely preferable to short spurts of matrimony, Rains set out to amass a peerless series of credits during the early twenties. His reputation grew and it wasn't long until he was offered a teaching position at London's prestigious Royal Academy of Dramatic Art. While his students included such future heavyweights as John Gielgud and Charles Laughton, his influence was also felt, in a decidedly different fashion, by many of the female members of his classes.

In 1924, the second year he was working as dramatics instructor, the heartthrob of the RADA married Beatrix Thompson, one of his students and herself the winner of the Academy's silver medal for being among its "most talented" performers. It would be a

**Still practicing his "aitches?" Claude would become as fervent an American and as devoted a Penn-sylvanian as he had been a Londoner.** *Courtesy Jessica Rains*

year of new associations. Norman MacDer-mott, founder and lifeblood of the *Every-man Theatre*, avidly sought Rains to join the new playhouse's resident troupe. The newly-wed's first appearance at the *Everyman* was as Napoleon Bonaparte in Shaw's *Man of Destiny*, and his presence in a half dozen subsequent productions helped keep the the-ater at capacity. While 1925's *Home Affairs* marked Rains' swan song at the *Everyman*, his friendship with Norman MacDermott would last a lifetime.

Late in 1926, Mrs. Rains ventured to New York City as the female lead in Basil Dean and Margaret Kennedy's *The Constant Nymph*; happy for his wife and content with

the secondary role of the butler, Rains quit RADA and went off with Beatrix. The move was motivated by more than the love he had for his bride, however. John Gielgud notes how

though he won praise from the critics for several years in plays of many kinds, Rains never achieved a big star position in London... "I can't eat my notices," he once said to me sadly, just be-fore he went away.... He left England to follow a long and distinguished career on Broadway....[1]

Playing butlers just didn't cut it, however, and within weeks, New York's theater-going public paid to see Claude Rains enact the title character in Henry Stillman's *Lally*. His impersonation of the bohemian composer won good notices, but was not of itself enough to keep the show from folding after 60 performances. Come September 1926, he was back in the *Nymph* company with the missus, but as the male lead, Lewis Dodd.

Next up for Mr. and Mrs. Rains was *Out of the Sea*, which was out of business by the end of the year. Beatrix's career slowed, while Claude's began to take off; the actor was invited to join New York City's unofficial "resident" company—the Theatre Guild. One production followed hot on the heels of another, and Beatrix and her husband agreed to separate, the actress returning to England where she labored to rekindle the spark of her career. Constant work was what Claude craved, and the variety of roles offered him by the Theatre Guild was very much to his liking. Also to his liking was the lovely Frances Propper, whom he first met while in Eugene O'Neill's *Marco Millions*.

All went well for a while, but in 1932 the Theatre Guild's future was beginning to look shaky, and the 43-year-old Rains found himself at an acting crossroads. Motion pictures might offer an alternative to unemployment, but he didn't see himself as a "collar ad" type and had little confidence in his physical appearance on camera. The Depression slowed new productions to a crawl, theaters closed for want of patronage, and the Theatre Guild temporarily disbanded. Apprehensive, Rains spent his life savings on a down payment on a small farm near Lambertville, New Jersey, figuring that if acting were no longer a viable vocation, he could always live on the crops he cultivated himself. When lightning destroyed his farmhouse, the actor entered a profound depression of his own.

The offer of a screen test at RKO temporarily lifted Rains' spirits; the studio was considering him for the part of Hilary Fairfield in the film adaptation of Clemence Dane's *A Bill of Divorcement*. As he had won good notices for the very same part back in 1921 and was allowed to select his own test material (he chose scenes from *The Man Who Reclaimed His Head*—his recent Broadway tour de force—and Shaw's *Man of Destiny*), things were looking up. Not familiar with any acting techniques specifically for use with sound motion pictures, however, he proceeded to overpower the camera and produced an almost surreal experience for the RKO executives. It was, in Rains' own words, "the worst screen test in the history of movie-making."

Out in Hollywood, James Whale got an eyeful of that RKO screen test. More importantly, he got an *earful*, and would settle for no voice other than Claude Rains' to articulate the swaddled ravings of *The Invisible Man*. The self-effacing actor later shared with interviewer Hubert Cole his initial reactions to Tinseltown's call:

I spurned their offers. They told me they wanted to take me away from my art, from the stage, to play in their beastly movies. I wouldn't listen; I resented the mere suggestion! Then they cabled me to say how much they would pay me and you couldn't see me for dust. I had my bags packed and was in Hollywood the next morning.
("Doesn't He Have Fun"; *Picturegoer* magazine, December 28, 1940)

Rains signed on for two pictures with Universal, which also optioned his services for a term of seven years. *The Invisible Man* was a huge success. Rains' first sound movie role had won him (or his voice, at any rate) great acclaim, and had landed in the ninth slot of *The New York Times'* "Ten Best Films" list for 1933. Whale's gamble on Rains had paid off in spades; the picture was a blockbuster, breaking box-office records and spraying studio ledgers with black ink. In a move that was as abrupt as it was inexplicable, Universal dropped its invisible star, who just as quickly headed back to Lambertville, his little farm, and a bout with despair.

Before long, Broadway beckoned, and Rains reappeared for first-nighters in John Wexley's *They Shall Not Die*, a production of the newly revamped Theatre Guild. The actor won his usual plaudits as Nathan G. Rubin, the powerhouse defense attorney who moves heaven and earth to save five innocent young black men from a rape charge. Impressed with Rains' bravura performance, writers Ben Hecht and Charles MacArthur personally invited him to headline their *Crime Without Passion*, about to start filming at Paramount's Astoria studios, just across the river from the Great White Way.

*Then* who should call but Universal, proposing that the actor reprise his role as pacifist Paul Verin for the studio's *The Man Who Reclaimed His Head*. Albeit devoid of the deformities which plagued the character in the 1932 drama, the role was a familiar one, and Rains played it to the hilt in exchange for $2,000 weekly and a two-picture contract. The second picture was to have been *The Return of Frankenstein*, with Rains as the insane Pretorius, Boris Karloff (and perhaps Bela Lugosi) lurching about, and

The proud husband is all smiles; Frances seems ambivalent about being the center of attention so soon after her wedding day. *Courtesy Jessica Rains*

Whale once again at the helm. Before the smoke had even cleared, Ernest Thesiger replaced Rains, who returned to the scene of his first ever theatrical triumph—the choir—for his role as John Jasper in *Mystery of Edwin Drood*. As the lustful, opium-addicted choirmaster, the actor was "brilliantly repellent" (per Brooks Atkinson). The picture was not as profitable as the bean counters had hoped, however, so Universal passed on Rains' option and dropped him once again.

A trip to London in January of 1935 proved to be a media event for the actor, who had not, save for the briefest of stays in 1930, seen his homeland since the early twenties. Gainsborough Pictures had fueled the prodigal son's return with an offer to star in the film adaptation of Ernst Lothar's *The Clairvoyant*. The film didn't make much of an impact on either side of the pond, but it gave Rains the chance to act opposite Fay Wray, then one of America's most popular stars.

On March 9, 1935, the deed to Glen Mills, a 40-acre farm dating back to 1710, was signed and filed in the name of Claude Rains. There was no doubt that the actor was moving up in the world, or that movie money had paved the way for the move to Pennsylvania. After years of separation, Rains had filed for divorce from Beatrix Thompson, citing grounds of desertion. The decree came through on April 8 of that year, and the 45-year-old actor took the 25-year-old Frances Propper as his bride the very next day. (In his native England, however, the marriage to Frances made Rains a bigamist. English law didn't recognize the New Jersey divorce, so Beatrix was forced to initiate her own proceedings in the U.K. upon hearing that Claude had wed Miss Propper; for all that, the British divorce court didn't make absolute the *decree nisi* it had granted to Miss Thompson until July 26, 1937.) About this time, the *Hollywood Reporter* announced that Rains and Virginia Bruce would top the cast of MGM's macabre *Mad Love*, but the scoop was both premature and completely inaccurate. The actor's next (and last) feature for 1935 would be Paramount's *The Last Outpost*; he wouldn't darken the Metro-Goldwyn-Mayer doorstep until his penultimate film, *Twilight of Honor* (1963).

The door to Warner Bros. opened in 1936, though, and a long term contract lay on just the other side; that meant job security, relief from financial worry, and respite from eternal vigils by the phone. Before Jack L. Warner loaned him out to Frank Capra and Columbia for *Mr. Smith Goes to Washington* in 1939, Rains graced an even dozen of Warners' most eclectic pictures with acclaimed performances, and the forties saw him prominently featured in nearly a dozen more. Among the plethora of challenging roles to be had, the scheduled salary increases, and the opportunities to freelance, Rains' becoming a ward of Warner Bros. was, for him, something of a milestone.

**Father and daughter had a mutual admiration society. Claude sired Jennifer late in life, and adored her until the day he died.** *Courtesy Jessica Rains*

The year 1938 saw two more milestones for Rains. While playing Prince John in *The Adventures of Robin Hood*, the 48-year-old actor became a father; Frances gave birth to their daughter, Jennifer, on January 24th. Rains found fatherhood to be an absolute joy and gushed about his baby to Irene Thirer of *The New York Post*:

I think she is the most wonderful of children. I don't know if it is because I waited so long to be a father, but I think she is unique.

Few fathers doted on their daughters as did Claude Rains on his Jennifer and, obsessed about her security—some six years after the fact, the horror of the Lindbergh kidnapping still occupied his mind—he had the farmhouse attic outfitted as a safe haven for her and enclosed the garden just off the living room with a high picket fence.

A new and jubilant (if anxious) father, Rains then became a new and enthusiastic citizen of the United States; one of his first "official" acts was to sign a petition (along with Myrna Loy, Melvyn Douglas, Groucho Marx, Jimmy Cagney, Henry Fonda, fellow naturalized countryman Carl Laemmle, and a host of other concerned movie people) urging the United States to break off all

**Stock Grange, Claude's idea of heaven.** *Courtesy Jessica Rains*

contractual films he made that year at Warners, but in *Mr. Smith Goes to Washington*, the Columbia loan-out. Although his portrayal was cheered, he lost the Best Supporting Actor statuette to his *Mr. Smith* co-star, Thomas Mitchell, for *his* performance in *Stagecoach*. No matter; with roles which ran the gamut from the kindly Mr. Halevy of *Saturday's Children* to the devilish Don José of *The Sea Hawk* to the arrogant and contrary David Belasco in *The Lady with Red Hair*, the actor's steady work was more than consolation. (The *Hollywood Reporter* noted that RKO had considered Rains—amid a playing field including Orson Welles, Lon Chaney, Jr., Bela Lugosi, and Robert Morley—for the title role in its production of *The Hunchback of Notre Dame*, before settling on Charles Laughton.)

As Claude's salary increased, the Rains family said goodbye to their small farmhouse in Glen Mills and moved onto the 329-acre spread of Stock Grange, near Romansville, Pennsylvania. The colonial farmhouse, dating back to 1745, was the perfect choice for the history- and antique-loving Rains who, with the help of construction specialists, restored it to its original form. "I find the country a bit like Sussex in England," he would tell a reporter some years later, "but I like it for itself and I think it's the best place in the world to live." He would buy more acreage as the years passed.

Between planing logs, pounding nails, cultivating assorted grains, and raising pigs and Hereford steer, the actor (listed in the county agricultural register as "Claude Rains, farmer") still found it necessary to augment his income via the occasional rail journey to Hollywood. Besides his duties at Warners, he was approached once again by the Universal brass, who had determined that his Oscar nomination and immense popularity made him worth another gamble. He was signed to play Sir John Talbot, father of *The Wolf Man*, and while he rolled his eyes at the movie, he enjoyed his role; per

economic relations with Hitler's Germany. Over the years to come, the dutiful Anglo-American actor appeared in concerts of tribute to his adopted country's musical heritage, broadcast his views on what America meant to him, and addressed patriotic, religious, and civic-minded organizations—gratis. The only trouble with the British, he would say on occasion, is "they're so damned British."

The year 1939 saw Rains' first (of four) Academy Award nominations, but, ironically, his celebrated performance (as Senator Joseph Paine) didn't occur in one of the four

John Brunas, Michael Brunas, and Tom Weaver (*Universal Horrors*), farmer Rains' "crisp performance is one of *The Wolf Man*'s major assets." At the very least, owning up to the bulky and hirsute Lon Chaney, Jr. was a nice departure from the array of off- and onscreen daughters he had sired since 1934.

Back at Columbia, Rains made a foray into comic fantasy with *Here Comes Mr. Jordan* (1941) and was delightful as the eponymous angel who helps prizefighter Joe Pendleton (Robert Montgomery) find a new body after having lost his own to Edward Everett Horton's cosmic blundering. Rains was pleased with the picture, feeling privileged to work with James Gleason, one of his favorite comedians. *Picturegoer* magazine revealed how

The scene in which an invisible Montgomery tried to explain the complicated situation to Gleason was made so irresistibly funny by Gleason's acting that Claude Rains had to be led off the set, because his laughter held up shooting.

The actor then ventured over to 20th Century–Fox, where, as Nutsy, the philosophical tramp, he rendered support in *Moontide* to Jean Gabin, a stocky French actor—late of the *Folies Bergère*—for whom the studio had great plans. Gabin went on to international fame apart from Fox, and Rains went back to Warners for two of his greatest roles.

His compassionate Dr. Jacquith was quite a contrast to his pompous, underhanded Napoleon III, and Bette Davis must have appreciated the difference. *Now, Voyager* reunited the actress with Rains, whom she had encountered first—and frighteningly—when he had impersonated Napoleon III in *Juarez* (1939). As she stated in her autobiography, *The Lonely Life*:

This was the third time I was in awe of an actor. I was again thrown for a loop. By this time, it must be clear that I was hardly a meek and obscure young actress. Still [Rains] scared the life out of me. When he looked at me during our scene as Napoleon would look at Carlotta, with loathing, I thought he Claude Rains held loathing of me Bette Davis as a performer! We have laughed about it many times since.[2]

Before *Now, Voyager* could be released to tremendous acclaim, Paul Henreid and Rains sauntered over to participate in a project which, despite in-fighting, second guessing, and constant, maddening script revisions, went on to become one of the most celebrated of all motion pictures: *Casablanca*. Trading in his conservative business suit for a French military uniform and pencil mustache, Rains was flawless as Louis Renault: poor, corrupt police official and closet patriot. A second nomination for Best Supporting Actor resulted in a second loss; this time, to Charles Coburn, in *The More the Merrier*. Still, $4000 a week bought an awful lot of handkerchiefs to cry into.

War bond rallies and Stock Grange kept the actor busier than did Hollywood in 1943. A cameo as villainous Ambrose Pomfret in RKO's all-star extravaganza for the British war effort, *Forever and a Day*, was followed by another call from Universal. Erratic as ever, the studio had briefly considered Broderick Crawford and had actually approached Charles Laughton before casting Rains as the titular menace in the remake of *Phantom of the Opera*, a role that had been a triumph for Lon Chaney in 1925. Despite Rains' being thought miscast by many, the picture went on to be a great financial and popular success, garnering five Academy Award nominations and winning in three categories.

Radio was another venue for farmer Rains, and he appeared on many of the most popular shows of the day. Found everywhere from the horrific *Inner Sanctum* to the patriotic *Cavalcade of America*, he also found time to exchange barbs with some of showbiz's greatest clowns. Rains and Fred Allen performed "The Phantom of Carnegie Hall," a parody on the actor's upcoming Universal release, and, despite some less-than-raucous punch lines, the quick-witted Allen and his uncontrollably giggling guest star came off splendidly.

In 1944 *Passage to Marseille* tried (and failed) to duplicate the magic of *Casablanca* by bringing back wholesale quantities of cast

The "real" Claude mugs with a studio portrait. *The Wioskowski Collection*

members, but the chemistry of Rains and Davis was enough to win big box-office bucks with *Mr. Skeffington*, and a third Best Supporting Actor nomination. Once again, Oscar bypassed Rains in favor of Barry Fitzgerald's work in *Going My Way*. Davis lost out, too.

A late '44 trip to England to star opposite Vivien Leigh in a film adaptation of Bernard Shaw's *Caesar and Cleopatra* resulted in a well-publicized $1 million–plus salary, headaches with director Gabriel Pascal, and a slew of mixed reviews. The director himself called the film "a gorgeous bore." Between Universal's *This Love of Ours*—the first non-macabre film that studio had ever offered him—and the marathon difficulties of Pascal's ersatz epic, Rains made it through 1945.

Back on track in 1946, Rains was reunited with big stars in big movies: Paul Muni in *Angel on My Shoulder*, Davis and Henreid for *Deception*, and Ingrid Bergman and Cary Grant in *Notorious* in which he played Alexander Sebastian, the Nazi with a conscience. (*The Los Angeles Times*' feature writer, Philip K. Scheuer, kidded the actor: "I half expect you in every picture I see." "If you do," Rains shot back, "you'll get plenty tired of this face of mine—especially that left eyebrow!") A bit trimmer than of late, the actor was now finding a new venue to explore—the mature romantic figure. Bette Davis commented wryly on the direction in which his career was shifting: "He began with a beard and a belly. Now, he's shaved off both and gets the girls, too." One thing he didn't get was the Oscar; neophyte actor and former serviceman Harold Russell of *The Best Years of Our Lives* displaced the frequent nominee. This, his fourth and last Oscar loss, devastated Rains and angered many of Hollywood's old guard, who felt that Russell had been awarded the statuette out of patriotic sentiment. Still, the Rains charm was on display in *Caesar and Cleopatra*, which finally opened in the United States. Critical opinion was sharply divided, as were audiences (Vivien Leigh had her many admirers; Stewart Granger, his groupies); nevertheless, Claude Rains' Caesar won the approval of movie lovers throughout America.

It was about this time that Rains was asked whether he might ever consider an active role *behind* the camera. *Deception* had marked the end of his long-term contract at Warner Bros. (the actor had been briefly considered for the villainous de Lorca in Errol Flynn's *Adventures of Don Juan*), and many of his colleagues had turned to producing or directing when studio ties came otherwise undone. "I am content merely to act," he responded, more than once; "besides, I'm convinced that mastery of one craft is better than a lesser ability in several." As if on cue, Michael Curtiz, who had directed Rains in nearly half of his Warners' pictures, invited him back to the studio to star in *The Unsuspected*, the premier effort of Curtiz's own production company. The noirish thriller—Rains' first—was also his last turn under Michael Curtiz's sure but quirky hand. With his popularity as assured as ever—Warners had been reissuing many of their past hits to theaters since 1943, and that sardonic smile and cocked eyebrow were everywhere—and his finances under control, farmer Rains could now spend more time at Stock Grange, in the company of his wife and beloved daughter. He donated his services to various organizations and lived up to what comprised his understanding of civic responsibility in one's own community; on September 17, 1947, for example, he led 5,000 school children in a "Freedom Pledge" which was broadcast throughout the country.

His "mature romantic" image got him an invitation to return to England at the tail end of 1948, and *The Passionate Friends* saw the 59-year-old actor competing with Trevor Howard for the love of Ann Todd under David Lean's watchful eye. The year 1949 found him back at Paramount (for the first time since 1935), where he vied with Mac-Donald Carey for Wanda Hendrix in *Song of Surrender* and indulged in an enjoyable adventure programmer, *Rope of Sand*, with Burt Lancaster, Peter Lorre, and his old co-star, Paul Henreid. Consideration of a couple of British projects (*Above the Dark Tumult* and a modernized version of *Crime and Punishment*) lost out to a three-picture contract with RKO that had the Rainses heading west en masse. The RKO trio—*The White Tower* and noir *Where Danger Lives* (both 1950), and 1951's *Sealed Cargo*—were unequivocally B pictures, produced as the top halves of double bills headed to help neighborhood movie houses combat the threat of television. They were also enormous fun. As the Warners' re-releases (mentioned above) continued to reach screens until 1953, it became something of a challenge to take in a double feature in the early fifties and *not* see Claude Rains.

While the prestige of his films may have slipped a notch or two, his actor's craft was as sharply honed as ever. On January 13, 1951, Rains opened in *Darkness at Noon*, Sidney Kingsley's drama of bolshevism, communism, conscience, and decay, at New York's *Alvin Theater*. When the performance ended, Rains was given a tumultuous standing ovation; as it had been 17 years earlier, Broadway was his once again. "They wouldn't let me go," Aljean Harmetz quotes him as saying.

They kept me on stage, bowing and bowing. God almighty, it was one of the most wonderful nights any actor ever had in the theater.[3]

Although the role of Rubashov was both physically and mentally draining for the aging actor, he reveled as he always had in hard work and continued to keep busy with a variety of stage, film, and radio projects over the next few years. Among the roles he has to pass on due to conflicting commitments was that of Klaatu, intergalactic messenger of peace—or else!—in 20th Century-Fox's classic *The Day the Earth Stood Still*. As the film's director, Robert Wise, told author Edmund G. Bansak:

All of us—Eddie North, the screenplay writer, Julian Blaustein, the producer, and I—thought that Claude Rains would be just right for this role. Unfortunately, he was tied up in a play in New York and we couldn't get him.[4]

Television had begun its juggernaut-like takeover of America in the early fifties, and CBS was the first network to tap Rains for an appearance. A brief segment from *Darkness at Noon* not only gave the play some excellent free publicity, but also did a world of good for its host program, *Toast of the Town*, Ed Sullivan's first crack at the variety format he would later master. In 1952 Rains was off to England for a spell of theatrical nostalgia in *Merely Players*—a star-studded dramatic review/tribute to old friend Sir Godfrey Tearle, and the starring role of Kees Popinga, *The Man Who Watched Trains Go By*, for Eros Films. Returning to the USA (and NBC radio) later that year, he impersonated the title character in the extended series, *The Jeffersonian Heritage.*

CBS recalled the actor for a brief bit on *Omnibus* and a couple of episodes of *Medallion Theatre* in 1953, and *Variety* reported he was all set to take a one-man show, "Claude Rains, the Strolling Player," up and down the coast. Retitled "Claude Rains: Great Words with Music," the show reached Los Angeles in November, where it opened to appreciative reviews. It was still filling California's medium-sized auditoriums when along came the call for T. S. Eliot's *The Confidential Clerk*, set to open on Broadway scarcely six weeks into 1954. Save for some radio work (including a daily 15-minute dramatic anthology broadcast over his own name), 1955 was spent puttering about the farm and recovering from a spell of liver trouble. By way of contrast, in 1956, Rains' plate was filled: Among a quartet of television programs, a trip to Portugal (where he stole *Lisbon* out from under Ray Milland and Maureen O'Hara's noses), and an ill-fated turn in Arch Oboler's *Night of the Auk*, there seemed little time for anything else to transpire.

Somehow, they found the time. To the intense surprise of many family and friends, Claude and Frances Rains were divorced after 20 years of marriage. The age difference between Claude and her, combined with his increasing health problems—some of which were alcohol related—conspired to have Frances call it a day after two decades. With his wife gone and Jennifer off to college in Vermont, Rains sadly decided to sell Stock Grange. "He told me the house had too many memories," related buyer Harrison Wetherill to the *West Chester* (PA) *Citizen*, "and that he could not live here anymore." On the day of the settlement, those memories must have caught up with him; Rains wrecked his Bentley while under the influence of alcohol.

In 1957 he accepted roles in television's *Alfred Hitchcock Presents* and the *Hallmark*

By 1956, when the smiles were illusory, Claude and Frances went their separate ways.

*Hall of Fame.* In the November 26 color special, *The Pied Piper of Hamelin*, he sang for the public for the first time since *Sweet Nell of Old Drury*, more than a half-century earlier. Pennsylvania remained home, but Rains downsized from the multi-acre farmstead to the antiques-filled Hawthorne House, built in one of West Chester's best neighborhoods back in 1839. In conjunction with his appearance on *The Outpost* for the *Du Pont Show of the Week*, Rains granted an interview to Margaret McManus of the *New York World Telegram and Sun*, wherein he confessed to missing Stock Grange even then:

I loved that farm. It was something to come home to. When the play closed, or the movie was finished, I went right back to that farm. Knowing it was there sustained me. But my doctor convinced me about five years ago that I didn't need the burden of all that land.

(September 8, 1962)

No longer buffered by hundreds of acres of farmland-cum-privacy, he found his celebrity to be a two-edged sword in town. "He complained that he would be mobbed for autographs," observed a neighbor, who later purchased the home at 400 South Church Street, "but he would have been more upset had he not been approached for them."

It was an airplane, rather than a train, that took the actor from Pennsylvania to Hollywood in 1959, where another stint on *Alfred Hitchcock Presents* and a plum role on *Playhouse 90* brought him into America's living rooms, and Universal-International's *This Earth Is Mine* put him back into movie theaters. His hair gone completely white and sporting a flattering Van Dyke, Rains looked heartier than he had in quite some time.

Madame Agi Jambor may have had something to do with that renewed vigor. The 50-year-old Jambor, renowned concert pianist and professor of music at Bryn Mawr College, married the actor—some 19 years her senior—at Hawthorne House on November 4, 1959. Scarcely nine months later, however, there was another ex–Mrs. Rains on the already lengthy list, as Mme. Jambor sued her husband for divorce, on the grounds of "indignities."

The new decade was one of many transitions. Not long after her mom had herself remarried, the 22-year-old Jennifer became Mrs. Edward Brash in a ceremony held in Philadelphia; her father was on hand to give her away. Meanwhile, Irwin Allen unleashed *The Lost World*, a ghastly remake of the 1925 silent original, against an unsuspecting public. The producer, who would come to be known as "The Father of the Disaster Movie" in the seventies, anticipated that honor by a decade with his disastrous version of Arthur Conan Doyle's popular novel.

A quick trip to Italy produced yet another science-fiction headache: *Il Pianeta degli Uomini Spenti* (*The Planet of the Lifeless Men*), filmed by upstart director Antonio Margheriti in 1960 and released (as *Battle of the Worlds*) to limited U.S. markets in 1963. *Battle*'s plot concerned the quest of Rains'

character for cosmic secrets and universal truths; on July 29, 1960, Rains' divorce battle had ended, but less than a month later, newspapers were reporting that the 70-year-old actor wasn't being totally truthful about the *sixth* Mrs. Rains—the former Rosemary Clark Schrode (née McGroarty)—whom he had wed "about three weeks ago." The wire services were able to ascertain that the 42-year-old mother of three children was a Wilkes-Barre (Pennsylvania) native, had herself been married twice previously, and had been hired by the actor to help him ghost write his autobiography, but neither of the newlyweds would go into detail about the courtship or the ceremony.

Television guest shots would take the lion's share of the aging actor's time from this point on, but the limited release to theaters of the earlier TV special *The Pied Piper of Hamelin* in the early part of the decade was a jot of financially welcome double-dipping. "I'm a frightened actor and I shall die a frightened actor," he had been quoted as saying,

but I do enjoy acting so much. I very much enjoy acting on television, but I do wish the pressure was a bit less. There is such a short time to get ready, and I must have time for preparation.
(*NY World Telegram and Sun* interview, September 8, 1962)

Nestled among his spots on *Rawhide*, *Wagon Train*, and the like, his turn as the calculating Mr. Dryden in *Lawrence of Arabia* showed him still a past-master at subtlety and technique. Critic Stanley Kauffmann reminded audiences that "Playing a diplomat, Claude Rains, always a fine and now a vintage actor, is simply not on the screen long enough to suit us."

In the summer of 1963, Claude and Rosemary Rains moved from Pennsylvania into what residents of Sandwich, New Hampshire, called the Weed house, in Lower Corner. Bracketing the move had been Rains' film work in *The Greatest Story Ever Told* and MGM's *Twilight of Honor*, a vehicle designed to make a movie star out of Richard

**Claude late in life, as the venomous Herod the Great.** *Courtesy Jessica Rains*

Chamberlain, TV's young Dr. Kildare. It failed to do so. The following February, Rains enjoyed appearing on Chamberlain's program in an episode entitled "Why Won't Anybody Listen?"

An anticipated return to the stage had to be postponed due to illness of both Claude and Rosemary; the sixth Mrs. Rains had earlier been diagnosed with pancreatic cancer and was in fact beginning to fail. For most of 1964, solicitous of Rosemary and under doctor's care himself, the actor took it easy. Puttering in the garden had always been a joy and now became a welcome therapy. The enforced respite from work gave Rains more time with his books—despite his having quit school in the second grade, he had become a voracious reader while associated with Beerbohm-Tree—and he frequently read aloud to his wife. Only partly in it for the exercise, he was also given to meandering in and about town; he'd grouse about being recognized, about being approached to sign

scraps of paper and pose for photographs, yet he'd become such a familiar figure that to trundle about incognito was impossible.

On the last day of the year, Rosemary Rains died; she was only 48 years old. For a while, her bereaved husband became something of a recluse; he had married and divorced a handful of wives, but only Frances and Rosemary had touched his soul. As it had throughout his life, an offer of work helped to lift his spirits and bring him out of his grief.

Director Edward Parone and the prospect of a tour of Henry Denker's *So Much of Earth, So Much of Heaven* then beckoned, with the added hook of a Broadway berth at tour's end. It was an iffy situation from the start, with Rains still given to periods of melancholy and weakened by a brace of surgical procedures on his damaged liver. Nonetheless, the old trouper made it through the larger part of the tour before an extended bout with internal bleeding finally put him out of the action. Due to his continued poor health and the cumulative effect of a series of less than enthusiastic notices, the play's eventual move to Broadway was out of the question.

His stage career ended, the failing actor was forced to nay-say what might have extended his film catalogue: 1965's *The Curse of the Fly*, shot in Britain for Robert Lippert, and *Blind Man's Bluff*, filmed in Madrid in 1967 by Robert D. Weinbach. (The latter picture wasn't released until 1971, which made it—under its final title, *Cauldron of Blood*—a posthumous credit for *Boris Karloff*, who had replaced Rains in the Spanish production.) Back in February, "Cops and Robbers," a comic turn with Bert Lahr and Ken Murray on *The Bob Hope Chrysler Theatre*, had spelled the end of his television work, as well.

### La commedia era finita.

Feeling the weight of his years and troubled anew by the chronic liver problems which had plagued him incessantly since his days at Stock Grange, Rains retired to the Weed house and seldom ventured out farther than the length of his brick path. In late May 1967, he collapsed while walking through his little garden. Rushed to Lakes Region Hospital in nearby Laconia, he was found to be suffering from severe internal bleeding caused by an intestinal hemorrhage. The condition was unstoppable and irreversible, and Claude Rains died on the 30th of May.

The memorial services held for Rains were private, and the actor was laid to rest next to his wife, Rosemary, in the Red Hill Cemetery, a rustic country graveyard a few miles due west of Sandwich, New Hampshire. News of his death drew worldwide

**At rest.** *Courtesy Joyce E. Ashcroft*

reactions, and his legions of fans went into mourning. *Variety* noted with satisfaction that the Actors' Fund of America was left a $25,000 bequest, and a trust fund was set up for Rains' beloved Jennifer—now Jessica, an actor in her own right. No other terms were made public, and the total amount of the estate was not disclosed.

Rains chose his epitaph, but arduous poring over world drama, classical literature, and religious texts has failed to disclose its source:

"All things once are things forever. Soul once living, lives forever." The words are a profession of belief in immortality whatever their origin, and Rains' anima continues to live on through his family and friends.

For the eulogy of the film actor, rather than the man, it's nearly impossible to improve on the simplicity of Robert A. Juran (*Old Familiar Faces*), who speaks volumes in a sentence:

He was a colossus of his profession—not merely one of the greatest of character actors, but one of the finest actors the screen has ever seen.

Nowadays, when savvy movie buffs are wont to make comparisons between the best of the contemporary lot and the greatest stars of the Golden Age of the Silver Screen, Tom Hanks is heralded as this generation's Jimmy Stewart. Harrison Ford, we are told, is a meld of Bogart and Errol Flynn; Ralph Fiennes, a modern day Basil Rathbone; and Emma Thompson is regarded as a reflection of Katharine Hepburn's light.

No one has ever been acclaimed as another Claude Rains.

# The Films

## *Build Thy House* (1920)

After being demobilized following the Great War, Arthur Burnaby (Henry Ainley) returns home to take up the partnership left vacant by the death of his father of the firm of Dawson and Burnaby, world-class iron-founders. The senior partner, Dawson (Jerrold Robertshaw), is also the owner of Happy Valley, a collection of slums in which his workers live; the ill-named property is in such a state of neglect that the residents are seething with discontent. Led by Medway (Reginald Bach), one of the hands, they decide to strike after Dawson gives notice of a reduction in wages. Arthur Burnaby espouses their cause and declares that unless the notice of reduction is withdrawn, he will himself lead the men on strike; Dawson is obliged to give way. Burnaby then decides to contest Dawson's seat in Parliament in the Labour interest.

Clarkis (Claude Rains), a drunken loafer who is applying for a job, informs Dawson that he was Burnaby's batman in France, and that Arthur is not that man! A woman who claims to be Burnaby's wife also denounces Arthur as an impostor. Arthur invites Dawson to his committee rooms, where he announces publicly that Burnaby, who had been killed in France, had left his business interests to Arthur on condition that he should do all in his power to better the treatment of the workingmen. The real Burnaby is discovered in a military hospital, where he has been suffering from loss of memory. He is able to confirm Arthur's statements,

and a reconciliation takes place with Dawson, which is further cemented by Arthur's marriage to Helen Dawson (Ann Trevor).

The undisputed film debut of William Claude Rains, *Build Thy House*—like so many other silent curiosities—has slipped noiselessly into the winding corridors of time. The hows and whys of the film are sketchy, as those few news items found in the files of the British Film Institute are themselves vague and redundant. A nebulous theory—tossed about by cognoscenti aware of the picture—maintains that leading man Henry Ainley was instrumental in getting his young protégé and others to strut their stuff before the camera as a lark, but there is no extant documentation to support such a stand. More probably, Ainley and his wife (billed onscreen as "Mrs. Ainley") agreed to appear in *Build Thy House* in order to spur on Britain's post-war economy and to incite to immediate and selfless action those entrusted with her reconstruction. Such noble motives are partially supported by one of the film's preliminary subtitles, wherein the thrust of the picture is explained as an effort "to make Britain a happier place, after the war, for the toiling masses of the people." A second title hesitantly opines that the film also offers "a hint how to deal with the labour claims."

Thus meant to serve two masters—base melodrama and social reform—*Build Thy House* did justice only to the former, if the accuracy of surviving critiques is in any kind of proportion to their woeful tedium. *Kine Weekly* found that

25

The failure of the film as a contribution to social discussion effects [sic] its merits as an entertainment, and this is a pity, for just when its dullness in the first particular has become painfully obvious, it develops into a quite ingenious, if rather mechanical, war melodrama, with a lost memory as a motif, and with quite good "suspense" value.
(October 21, 1920)

*The Bioscope* of the same date (whence was adapted the above synopsis) perceived the same weaknesses and strengths:

Its author has selected as his subject a problem for which he has no solution beyond the usual truism that labour troubles would cease if employees were all happy and content.... The story, however, is less an attempt to solve an industrial problem than to provide an effective drama, and with slight weakness of construction, the story of the pseudo Arthur Burnaby is not without interest.

The author of the rather poorly integrated tale was one S. Trevor Jones, about whom virtually no information has survived. A panel of three Ideal Studios judges awarded Jones' manuscript the top prize of £200 in a writing competition, but the author's greatest reward may well have been his watching his masterpiece set down on celluloid. Before director Fred Goodwins could conspire with the uncredited cameraman, however, scenarist Eliot Stannard was handed the deathless prose, and to him fell the unenviable task of wedding the hogwash with the soap box. As it's impossible to compare Stannard's cutting continuity with Jones' prize-winning narrative, the final words on the picture's split personality have to be "contributory negligence."

Stannard was no novice at adapting original stories for the silent screen, though; his numerous credits stretched back to 1914—as did Ainley's. Pegged by John Gielgud (in his *Early Stages*) as "among the most popular stars of the period," Henry Hinchliffe Ainley had, by 1920, become as adept in the bastard art as he had in the legitimate theater. He was, in fact, something of a cinematic veteran, having starred in a good dozen prestige motion pictures, beginning with Gau-

mont's *She Stoops to Conquer*, in 1914. (In 1916, the perennial leading man had toplined a couple of films—*The Great Adventure* and *The Marriage of William Ashe*—which had featured Rains' *governor*, Fred.)

Naturally, the renowned Ainley got the lion's share of the *Build Thy House* press, which nodded approvingly if not overly enthusiastically. (One nameless critic found the actor inclined "somewhat to over-emphasize the part of the earnest young demagogue," a stylistic sin typical of stage actors seeking to adapt their traditions to the screen.) Tossed into the critical hopper with the rest of the second cast, Rains (et al.) ran the collective gamut from "stagey" [sic] to "excellent." The fact that he wasn't singled out for mention in the extant film reviews (as he usually was in theatrical notices) may have helped shape Rains' decision to steer clear of motion pictures for more than a decade to come.

Without either the film itself or stills of the 30-year-old Rains photographed while spilling the dramatic beans or lurching about drunkenly—further appraisal is impossible. A dozen years would separate *Build Thy House* from *The Invisible Man*, and that period would witness the honing of the diminutive actor's techniques and the perfection of his art. The Claude Rains who was literally unwrapped in James Whale's comic melodrama was vastly different from the journeyman performer who was still unsure of himself and unsettled in his craft at the beginning of the earlier decade. Thus, although we are grateful to the shades of the Messrs. Ainley, Goodwins, Stannard, and Jones for giving our lad a chance, we must continue to regard the 1933 Universal science fiction sensation as Rains' official movie debut.

***Build Thy House*** Ideal Film Company. Released October 1920. 5230 feet (5 reels).

Henry Ainley (Arthur Burnaby); Ann Trevor (Helen Dawson); Reginald Bach (Jim Medway); Warwick Ward (Burnaby); Jerrold Robertshaw (John Dawson); Adelaide Grace (Mrs. Medway);

Howard Cochran (Marshall); CLAUDE RAINS (Clarkis); R. Van Courtlandt (Mr. Cramer); Mrs. Ainley (Miss Brown); V. Vivian-Vivian (Florence Burnaby)

Director: Fred Goodwins; Screenplay: Eliot Stannard; based on an original story by S. Trevor Jones

## *The Invisible Man* (1933)

Winter in Iping, England. The bandaged apparition seeking shelter at a small inn is Jack Griffin (Claude Rains), a scientist who has rendered himself invisible and is now struggling desperately to find an antidote. While Griffin battles the mind-distorting properties of the drug monocane and the intrusiveness of the local population, his fiancée, Flora (Gloria Stuart), and her father, Dr. Cranley (Henry Travers), are searching for him, so as to restore him to sight and safety.

Enraged at the constant interference with his work, Griffin attacks the innkeeper (Forrester Harvey) and, in the presence of the local constable (E. E. Clive) and some of the barflies, strips down to his transparent skin and escapes. While news of an invisible man spreads quickly throughout the countryside, Griffin visits his colleague, Dr. Kemp (William Harrigan) and coerces him into helping him in his mad plan to rule the world. The men retrieve the notes and books Griffin had left at the inn; in a spontaneous display of his power, the invisible man kills a policeman in the midst of a meeting of frightened citizens.

That night, Kemp advises Dr. Cranley and the police of Griffin's whereabouts. Flora meets with Griffin; she is unable, however, to convince him to return home with her. The arrival of the police forces the invisible man to flee, but not before he vows to kill Kemp at ten o'clock the next night for his betrayal. The next day witnesses a series of murderous incidents, and, despite the every effort of the police force, Kemp is hogtied and sent hurtling to his death at the appointed hour.

Everyone is terrified, and the police seem incapable of discovering a means of locating and immobilizing the invisible one, when—providentially—a farmer informs them that he has heard "breathing" in his barn. Surrounding the rickety old structure, the police set it afire, and a bullet targeted above a line of footprints appearing on the snowy ground does the trick. Griffin is hospitalized; he confesses the error of his ways to Flora and becomes visible again in death.

Just as Boris Karloff never tired of regaling interviewers with his account of how he came to be cast as Frankenstein's Monster, so also did Claude Rains get a lot of mileage out of retelling the circumstances surrounding his major-film debut. The actor had always been director James Whale's first choice for the role, even after the ludicrous screen test he had taken over at RKO for *A Bill of Divorcement*. Virtually a cinematic innocent at the time, Rains later confessed to interviewers that he had been unaware that the last row of the audience was never farther away than his own distance from the lens,

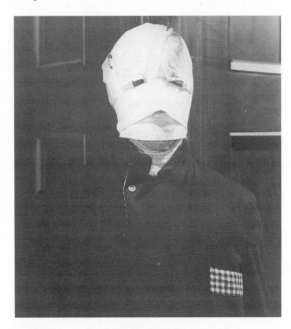

**Denied even the capacity to raise an eyebrow, Claude makes Griffin seem all too human largely by dint of his magnificent voice.**

and had exhibited an array of stage techniques which had sent RKO's head honchos into hysterics and him back to his New Jersey farm. In the end, rolls of gauze and John P. Fulton's optical magic covered any residual tendencies towards over-theatricality (the actor's next several films would allow audiences to witness the excesses winnowed still further), and the first and only glimpse moviegoers got of him was as a corpse at the picture's close. As had Errol Flynn (in *The Case of the Curious Bride* [1934]), Rains' brief turn as a cadaver would lead to a bright future in motion pictures, and no one was more surprised than he was.

With the release of *The Invisible Man*, it appeared that Herbert George Wells was going to have a bright future in motion pictures, too. The film was a smash—audiences and critics alike were amused, amazed, and, most importantly, *entertained* by the Universal feature—so the 1897 source novel was reprinted (in a photoplay edition, of course). Its author, to his distress, became regarded as an *homme d'esprit* more for his sensational fiction than for his portentous world views.

Although Britain had already banned Paramount's *Island of Lost Souls* (1932; née, in print, as *The Island of Doctor Moreau*), London Films rushed to have the Great Man sign on the dotted line, only to discover that having Wells' name on a contract meant having Wells as a very vocal partner; things slowed to a crawl immediately. By 1936, only *Things to Come* and *The Man Who Could Work Miracles* had ventured through that studio's portals, and neither made enough of a noise at the box-office to warrant continuing to put up with Wells' demands. With the disappointing results of these items from the author's science fiction and fantasy catalogue, British cinema returned to its more traditional stance—playing it safe—and contented itself with a remake of Wells' comedy, *Kipps* (in 1941) and a well-received version of his *The History of Mr. Polly* (also a comedy) some eight years later. It remained for Hollywood to rediscover the potency of the man's vision via the George Pal connection (*The*

*War of the Worlds* and *The Time Machine*) in 1953 and 1960, respectively.

Still, in 1933, the big noise was Wells. R. C. Sherriff, who had labored long and hard on Whale's earlier *Journey's End*, now worked on melding elements of Philip Wylie's sensational *The Murderer Invisible* (which Universal had previously bought, both for its lurid episodes and in order to forestall any later charges of plagiarism) with the narrative and characters of the titular novel. Virtually nothing from the former would make it to the screen; nor would either the director originally cited in early trade blurbs (Cyril Gardner), or Ur-leads Boris Karloff and Chester Morris. (In *James Whale: A New World of Gods and Monsters*— a revised and expanded version of his 1982 biography of the director—James Curtis reveals that Colin Clive had likewise been approached for the role of Jack Griffin.) It took Wells, Whale, Fulton, and Rains to concoct the masterpiece among them, although Wells would later grouse to *The New York Times* that while he liked the picture, he couldn't condone how the screenplay had changed a brilliant scientist into a lunatic. Universal's taking such a liberty, he grumped, was the film's "grave fault."[5]

Rains had been chosen for his voice and his presence, the two qualities which were considered paramount when casting the role of Jack Griffin. The stage mannerisms which had made viewers of that first screen test wince helped immeasurably with the more pantomimic aspects of the scenes wherein the character was bandaged to the nines, and the arduous vocal training—which the actor had undertaken to overcome the speech impediments and regional peculiarities of his youth, and which had conspired with his God-given timbre to produce one of the most distinctive and distinguished voices in theater and motion pictures—couched the most melodramatic of lines in the most convincing of tones. The impersonation was wildly successful and Rains, who had sped east to the comfort of his Lambertville acreage immediately after the production had wrapped, found himself (as Karloff had in 1931) being heralded as a "new face" despite his years of dedication to his craft.

Not surprisingly, contemporary reviews were more taken with the novelty of the situation and the remarkable special effects than they were with the perambulations of the cast members. The unanimous critical huzzahs covered individual performances, of course, but none of the actors—including Rains—was consistently singled out for special praise. The technical scope of *The Invisible Man* merited coverage in numerous trade, fan, and scientific periodicals, and the February 1934 issue of Hugo Gernsback's *Everyday Science and Mechanics* made the special effects its cover story.

Most of the leads were tapped for interviews during the film's initial release, and great fun can be had in perusing the various actors' impressions on how Whale and John P. Fulton managed their magic. In a brief chat with *New York Times* journalist Andre D. Sennwald, Rains revealed that, in order for him to do many of the feats required of him by the screenplay,

> … they really photographed me straight and then took me through the pink, green and blue rooms, or whatever they are, in the laboratories, and made me disappear…. Sometimes they didn't get total invisibility. At night, in the projection room, I would come out opaque, or just the outline of my figure would be visible. But after the film went through the laboratory I just disappeared.
> (December 3, 1933)

*The Invisible Man* was Gloria Stuart's second James Whale thriller in a row (1932's *The Old Dark House* being the first), and the beautiful actress went on to infrequent film appearances until 1946, when she forswore film for art and settled into happy domesticity with comedy scenarist Arthur Sheekman. (As this chapter is being written, the 88-year-old Miss Stuart is again in the spotlight, universally celebrated for her Oscar-nominated performance in James Cameron's 1997 epic, *Titanic*.) Miss Stuart has gone on record more than once about her early-thirties Universal thrillers, and has expressed her

honest surprise that the films—which neither she nor her coworkers had regarded as remarkable in any way—have increased in popularity over the ensuing decades. Durability on the screen, however, did not necessarily mean compatibility in the studio. The first of several actresses who saw eye-to-eye with Rains

Moviegoers were curious about the actor who was glimpsed for a moment at the film's close. This is one of the first publicity shots issued by Universal to satisfy audience curiosity. *The author's collection*

only when he was perched on a box, Stuart recalled that the man and the production were somewhat less than fun:

> It was a very serious set, and we put in long hours. Claude Rains was an actor's actor. I think all actors are egotistical in nature, perhaps women somewhat less than men. Claude was a big ego. One could sense a tenseness with him. No jokes; very little relaxation.[6]

For Rains, of course, the picture was the true beginning of a film career which would extend through the mid-sixties. Madness in one form or another would rear its head for each of his next few features, and then the actor would branch out into melodramas, historical adaptations, action films, horror movies, and tearjerkers. Capable of heroics, he was far more credible as the heavy; in most cases, however—as in *The Invisible Man*—he richly layered his characterizations, thus making facile assessments difficult and one-dimensional critiques impossible.

*The Invisible Man* Universal. Released November 13, 1933. 71 minutes.

CLAUDE RAINS (The Invisible One/Jack Griffin); Gloria Stuart (Flora Cranley); William Harrigan (Dr. Kemp); Henry Travers (Dr. Cranley); Una O'Connor (Mrs. Hall); Forrester Harvey (Mr. Hall); Holmes Herbert (Chief of Police); E. E. Clive (Constable Jaffers); Dudley Digges (Chief of Detectives); Harry Stubbes (Inspector Bird); Donald Stuart (Inspector Lane); Merle Tottenham (Milly); Dwight Frye (Reporter); John Carradine (Informer); Jameson Thomas (Doctor); John Merivale (Boy); Walter Brennan (Man with Bicycle)

President: Carl Laemmle; Producer: Carl Laemmle, Jr.; Director: James Whale; Assistant Director: Joseph A. McDonough; Screenplay: R. C. Sherriff, based on the novel, *The Invisible Man*, by H. G. Wells; Director of Photography: Arthur Edeson, ASC; Camera Operator: King Gray; Assistant Camera Operator: Jack Egan; Special Effects: John P. Fulton; Art Director: Charles D. Hall; Editor: Ted Kent; Supervising Editor: Maurice Pivar; Sound Supervisor: Gilbert Kurland; Recording Engineer: William Hedgecock

# *Crime Without Passion*
(1934)

A brief prologue to the film explains that those who commit crimes of passion will be subject to the whims of the three Furies, terrible female spirits who, according to myth, punished the doers of unavenged crimes.

Successful but unscrupulous defense attorney Lee Gentry (Claude Rains) is as dishonest in love as he is in court, where his tampering with evidence has gotten his latest client off the hook. With a lustful eye on socialite, Katy Costello (Whitney Bourne), Gentry schemes to end his two-year relationship with Carmen Brown (Margo), a Spanish dancer at the *El Bravo Club*, a Manhattan nightspot.

A master of deceit, the lawyer meticulously arranges matters so that he can claim that Carmen is two-timing *him* with Eddie White (Stanley Ridges), the dancer's old boyfriend. Feigning outrage, Gentry storms out of the cabaret, but fellow headliner

Buster Malloy (Paula Trueman) informs Carmen that the whole thing had been a set-up.

Threats of suicide bring Gentry to Carmen's apartment, where, unaware that he has pocketed her pistol, she rages at her ex-lover for his dishonesty before grappling with him. The gun goes off, and Carmen falls to the floor. Fearing that he has killed her, Gentry is aghast, but a ghostly version of himself—as smug and deceitful as ever he was in the flesh—leads him step by step through the cover-up of the murder.

Gentry confesses to Katy that he has killed Carmen, and the horrified socialite rejects him. Stopping by the *El Bravo* so as not to blow his cover, the attorney soon becomes drunk and is disconcerted when Della (Greta Granstedt), a friend of Carmen's, mentions his earlier—and suspiciously brief—trip to a movie house, which he had made for purposes of establishing an alibi. While Gentry tries to bully the woman into remembering things differently, her boyfriend, Eddie White, returns to the table. Angered that the lawyer is again coming between him and a woman, Eddie knocks Gentry to the floor, whence Gentry, firing through his jacket pocket, shoots Eddie in cold blood.

As the police take him away, Gentry is astounded to see Carmen whirling out onstage; she had, in fact, only been grazed by the bullet back in her apartment. At the station house, the police regard the shooting as premeditated murder due to Gentry's prior treatment of Eddie White. His ghostly alter-ego exhorts the attorney to commit suicide with the gun with which he had shot his erstwhile rival, but State's Attorney O'Brien (Leslie Adams) disarms him, while reminding him that the state will take care of his execution.

*Crime Without Passion* was a Ben Hecht–Charles MacArthur tour de force from start to finish, even to the point of having Mrs. MacArthur—Helen Hayes—sitting prettily (along with Fannie Brice) on a divan in a hotel lobby. (Nor did it stop there; both writers had cameos as reporters in the interview scene held outside the courtroom.) Based on Hecht's *Saturday Evening Post* short story, "The Caballero of the Law," the screen treatment was the first collaboration at Paramount for the award-winning team, who not only plotted the picture *ab initio*, but produced and directed it as well.[7]

Witty lines and clever exchanges wrought by characters who are at once fascinating yet less than totally three-dimensional were Hecht and MacArthur's trademarks, and their prior successes (including *The Front Page* [1931] and *Twentieth Century* [1934]) paved the way for the kind of autonomy they enjoyed with *Crime*. There is less impossibly affected dialogue here than in these earlier milestones, yet, even when over-enunciated or minced superciliously (as Rains does in his courtroom summation, when the intolerably smug Gentry belittles the police and jousts with the jury), the sharpness of those scripted barbs survives intact.

The film's title can get you going, though. The posters and trade ads trumpet hatred and revulsion—there's nothing like a good case of loathing to make one passionate—so the picture's nomenclature *can* cause a bit of bewilderment. Even the studio pressbook finds it necessary to examine the phrase:

The "crime without passion" of the title is the cruel, premeditated, calculated effort of a famous trial attorney to break a woman's heart, to kill her love for him, so that she voluntarily will leave him free to love another woman.... "A dead heart in a living woman"—that is Lee Gentry's (Claude Rains's) aim.

The distinction being made, however—that Gentry keeps his wits about him during his ongoing charade with Carmen rather than becoming caught up in the "passion" of any given moment—may not be readily apparent to the casual viewer, though attorneys, law clerks, and other judicial types would doubtless chuckle knowingly at the splitting of such legalistic hairs.

First-time viewers are usually taken

The quotes at the top of this pressbook ad certainly *seem* passionate enough. *Courtesy Buddy Barnett*

aback by the appearance of the Furies: "The three sisters of Evil who lie in wait for those who live dangerously and without Gods". Despite their being carefully interwoven with the storyline (meriting both an edgy reference from Rains mid-plot and a reprise at the wrap), they *do* seem more appropriate to one of the horror pictures over at Universal than to a kinky crime tale from Paramount. (And, lest anyone think that the inclusion of the harpies put the Messrs. Hecht and MacArthur off their mark, be advised that the former penned the original story for *The Great Gabbo*, a 1929 musical dissertation on kinkiness, while the latter helped adapt one of the more infamous instances of historical debauchery for Lionel Barrymore, in *Rasputin and the Empress* [1932].)

The malignant spirits issue forth from the blood of murdered women, but lead to sundry instances of ill-advised amour, rather than to crimes of violence; if the screenplay holds any water, *those* atrocities inevitably occur sometime later. In fact, while Lee Gentry's duplicity regarding evidence and police procedure presented no little headache to the avatars of the new Production Code, it was the assorted "Come hither" glances, sensual smirks, and illicit embraces which shared prologue time with the airborne Furies (themselves flirting with charges of indecent exposure) that caused the lion's share of rewrites and restructuring.

*Crime Without Passion* marked the cinematic debuts of both Margo and Whitney Bourne. Margo (María Marguerita Guadalupe Boldao Castilla y O'Donnell) possessed a dusky beauty, genuine thespic ability, and a talent for dance; she had been tutored by Margarita (Rita Hayworth) Cansino's father. Her Carmen Brown is lovely, honest, popular—and fiery: the diametric opposite of Lee Gentry, that passionless legal eagle. Compared with her, Whitney Bourne's Katy Costello comes off as a drip of the first order; while Rains oils his way through the film's mundane meld of romantic rot and exposition, Bourne bites her lip, rolls her eyes, pouts, blows cigarette smoke in the au courant fashion, and otherwise reacts noiselessly until her partner comes up for air and the drama proceeds. The novice actress hadn't enough experience to pull off this kind of stuff, however, and until she finally opens her mouth and the

writers' give-and-take magic builds up steam, the scene remains more aggravating than enlightening. Later, away from the rigors of close-up eyebrow-cocking and nostril-flaring, Bourne is better.

His notoriety as *The Invisible Man* advertised as heavily as the Hecht/MacArthur connection, Rains makes the arrogant wonder-lawyer his own. Devoid of compassion and understanding, Lee Gentry exhibits Jack Griffin's megalomania without having recourse to any of his sympathetic circumstances. In a February 22, 1935, article on the film in *Film* Weekly, a British movie magazine, the actor revealed how uncomfortable he was in discovering his character to be "a terrible scallywag." Hecht (per Rains) was unimpressed: "That guy's a heel! I know he's a heel," cried the scenarist. "And that's my idea of a hero! Play him just as he is—and don't take the edge off anything!" The actor's acclaimed performance as attorney Nathan Rubin in The Theatre Guild's *They Shall Not Die* earlier in 1934 had won him the team's invitation to topline *Crime*, and the writers had little doubt that he would be a quite convincing scallywag.

Unlike most of his cadre of scoundrels, there's virtually nothing redeeming about Rains' Lee Gentry. Sneering at integrity to Katy ("I live by lies, make money by lies, I've become famous by lies"), he seeks to explain away his seeing her rival every night as a form of chivalry! ("Even after you've grown to hate a woman," he murmurs, "you can't pick up your hat and go; you've got to do it like a gentleman.") In court, he doctors exhibits, manufactures evidence, insults his opponents, and talks down to the jury as if it were a band of moronic school children.

In addition, having gone from a role which was all voice and no "body," Rains found himself in a part which further challenged his velvety pipes, while demanding that he appear (literally) alongside himself. The Rains temperament (which had been as slow to manifest itself as had been the Rains physique during the shooting of *The Invisible Man*) now came to the fore:

One day we had a lot of difficulty with one of my scenes. It was the tricky double-exposure sequence in which my logical mental self argues with my illogical emotional self. I played it through once and something went wrong with the lights. I played it through again and something went wrong with the camera. I played it through a third time and something went wrong with the sound. And then I started making mistakes myself. I became mechanical. There was no feeling in my expressions, no meaning in my lines. I blew up.

"I'm not going on with this!" I shouted. "I'm not a puppet!"

There was an awed silence. Everybody waited respectfully for me to cool down. Then Charlie, quite unperturbed, said quietly, "O.K., puppet. Let's take a rest." From then on he always called me his "little puppet." How can you get temperamental with a man like that?

(*Film Weekly*, op. cit.)

For some critics, like *The Family Circle*'s Harry Evans, the newly visible Rains took some getting used to:

During the opening scenes of "Crime Without Passion" I was pretty sure I was going to find Mr. Rains' acting boring, due to his inclination to strut and make fussy gestures. However, as the film progresses, Mr. Rains becomes a more and more interesting character. He's one of those birds who gets under your skin, and it's difficult to explain because he's not an impressive-looking man, nor is his voice particularly easy to take. Maybe it's because he is a good actor. That often has something to do with it.

[October 5, 1934]

Others, however, found the actor distinctly more palatable from the get-go, although *Variety* faulted his voice for its British cadence rather than for its being hard to take. *The New York Times*' Mordaunt Hall heard nothing amiss whatsoever, and, in fact, wrote that Rains "gets full effect out of the cleverly written speeches and gives an extraordinarily clear characterization." (September 1, 1934)

All in all, *Crime Without Passion* was a wonderful follow-up to the more outlandish excesses of *The Invisible Man*. Lee Gentry was Rains' first step at overcoming the blatant theatricality that had been concealed by

Jack Griffin's bandages, and the smug attorney's ghostly alter-ego bridged the gap between the literal transparency of Wells' novel and the transparent literalness of Rains' next film, *The Man Who Reclaimed His Head*. Even now, after so many years, the Hecht-MacArthur magic still either excites or estranges viewers; the authors had purposefully left very little middle ground upon which to tread.

*Crime Without Passion* Paramount. Released August 17, 1934. 70 minutes.

CLAUDE RAINS (Lee Gentry); Margo (Carmen Brown); Whitney Bourne (Katy Costello); Stanley Ridges (Eddie White); Leslie Adams (State's Attorney O'Brien); Greta Granstedt (Della); Esther Dale (Miss Keely); Charles Kennedy (Lieut. Norton); Fuller Melish (Judge); Paula Trueman (Buster Malloy); Betty Sundmark, Fraye Gilbert, Dorothy Bradshaw (Furies); Ben Hecht, Charles MacArthur (Reporters); with Helen Hayes, Fannie Brice, Mickey King, Alice Anthon, and The Bobby Duncan Troupe

Producers/Directors: Ben Hecht and Charles MacArthur; Associate Director: Lee Garmes; Screenplay: Ben Hecht and Charles MacArthur based on the short story, "Caballero of the Law," by Ben Hecht; Director of Photography: Lee Garmes; Camera Operator: Leo Lipp; Special Effects: Slavko Vorkapich; Film Editor: Arthur Ellis; Scenery: Albert Johnson; Musical Score Composer and Arranger: Frank Tours; Sound Recording: Joseph Kane

## *The Man Who Reclaimed His Head* (1934)

France, during the Great War. Paul Verin (Claude Rains) arrives at the office of his attorney (Henry O'Neill) carrying his little daughter Linette (Baby Jane Quigley) and an ominous-looking satchel. In flashback, he reveals how he and his wife Adele (Joan Bennett) had been poor but happy before his association with Henri Dumont (Lionel Atwill), an ambitious politician with lofty aspirations. Dumont had hired Paul to ghostwrite pacifist editorials for him, and these had won Dumont tremendous acclaim and respect.

Behind Paul's back, Dumont had also been courting Adele, using her desire to return to Paris from the countryside to sway Paul's writings to Dumont's changing views. Archduke Ferdinand's assassination ignited the hostilities and Paul, unwilling to sell out his ideals for Dumont, soon found himself on the front lines. Dumont collaborated with war profiteers, who plotted to prolong the fighting so long as there was money to be made. Paul was on his way to Verdun when news of Dumont's betrayal and the danger to Adele's honor brought him back to Paris. With his bayonet, Paul killed Dumont, claiming that he wanted to get back what had been stolen from him: his wife and his mind.

The attorney glances at the satchel, aware that, in a very literal way, Paul has "reclaimed his head." He counsels his client to turn himself over to the police and to trust in justice, mercy, and Adele's love to see him through his ordeal.

This intriguing but uneven film is a bowdlerized version of the Jean Bart play that had lingered for 28 performances at New York's Broadhurst Theater in 1932. Bart (real name: Marie Antoinette Sarlabous) divvied up the duties of adapting her drama to the screen with Samuel Ornitz, and it's not clear which of the screenwriters (or which outside force) opted to divest Rains' movie Paul Verin of the sundry ailments and deformities which his legitimate Paul Verin had had to endure. This decision was both perplexing and ironic in that Universal was already notorious as the home to ghoulies and beasties (including Rains' own macabre Invisible Man). Why, of all the studios in Hollywood, would the House that Carl Built purchase a property that revolved around the anguish of a brilliant goblin and then pare away the very quality for which the company had become known? Strange are the ways of real life.

The play had suffered not only from

over-writing, but also from poor timing; by 1932, the specter of the Great War had been supplanted by the bugbear of the Great Depression. While every mother's son and daughter craved some form of entertainment as a respite from frustration and to ward off despair, very few had the financial or psychological wherewithal to sit through such a lengthy session of political moralizing in the hopes of finding it enjoyable rather than therapeutic. While the advent of talkies a few years earlier had mined the vein profitably—moviegoers were still arguing whether Lewis Milestone's *All Quiet on the Western Front*, Howard Hughes' *Hell's Angels*, or James Whale's *Journey's End* (1930, all) was the thematic *pièce de résistance*—and while audiences would always sit enrapt by wartime tales of intrigue, romance, or heroism (especially if enlivened by the breath of scandal [like *The Last Outpost*, 1935], or fascinating special effects [a la *The Dawn Patrol*, 1938]), they had little patience for the attendant politics.

The greatest irony of all was that the work's underlying warning—through indifference, man risks disaster by having others think and act in his stead—went largely unheeded, as the theme failed to attract enough ticket-buyers (in either medium) to make an impact.

Rains was a veteran of World War I, of course, and was no stranger to either the horrors of the front lines or the sacrifice and suffering which marked the home front. Probably because of this, his character takes on considerable dramatic weight only after the outbreak of hostilities, when he suddenly realizes that jingoism and pacifism are more than theoretical constructs. Forces beyond his control compel him to take up the sword, leaving the pen and his earlier rhetoric aside until such time that one may again argue for peace on purely philosophic terms. But there are choices to be made even in the heat of battle: On his way home to avenge his honor, Verin collides with a nun, and some hamfisted symbolism—the crucifix or the bayonet?—gives pause to the erstwhile pacifist, before he opts to move ever farther afield. Intellectually, such an ideological about-face is less than reassuring; emotionally, it's the ticket to catharsis and a block or two into the neighborhood of a happy ending. If it be true that without conflict, there can be no drama, then Rains, who thrived on drama, does his best work in the picture here.

Early in the film, though, he is called upon to demonstrate near imbecilic complacence with his livelihood and his lifestyle, and he is rather less successful. The Verins are obviously poor as church mice and supposedly happy as clams, but church mice and clams can co-exist peaceably only in Paul's mind. Adele is less than thrilled with their living on the edge, and virtually everyone on either side of the screen is aware of this, save for Paul. That Verin is thought to have his finger on the ethical pulse of Western Civilization, yet cannot sense disappointment in his bed or danger at his door, is not the stuff of pacifist drama, but fodder for soap opera.

Bart and Ornitz are guilty of changing horses midstream, of shifting the stylistic emphasis of what had essentially been (in the worst sense of the phrase) a "woman's picture" to a (very) old-fashioned melodrama, complete with damsels in distress, imperiled tots, mustachioed villains, heroes rushing to the rescue, mysterious packages, the power of the cross, railroad tracks, and the snatching of the fair-haired heroine from a fate worse than death in the nick of time. Once war is declared, the film frees itself from the sort of gabby oversimplification that marked the worst of dime novels and daytime radio and assumes the visually oriented narrative style proper to motion pictures. People stop being symbols and start acting like people; such symbols that do remain advance the plot, rather than embody the plot.

Rains—hell, everyone (with the exception of the highly irritating Baby Jane Quigley) —fares better when the call to arms at last introduces some action into the verbose screenplay, and they fare best when they rise above the importance of the message and indulge in the dynamics of the medium. In fact, the second half of *The Man Who Reclaims His Head* is very nearly the stylistic preamble to the halfpenny thrills of *Mystery of Edwin Drood* that were to follow. The three leads are pretty much impeccable, paying the thin but convoluted material more attention than it deserves.

Andre Sennwald of *The New York Times* felt burdened by the portent of the picture, but found the experience satisfying enough because of Rains' performance:

> The new photoplay at the Rialto has the overwrought and underdone look of a theme which has caused its author's head to whirl with the magnitude of its implications.... This cautious reporter is not prepared to admit that Mr. Rains' portrait of applied hysteria is the brilliant piece of acting that some of his disciples appear to believe. But it is certainly arresting, and it is dosed with the kind of virtuoso terrorism that makes it difficult for you to breathe when he is on the screen.
>
> (January 9, 1935)

The December 8, 1934, issue of the *Motion Picture Herald* waxed enthusiastically about the film's potential to exhibitors; would that the critic have been a better prognosticator:

> ...It is gripping entertainment. Because of its provocative premise, Claude Rains' outstanding characterization, the performances of the principal supports, Joan Bennett and Lionel Atwill, together with story significance, it potentially is to be one of the season's most talked about productions.

Char, over at *Variety*, homed in unerringly on the picture's gear-shifting excesses when he noted that "Depending on the occasion, [Rains] can be as sweet as a little boy or as mad as a butchering murderer."

*The Man Who Reclaimed His Head* Universal. Released January 8, 1935. 82 minutes.

CLAUDE RAINS (Paul Verin); Joan Bennett (Adele Verin); Lionel Atwill (Henri Dumont); Baby Jane Quigley (Linette Verin); Henry

O'Neill (Fernand DeMarnay); Henry Armetta (Laurent); Wallace Ford (Curly); Lawrence Grant (Marchand); Ferdinand Gottschalk (Baron); William B. Davidson (Charlus); Gilbert Emery (His Excellency); Hugh O'Connell (Danglas); Rollo Lloyd (Jean); Bessie Barriscale (Louise); G. P. Huntley (Pierre); Valerie Hobson (Mimi); Doris Lloyd (LuLu); Noel Francis (Chon-Chon); Walter Walker, Edward Martindel, Craufurd Kent, C. Montague Shaw (Dignitaries); Edward Van Sloan, Purnell Pratt, Jameson Thomas (Munitions Board Directors); Judith Wood (Margot); Lloyd Hughes (Andre); Bryant Washburne, Sr. (Antoine); Boyd Irwin (Petty Officer)

Producer: Carl Laemmle, Jr.; Executive Producer: F. R. Mastroly; Director: Edward Ludwig; Associate Producer: Henry Henigson; Screenplay: Jean Bart, Samuel Ornitz; based on the drama, *The Man Who Reclaimed His Head*, by Jean Bart; Additional Dialogue: Barry Trivers; Director of Photography: Merritt Gerstad; Asst. Cameraman: Paul Hill; Process Photography: John P. Fulton; Musical Director: Heinz Roemheld; Art Director: Albert S. D'Agostino; Film Editor: Murray Seldeen; Supervising Editor: Maurice Pivar; Recording Engineer: Gilbert Kurland; Assistant Directors: W. J. Reiter, Fred Frank; Wardrobe: Vera West; Make-Up: Jack P. Pierce

# *Mystery of Edwin Drood*
(1935)

Young Edwin Drood (David Manners) and Rosa Bud (Heather Angel) have been betrothed since they were children, but each has come to regard the other more as a friend than a potential life partner. Thus, as their long-awaited wedding approaches the two dissolve all emotional bonds and agree to look elsewhere for romance and fulfillment. Unfortunately, neither has the chance to reveal this to John Jasper (Claude Rains), Drood's uncle and choirmaster of Cloisterham cathedral, who has taken to opium to quell his secret passion for Rosa. Edwin suddenly disappears, and Jasper stirs up local fires, recounting how his nephew and Neville Landless (Douglass Montgomery), a hot-headed Ceylonese youth who has come to live with the Reverend Dr. Crisparkle (Francis L. Sullivan), had nearly come to blows over Rosa on the very night before Drood had vanished.

The choirmaster's testimony cinches public sentiment about Landless, who—still proclaiming his innocence—manages to escape from prison and make for parts unknown.

Not long after, Cloisterham is visited by Mr. Datchery, an old man with an uncommon interest in the mystery of Edwin Drood. Datchery makes it his business to question anyone who might shed some light on the matter, including Durdles (Forrester Harvey), the usually besotted caretaker of the cathedral's cemetery and mausoleum and the old woman (Zeffie Tilbury) who supplies the town's addicts with opium and privacy. Deducing that his obsession with Rosa had led Jasper to kill Drood and then to seek to dispose of his body with quicklime in an empty, unmarked crypt, Datchery confronts the choirmaster, revealing himself as Neville Landless. Horrified that he had murdered his nephew needlessly, Jasper makes for the spires of the cathedral. There, he throws himself to his death in the sight of the pursuing townspeople.

To aficionados of barnstorming melodrama from the old school, *Mystery of Edwin Drood* is a most enjoyable way to kill an hour and a half. There's not for a moment any mystery as to who did it, or why; the scripted mechanics steer Charles Dickens' last (and unfinished) novel to an obvious conclusion, and very few of those familiar with the work have ever groused about the move. With all that poking about on the atmospheric crypt set (thank you, Charles D. Hall and *Dracula*), neither is the savvy viewer ever truly perplexed as to where poor Edwin has gone. For all that, the glimpse of the lime-charred outline of the *corpus delicti* still takes one's breath away, as it rings down a ghastly final curtain on the crime and provides a stark,

Claude *(to lower right of boom operator)* watches as David Manners *(behind clapper)* sets to meet Heather Angel *(back to camera)*. The scene depicts Cloisterham *á la* the San Fernando Valley. *Courtesy of the Pentagram Library*

visual image of the profound hollowness of Jasper's "love" for his nephew.

The book—like most of Dickens' novels—is a screed about the hypocrisy of Victorian society, but the characters—like most of Dickens' *later* characters—are less whimsical and more earnest than their earlier counterparts. Their names may still verge on the onomatopoeic (Crisparkle, Grewgious), the ominous (Drood), or the symbolic (Landless), but the sly humor with which their author had imbued their literary ancestors is nowhere to be found in Cloisterham. As popular as the unfinished work was (and *is*), it really was one of Dickens' lesser flashes of brilliance. With snarling bouts of fisticuffs, flashing knives, raging tempests,

nocturnal prowlings, whited sepulchers, opium dreams, and enigmatic intruders, *Mystery of Edwin Drood* seems more the spiritual child of Sax Rohmer than of the self-styled critic of the Industrial Revolution. The wonder is that the work—to which Gaumont Studios had devoted some two and a half reels back in 1909—was never later revamped to suit the blood and thunder ministrations of Tod Slaughter, Britain's specialist in the macabre.

Substantial amounts of money were invested to ensure that the plot would unwind against a solid and authentic background, and everyone—from Rains to Louise Carter, bringing up the rear as Mrs. Crisparkle—did a bang-up job in keeping a straight face.

Mindful of the very real danger of having this sort of thing descend into self-parody, director Stuart Walker—who had just finished helming Universal's *Great Expectations*—succeeded in eliminating all traces of the tub-thumping which would have dated (and thus, doomed) the picture immediately. With film a primarily visual medium, the Dickensian prose had to yield to George Robinson's canny lens, with the happy result that the effusiveness of the novel's language—which had been deplored as "old fashioned" by the majority of literary critics when the unfinished manuscript was first published—was reined in on the screen. Still, John L. Balderston (who had brought *The Mummy* to the screen in 1932) and Gladys Unger crafted a screenplay which nimbly balanced the story's futile tragedy with the piecemeal revelation of Jasper's pathetic yet despicable personality, resulting in *Drood* emerging as one of the best quasi-horror films of the period. The downside was that the structure of the narrative assured the film's relative lack of suspense; for the ticket-buyer, the only mystery was how the choirmaster was going to get his at the end.

*Mystery of Edwin Drood* marked Rains' fourth consecutive venture into the neighborhood of madness, and three of those had been for the Laemmles. The actor would leave the studio—but not the throes of cinematic dementia—after the picture opened to less than total enthusiasm. In light of the varied opportunities which were his during his lengthy stay at Warners, however, Universal's unwillingness to commit for the long haul was a blessing in disguise. The roles of Jack Griffin, Paul Verin, and John Jasper had been verified and yet it seemed that the studio was grooming Rains to be a tertiary bogey, on call to fill in the spaces left vacant by Karloff and Lugosi.

As Jasper, there is never a moment when Rains is not called upon to speak volumes with his face. The degenerate churchman is forever shifting facial gears over the shoulders and behind the backs of the other dramatis personae, and the audience—privy both to these constant, instantaneous transformations *and* to the break-up of Drood and Rosa at the eleventh hour—becomes an impotent bystander, a silent witness to circumstances which, in reality—or under the proscenium arch—would cry out for crying out. John Jasper is certainly not among the subtlest of the actor's screen portraits, but the residual theatricality that is still pretty much evident here is in sync with the larger-than-life parameters of the character himself. In light of this, *Variety* applauded Rains for imparting "a wealth of weirdness and intensity to the production." Taking a wider tack, the *Motion Picture Herald* also gave him the okay, while acknowledging that the actor "has made for himself a reputation for strongly dramatic portrayals."

Neither *Great Expectations* nor *Drood* did enough business to convince the bean-counters that Universal and Charles Dickens were meant for each other the way that, say, Universal and Edgar Allan Poe were. (Of course, the reaction of the outraged British critics later in 1935 to *The Raven* would see not only that author but the entire horror genre take a flyer for a while.) Nevertheless, *Drood* entertained audiences sufficiently well to go into the black before it and *Great Expectations* were pushed into the shadows by *David Copperfield* and *A Tale of Two Cities*, upscale Dickens produced by MGM.

It was at this juncture that Rains was again released by Universal; he cared not a whit. His professional and personal sensibilities otherwise engaged (a British-Gaumont contract for *The Clairvoyant* shared pocket space with divorce papers from Beatrix Thompson), the actor had England, Warner Brothers, and Frances Propper in his future. They helped ease his pain.

*Mystery of Edwin Drood* Universal. Released February 4, 1935. 87 minutes.

CLAUDE RAINS (John Jasper); Douglass Montgomery (Neville Landless/Mr. Datchery); Heather Angel (Rosa Bud); Valerie Hobson (Helena Landless); David Manners (Edwin Drood); Francis L. Sullivan (Crisparkle); Zeffie Tilbury

(Opium Den Woman); Ethel Griffies (Mrs. Twinkleton); E. E. Clive (Thomas Sapsea); Walter Kingsford (Mr. Grewgious); Forrester Harvey (Durdles); Vera Buckland (Mrs. Tope); Elsa Buchanan (Mrs. Tisher); George Ernest (Deputy); J. M. Kerrigan (Chief Verger Tope); Louise Carter (Mrs. Crisparkle); Harry Cording, D'Arcy Corrigan (Opium Fiends); Anne O'Neal (Crisparkle Maid); Will Geer (Villager)

Associate Producer: Edmund Grainger; Director: Stuart Walker; Screenplay: John L. Balderston and Gladys Unger, based on the novel, *The Mystery of Edwin Drood*, by Charles Dickens; Adaptation: Bradley King and Leopold Atlas; Special Effects: John P. Fulton; Director of Photography: George Robinson; Editor: Edward Curtiss; Musical Score: Edward Ward; Art Director: Albert S. D'Agostino; Assistant Directors: Phil Karstein and Harry Mancke; Recording Engineer: Gilbert Kurland; Technical Advisor: Mme. Hilda Grenier; Makeup: Otto Lederer; Hair: Margaret Donovan

# *The Clairvoyant* (1935)

Maximus the Great (Claude Rains) and his wife, Mlle. Rene (Fay Wray), are small-time music-hall mind readers. Together with his mother, Topsy (Mary Clare), and his partner, Simon (Ben Field), Maximus and Rene discover—to mixed emotions—that Maximus is subject to moments of genuine clairvoyance, but apparently only when in the presence of Christine Strawen (Jane Baxter). After his prediction of a train wreck has earned him notoriety (and an extended engagement at the London Palace Theatre), the occasional seer foretells the winner of the Derby. This success catapults him to national renown and a position on the staff of *The Daily Sun*, a newspaper published by Lord Southwood (Athole Stewart), Christine's father.

Maximus is troubled by the responsibility imposed upon him by this "gift," and Rene is distressed at the relationship which is blossoming between her husband and Christine. Things get worse, as Topsy is killed by a fall downstairs, a portent of which

Maximus had experienced but ignored. The distraught prophet is torn between loyalty to his wife and his "duty" to humanity. While in the act of resigning from *The Daily Sun*, Maximus has a premonition of a mining disaster which will cost hundreds of lives. When Lord Southwood refuses to publish an account of this vision, Maximus and Christine make for the mine and frantically try to warn the workers themselves. Foreman MacGregor (Frank Cellier) bullies the men back to work with threats of firings; within moments, an ill-timed explosion has caused a cave-in, and most of the miners lose their lives in the Humber River shaft.

Maximus is arrested and charged with instigating the state of panic which led to the disaster. As an angry mob gathers outside the Court of Assizes, both Rene and Christine testify to Maximus' gift as being genuine. For the last time, the clairvoyant and the publisher's daughter bond psychically, and the courtroom is hushed as the prediction that 110 survivors of the catastrophe are making their way to safety. Corroboration of the vision is soon in coming, and Maximus is declared *Not Guilty* by both judge and jury.

*The Clairvoyant* marked a departure from Rains' previous screen roles, all of which found him dancing about somewhere in the throes of madness; here, his Maximus is aghast at the insane reactions of others to his gift of second sight. Still, for some viewers, the distinction is not worth mentioning.

The picture was a prestige effort for Gainsborough, a British company which, like most of its competitors at this time, usually proffered the public insipid renditions of obscure literature (not that Ernst Lothar's source novel was sitting on anybody's bedstand), or overblown adaptations of antiquated dramatic works. Still, frugality being a national virtue, there was no shame in the studio's plundering the stock footage library (the film opens with an ocean liner cruising *backwards* into port) or utilizing extant sets. Nor was there anything apart from praise in

Original theater promo art for Claude's second British picture.

its employing the *crème de la crème* of the country's supporting artists; the secondary cast list reads like a Who's Who of Early British Talkies.

The top-billed ensemble is a bit uneven, however. At scarcely 40 years of age, Mary Clare was a half-decade younger than her onscreen son, and while the actress would go on to embody an impressive array of dowagers and grand dames, she is—despite the efforts of the uncredited makeup man— clearly not of an appropriate vintage here. The character of Topsy is equal parts stage mom, marriage counselor, and Border Collie—with just a dash of Cassandra thrown in—and would probably have been better served by Miss Clare had she come upon the role some 20 years down the line.

Ben Field is just splendid as Simon, Maximus' partner and—just possibly—Topsy's significant other. Likewise, Fay Wray brings beauty and class to Mlle. Rene, although *her* growing unease about the future of her professional and personal life comes a little too early in the proceedings for some people's taste. Jane Baxter is adequate as Christine Strawen, the psychic "battery" who powers Maximus' conduit to the future. It's hardly a surprise that Christine falls in love with the bewildered seer, and that Rene fans the dramatic fires by jumping to the sorts of conclusions normally associated with heroines in mid-contrivance. But, even so, the supposed *menage a trois* generates no real electricity. Realistically, Baxter is neither attractive enough to supplant the darkly beautiful Wray, nor intense enough to out-emote her. And, despite the script's forcing Rains to admit that a "queer sort of sympathy" links Baxter's character to his, or its having him ponder aloud whether Maximus' love for Rene can withstand such a psychic onslaught, one never doubts for a moment that Baxter will end the film in Fay Wray's shadow.

Even with his eyebrow-elevating shtick a tad overdone, Rains offers a wonderful portrait of a good-hearted fellow (of limited talent), who glimpses the appalling responsibility that true clairvoyance can bring. The recent availability of the film in its original form[8] adds dimension to one's appreciation of the King of Mind Readers. The opening sequences, aboard ship and on the customs line, reveal a man who is much more in sync with his lovely wife's heart than with the cues which supposedly lead him to her mind. These vignettes, and the boardinghouse scene wherein Maximus impishly delights in having landed his little troupe a whale of an engagement, hand Rains the opportunity (not had in any of his earlier features) to create a person of whole cloth. Maximus' trances are all the more striking and his frustrations all the more profound for the knowledge that the man behind them is normally given to pranks, gags, and kisses.

Along with Rains' early-thirties' Universal melodramas, *The Clairvoyant* has always been considered as something of a horror picture, but that tag is as ill-suited here as it is for *The Man Who Reclaimed His Head*. (In a ghost-written publicity puff-piece in Britain's *Film Weekly* magazine, however, Fay Wray maintained that whenever Rains pantomimed going into a trance, she felt "a horrible cold shiver run down [her] spine.") Madness does indeed attempt to rear its ugly head, but, for all his near-hysterics, Maximus is ultimately shown to be the sanest man in a society at once anxious for word of the future and terrified at its portent. The horror—such as it is—lay not so much in the varied disasters which befall the populace as in the guilty awareness that these tragedies might have been averted had people only heeded the warnings. Only moments before his timely vindication in the courtroom, Maximus himself is made to wonder whether the most devastating of his prophecies was not self-fulfilling.

Charles Bennett, Bryan Edgar Wallace, and Robert Edmunds got the screen writing credit here, and theirs was the requisite task of transforming Ernst Lothar's tale of an impecunious Austrian seer into the more readily understandable milieu of the English music hall. The picture was assigned to

Maurice Elvey (*nee* William Folkard), a craftsman who had been around since the *very* early days of silent film, and who went on to become one of the most prolific of British directors. Elvey helmed almost 300 films in a career which exceeded 50 years, among them the Eille Norwood version of *The Hound of the Baskervilles* (1921) and Gaumont's science fiction/fantasy, *The Tunnel* (1935).

Distributors of the Gainsborough product, Gaumont-British, went whole hog in publicizing the film, going so far as to issue *two* pressbooks, one aimed at a decidedly more upscale market than the other. Much of the usual claptrap and more than enough hyperbole can be found in both pieces, but it's doubtful whether Rains could have been thrilled by such biographical observations as "...looks taller on screen than he really is," and "...is one of the few short men who doesn't possess a collection of Napoleana."

The British press was pleased enough with *The Clairvoyant*; while they were aware of the production's shortcomings, they were effusive in their plaudits for their diminutive countryman:

First, last and all the time, the honours belong to Claude Rains. He dominates every foot of the action, almost, with another of his compelling studies of abnormal mentality.... Jane Baxter is scarcely strong enough as the girl from whom the Clairvoyant derives his mysterious powers, but Fay Wray plays the faithful wife with characteristic efficiency, and the support is generally good.
(*Film Weekly*; August 9, 1935)

Their American cousins were downright penurious in their praise of anything/anyone other than Claude. Typical of the reception the picture received was this comment by *The New York Times*:

Had the producers elected to stress the danger of knowing too much about the future, rather than building so long upon the issue of the wife's jealousy, "The Clairvoyant" would have been more effective drama. In its present form it is a rather meandering melodrama which would be utterly unimportant except for Mr. Rains's' [sic] presence.

His vigorous and sensitive performance is about all that holds a faulty story structure together.
(June 8, 1935)

Not caring to stay over in the UK longer than anticipated, Rains refused additional picture offers from other English film companies.

Despite the overall lack of critical enthusiasm, *The Clairvoyant* helped Gainsborough meet the notes, and is still a painless way of easing into the future.

*The Clairvoyant* Gainsborough/Gaumont-British. Released June 7, 1935. (New York premiere). 81 minutes.

CLAUDE RAINS (Maximus); Fay Wray (Rene); Mary Clare (Topsy); Ben Field (Simon); Jane Baxter (Christine); Athole Stewart (Lord Southwood); C. Denier Warren (James J. Bimeter); Frank Cellier (MacGregor); Donald Calthrop (Derelict); Felix Aylmer (Counsel); Jack Raine (Customs Official); Graham Moffat (Page); George Merritt (Guard); Eliot Markeham (Man); Percy Parsons (Showman); Margaret Davidge (Lodging Housekeeper)

Producer: Michael Balcon; Director: Maurice Elvey; Screenplay: Charles Bennett, Bryan Edgar Wallace, Robert Edmunds, based on the novel, *The Clairvoyant*, by Ernst Lothar and the English-language translation by B. Ryan (New York, 1932); Director of Photography: G. MacWilliams; Editor: Paul Capon; Musical Director: Louis Levy; Dresses (Set Decoration): Joe Strassner; Wardrobe: Marianne; Recording: Harry Hand; Music: Arthur Benjamin

# *The Last Outpost* (1935)

During the Great War, armored car patrol officer Michael Andrews (Cary Grant) is captured by the Kurds, and the cruelest of his captors turns out to be a member of British Intelligence, who owns up to the name "Smith" (Claude Rains). Smith frees Andrews and together the men help save the Balkari people from the bloodthirsty Kurd irregulars, despite the treachery of Cullen (Jameson Thomas), an English spy working

**Helmets and mustaches, wherever you look: the title card from** *The Last Outpost*. *Courtesy The Morris Everett Collection*

for the enemy. Smith rides off to new adventure while Andrews, his leg fractured, is taken to a hospital in Cairo.

At the end of a couple of months, Andrews has his cast removed and immediately declares his love for his nurse, Rosemary Hayden (Gertrude Michael). In love with him as well, Hayden reveals that she has been married for three years to a man she scarcely knows, and that, a week after their wedding, her husband had been whisked off into the war. Meanwhile, Smith, whose real name is John Stevenson, is given six months' leave for his splendid work among the Kurds, and he makes for Cairo and Rosemary, his wife. Stevenson quickly senses that something is amiss and Rosemary confesses that she loves Andrews; Stevenson is bent on revenge.

Andrews, though, has been assigned to the Sudan, where he is to help rout rampaging natives. Stevenson tracks him down and is within a hair of shooting him when their fort is attacked, prompting the men to put aside their differences for the moment. Hoping to intercept the relief troops and warn them of an impending ambush, the soldiers abandon the fort during the night. The next day, all are slaughtered except for Andrews and Stevenson, who must cross the desert if they are to alert the unwary British. Stevenson reaches the column in time, and then returns to save Andrews' life once again—this time, at the cost of his own.

One of the first pictures to really posit Cary Grant in a rough-and-ready action role, and Claude Rains' last non–Warner

Bros. film for some years to come, *The Last Outpost* is an only partially successful blend of genuine excitement, formulaic lovemaking, and the kind of impossible coincidences that characterize grand opera and women's movies. Upon reflection, it's also an uncomfortable sort of picture, depicting as it does the efforts of the British to keep their various "subjects" from taking advantage of the Great War and freeing themselves of the yoke of the Empire. If Rains' mission in the first third of the film is grounded in altruism and nobility, his (and Grant's and the whole damn army's) quest in the final third is nothing less than the re-subjugation of an unhappy native populace.

Nonetheless, it's fascinating to watch Rains prowl about the opening reels of the picture, every inch an action hero. Whether he's barking commands in some godforsaken patois, plunging his dirk into the chest of the despicable Jameson Thomas, or even kicking in Mr. Grant's sweaty but handsome ribs, Rains makes the sort of impression he hadn't ever made to that point in his film career and would seldom make again. While he's enthusiastically acting against type, nominal star Grant gets the ball rolling by pretty much playing a variation on his typical persona; here, in the words of Graham Greene, he's an "incurably light-minded and rather stupid British officer."

Gertrude Michael is perfectly acceptable as the object of the soldiers' adoration, but her part really wasn't much more than a cannily constructed bridge, separating the two disparate wartime sequences. Frank Nugent of *The New York Times* wrote that "*The Last Outpost* is at its best during those spirited moments at the beginning and the end when Cary Grant and Claude Rains are upsetting the plans of the Turks or exchanging leaden compliments with the tribesmen" (October 5, 1935). Other critics argued that Miss Michael and her romantic dilemma were of (*ahem*) paramount importance in assuring the picture a healthy female audience. As any woman who plunked down her quarter to witness the plot twists of *The Last Outpost*

would have just as eagerly done so to watch Cary Grant spend an hour folding socks, this evaluation may well be discounted. (Just how many *male* ticket-buyers gave a hoot as to who ended up with whom?) Still, had the actress been required to demonstrate a preference for, say, Akim Tamiroff (instead of Grant) over Claude Rains, she would definitely deserve greater praise than she has received to date.

*The Last Outpost* would be *the* big picture for director Louis Gasnier, whose career was otherwise highlighted by an armful of Spanish-language musicals of the thirties that starred Argentine tango singer Carlos Gardel. Gasnier's co-director was Charles Barton, who had started out in sound films with the Marx Brothers, and who later found his most comfortable niche with Abbott and Costello. Which one of the two okayed the overabundance of undercranked stock footage to supplement Rains' strutting among the Balkari, or ordered some ludicrous post-dubbing for the chief of a Sudanese battle strategy confab, is anybody's guess. The photography is adequate, except for scenes of the nighttime attack on Fort Safar, which are too dark. Because cinematographer Theodor Sparkuhl had cut his professional teeth back in 1918 (with Ernest Lubitsch and *Die Augen der Mumie Ma*), this deficiency is hard to accept.

A truckload of writers worked on adapting the original story (F. Britten Austin's "The Drum," which had been kicking around since 1923), and two dialogue directors were needed, not only to provide Grant's ghastly come-on lines ("Do you happen to know I love you?"), but also to work up an ersatz-Kurdish dialect which didn't sound like gobbledygook when mouthed by the featured players. Rains comes across so glibly as to seem bilingual; to Georges Renavent's Turkish major, similar phrases ring falsely.

Reviewing the film for *The Spectator* magazine, Graham Greene made a point of lauding Rains' vocal (rather than physical) prowess:

Mr. Rains's low husky voice, his power in investing even commonplace dialogue with smoldering conviction, is remarkable. He never rants, but one is always aware of what a superb ranter he could be in a part which did not call for modern restraint but only for superb diction.

(October 1935)

Most of the other reviewers expressed gratitude that Rains and Grant spent twice as much time keeping the various deserts and jungles safe for civilization than they did indulging in that selfsame "commonplace dialogue."

*The Last Outpost* Paramount. Released October 11, 1935. 75 minutes

Cary Grant (Michael Andrews); CLAUDE RAINS (John Stevenson); Gertrude Michael (Rosemary Hayden); Kathleen Burke (Ilya); Margaret Swope (Nurse Rowland); Jameson Thomas (Cullen); Nick Shaid (Haidar); Colin Tapely (Lieut. Prescott); Billy Bevan (Pvt. Foster); Claude King (General); Akim Tamiroff (Mirov); Georges Renevant (Turkish Major); Harry Semels (Amrak); Elspeth Dudgeon (Head Nurse); Robert Adair (Sergeant); Meyer Ouhayoun (Armenian Patriarch); Olaf Hytten (Doctor); Frank Elliott (Colonel)

Executive Producer: Henry Herzbrun; Producer: E. Lloyd Sheldon; Directors: Louis Gasnier, Charles Barton; Assistant Director: Edgar Anderson; Dialogue Directors: Max Marcin, Henry C. Potter; Technical Director: Lieut. Col. Wynn E. Wynn, OBE; Screenplay: Philip MacDonald, based on the short story, "The Drum," by F. Britten Austin; Adaptation: Frank Partos and Charles Brackett, with Marguerite Roberts, Arthur Phillips, Eugene Walter, and Max Marcin; Director of Photography: Theodor Sparkuhl; Art Directors: Hans Dreier, Earl Hedrick; Editor: Jack Dennis; Sound: A. W. Singley, J. N. Cope

# *Hearts Divided* (1936)

Napoleon Bonaparte (Claude Rains) has been approached by emissaries of Thomas Jefferson (George Irving), who is looking to buy France's substantial Louisiana territory for the United States; such a purchase would effectively double the size of the fledgling nation. Not at all unwilling to part with the indefensible expanse, Napoleon sends his younger brother Jerome (Dick Powell) to America to act as intermediary. At the horse races in Baltimore, an incognito Jerome meets and becomes enamored with Betsy Patterson (Marion Davies), daughter of Charles Patterson (Henry Stephenson), the most vocal advocate of the purchase. Jerome becomes Betsy's French tutor, and the two fall in love, despite the young Frenchman's being dismissed from his position of tutor for being too forward in his defense of Napoleon.

When the purchase is a fait accompli, Jerome's true identity is revealed at a soiree at the Patterson home; in the presence of President Jefferson and most of the polite society of Virginia and Washington, Betsy and Jerome's engagement also is announced. Only then does the couple become aware of a missive from Napoleon ordering Jerome back to France to wed the Princess of Wurtenberg for reasons of French national security. Jerome is all for staying in America and renouncing his heritage, but he and Betsy sail for France, fully intending to inform the emperor that they will not be parted.

As their ship lies at anchor in a port of France, Napoleon boards and discusses the *affaire du coeur* privately with Betsy. The Little Corporal convinces the young woman to give up her beloved for the sake of the good he can do France. Leaving Jerome on the spot, Betsy returns to the Patterson homestead in Maryland and struggles to get by without him. Back in France, Mme. Bonaparte manages to effect a reconciliation of sorts between her sons while persuading Napoleon to allow Jerome to return to America—for her sake, if for nothing else.

Permission is given and Jerome—now wearing the uniform of a simple seaman—is reunited with Betsy in the garden of her Baltimore home.

Missing from the synopsis is any indication that *Hearts Divided* is an historical drama set to song, or that it suffers from some of the most irritating comedy relief ever seen on the screen.

Released in the summer of 1936—and thus some eight years before *Murder My Sweet* and Philip Marlowe would forever change the audience's perspective of Dick Powell—the picture was another in a series of ersatz, semi-, and full-blown musicals involving the actor and his tenor pipes. As Jerome Bonaparte—surely the last and least of the brothers whom history has rightly delegated to Napoleon's shadow—Powell shines as the traditional light juvenile who falls in love at the drop of a *chapeau*, but who has got to be everyone's absolute last choice as the right man to send on an important mission of international diplomacy. This, however, matters little; a schoolboy's knowledge of the Louisiana Purchase relieves one of any dramatic tension as far as its successful completion is concerned. What's left—your basic boy meets girl, boy loses girl, boy gets girl light musical baloney, extracted in essence from Rida Johnson Young's 1908 drama, *The Glorious Betsy*, and tailored to suit predictable and undemanding 1936 conventions—is mostly pap, and *inaccurate* pap, at that.

The picture had originally been slated to star Leslie Howard and Jean Muir and had borne, albeit briefly, the working title of *Glorious Betsy* (as had the 1928 part-talkie version with Dolores Costello). When William Randolph Hearst brought his Cosmopolitan Productions over to Jack L. Warner's place, extant footage was scrapped, Marion Davies replaced Muir, and Powell was brought in (at Davies' request) to supplant Howard. Songs were added to allow the leading man to play to his strengths, and the tale of Jerome and his Betsy—never a big gun in the canon of historical liaisons—sparked uncertainly without leaving much damage.

Miss Davies had been active in films since the late teens, but *Hearts Divided* would prove to be her last motion picture but for two. Followers of the actress have al-

ways maintained (as did Charlie Chaplin) that her forte was comedy, not weepy and melodramatic treacle, and that she might very well have really come into her own had she not allowed Hearst to dictate her professional life. If one were to judge the truth of that statement solely by *Hearts Divided*, though, one might come away feeling that while the estimable Mr. Chaplin was a comic genius in his own right, he wasn't worth a brass farthing when it came to assessing others. As Betsy, Davies' best moments come when she has tears in her eyes; most of her scripted wit suffers from an absence of discernible comic technique. Likewise, the actress was a bit long in the tooth for a juvenile (she was almost forty at the time); still, despite several unflattering bonnets, an apparent problem with avoirdupois (several gowns show her to be distressingly thick-waisted), and an occasional tendency to stumble about with the grace of an asphalt-spreader, she's no less credible as a romantic lead than Dick Powell is as the brother of Claude Rains.

One's suspension of disbelief gets a well earned respite whenever Rains is on the screen. His turn as Napoleon is simply magnificent, and cinema's loss is that the actor—despite an abundance of Warners' publicity to the contrary—never got to enact *Le Petit Corporal* in a movie biography worthy of both the subject and the impersonator.

The heady title of Emperor of France notwithstanding, Napoleon is a relatively minor figure in this tale of crushes and crooners, but director Frank Borzage makes certain that his every appearance is clever or dramatically valid. The emperor is introduced via an adroit segue from Jefferson's map of the territories in question to its twin some 3000 miles away. We see his back, we hear his voice—wisely, Rains opts not to affect a French accent—and, once he turns into the camera, the blend of makeup, stature, wit, and interpretation gives us a Napoleon who might very well have stepped from a portrait by Jacques Louis David.

**Betsy Patterson (Marion Davies) matches wits with *Le petit corporal*. Plans to star Claude as Napoleon in a full-length biography came to naught.** *Courtesy Buddy Barnett*

When Jerome later snarls to his aides that his brother can "go soak," Borzage cuts to the conqueror signing documents and waxing philosophically of women and war while nestled in his bath. For sheer impact, however, nothing matches Napoleon's unexpected and chilling appearance at the cabin door an instant after Jerome—in another fit of love-inspired pique—has remanded him to the devil. Clad in that famous black military hat and greatcoat, Rains *is* Napoleon.

There is a handful of memorable lines in the Laird Doyle-Casey Robinson screenplay, and they are (like those eponymous hearts) divided—mainly, between the lovebirds; still, Rains gets off his share of bon mots. Seemingly sympathetic to Betsy's outpourings of love and frustration—she avers that

she would die for Jerome—the emperor reminds her that "To die for him is easy; to live without him is hard." Then, having won her over to his way of thinking, he disarms her completely with the most obvious of flattery. "You were very sure of yourself, M. le Emperor," the defeated woman observes. "No," rejoins Napoleon, "only certain that any woman whom Jerome would love would be a gallant lady." Glib, perhaps, but totally believable when purred in Rains' honey-laden tones.

There would be no place in a serious picture about Napoleon Bonaparte for heavy-handed comic relief; in an innocuous take on the adventures of *Jerome* Bonaparte, however, anything goes. Pitching in to destroy whatever weight and verisimilitude Rains and George Irving have lent to the production are Charlie Ruggles and Edward Everett Horton as a couple of dim bulb U.S. senators, and Arthur Treacher as the equally obtuse and foppish Sir Harry, apparently on permanent loan from the House of Lords. The idea that these imbeciles could be front-runners in the race for Betsy Patterson's hand was doubtless hoped to be amusing—God knows, it wasn't meant to be *flattering*—yet it's all the veteran comedians can do to avoid being seen as other than tiresome in the course of their many laborious scenes.

Yawning a bit when *Hearts Divided* came their way, the critics were anything but divided in their reactions. (At this stage in the game, the reviewers for the Hearst empire had retired the superlatives they had paraded ceaselessly since *Cecilia of the Pink Roses*, back in 1919.) Marion Davies *and* Dick Powell were thought to be miscast (although no one longed in print for the original team of Leslie Howard and Jean Muir), but praise for the fine supporting team (*including* the Messrs. Horton, Ruggles, and Treacher) and Frank Borzage's stylish leadership seemed to balance it all out. Tipping the scales in favor of a "Go see" was, of course, CR's tremendous Napoleon. Even when ensnared in one of cinema's most ludicrous vignettes—the anticlimactic scene in which Jerome tells his mom on his big brother—Rains shines, while appearing only *slightly* embarrassed.

Some 18 minutes were excised between the film's Hollywood preview and its New York opening, yet nothing of dramatic portent (all things being relative) seems to be missing. Even nowadays, many viewers feel that the wit, thrust, and merit of the entire film are best summed up in the brief exchange Rains has with Halliwell Hobbes, who's playing Napoleon's second consul, Cambaceres. Having cowed the American heroine with a display of logic and patriotic sentiment, the Little Corporal is quizzed by his right hand man as they prepare to disembark from the ship:

Cambaceres: "Success?" Napoleon smiles.

Cambaceres: "Strategy?"
Napoleon: "Dramaturgy. An amazingly good actor met an amazingly receptive audience."

Amazingly, in this case, brevity is the soul of wit *and* truth.

*Hearts Divided* Warner Bros. Released June 20, 1936. 70 minutes.

Marion Davies (Betsy Patterson); Dick Powell (Jerome Bonaparte); Charles Ruggles (Henry); CLAUDE RAINS (Napoleon Bonaparte); Edward Everett Horton (John); Arthur Treacher (Sir Henry); Henry Stephenson (Charles Patterson); Clara Blandick (Aunt Ellen); John Larkin (Isham); Walter Kingsford (Pichon); Etienne Girardot (Du Fresne); Halliwell Hobbes (Cambaceres); George Irving (Thomas Jefferson); Beulah Bondi (Mme. Letizia Bonaparte); Freddie Archibald (Gabriel); The Hall Johnson Choir; Hattie McDaniel (Mammy); Sam McDaniel (Servant); Phillip Hurlic (Pippin); Hobart Cavanaugh (Innkeeper); Granville Bates (Livingston); John Elliott (James Monroe); Clinton Rosemond (Black Man); Wilfrid Lucas (Footman)

Executive Producers: Jack L. Warner and Hal B. Wallis; Producer and Director: Frank Borzage; Supervisor: Harry Joe Brown; Assistant Directors: Lew Borzage, John Gates; Screenplay: Laird Doyle, Casey Robinson, based on the play, *Glorious Betsy*, by Rida Johnson Young; Director of Photography by George Folsey; Art Director: Robert Haas; Editor: William Holmes; Gowns: Orry-Kelly; Conductor of Vitaphone Orchestra: Leo F. Forbstein; Incidental Musical Score: Erich Maria Korngold; Original Music and Songs ("My Kingdom for a Kiss" and "Two Hearts Divided"): Harry Warren and Al Dubin; Traditional Spirituals: "Nobody Knows the Trouble I've Had" and "Rise Up Children and Shine"

A Cosmopolitan Production

A First National Picture

# *Anthony Adverse* (1936)

Maria Bonnyfeather (Anita Louise) has been consorting with her true love, Denis Moore (Louis Hayward), while her husband Don Luis (Claude Rains) has been receiving treatment for his gout. Fully recovered, Don Luis discovers his wife's infidelity and kills Moore in a duel. When Maria subsequently dies in childbirth, Don Luis abandons the infant at the Convent of the Holy Child; the nuns christen the boy Anthony. At the age of 10, Anthony is taken by Father Xavier (Henry O'Neill) to be apprenticed at the Casa de Bonnyfeather, a mercantile company. Although John Bonnyfeather (Edmund Gwenn) has been told that both his daughter and grandson lie buried together somewhere in the Italian Alps, he recognizes that his own blood flows in the orphan's veins, and gives the boy the surname Adverse, for the hardships he has had to endure.

Growing into manhood, Anthony falls in love with Angela Giuseppi (Olivia de Havilland), the daughter of the cook, and, after a bit more adversity—Napoleon Bonaparte has invaded Italy—they are married. Anthony agrees to sail for Cuba to ward off ruin for the Casa de Bonnyfeather, but does so without Angela; a note she has left for him has blown away, and neither knows where the other is. Angela decides to pursue an operatic career. From Havana, Anthony sails for Africa, where he joins the slave trade and recoups the monies owed Bonnyfeather. Three years in the trade, however, have corrupted Anthony, who has also grown embittered that neither his wife nor his employer has seen fit to communicate at all with him. The death of the steadfast Brother Francois (Pedro de Cordoba) restores Anthony's soul to him, and he returns to Italy.

In the interim, Bonnyfeather has died, and his housekeeper-cum-mistress, Faith Paleologus (Gale Sondergaard) is due to receive the bulk of his estate, unless Anthony can claim his rightful inheritance in Paris. He does so, but immediately offers his newly found wealth to his old friend Vincent Nolte (Donald Woods) to help *his* firm stave off bankruptcy. As if in reward for his generosity, Anthony locates Angela—now a famous diva—and discovers that he and his wife have a young son. He also discovers that,

under the stage name of Mlle. Georges, Angela has become Napoleon's mistress. Anthony decides to head for America and a new life; he is accompanied by his son—nobly surrendered by Angela, who has resolved to stay in Europe with her career and her Emperor.

The greatest danger in adapting literature to the screen lies in the finesse (or lack thereof) with which one wields the editorial red pencil. If too much verbiage is excised, the resultant film risks being criticized for not being "faithful" to its source, and the pertinence and legitimacy of its extraneous material—usually added by the scenarists to plug up the holes created by "abridgment"—is brought into question. If too *little* editing is done—and this normally holds true of sprawling adventure novels originally commissioned by weight—one has a picture with an alarming tendency to sag in spots and an overabundance of narrative intertitles. In the dark days of yore—before the dawn of the videocassette and pre-dating even the TV mini-series—one could set the book aside when fatigue became overwhelming; one's only option where film was concerned was to repair to the lobby for a smoke and hope to God nothing crucial transpired in the meantime.

Hervey Allen's *Anthony Adverse* was a best seller of high romance and substantial heft, and Hal Wallis had to fabricate a 1200 word synopsis for Jack L. Warner in order to get the studio chief to pay Allen $40,000 for the whole 1200 pages. Sheridan Gibney was assigned to winnow the novel's dramatic highlights to fit the confines of a two-hour motion picture, and he came within a hair's breadth (actually, 19 minutes) of succeeding. Although the end result *was* protracted, the movie became a veritable cash-cow, breaking box-office records for opening revenues and length of runs.

If the film's episodic nature mildly disconcerted the reviewers, it went unnoticed by the masses. Still, it was argued that whole segments—the lengthy sequence devoted to

**Don Luis has caught his bride (Anita Louise) signaling his rival from the window. Nothing good can come of this.** *Courtesy the Wioskowski Collection*

Anthony's African misadventures, for example—could have been somehow shortened, if not eliminated entirely, to the ultimate betterment of the picture. The globe-hopping propensities of the title character may have kept the audiences on their toes, but they also created a raft of sub-plots which detracted from the overall cohesiveness of the work, while adding little other than pages to the novel and running time to the film. Referring to the picture's "kaleidoscopic nature," *The New York Times'* Frank S. Nugent observed that:

Many of these episodes have dramatic virtue, particularly those involving Don Luis, who has been played to perfection by Claude Rains, and those centering upon John Bonnyfeather, drawn to the life by Edmund Gwenn, but a series of dramatic episodes does not make a drama.
(August 27, 1936)

The glue that holds the unwieldy framework together is Fredric March who is, as he always was, magnificent, even in his excesses. (Keeping a close eye on those excesses was director Mervyn LeRoy, for whom *Anthony Adverse* would be the last of his great Warners' productions.) March's Anthony may look off into the depths of his soul or the uncertainty of his future a bit too often for some tastes, but that sort of introspection comes with the territory. He rebounds admirably from any number of personal and professional disappointments, and is preternaturally calm at discovering that a six-year-old son awaits him on his return from a three-year hiatus on the Dark Continent.

The rest of the players—big and not-so-big names alike—do their perukes and period costumes proud, although Steffi Duna tries much too hard as an African femme fatale, and Paul Sotoff is laughable as Ferdinando, striving as he does to match the cavernous vocal reaches of John Carradine, who had initially been signed for the part. Scotty Beckett, late of Hal Roach's Rascals, keeps little Anthony's few lines retch-free, but it's difficult to understand how Gale Sondergaard, given largely to widening her eyes, flaring her nostrils, and hissing her lines through clenched teeth, walked off with the Oscar for best supporting actress.

The lengthy, self-congratulatory trailer that preceded the film into theaters divided its footage nearly equally between hosannas to Hervey Allen and stacks of impressive statistics: 400 screen tests, 5000 extras, 8 million readers, etc., etc., etc. If there were, indeed, some 98 "principal players" (in addition to the 14 "stars") to be captured, identified, and tagged, more than a handful of excruciatingly poor casting choices were made among them. *The AFI Feature Film Catalog* reports on but one of them when it reveals that J. Carroll Naish had tested for the part of Napoleon, only to lose out to Rollo Lloyd, as nondescript a Bonaparte as ever graced a movie screen. *Daily Variety* claimed that Humphrey Bogart had also tried for the Little Corporal, while its weekly sister publication forewent additional names and settled for kvetching about the casting of the role:

Claude Rains does a splendid job as Don Luis. It is curious to see him there, incidentally, since he has almost become the official Warner Bros.' Napoleon, having played that as a bit in a previous WB picture, and is assigned to it as a full-length feature to come.
(September 2, 1936)

The "previous WB picture" was, of course, *Hearts Divided*, the "full-length feature to come" was never made, and this was Rollo Lloyd's only shot at empire-building.

Rains is the blackest of blackguards as Don Luis: He bludgeons footmen with his cane, dispatches Denis Moore with an unerring saber thrust between side and left arm, and outright lies to saintly John Bonnyfeather. For Rains' fans, the absolute highlight of the film has the actor standing alongside Gale Sondergaard on a twisted and treacherous Alpine stretch. The two villains have commanded their snaggle-toothed coachman to force Anthony's carriage into the precipice, thus ridding them of any further competition in the race for the Bonnyfeather fortune. Anthony has anticipated the move, however, and uncouples his own horses at a crucial moment; it is Don Luis' henchman who hurtles to his death. Rains and Sondergaard witness the whole fiasco impassively, like spectators at a flower show. Without looking away from the scene, without so much as moving a muscle, the two bring down the house.

Rains: "He was the best servant I ever had."
Sondergaard: "The coach was rather handy, too."

But the role of Don Luis was not without its potential pitfalls. In one of the most perceptive profiles* ever published on the actor, *Film Weekly* writer W. H. Mooring noted Rains' ability to provide the ideal nuance so crucial to the creation of a masterful portrayal:

I recall, for instance, that wonderful scene in *Anthony Adverse* in which he proclaimed with almost devilish glee that, his gout having departed, he was about equal to the obligations of a deferred honeymoon.

In the hands of an actor who was anything less than a genius, the whole scene might have been transformed into a most disgusting spectacle of senile passion gone riot. Mervyn LeRoy was so afraid of that scene that he wanted to cut it out of the script.

It took Claude Rains half an hour to work out the exact routine for that scene.

Rains carried the scene right to the very edge of that narrow border which divides good drama from bad taste and, extracting every ounce of meaning from the situation, he presented it to us, not as so many actors would have done, with an unpleasant reek about it, but as a perfect exposure of the true emotions of the character he was playing.

That was just what the man would have done; just how he would have been thinking and just the way he might have acted, but not one

**Claude at the wrap party: happy, exhausted, or just glad it's over? Gale Sondergaard is seated to Claude's left.** *Courtesy Richard Bojarski*

actor in a thousand could have suggested it without a suggestiveness which would have turned our stomachs.

(April 2, 1938)

When Rains drives off early in the picture, a good bit of the film's bite disappears with him. Sure, there are plenty of snarls and lots of noise and a punch or two is thrown, but, until the aged Grandee of Spain reappears some two reels before the end credits, there is very little crackle to the narrative. "Things happen, changes come, subtitles assure us that Anthony is at the crossroads," Mr. Nugent wrote, "but somehow we are not convinced that a real crisis impends."

Tough to have a real crisis when the one true villain of the piece is given most of the picture off.

*Anthony Adverse* Warner Bros. Released August 29, 1936. 139 minutes.

Fredric March (Anthony Adverse); Olivia de Havilland (Angela Giuseppi); Donald Woods (Vincent Nolte); Anita Louise (Maria); Edmund Gwenn (John Bonnyfeather); CLAUDE RAINS (Don Luis); Louis Hayward (Denis Moore); Gale Sondergaard (Faith Paleologus); Steffi Duna (Neleta); Akim Tamiroff (Carlo Cibo); Ralph Morgan (Debrulle); Fritz Leiber (Ouvrard); Luis Alberni (Tony Giuseppi); Billy Mauch (Anthony, aged 10); Henry O'Neill (Father Xavier); Pedro de Cordoba (Brother Francois); Joseph Crehan (Captain Jorham); Rafaela Ottiano (Signora Bovino); Rollo Lloyd (Napoleon Bonaparte); Eily Malyon (Mother Superior); Clara Blandick (Mrs. Jorham); Scott Beckett (Anthony's Son, Anthony); J. Carroll Naish (Major Doumet); Frank Reicher (Coach Driver); Ann Howard (Angela, as a Child); Leonard Mudie (De Bourriene);

Addison Richards (Captain Matanaza); Egon Brecher (Innkeeper)

Executive Producers: Hal Wallis, Jack L. Warner; Director: Mervyn LeRoy, Michael Curtiz (uncredited); Production Supervisor: Henry Blanke; Assistant Director: William Cannon; Screenplay: Sheridan Gibney, based on the novel, *Anthony Adverse*, by Hervey Allen; Director of Photography: Tony Gaudio, ASC; Special Effects: Fred Jackman; Art Director: Anton Grot; Editor: Ralph Dawson; Musical Score: Erich Maria Korngold; Conductor Vitaphone Orchestra: Leo F. Forbstein; Opera Sequences: Natale Carossio; Operatic Passages: Aldo Franchetti; Gowns: Milo Anderson; Makeup: Perc Westmore

## *Stolen Holiday* (1937)

Looking to break in to the world of *haute couture* in 1931 Paris is American Nicole Picot (Kay Francis), currently a mannequin in the employ of Mme. Delphine (Kathleen Howard). The young woman is engaged for a private showing by Stefan Orloff (Claude Rains), an expatriate Russian claiming to be personal secretary to one of the local nobility. Nicole quickly sees through this ruse, but Orloff convinces her that they should pool their professional strengths in order to achieve success in their respective fields. They do and within five years Nicole has become a world-famous designer (*La Maison Picot*) and Orloff has the nation's ear regarding financial matters.

Without Nicole's knowledge, but with the media (publisher Francis Chalon [Walter Kingsford]), the mercantile lobby (Charles Ranier of Le Credit Municipal [Frank Reicher]), the diplomatic corps (Deputy Bergery [Egon Brecher]), and the police (Inspector Dupont [Frank Conroy]) all in cahoots, Orloff has engineered a series of schemes to defraud the public. Investigations into these matters are underway, however, and as they begin to take their toll, Nicole meets and falls in love with Anthony Wayne (Ian Hunter), an attaché at the British embassy in Paris. Nonetheless, she

agrees to marry Orloff in order to help him weather increasingly adverse publicity and salvage his reputation. This ploy fails miserably, and Orloff goes into hiding.

With the disgraced financier the object of a nationwide manhunt, the Paris mob erupts violently; *La Maison Picot* is stormed, and people are trampled in the ensuing melee with mounted gendarmes and the fire brigade. Citing this deplorable violence, the prefect of police (Robert Strange) offers Dupont the opportunity to ease his conscience and reduce the severity of the charges leveled against him; the ex-conspirator agrees.

When Nicole receives a note from Orloff, she runs to him, not dreaming that she is being followed by Dupont. At his chalet hideout, Orloff confesses his fiscal sins to Nicole; her willingness to help him touches his heart. Aware that the police have encircled the chalet, Orloff leaves the young woman and walks out into their midst. A shot rings out—the police have "executed" the rogue investment broker—but Dupont, warning Nicole to return to Paris, arranges for the murder to appear as suicide.

Having liquidated all of her assets to reimburse those cheated by Orloff and his accomplices, Nicole prepares to leave Paris forever. She is joined, however, by Mr. Wayne, with whom, it appears, her journey will end at the altar.

With all those chic hats, gowns, and ensembles paraded through miles of cavernous Art Deco salons, there's no way that 1937 viewers could have regarded *Stolen Holiday* as anything other than yet another woman's picture. Despite the well-choreographed riot in front of *La Maison Picot*, there just isn't enough action to merit a genre tag with wider audience appeal. Although based on the real-life exploits of France's notorious "king of crooks," Serge Alexandre Stavisky (despite an opening disclaimer about the characters and events being fictitious), the screenplay refuses to allow one to watch the sundry schemes as they unfold, preferring to confine the dishonesty to pre- and post-scam exposition. It may be true that white-collar crime is less physically compelling than its more brutal counterpart, but film is primarily a visual medium, and when the only relief one has from clutches of gabby—if undeniably clever—narrative is a glimpse now and again of silken chemises loping languidly across an overwaxed floor, there is very real danger of losing the less fashion-conscious portion of the audience. (Had the film been released under its working title—*Mistress of Fashion*—Warners could have counted on one hand the tickets bought with greenbacks nestled in wallets rather than in purses.)

Rains and Kay Francis interplay so delightfully and so well, though, that we're tempted to wave away the fuzzy attention to detail and accept their ascendancy to the heights with a shrug and a smile. Shop windows and office doors metamorphose into fashion and financial command centers, and … *voila!*—in terms of screen time, instant success, and all without having to endure a wearying and clichéd parade of newspaper headlines. (These wait until the next to last reel, when the dailies fall all over themselves to spill the beans.) Since the film doesn't dwell much on Nicole and Orloff's rather modest status in 1931, several potent bits of characterization must be hurled quickly at the outset and hung onto until the end. Suzanne the dresser (Alison Skipworth) thus not only provides a counterbalance to the wholesale quantities of ravishing young models, but also acts as Nicole's friend, confidante, and prognosticator. We might not need her to recognize Nicole's big dreams, but she's a painless way of learning about Nicole's big heart. Before Stefan Orloff can make the ambitious young woman an unwitting accomplice, he *has* no confidante, so Rains must work his smile and his nostrils overtime if the charm that will soon seduce a nation away from its collective common sense is to be visible to the back row.

At different moments before the picture

ends, each of the protagonists is stripped of the fruits of his/her five years' labor. Nicole—not totally innocent of complicity even if ignorant of the scope of Orloff's corruption—atones by voluntarily dissolving her fashion empire in order to make restitution. Orloff, who never *was* anything other than the flim flam man he remains throughout the film, loses his fortune and his life. Still, his innermost feelings for Nicole dictate that, when the two partners meet in the chalet hideout that one last time, there *is* catharsis for Orloff. His knowledge of the police cordon outside and his being moved by Nicole's offer of help (even under such desperate circumstances) makes Orloff's confession to her in essence a deathbed recantation; he receives personal forgiveness for his sins, even if official mercy is to be denied.

The presence of a hale and chubby Anthony Wayne might bring stirrings of the heart to Nicole, but until the last reel neither she nor Orloff undergoes any real transformation. Nicole appears softer, perhaps; she's definitely more feminine than she had been at the outset. (At the initial showing at Mme. Delphine's, a patron finds Nicole's short coiffure "shocking" and "mannish," and the model herself lumbers about lugubriously in a gown which, despite being cut to below the rib-cage, reveals no bosom whatsoever.) This "feminization" can't be what *love* does to one, as the cigarette-puffing virago of the opening scenes vanishes soon after taking up with Orloff; can money and success bring a woman to physical fruition without any *affaires de coeur*?

Orloff is, if anything, more self-assured and suave than he had been earlier, a factor due as much to his warm and profitable relationship with Mlle. Picot as to the well-oiled machinery of corruption he has masterminded. The schemes may have proliferated and the stakes may have risen, but there is little but physical appearance to distinguish the dapper young con man from the sophisticated embezzler.

Lovely Kay Francis had survived the

Marx Brothers (*The Cocoanuts*, 1929) to become one of the leading lights in women's pictures through the mid-thirties. She had moved early in the decade from Paramount to Warners, where each year she would star in four or five romantic dramas targeted at the daydreams of the American housewife and the contemporary working woman. According to biographer Michael Freedland, it was about the time of *Stolen Holiday* that Francis, who had been faithful to Warner Bros. amid a raft of colleagues' defections, was perversely "rewarded" for her loyalty by Jack L. Warner with a *demotion* to B pictures.[9] The doe-eyed actress suffered through a few years more of tolerable if hardly outstanding assignments, and then retired from the screen after 1946's *Wife Wanted*; she may have chosen to co-produce her last three features more for the gratification than for the credentials. Nicole's passions may be a tad too staid for nineties' tastes, but Francis' heroine raises all the emotional flags, necessary to assure the sympathy and admiration of her contemporary sisters.

To all outward appearances, Rains is a clone of *Crime Without Passion*'s Lee Gentry; that little pencil-line mustache would write "scoundrel" all over his face until it found redemption through the patience of Job (as in *Skeffington*). The actor's "twinkle" and Casey Robinson's dialogue assure that no one doubts that Stefan Orloff could talk the furs off an Eskimo, and one is left with the feeling that had his accomplices been possessed of greater intellect or gall, the ex–Russian would still be sitting pretty. A couple of inadvertent chuckles can be had by noting Rains' height increase in myriad two shots with the taller Francis, but one feels for the actor when he's referred to caustically as "that little pip-squeak" by husky Ian Hunter.

As with most pictures set abroad, the printed word always presents a quandary to the production team. Everyone in *Holiday* is supposed to be speaking French, but cinematic convention allows an understanding deaf ear to be turned in this direction; one is especially grateful for the liberty when Egon Brecher is concerned. Legitimate local newspapers *write* in French, however, so audiences desperate to stay in the know have first to wade through the Gallic originals, which are then translated—only the relevant parts, *naturellement*—as one looks on. Impressive bits of work, indeed, but the same fastidiousness doesn't extend to the rest of the picture, wherein (for example), M. LeGrand's family name enjoys a variety of renditions, the municipality of Courney suffers through three different spellings, and the signs hoisted aloft by the vulgar Parisian mob denounce Orloff and all he represents in idiomatic English. A gratifying bonus, though, is having the American heroine already outfitted for the trade with the name of Nicole Picot.

But these are quibbles. Every picture has its silly moments, so these minor discrepancies and the almost embarrassing vignette in which Nicole and Anthony realize their true feelings for each other while ransacking a chalet and taking an impossibly cute hay ride in front of the rear projection screen should be noted and forgotten. A bit more action, character development, or narrative detail certainly couldn't have hurt, but, running only some 76 minutes, *Holiday* is extremely compact for a picture of its type.

*Variety* was satisfied to note that Kay Francis "and [Ian] Hunter are opposite each other for the third time," and took the trouble to proffer that "Rains gives the swindler-romancer a high polish." *The New York Times* was much more effusive in its praise for the leading lady, but split no hairs when it said: "If the picture is at all distinguished, it is because Claude Rains does a superb job with the character." For the record, this marked Rains' first of many encounters with Hungarian director Michael Curtiz, with whom he would make some of his most successful films.

With high-level scandal and corruption commonplace nowadays, *Stolen Holiday* should no longer be perceived of as solely a film for the fair sex. We've all come a long way.

*Stolen Holiday* Warner Bros. Released February 6, 1937. 76 minutes.

Kay Francis (Nicole Picot); CLAUDE RAINS (Stefan Orloff); Ian Hunter (Anthony Wayne); Alison Skipworth (Suzanne); Alexander D'Arcy (Leon); Betty Lawford (Helen Tuttle); Walter Kingsford (Francis Chalon); Charles Halton (LeGrande); Frank Reicher (Charles Ranier); Frank Conroy (Dupont); Egon Brecher (Deputy Bergery); Robert Strange (Prefect of Police); Kathleen Howard (Mme. Delphine); Wedgewood Nowell (Borel)

Executive Producer: Hal B. Wallis; Associate Producer: Harry Joe Brown; Director: Michael Curtiz; Assistant Director: Sherry Shourds; Screenplay: Casey Robinson; Original Story: Warren Duff and Virginia Kellogg; Director of Photography: Sid Hickox; Camera Operators: Wesley Anderson, Vernon Lawson; Special Photographic Effects: Fred Jackman; Art Director: Anton Grot; Editor: Terry Morse; Gowns: Orry-Kelly; Musical Director: Leo F. Forbstein; Sound: Stanley Jones; Makeup: Ray Romero; Unit Manager: Robert Fellows

A First National Picture

# The Prince and the Pauper
## (1937)

A son is born to England's King Henry VIII (Montagu Love) on the same day that beggar John Canty (Barton MacLane) becomes the father of a boy of his own. Ten years later, young Prince Edward (Bobby Mauch) and Tom Canty (Billy Mauch) meet by accident in the palace courtyard; Edward invites the beggar boy to play with him. Noting their remarkable resemblance to each other, the boys change clothes; Edward is beaten and thrown into the street when later caught in the courtyard in Tom's ragged clothes, and the bewildered young Canty finds himself taken for the Prince of Wales.

Tom tries to confess the switch to King and to the Earl of Hertford (Claude Rains), but the dying king thinks his son has become addle-pated, and the villainous Hertford angles to be declared the prince's Lord High Protector. When Tom's story is borne out both by the testimony of the Captain of the Guard (Alan Hale) and by the fact that the prince's dog growls at his apparent master, Hertford understands that, in order for him to keep his hold on the throne, the real prince must be found and killed.

Meanwhile, Edward has been unsuccessful in making the English lower classes believe that he is, in fact, the prince, and has to be rescued from a beating from the outraged peasants by Miles Hendon (Errol Flynn), a good-hearted soldier of fortune. With Hendon's help, Edward escapes the clutches of the brutal John Canty and a murderous attack by the Captain of the Guard; on the very day Tom Canty is to be crowned to succeed the deceased Henry as king, Miles manages to get Edward into the palace.

Disrupting the coronation, Edward proves his identity by remembering the location of the "mislaid" Great Seal of England and is crowned. Hertford is banished from England, Miles is rewarded for his loyalty and bravery, and Tom Canty is made a ward of the Court.

Mark Twain's glorious tale of honor and justice and the dangers of attempting to tell books by their covers had been heralded as one of the humorist's greatest concoctions from the moment it was published back in 1881. Prior to the Warners' rendition, the yarn had been filmed by Thomas Edison's people (in 1909) and by Adolph Zukor's (for Paramount) in 1915. A story about children, but not solely for children (the author had subtitled the novel—his favorite, if least typical—"A Tale for Young People of All Ages"), *The Prince and the Pauper* ended with a corker of a coronation scene in Westminster Abbey, and this, as much its literary virtue, captured Hal Wallis' attention in late 1936.

More than a few Americans were closet Anglophiles, wistful about the pomp and circumstance which attended the monarchical system their ancestors had overthrown in

1776. Twain's tale centered on familiar territory, turning on the oversized figure of Henry VIII and his struggle to have one of his wives produce a son for the throne. The fictional Edward (and the resultant confusion) stood in for the factual Elizabeth: all the rest—class struggles, court infighting, betrayal and complicity—were as right as rain and English tradition saw to it that, when order was finally restored, it would be restored in accordance with the divine right of kings and amid glorious spectacle.

From pre-production to answer print, the picture was more than a half-year in the making, and serendipity—the quality of being in the right place at the right time—struck Warners as it seldom had before: The British were set to crown King George VI hard on the heels of Edward VIII, who had abdicated to wed American Wallis Simpson. (Cf. *Casablanca* for a similar happy coincidence.)

Errol Flynn got top billing, of course; even with virtually no love interest in the picture (apologies to Phyllis Barry's brief turn as an amorous barmaid) and the dramatically important Miles Hendon a secondary role in terms of footage, the handsome star's presence opened more purses than it did even bedroom doors. Flynn breezes through his paces, sensing, no doubt, that it would take a far more cunning actor than himself to snatch the attention from the Mauch twins, whose refreshingly unsentimental portrayals of the titular youths make the film theft-proof.

Not that there weren't two very real, very substantial efforts at larceny going on under their young noses. Montagu Love was seldom given a meatier bone on which to gnaw as his Henry VIII. The veteran heavy makes Henry's every line seem worth committing to memory. "Never trust so much, love so much, or need anyone so much," he counsels Edward, "that you can't betray them with a smile." Love seems at once bothered yet proud of that philosophy as he concludes: "That is the paradox of power." Given both a deathbed scene and then allowed to rise

up and die, in ermine, on his throne, Love spews a venom at his court that is terrifying in its import and all the more powerful for its underlying truth. "The old dog dies," he snarls, "and the lice daren't desert his pup, lest they starve." Magnificent.

It takes Henry's death for Hertford to emerge from the king's shadow and become the prince's, yet the man's goals are transparent from the beginning and, frighteningly, appear to be in sync with the king's own plans for his son. Rains' ignoble earl is not so much distressed by his monarch's contempt as by his twice failing to name Hertford publicly as protector.

Henry: The protector will be a man who nibbles at the hand of the court, whose power frightens only the ladies, whose chief ambition is to build a safe nest in the throne. You'll forgive me if I say the description greatly resembles that of a palace rat!
Hertford: You mean…
Henry: I mean you!
Hertford: I am unable to tell my gratitude for this honor, Sire.

It's an honor the unscrupulous earl must cadge via Tom Canty's innocence, as the untimely arrival of the court physicians cuts Henry off in mid-sentence the first time around, and death itself foils the earl later.

Rains may not have the eminently quotable dialogue the scenario doles out to Love, but his Hertford enjoys an advantage denied to Twain's character: He learns of the switch and plots accordingly. In the act of seeking to remain Lord High Protector, the earl is thus a traitor to the crown. Nonetheless, as he convinces the terrified beggar boy, treachery is as easy to slip into as an old shoe:

Tom Canty: Then you know who I am?
Hertford: Yes.
Tom Canty: When can I go?
Hertford: Never.
Tom Canty: Never? But if I am not the king…
Hertford: You *are* the king. The only way to lose the crown now is to lose your head with it.
Tom Canty: But I told the truth…
Hertford: …and committed treason. You don't

**Director William Keighley** *(seated)* **puts Claude and Billy Mauch through their paces.** *Courtesy Richard Bojarski*

want that pretty little head of yours chopped off, do you? Nor to have your mother see the crows tearing tufts from a skull on London Bridge and know that it's her son's hair in which they will nest? Then never forget that you are Edward the Sixth of England and that to ever again become Tom Canty is to die!

Naturally, the crown sits on the correct head once the coronation has come and gone, and Hertford, like Prince John in the Robin Hood saga, is banished rather than beheaded. "May I learn generosity from you, Sire," Rains purrs wearily, his voice dripping with sarcasm, and off he goes, leaving behind a pair of boys cracking walnuts with the Great Seal of England. Makes you want to run after him, doesn't it?

*The Prince and the Pauper* Warner Bros. Released May 8, 1937. 118 minutes.

Errol Flynn (Miles Hendon); CLAUDE RAINS (Earl of Hertford); Henry Stephenson (Duke of Norfolk); Barton MacLane (John Canty); Billy Mauch (Tom Canty); Bobby Mauch (Prince Edward); Alan Hale (Captain of the Guard); Eric Portman (First Lord); Lionel Pape (Second Lord); Halliwell Hobbes (Archbishop of Canterbury); Phyllis Barry (Barmaid); Ivan Simpson (Clemens); Montagu Love (Henry VIII); Fritz Leiber (Father Andrew); Elspeth Dudgeon (Grandmother Canty); Mary Field (Mrs. Canty); Helen Valkis (Lady Jane Seymour); Lester Matthews (St. John); Robert Adair (First Guard); Harry Cording (Second Guard); Lionel Braham (Ruffler); Lionel Belmore (Innkeeper); Harry Beresford (The Watch)

Executive Producers: Jack L. Warner and Hal B. Wallis; Associate Producer: Robert Lord; Director: William Keighley (and William Dieterle, uncredited); Assistant Director: Chuck Hansen; Screenplay: Laird Doyle, based on the novel, *The Prince and the Pauper*, by Mark Twain; Dramatic Version: Catherine Chisholm Cushing; Director of Photography: Sol Polito and George Barnes; Special Effects: Willard Van Enger, James Gibbons; Art Director: Robert Haas; Editor: Ralph Dawson; Gowns: Milo Anderson; Musical Director: Leo F. Forbstein; Orchestrations: Hugo Friedhofer, Milan Roder; Sound: Oliver S. Garretson

A First National Picture

## *They Won't Forget* (1937)

When beautiful young student Mary Clay (Lana Turner) is found dead at the bottom of the Buxton Business College elevator shaft, it appears that the Yankees and the Rebels are set to have at it once again, with the courtroom subbing for the battlefield this time around. District Attorney Andy Griffin (Claude Rains), his eye on the state senate seat, hopes for bigger fish to fry than Tump Redwine (Clinton Rosemond), Buxton's Negro janitor, and is ecstatic when circumstantial evidence points to Robert Hale (Edward Norris), Mary's teacher and—Thank you, God!—a Northerner.

The murder case holds the nation enthralled, with the South decrying Northern interference and the North responding with accusations of prejudice. Renowned New York detective Pindar (Granville Bates) comes to the aid of Hale and his wife, Sybil (Gloria Dickson), but makes little headway in his investigation before he is found beaten by a mob. Famed New York attorney Michael Gleason (Otto Kruger) needs a police escort as he arrives at the railroad station; he's stoned before he can reach his car.

The trial is the biggest thing to hit the town of Flodden since the War Between the States, and, despite Mary's three vengeful brothers ominously muttering "We know

how it's gonna end," the excitement is palpable. Local reporter Bill Brock (Allyn Joslyn) gleefully tallies the "points" scored by each of the lawyers while pulling double duty by keeping Flodden in the know via both print and radio. Griffin's grandstanding strikes the right chord with the edgy townspeople, while attorney Gleason—methodically refuting his opponent's accusations and meticulous in cross-examination—cannot put a dent in the stone wall that confronts him in the jury box. Hale is convicted and sentenced to die.

Only Governor Mountford (Paul Everton) can save Hale now, but sparing his life is tantamount to betraying the Stars and Bars, and the governor is as Southern as the next man. Still, Mountford has a conscience, and—political suicide or no—he commutes Hale's sentence. Under cover of darkness, the teacher is being transported to a state prison some distance from the town when his train is commandeered by a mob of passengers, his police guards are overcome, and Mary Clay's three brothers lead him off to be lynched.

Despite this tragic aftermath, Griffin rides the crest of the trial's publicity right into his campaign for senate. The attorney is forced by Hale's widow to consider briefly that he had railroaded the teacher and had thus indirectly precipitated the lynching, but, in the face of his bright political future, this makes little impression on him.

As a reporter for *The Atlanta Journal*, Ward Greene had covered the 1913 trial of Leo M. Frank—a Northerner wrongfully convicted of murder, whose death sentence was commuted by Gov. John M. Slaton of Georgia, and who then was subsequently lynched by a mob 1915. Frank's trial and treatment haunted the journalist for decades, and his resultant novel, *Death in the Deep South*, served as the basis for Mervin LeRoy's classic motion picture. *They Won't Forget* was both a critical sensation and a box-office success, although it never played in parts of the Deep South (as rancor ran deep over a similar and more recent real-life situation in Scottsboro, Alabama). Nonetheless, many viewers south of the Mason-Dixon line swallowed the attendant Warners' propaganda—that the film was really more an indictment of small-minded prejudice, mob rule, and mass hysteria than a wholesale condemnation of Southern justice—and comparatively little backlash on the part of Southern extremist organizations materialized.

While the film was being shot, Rains admitted to *New York Times* interviewer John T. McManus in the July 11, 1937, edition that he was "frightened to death" at the thought of portraying the ambitious prosecutor. Impersonating unscrupulous lawyers didn't much trouble him—he had done just fine in Paramount's *Crime Without Passion* a few years earlier—but he was totally unfamiliar with the customs and culture of the Deep South, and this was discomfiting. Either Rains or McManus was prone to flights of fancy, for the readers were then advised that the actor "had lived for several months with a professor from the University of Louisiana, learning lots about the late politician Huey Long and about pot-likker." Colorful, perhaps, but a far cry from the sterile pre-production announcement in *The Hollywood Reporter* that a certain Professor Dalton S. Raymond would be the film's technical director. (To date, the AFI has been unable to confirm whether Prof. Dalton ever showed up.)

Another bone of contention was the requisite Southern drawl; this, the actor moaned, "seemed impossible of achievement." Perhaps sympathetic to their star's vocal difficulties—more likely, taking no chances whatsoever—scenarists Aben Kandel and Robert Rossen established at the outset that the ambitious Griffin was *not* a local and masterfully avoided any subsequent reference to his background or origin.

The action centers in the fictional Southern "everytown" of Flodden—surely a dull, unpleasant name for the amalgamation of clean streets and small businesses we see

before us. A benchful of geriatric Johnny Rebs—graybeards all, the last of their kind—muster their energies before marching in the Memorial Day parade. The antique veterans are both a visual metaphor of the tensions which had divided the nation for five ghastly years and a portent of things to come. When one of the men sighs that, after the last of them has passed on, the townsfolk will forget them and what they stood for, his companion strongly objects: "They won't forget! They won't never forget...." And, lest anyone be lulled into thinking that Southern passions and Southern biases have withered like these once strapping soldiers, he trumpets: "...and if they do, we'll get up out of our graves and remind them!" As the picture demonstrates, all it takes to have *this* South rise again is the battle cry of "Outrage!" thundered by a couple of opportunists, driven by either political ambition or ennui.

Once the beams of the flashlights catch Lana Turner holding her breath at the bottom of that elevator shaft, things begin to take off. Albeit crying bloody murder, "Little Andy" (an appellation Rains must have just loved) Griffin demurs from rounding up his "usual suspects"—Detective Laneart (Cy Kendall) et al give us to understand that blacks are very much the suspects of choice—as convicting the Negro janitor who had discovered the body would add nothing to the ambitious lawyer's prestige. "I'm out for bigger game," the D.A. crows.

Rains couldn't have asked for bigger game than this. It makes little difference that a drawl was beyond him; vows are taken, threats are hurled, lies are spun, and venom is spewed, and all in a performance of such energy and intensity that a spate of "Y'alls" and such might well have been distracting and counterproductive. The actor imbues Kandel and Rossen's crisp lines with his trademark flair, and in his hands Griffin's ubiquitous cigar nearly takes a life of its own, metamorphosing from maestro's baton to exclamation point to the dreaded finger of accusation. Whether he is massaging the merits of circumstantial evidence for the jury or triumphantly flourishing the murdered girl's bloodied clothing to the tearful outcry of her mother and the futile objection of the defense, Rains draws a character who is not so much concerned with the truth as with appearances, for whom the message is of much less importance than the method.

So appalling and transparent is Griffin's scheme, so frustrating and irate is the viewer's reaction, that the fact that it's never made clear whether Edward Hale is, indeed, *innocent* of the crime doesn't register for some time. In fact, the film's most powerful moment belongs to Griffin, and the end credits coming hard upon it makes it seem almost an afterthought. Having been denounced by Sybil Hale, Brock and Griffin watch out the window as her forlorn figure moves out of their lives. "Now that it's all over, Andy," murmurs the reporter, "I wonder if he really did it." And little Andy Griffin, who had "staked his reputation" on Hale's guilt to Flodden's old money, looks out on the shattered woman and sighs, "I wonder."

Not once in the picture is the murderer's *motive* discussed, and whether this was an inadvertent oversight or a carefully engineered ploy on the part of Kandel, Rossen, and LeRoy is the stuff of which great arguments are made. Had Tump Redwine been selected as scapegoat, the motive would doubtless have involved unrequited lust (and no one watching the buxom Lana Turner sashay about in her few scenes can be left to puzzle over why she became known as "The Sweater Girl"). With Hale seemingly unable to keep his hands off his wife of six months, however, that doesn't fly in his case. Even *had* some moves been made, Mary's "being crazy about him" would seem to preclude any need of violence in Hale's pursuit of passion. Considering, too, that Mary's sometime fella, Joe Turner, is none other than Elisha Cook, Jr.—impossibly young, but, as always, a weasel—the chances that the lovely young woman would reject the advances of the mature and handsome Hale plummet from slim to none.

Rains was the biggest name in *They Won't Forget* and the lion's share of the excellent notices, of course, singled him out for praise. Nonetheless, many of the critics regarded the drama as a wildly successful team effort. Frank Nugent of *The New York Times* opined that "From Claude Rains and Allyn Joslyn and Gloria Dickson right on down the list of players heading this review, you will not find one whose performance does not deserve commendation."

"Bert" in *Variety* took up the banner when he proclaimed that

The cast, while not boasting any names of much marquee magnetism, is uniformly fine. Rains especially stands in one of the very best parcels of playing he has yet delivered in films. Newcomers to pix, Edward Norris, Allyn Joslyn and Gloria Dickson are swell. Elisha Cook, Jr., Trevor Bardette and Lana Turner (as the girl murdered), in subordinate assignments, give splendid accounts of selves.

(June 30, 1937)

The picture made all kinds of money and was on the top ten lists of both *The New York Times* and The National Board of Review. A minor masterpiece—thanks to an adept cast, excellent writing, Mervyn LeRoy's expert direction, and the canny eye of ace cinematographer, Arthur Edeson—*They Won't Forget* deserves to be dusted off and screened time and again. Its caveats on prejudice and ambition are, unfortunately, timeless; thankfully, so is its artistry.

*They Won't Forget* Warner Bros. Released October 9, 1937. 92 minutes.

CLAUDE RAINS (Andy Griffin); Gloria Dickson (Sybil Hale); Edward Norris (Robert Hale), Otto Kruger (Michael Gleason); Allyn Joslyn (Bill Brock); Lana Turner (Mary Clay); Linda Perry (Imogene Mayfield); Elisha Cook, Jr. (Joe Turner); Cy Kendall (Detective Laneart); Clinton Rosemund (Tump Redwine); E. Alyn (Fred) Warren (Carlisle P. Buxton); Elizabeth Risdon (Mrs. Hale); Sybil Harris (Mrs. Clay); Clifford Soubier (Jim Timberlake); Granville Bates (Detective Pindar); Ann Shoemaker (Mrs. Mountford); Paul Everton (Governor Mountford);

Donald Briggs (Harmon Drake); Wilmer Hines (Ransom Clay); Trevor Bardette (Shattuck Clay); Elliott Sullivan (Luther Clay); Eddie Acuff (Soda Jerk); Frank Faylen (Reporter); Leonard Mudie (Judge Moore); Henry Davenport, Harry Beresford, Edward McWade (Confederate Soldiers)

Executive Producer: Jack L. Warner; Director: Mervyn LeRoy; Assistant Director: Lee Katz; Screenplay: Robert Rossen and Aben Kandel, based on the novel *Death in the Deep South,* by Ward Greene; Director of Photography—Arthur Edeson, ASC; Art Director: Robert Haas; Editor: Thomas Richards; Gowns: Miss MacKenzie; Musical Director: Leo F. Forbstein; Music and Arrangements: Adolph Deutsch; Hair: Helen Turpin; Makeup: Al Bonner; Grip: James Hicks; Properties: L. S. Edwards

A First National Picture

## *Gold Is Where You Find It* (1938)

In 1868, Colonel Christopher Ferris (Claude Rains), his brother Ralph (John Litel), and scores of others had found peace and prosperity farming wheat in the Sacramento Valley. In 1877, however, hydraulic mining—a process whereby gold is blasted from the porous hills by high-pressure hoses—has turned the wheat fields into rivers of mud. The farmers are helpless to combat the "slickens" as it covers their topsoil and destroys their crops. For the nonce, they agree to follow Colonel Ferris' advice and let the courts settle the matter.

Complicating affairs is the arrival of Jared Whitney (George Brent), a mining engineer who soon falls in love with Serena (Olivia de Havilland), the colonel's daughter. Ralph, feeling that easy riches can be had through mining, sells his interests in the family lands to his brother and heads to San Francisco to work for his father-in-law, Harrison McCooey (Sidney Toler), who heads up the Golden Moon mining company. When the colonel's son, Lance (Tim Holt), likewise leaves the homestead for the glamour of the

big city and the allure of gold, Ferris orders Jared never to darken his doorstep or see Serena again.

Jared heads for San Francisco, where he convinces McCooey and his partners that building a dam above the Sacramento Valley will help the Golden Moon triple its production. The gold magnates agree, also seeing the plan as a way to force their competitors to sell out or go bankrupt. Jared's dam does what he claimed it would and also drives both the Sunrise and Inspiration mining companies into insolvency while sending the farmers into apoplexy. When the Sacramento District Federal Court grants the farmers an injunction against the mining concern, though, McCooey orders low-life mining foreman Slag Minton (Barton MacLane) to arm the men and defies anyone to deliver the injunction.

Jared rides to the mine, but is too late to prevent Lance Ferris from being shot in the back as he attempts to serve the papers. When the colonel and the farmers gather their rifles and head for a shootout, Jared dynamites the dam: The mining camp (and Slag Minton) are washed into oblivion. Not long after, the California Supreme Court upholds the injunction; the days of hydraulic mining are over and the wheat farmers are victorious. Serena and Jared see their future tied to innumerable orchards which will cover the state for generations to come.

There don't seem to be any surviving memos a la *They Made Me a Criminal* wherein Rains pleaded to let this cup pass, so we've no choice but to believe that the actor had few gnawing doubts about taking part in an oater. *Gold* isn't really a *western* Western—Warners wasn't much at home with those—despite the presence of horses, rifles, and Gabby Hayes; it's an ideological period piece with a no-nonsense ecological theme that's articulated in the first reel and vindicated in the last. Everything in-between is largely enjoyable window dressing, obfuscated by mud and dust, enlivened by splendid miniatures and hurt by execrable rear screen projection, and done up all fancy-like on some of the most cavernous sets this side of *Gone with the Wind*.

The opening montage, which culminates with images of those fabled amber waves of grain sinking in rivers of sludge, leaves no doubt in anyone's mind that the production team sits on the side of the gods. As the portentous narrator warns:

For every precious yellow lump, tons of mud, gravel, and rubble are dumped into the streams that feed the golden wheat empire below. The floods spread, the wheat ranchers protest, but up in the mountains, the monitors lash out their yelling tongues: "Where there is gold, men are going to get it!"

Not deathless prose, perhaps, but we get the picture.

There are no gray areas in this Technicolor romp. As depicted in Clements Ripley's source novel and the screenplay, the wheat farmers are reasonable men who suffer the tortures of the damned while awaiting a lawful solution to their seemingly hopeless situation. By way of contrast, with the exception of Jared Whitney, everyone working for the Golden Moon company is depicted as either an anal retentive—fixated on nuggets, dust, and the good life—or an immoral goon, given to shooting first and asking questions never. If Colonel Ferris and the leaders of the farm contingent spend most of their time debating the law and wringing their hands over man's inhumanity to man, Harrison McCooey and his ilk keep themselves busy raping the land and bellying up to the bar. Of course, cinematic convention of the thirties dictated that prodigal son Lance would return the fold, and that Jared would have his eyes opened to the greed and callousness of his employers, all before that flood of near-biblical proportions would wipe evil from the face of the earth and make California safe for agriculture.

George Brent and Olivia de Havilland are the romantic leads. In this, the second of her three on-screen adventures with Rains,

Miss de Havilland was 21 years old, but looks (more or less) the 16 she's supposed to be. Mr. Brent was 34 and looks 40, even with the judicious application of Max Factor; *he's* supposed to be instantly irresistible. There's a whiff of compromise in that his hair has been blue-blacked (so that comparisons with the 49-year-old Rains—who has been outfitted with a gray bouffant appliance—are not forthcoming), but there's no denying that by the time he first lays eyes on Olivia, he has already decked two guys (including burly Barton MacLane). Hell, his Jared Whitney *must* still be in his prime.

For one of the few times in his thirties' movie career, Rains gets to embody forthrightness and integrity. While the indisputable leader of the put-upon farmers, he is (his expansive mansion apart) one of them—an equal among equals. His eyes mist up and the corners of his mouth curl into an appreciative smile at the sight of an excerpt from the Gettysburg Address. He counsels patience and adherence to the law when every mother's son is chafing at the bit for the miners' blood. Clad in a variety of 6 or 7-gallon hats, he strides through scenes of desolation and stands tall during moments of strife. He is the farmers' spokesman at the hearing, and while the Golden Moon attorney may have the last word, Rains' Colonel Ferris has already cut the lawyer's legs out from under him:

We have only one question to ask: Does the law of this country give one man the right to ruin another man's land? To stand on a mountain and throw mud in his face? Because that's what the miners are doing to us.

No judge can harden his heart to such a simple yet eloquent appeal, especially when limned in that velvet purr.

Later, his son Lance having died in front of him, Ferris narrows his eyes, widens into a full grimace his slit of a mouth, and quietly calls his friends to arms. Theirs is the task of giving the law the teeth it needs. It's a sad moment, subtle and powerful; more importantly, it's completely credible.

*Variety*'s Bert held that Rains

does by far the best job in the film as the sincere, fearless, justice-seeking planter. It's a nice break for him, getting away from the unsympathetic roles he's been doing on end.

(February 16, 1938)

It would be nice to report that *Gold Is Where You Find It* struck a box-office bonanza; truth is, it didn't do half as well as producer Hal Wallis would have liked. Warners had hoped to repeat the success it had enjoyed with 1937's *God's Country and the Woman*, another Technicolor extravaganza featuring George Brent, Barton MacLane, and a sumptuous array of natural resources, but *Gold* came up short. One problem may have been that the post-Civil War Reconstruction Era was neither fish nor fowl: not nearly "westernish" enough to attract followers of that genre, nor cozily familiar enough to the historically minded to strike the right chords. For some, the predictable story line offered nothing new; for others, being able to sort out the righteous from the rotters within moments freed them up to appreciate the action, which was then perceived as being long in coming, unconventional, and unsatisfying.

(And mystifying. When it's been carefully established that the *monitored* flow of water by the mining company has wrought near total destruction to the valley below, how in God's name can the hero's dynamiting the dam—an action which sends an uncontrollable deluge sweeping through the area, washing away everything in its path—be seen as any kind of solution to the problem confronting the wheat farmers?)

The screenplay does have its clever moments. En passant references to Alexander Bell and Tom Edison, along with disparaging comments on their signature inventions, are fun. Similarly, Senator Hearst's moaning about his son Willie and his interest in journalism must have been regarded by savvy viewers as a wonderful in-joke. As author Ripley's eponymous novel had been serialized back in 1936 in Hearst's *Cosmopolitan*

magazine, and as the motion picture was itself a "Cosmopolitan Production," more's the pity that the usual Hearst ballyhoo wasn't enough to ensure a mother lode in ticket sales.

*The New York Times'* Frank Nugent felt that the misuse of Technicolor actually *detracted* from the impact of the picture:

"Gold Is Where You Find It" is a story of ugliness - of greed and mud, exploitation and destruction. Its burden is tragic, no matter the sunburst happy ending, and Technicolor's roseate approach is as indecorous as a Maypole dance at a funeral.

(February 14, 1938)

There may be dozens of reasons why *Gold Is Where You Find It* didn't cut the mustard—and maybe poor judgment regarding Technicolor ought to be considered seriously—but Claude Rains was not one of them. His Colonel Ferris may have clamored against injustice while wearing high-heel boots, but Rains' voice and presence were tailor-made to express the man's moral outrage. (His voice, even denuded of vestigial Britishisms, didn't fit the geographical profile as comfortably as John Litel's; still, it was certainly no farther off the mark than either the occasional remnant of George Brent's Irish lilt or the wheezing of Gabby Hayes.) One comes away from the film, not marveling that the actor had "pulled it off" in a western setting, but wondering why he wasn't given similar assignments—in more fortuitous circumstances—and allowed to reach wider audiences.

*Gold Is Where You Find It* Warner Bros. Released February 12, 1938. 91 minutes.

George Brent (Jared Whitney); Olivia de Havilland (Serena Ferris); CLAUDE RAINS (Colonel Chris Ferris); Margaret Lindsay (Roseanne Ferris McCooey); John Litel (Ralph Ferris); Marcia Ralston (Molly Featherstone); Barton MacLane (Slag Minton); Tim Holt (Lance Ferris); Sidney Toler (Harrison McCooey); Henry O'Neill (Judge); Willie Best (Joshua); Robert McWade (Mr. Crouch); George "Gabby" Hayes (Enoch Howitt); Harry Davenport (Dr. Parsons); Russell

Simpson (McKenzie); Clarence Kolb (Senator Walsh); Moroni Olsen (Senator Hearst); Granville Bates (Nixon); Robert Homans (Grogan); Eddy Chandler (Deputy)

Executive Producers: Jack B. Warner and Hal Wallis; Associate Producer: Sam Bischoff; Director: Michael Curtiz; Screenplay: Warren Duff and Robert Buckner, based on the novel, *Gold Is Where You Find* It, by Clements Ripley; Screenplay Contributors: William Wiser Haines and Michael Jacoby; Dialogue Director: Irving Rapper; Assistant Director: Jack Sullivan; Director of Photography: Sol Polito; Special Effects: Byron Haskins; Technicolor Consultant: Natalie Kalmus; Technicolor Photographic Advisor: Allen M. Davey; Art Director: Ted Smith; Editors: Clarence Kolster and Owen Marks; Costumes: Milo Anderson; Musical Director: Leo F. Forbstein; Musical Score: Max Steiner; Sound: E. A. Brown; Makeup: Perc Westmore

A Cosmopolitan Production

A First National Picture

# *The Adventures of Robin Hood* (1938)

While King Richard the Lion-Heart (Ian Hunter) has had the misfortune of being taken captive at the Crusades, England has been suffering under the pro-tem rule of his brother, Prince John (Claude Rains), who oppresses the Saxon end of the populace and plots to hang onto the throne ad infinitum. Aiding the would-be usurper in his scheme is a group of opportunistic Norman knights, led by the redoubtable Sir Guy of Gisbourne (Basil Rathbone).

Fighting to restore their rights to the poor and freedom to the country is Robin of Locksley, aka Robin Hood (Errol Flynn), who, with his band of "merry men" (including Friar Tuck [Eugene Pallette], Will Scarlett [Patric Knowles], and Little John [Alan Hale]), inspires the common folk and confounds the treacherous nobles. Losing her heart in the act of being won over to this cause is Maid Marian (Olivia de Havilland), whose outrage at Prince John's abuse of power grows simultaneously with her love for Robin.

With his foes a strong and wily group, and with their haven, Sherwood Forest, unassailable by conventional means, the Sheriff of Nottingham (Melville Cooper) proposes an archery contest as a means of luring the outlaw chief into the open. Because the lovely Maid Marian will award the victor a golden arrow, there is no way that Robin Hood can resist the trap. As expected, Robin appears (in disguise), wins the prize, and is taken away to await his execution.

Robin is rescued from the gallows by his men and makes his way back to Sherwood. Unbeknownst to all save Prince John, Guy of Gisbourne and Dickon Malbete (Harry Cording)—and Maid Marian, who is eavesdropping—King Richard and his knights have returned to England. Having overheard the trio plan to have the king slain and Prince John crowned his successor, Marian is discovered, but not before she tells Bess (Una O'Connor), her lady-in-waiting, to get word to the men of Sherwood Forest. Robin's lady is then imprisoned.

The sham coronation gets underway, but, at the most dramatic of moments, King Richard, his fellow Crusaders, and Robin and his men shed their disguises and battle the treacherous Norman nobles into submission. Gisbourne is slain, Prince John is banished from the realm, Robin and Marian are united, and England once again knows peace and justice.

When your titular character is a legendary hero whose fabled exploits stretch back to 14th-century English ballads, little if any money is needed for royalty payments, and almost all of your budget should be evident on the screen. Warners went for Robin Hood in a big way, spending a lavish $2 million (a studio record) on what was, arguably, Errol Flynn's most popular vehicle. A small chunk of this came from MGM, which—with an eye to Jeanette MacDonald and Nelson Eddy—had purchased the book and lyrics to Reginald de Koven's Robin Hood *operetta* from Warners in 1935. MGM's grand vision proved to be myopic; the studio never produced the operetta, and 1936 saw Jack L. Warner and studio production chief Hal B. Wallis mulling over the immortal (and public domain) legend themselves.

The picture, of course, would rise or fall on the eponymous outlaw, and a Fairbanksian bundle of masculine energy was the ticket. James Cagney had originally been penciled in for the lead, but with the statuesque Flynn making favorable impressions on both male and female ticket-buyers with each successive feature, there was really little doubt who would be wearing the green tights as production started in September 1937. Flynn was a natural in the part; the rugged, impish, irresistible Robin Hood was basically an extension of his own persona. Despite a plethora of Robins over the years, generations of viewers have always regarded the devil-may-care Flynn as the personification of the mythic hero who robbed from the rich and gave to the poor.

Few "spectacles" ever enjoyed such impeccable casting as did *The Adventures of Robin Hood*. Warners had enough capable bit players under contract to populate Sherwood Forest and its environs, and most featured players were either long-term studio veterans, or members of Hollywood's British Colony, or both; anyway you sliced it, they could play off each other in their sleep. Patric Knowles had already worked with Flynn in *The Charge of the Light Brigade* (1936), and would arguably make his greatest impression in a spate of forties' Universal horror pictures. Irish banshee Una O'Connor already had *her* big horror films (*The Invisible Man* [1933] and *Bride of Frankenstein* [1935]) as well as a plum role in John Ford's *The Informer* (1935) behind her, but her pinched features and trademark wailing made her effectively comic here. Big Alan Hale came close to building a second career around Little John, a part he had played opposite Douglas Fairbanks 16 years earlier and would

play again, opposite John Derek (as Robin Hood, *Junior*, in *Rogues of Sherwood Forest*), some 12 years down the road.

Basil Rathbone, Olivia de Havilland, and a goodly portion of the secondary cast had already crossed paths (and swords) with Flynn in 1935's *Captain Blood*. (Per film historian Michael B. Druxman, Warners had shoehorned the fledgling actress and the buff Tasmanian nobody into the leads in *Blood*, when Robert Donat had proved recalcitrant.[10]) Miss de Havilland had made her debut as Hermia in the studio's mangling of Shakespeare's *A Midsummer Night's Dream* (1935; the studio also mangled her name in the credits), and only a couple of sports-oriented efforts [baseball with Joe E. Brown in *Alibi Ike*, and boxing with Jimmy Cagney in *The Irish in Us*, both 1935] separated her from Flynn, her soon-to-be most frequent of leading men. The lovely ingenue's Maid Marian is a noble woman in every sense of the word, and the chemistry between the outlaw and the King's ward is right out of the legend.

Resplendent in chain-mail and flowing hair appliances, Basil Rathbone was already one of the screen's finest heavies—Guy of Gisbourne was just icing on the snake—and his expertise at fencing assured him of meaty parts and splendid death scenes in many of the decade's swashbucklers. With the Sheriff of Nottingham essentially a comic foil and Prince John the brains behind the organization, the lion's share of the physical action is left to Rathbone's testy nobleman. As he had as Captain Levasseur in *Captain Blood*, and as he would as Captain Esteban Pasquale in *The Mark of Zorro* (1940), Rathbone enacts Gisbourne as arrogant and fatally overconfident. Nonetheless, the duels fought in each of these films (with the Gisbourne-/Locksley bout the best of them all) remain exciting, and the villains' deaths, wonderfully cathartic.

Claude Rains appears to have had a marvelous time as the conniving Prince John, although the disparity in size between him and the husky Ian Hunter has one ruminating on

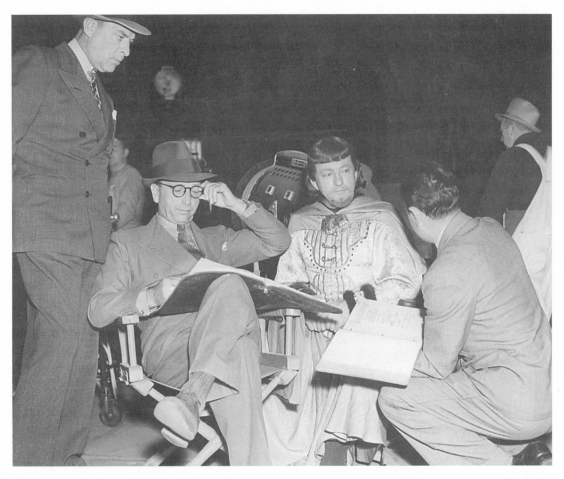

A between-scenes conference with *(from left to right)* assistant director Jack Sullivan, director Michael Curtiz, and dialogue director Irving Rapper *(back to camera)*. *The author's collection*

the fidelity of the brothers' sire to the brothers' mother. Yet, despite the character's title and delusions of grandeur, the part is fairly small and doesn't call for much in the way of subtlety. Nor is Rains tapped to do his patented personality reversal, where he would suddenly pull a 180 degree turn in temperament and thus surprise a good portion of the cast while gratifying the majority of the audience. The prince's schemes are so transparent that the picture's only head-scratcher is how the good (but apparently thick) King Richard could have handed him England on a silver platter.

John is cocky and self-certain—only that sudden epiphany of the Lion-Heart at the coronation moves his eyelids past half-

mast—as well as being by far the least physical of cultured scoundrels in pictures such as these. Forced by the legend (to say nothing of Norman Reilly Raine and Seton I. Miller's screenplay) to share his villainy with Guisbourne, Rains' half-a-blackguard stands in contrast both with the crafty, capable Sir Guy, and with Richard, every inch a king and a warrior, to boot. Bitchy and boastful, arch and effete, Prince John is quick to take refuge behind walls of armored humanity; his is the only sword to remain sheathed during the melee at the coronation. Years after the film's release, Rains confided to his daughter that he had purposefully sought to play the character as a homosexual.

Rains and Rathbone do make quite a pair,

though, clucking evilly as they plot amidst the flickering shadows. Complemented by Cooper's Sheriff of Nottingham—no man of action, either, but occasionally possessed of a good idea—the conspirators so much enjoy hounding the Saxons, taxing the arses off the peasants, and putting the screws to Friar Tuck and the Church, that their chief reason for wanting the throne in perpetuity can only be so that the fun never stops. If Flynn's Robin Hood came to epitomize heroism to school-age children, then Rains' Prince John and his evil retinue introduced the younger set to the joys of booing and catcalling.

Buoyed by Erich Wolfgang Korngold's Academy Award-winning score (art director Carl Weyl and editor Ralph Dawson also took home Oscars), the film received a nomination (but not the nod) for Best Picture of the Year, and made a couple of the Top Ten lists of 1938. The product of two directors (William Keighley, then Michael Curtiz) and two cinematographers (Tony Gaudio giving way to Sol Polito), the Technicolor romp is as close to ensemble theater as a costume spectacular can get.

Sparkling performances by everyone, splendid sets and gorgeous exteriors, rousing music, and the sheer visual beauty of much of the film has helped keep *The Adventures of Robin Hood* the best of its kind for over 60 years.

*The Adventures of Robin Hood* Warner Bros. Released May 14, 1938. 102 minutes.

Errol Flynn (Robin Hood); Olivia de Havilland (Maid Marian); Basil Rathbone (Sir Guy of Gisbourne); CLAUDE RAINS (Prince John); Alan Hale (Little John); Patric Knowles (Will Scarlett); Ian Hunter (Richard the Lion-Heart); Eugene Pallette (Friar Tuck); Melville Cooper (Sheriff of Nottingham); Una O'Connor (Bess); Herbert Mundin (Much); Montagu Love (Bishop of the Black Canons); Leonard Wiley (Sir Essex); Kenneth Hunter (Sir Mortimer); Robert Warwick (Sir Geoffrey); Colin Kenny (Sir Baldwin); Lester Matthews (Sir Ivor); Harry Cording (Dickon Malbete); Howard Hill (Captain of Archers); Ivan Simpson (Proprietor of Kent Road Tavern); Robert Noble (Sir Rafe); Charles McNaughton (Crippen); Lionel Belmore (Humility Prin); Austin Fairman (Sir Nigel); Crauford Kent (Sir Norbert); Wilfred Lucas (Archery Official); Holmes Herbert (Archery Referee); with Halliwell Hobbes, Olaf Hytten, John Sutton

Executive Producers: Jack L. Warner and Hal B. Wallis; Directors: William Keighley; Michael Curtiz; Dialogue Director: Irving Rapper; Screenplay: Norman Reilly Raine and Seton I. Miller; Assistant Directors: Lee Katz and Jack Sullivan; Directors of Photography Tony Gaudio; Sol Polito; Technicolor Photography: W. Howard Greene; Camera Operator: Al M. Greene; Technicolor Consultant: Natalie Kalmus; Technicolor Associate: Morgan Padelford; Art Director: Carl Jules Weyl; Technicolor Advisor: Louis Van Den Ecker; Editor: Ralph Dawson; Costumes: Milo Anderson; Musical Director: Leo F. Forbstein; Music: Erich Wolfgang Korngold; Orchestral Arrangements: Hugo Friedhofer; Recording Director: Major Nathan Levinson; Sound: C. A. Riggs; Makeup: Perc Westmore; Unit Manager: Al Alleborn; Stills: Mac Julian

## *White Banners* (1938)

On a snowy January morning in 1919, when Middale, Indiana, is struggling to rouse itself from slumber, Hannah Parmalee (Fay Bainter) shows up on the doorstep of the close-knit but mildly dysfunctional Ward family. Brought in to warm herself by Marcia Ward (Kay Johnson), Hannah is soon all but indispensable to the household: transforming leftovers into a feast worthy of praise from paterfamilias, Paul (Claude Rains); offering grooming tips and advice on boys to 14-year-old Sally (Bonita Granville); and taking over most of the housekeeping chores from Marcia. She's also quietly insistent that the Christian tenet of turning the other cheek in times of injury is the only way to live, and she shares her feelings with the Wards throughout her stay.

Hannah is concerned about Peter Trimble (Jackie Cooper), one of Paul's prize science students and the object of Sally's affections. Convincing Paul to take the young boy under his wing, she is pleased and gratified when, together, they invent an iceless ice-box. Peter asks his father, banker Sam Trimble (Henry O'Neill) for help in financing the invention, but, through the boy's thoughtless blunder, their design is stolen, and Paul turns his young partner out of the house.

Making matters worse, Peter had earlier disregarded Hannah's wishes that he not take Sally ice-skating, as the girl was coming down with a cold. Sally had gone through the ice and now lies near death, with pneumonia and a 105-degree fever. Worried sick about his daughter and outraged at the theft of his idea, Paul smashes his apparatus and vows to fight this injustice to the bitter end. When he points out that Hannah's beliefs demand that he raise "a lot of white flags," she responds that they're really white banners, which indicate that one has the courage to clean up what's passed and find new direction for the future.

Sally recovers, and Paul packs her and his wife and baby off on a trip to see their aunt. When Hannah brings Paul and Peter back together, the two concoct an even better iceless ice-box than before, and Sam Trimble arranges for his friend, millionaire Thomas Bradford (James Stephenson), to come in from Chicago to underwrite the invention. Distraught, Hannah reveals to Paul that Peter is really her son by Bradford; they had had an affair when they were younger, and Hannah had given up her baby when Mrs. Trimble's own son had died during childbirth. She prevails on Bradford not to take Peter away from his home and his past. With her son's safety assured, Hannah moves on, departing Middale as suddenly as she had arrived.

Claude Rains may be top-billed, but this Warners' drama of success in the face of adversity is really Fay Bainter's film. The actress had made the switch from the legitimate theater to film only four years prior to *White Banners*, yet she made an almost immediate impact on the industry. Nominated for the Oscar for Best Actress for Hannah, Bainter was also up for Best Supporting Actress for her work in *Jezebel*, and it was for *Jezebel* that she won. Although she had appeared in only four features prior to delivering her acclaimed performances, she was the first actress ever to be nominated in both categories during the same year.

As delineated in Lloyd C. Douglas's eponymous novel, Hannah Parmalee strives to set those with whom she comes in contact onto the straight and narrow path. Not so much proselytizing as convincing her listeners of the value of her message, the woman from nowhere provides some much-needed guidance to a variety of Middale's citizenry just when they need it most. Bainter's delivery of many of her more "uplifting" lines is the key here; by keeping her tone relatively matter-of-fact, there's nary a whiff of pontificating or condescension in the air. With Lloyd Douglas (and scenarists Lenore Coffee, Cameron Rogers, and Abem Finkle) making sure that the sagacity flows only *after* problems rear their ugly heads, Bainter has all the help she needs in keeping the housekeeper from being an omniscient buttinski.

Still, Hannah's near sanctity and knack at being a Jill-of-all-trades do verge on the supernatural. Her kitchen savvy means that the Wards can reduce their monthly food budget while eating better *and* can now afford to hire her on indefinitely. Her skill at restoring discarded furniture leads to much-needed cash with which to settle outstanding bills, and the deductions she makes about the history of Paul's old desk—now primed, polished, and on its way out the door with sundry other pieces—show that she possesses a capacity for ratiocination to rival Sherlock Holmes. Likewise, only a guardian angel could subtly move Paul Ward to turn from his propensity at tinkering to the serious pursuit of an "iceless ice-box," without once marveling that—Land o' Goshen!—the teacher and young Peter Trimble are that very day studying the principles of refrigeration over at the high school.

At first glance, the Wards appear to be very much in need of a Mary Poppins-like organizer. It takes the combined efforts of the three of them to determine whether it's Friday or Saturday, with the vague memory of fish for dinner the night before casting the deciding vote: "We always have fish for dinner on a Friday." No less an authority than the morning paper has to clear up the confusion: It's Friday. (Paul: "What about the fish?" Marcia: "It was canned salmon, on special.") Father and daughter scramble out to school, with the young girl pausing only to remove her shoes from the oven, where they have been baking since the previous evening.

Rains, Kay Johnson, and Bonita Granville play the Wards as one, not-so-big (albeit there's an infant safely nestled in a kitchen bassinet), happy family. Granville is a delight, and there's something nice about seeing a 14-year-old actress play a 14-year-old character. Sally Ward's mood swings—happy one minute, furious with her father over his treatment of Peter Trimble the next—are dead on, and the character passes the litmus test—does anyone in the audience really care whether she survives pneumonia?—due to the actress's native vivacity and natural reading of the role.

Kay Johnson does as well as she can as Marcia, the least well defined of the Wards (excepting, of course, the baby). Marcia may or may *not* be having health problems; early in the feature, Sally expresses concern for her mom, and we learn of visits to the doctor. This road leads nowhere, but Hannah's attention turns later to *Sally's* delicate constitution, thus stoking the dramatic fires when the young girl is feverishly fighting for her life. Johnson doesn't make much of an impression, but—as Paul ships his wife and brood into Aunt Nellie's arms and out of the picture to smooth the way for the grand finale—Marcia is pretty well expendable anyway once her daughter weathers the storm.

Rains *is* impressive, though, and for any of a number of reasons. For one thing, there's the novelty of the situation. Of all his pictures to that point, only *White Banners* freed him from madness, larceny, or period costume, and placed him at the head of a little family in a little town. There are no hints whatsoever of megalomania, usurpation of authority, or unbridled ambition; nor are there any rivals—real or imaginary—for the affections of his beloved. And, as earthshaking as it is to Paul Ward, the theft of the design is really only a minor dramatic pivot, tossed into the proceedings to bring Hannah's "white banners" philosophy to a succinct and quotable head.

For another, there's Mr. Ward's grandly affable nature. Paul Ward was Rains' most even-tempered portrayal to date (save for *The Man Who Reclaimed His Head*'s Paul Verin, who was as close to a complacent idiot savant as screenplays of the thirties were capable of delivering). Taking in stride this latest addition to his poverty-stricken household, he's willing to go along with the flow, even if he's not quite sure where the flow is headed. At the school, he's just another overgrown boy, modeling a false nose and mustache, and adding his own name to the role of dishonor (to good-natured laughter and applause) when he's caught wearing that getup by the dean.

At home, he's the least rigid of fathers, the least tolerated of inventors, and the least argumentative of employers. When Hannah tells him that he's getting both her services and a month's groceries for less than the price of the foodstuffs alone, he asks: "I say, aren't you just a little bit crazy?" "You ought to know, being a professor, I mean," she replies, and he swallows it whole. In the face of so much calm, Rains must have relished the chance to finally let off dramatic steam by ranting, raging, and ravaging the now useless Rube Goldbergesque assemblage of coils and tubing he had jury-rigged in the basement.

The turnabout in *White Banners* comes when Rains pulls a quiet reversal on Fay Bainter. As Hannah angrily vows that she will fight Bradford should he try to tell Peter about their old love affair or to reveal the truth concerning the Trimbles, Paul cuts her off at the knees. The science teacher has been totally converted by Hannah's homespun philosophy, and now reminds *his* teacher of the force of her own arguments. White banners, you know. It's a great and touching moment, and it sums up what's gone before it perfectly.

*White Banners* Warner Bros. Released June 25, 1938. 88 minutes.

CLAUDE RAINS (Paul Ward); Fay Bainter (Hannah Parmalee); Jackie Cooper (Peter Trimble); Bonita Granville (Sally Ward); Henry O'Neill (Sam Trimble); Kay Johnson (Marcia Ward); James Stephenson (Thomas Bradford); J. Farrell McDonald (Dr. Thompson); William Pawley (Joe Ellis); Edward Pawley (Bill Ellis); John Ridgely (Charles Ellis); Mary Field (Hester); Edward McWade (Sloan)

Executive Producers: Jack L. Warner and Hal B. Wallis; Associate Producer: Henry Blanke; Director: Edmund Goulding; Assistant Director: Frank Heath; Screenplay: Lenore Coffee, Cameron Rogers, and Abem Finkle, based on the novel *White Banners* by Lloyd C. Douglas; Director of Photography: Charles Rosher; Art Director: John Hughes; Editor: Thomas Richards; Wardrobe: Milo Anderson; Musical Director: Leo F. Forbstein; Musical Score: Max Steiner; Sound: Oliver S. Garretson; Technical Advisor: C. A. Meller

A Cosmopolitan Production

On June 12, 1939, *The Lux Radio Theatre* presented its adaptation of *White Banners*. Fay Bainter and Jackie Cooper repeated their screen roles, but Rains was replaced as Paul Ward by Lewis Stone.

# *Four Daughters* (1938)

Music professor Adam Lemp (Claude Rains) and his older sister, Etta (May Robson), head a household centered on Adam's four daughters, all beautiful, talented, and ranging in age from their very late teens to their very early twenties.

Thea (Lola Lane) has determined that she will marry Ben Crowley (Frank McHugh), but for money rather than out of love. The other girls—Emma (Gale Page), Ann (Priscilla Lane), and Kay (Rosemary Lane)—are as of yet uncommitted, although the family feels that Emma and shy florist Ernest Talbot (Dick Foran) make a nice couple. When young composer Felix Deitz (Jeffrey Lynn) comes to live with the Lemps, though, all four girls are hopelessly smitten.

Mickey Borden (John Garfield) also appears on the scene. Mickey is obviously talented at musical orchestration, but has a morose and pessimistic attitude; Aunt Etta and Ann see through this facade, however, and work to lift Mickey's spirits. They are nearly successful when Ann announces that she and Felix are engaged to be married. Mickey is shocked—he has fallen in love with her himself—and each of the other girls is crushed; Emma is particularly heartbroken.

In short order, Thea announces that she and Ben will wed in June, Kay announces that she's off to pursue a singing career, and Mickey elopes with Ann, who hopes that to remove herself from the picture will free up Felix for Emma. This sacrifice notwithstanding, Felix leaves for Seattle, and Ann and Mickey make for New York, where nothing goes their way. Christmas finds everyone back at the Lemp house (save for Kay, who can be found on the radio); Emma has fallen in love with Ernest, and Mickey notes how Ann and Felix are still very much in love.

After the celebration, Mickey offers Felix and Ben a lift and then later, while alone, runs his car into a tree. When Thea mistakenly believes that Ben is injured, she realizes that she does love him after all. The family rushes to the hospital, only to discover that Mickey is dying; he and Ann share his last moments together. Come springtime, Felix returns to the Lemps' and proposes once again to Ann.

*Four Daughters* is a satisfying little movie, but it's tough, some 60 years after the fact, to appreciate that it was up for the Oscar as Best Picture, or that it was named as one of the year's Ten Best by *The New York Times*. Tossed amidst lots of flute-waving and Beethoven-ranting by Rains, lots of fussing by cranky-yet-lovable Robson, and lots of carefully choreographed cuteness on the part of the Lane sisters (and Gale Page), is the predicament upon which the film (and a good portion of its sequel) turns: how is the prettiest of the Lemp gals going to accommodate *both* of the primary romantic leads?

The answer was transparently obvious to those addicted to soapy, "women's" novelist Fannie Hurst. Ann Lemp (the impossibly vivacious Priscilla Lane) merely had to give her consent to Felix and her body (after a proper elopement, of course) to Mickey. (Come *Four Wives*, and some 12 reels would be focused on her again giving her heart to the one but her *mind* to the other.) It would take Mickey's noble self-sacrifice (scripted and photographed to mute overt indications of suicide) to straighten things out and allow a happy ending. Before the film's success was apparent, Mickey was little more than a dramatic speed bump, slowing the momentum, changing the pace, and forcing the viewer to pay close attention to the narrative. After the receipts were in, he and his personal angst became the stuff that dreams (and obsessions and hallucinations and sequels) were made of.

This was *the* big break for John Garfield, whose tough-guy-you-feel-sorry-for persona was an instant hit with almost everyone who counted. The National Board of Review pegged him one of the year's best actors, and he was nominated for (but didn't win) the Oscar for Best Supporting Actor. He became an overnight sensation; men admired his flippant attitude and easy masculinity, while women perceived him as a figure of romance. His presence boosted the revenue of every picture he appeared in for some time to come, and, if you include his ghostly cameo in *Four Wives* (the studio's back-door method of getting the Garfield name into that film's publicity campaign), the actor

helped push five successive Claude Rains-Warner Bros. features into the black ink column.

Director Michael Curtiz once again proved that he could move easily from genre to genre, and his masterful melding of the unique Garfield persona with Fannie Hurst's take on sisterly interaction in white-bread, small town America won him his first Academy Award nomination. Few directors could swash buckles like Curtiz, and fewer still could juggle such potentially dangerous elements as were to be found in the picture at hand and not find themselves drowning in *Weltschmerz*. The hearts that were broken during the picture's sundry climaxes beat again with renewed vigor at the director's whim; only actress Leota Lane, whom Curtiz had naysayed in favor of Gale Page, was still unhappy when the production wrapped.

For a man whose every thought and/or action is apparently empowered by his passion for Beethoven or other of his classical colleagues, Adam Lemp is a Johnny one-note. Rains tempers his velvety voice with the edge appropriate to a crusty old curmudgeon, and earns whatever smiles, chuckles, or affectionate head-shakes are to be had. Watching him gobble hot dogs at the family picnic, you want to hug him to death, and his later verbalization that there may not be (*choke, sniffle*) too many more birthdays in his future (this mouthed by a 49-year-old actor as a man whose eldest child is supposedly but 23) has more sentiment than sappiness. (In this last, Rains is helped by May Robson; the two seasoned pros work off each other almost instinctively. Tragically, Robson *did* have less than a handful of birthdays left.) Still, Rains' performance skates close to caricature. *The New York Times* felt the picture was "a triumph ... for Claude Rains as the musical father," and *Variety* gushed that the actor was "terribly persuasive and attractive," but that was then and this is now. Nonetheless, the fact that you're not quite ready to toss Adam Lemp and his goddamn flute into the river by the closing credits is entirely thanks to Rains and, by "modern"

Priscilla Lane carried the ball most of the time in the series, with Claude (and May Robson) running interference. *Courtesy Susan Duic*

standards, that's more than enough. Hal Wallis must have also been grateful for Rains' winning ways, as the producer had overruled Michael Curtiz's decision that Charlie Winninger would play Lemp.

Besides a brace of sequels, *Four Daughters* inspired the filming of *Daughters Courageous*, a comprehensive reworking of everything and everyone (albeit with a bit of reverse English) and an out-and-out remake, *Young at Heart*, in 1954. For this latter film, scenarists Julius J. Epstein and Lenore Coffee would once again plunder Miss Hurst's "Sister Act" (this time, for Frank Sinatra and Doris Day), but that voodoo the writers had done in 1938 (when they were nominated for an Oscar for Best Screenplay) didn't do nearly so well.

*Four Daughters* Warner Bros. Released September 24, 1938. 90 minutes.

CLAUDE RAINS (Adam Lemp); Jeffrey Lynn (Felix Deitz); John Garfield (Mickey Borden); Frank McHugh (Ben Crowley); May Robson (Aunt Etta); Gale Page (Emma Lemp); Pricilla [sic] Lane (Ann Lemp); Lola Lane (Thea Lemp); Rosemary Lane (Kay Lemp); Dick Foran (Ernest Talbot); Vera Lewis (Mrs. Ridgefield); Tom Dugan (Jake); Eddie Acuff (Sam); Donald Kerr (Earl); Wilfred Lucas (Doctor)

Executive Producers: Jack L. Warner, Hal B. Wallis; Producer: Henry Blanke; Director: Michael Curtiz; Dialogue Director: Irving Rapper; Screenplay: Julius J. Epstein, Lenore Coffee, based on the story, "Sister Act," by Fannie Hurst; Director of Photography: Ernest Haller, ASC; Art Director: John Hughes; Editor: Ralph Dawson; Musical Director: Leo. F. Forbstein; Musical Score: Max Steiner; "Mickey's Theme" composed by Max Rubinowitsh; Orchestral Arrangements: Hugo Friedhofer, Ray Heindorf; Gowns: Orry-Kelly; Sound: Stanley Jones; Makeup: Perc Westmore

A Warner Bros./First National Picture

## *They Made Me a Criminal* (1939)

Supposedly clean-cut, sober, and apparently devoted to his sainted mother, boxer Johnnie Bradfield (John Garfield) slugs his way to the lightweight championship of the world. Later, however, while celebrating his win, a drunken Johnnie lets it slip before reporter Charles Magee (John Ridgely) that he doesn't even have a mother, and that he regards most people as suckers. Looking to prevent Magee from printing this explosive revelation, fight manager Doc Ward (Robert Gleckler) bludgeons the reporter with a liquor bottle and fixes it to look as if the champ—passed out on a nearby table—is responsible for the killing. Doc steals Johnnie's money, his wristwatch, and his girl, Goldie (Ann Sheridan), but the two perish in a car crash while leaving town. Because of the wristwatch, the police misidentify Doc's charred body as Johnnie's, and close the case.

Johnnie consults his lawyer, who advises him to change his name and make a new life for himself, someplace far from New York. Calling himself Jack Dorney, the champ is soon a drifter. In Arizona, he finds work on a date farm run by Grandma (May Robson); her brother, a priest, had established the place as a home where wayward boys would come to find themselves. Helping Grandma is Peggy (Gloria Dickson), whose younger brother Tommy (Billy Halop) and his pals (the Dead End Kids) come to mean a lot to the cynical Johnny.

Hard work, Peggy's devotion, and the kids' admiration put Johnny on the road to spiritual renewal. He proposes to fight a touring boxer at the local fairgrounds, hoping to win some money so that Tommy and his pals can open a gas station and have real jobs and real futures. Meanwhile, Detective Phelan (Claude Rains), has tracked Johnnie from New York to ringside, where he witnesses the boxer take a beating from Johnnie.

Later, as Phelan and Johnnie make for the train station, the policeman has a change of heart—he's always been doubtful that the champ had swung that fatal bottle—and tells his prisoner to keep his face out of the papers and to get on with his life. Phelan returns to New York alone.

August 31, 1938

Jack Warner
Vice President, Warner Brothers
First National Pictures

Dear Jack. Having thoroughly enjoyed my association with the studio and toed the line to cooperate to the best of my ability, I feel that you should know of my inability to understand being cast for the part of Phelan in "They Made Me a Criminal." Frankly, I feel that I am so poorly cast that it would be harmful to your picture. You have done such a good job in building me up that it seems a pity to tear that down with such a part as this, and I am confidant that your good judgment will recognize this. Dogs delight to bark and bite and I think I have been a good dog for three years, so perhaps you will give me five minutes to talk it over.

Claude[11]

It's not clear whether Rains ever got his five minutes, but his awareness of this dreadful piece of miscasting has been shared by almost everyone who has viewed this film since its debut in January 1939. *Criminal* marked John Garfield's first real headlining role in motion pictures and was another blow struck for fans of the Dead End Kids; for Claude Rains, however, no-first-name Phelan, with his ersatz Noo Yawk accent and simplistic mindset, was little more than an embarrassment.

Back in 1933, Warners had filmed the Bertram Millhauser-Beulah Marie Dix play, *Sucker*, as *The Life of Jimmy Dolan*, with Douglas Fairbanks, Jr., Loretta Young, and Guy Kibbee in the roles that Garfield, Dickson, and Rains would take a half-decade later. Decidedly one of Fairbanks' lesser efforts, despite its being released amid a plethora of boxing tales and its being helmed by the no-nonsense Archie Mayo, *Dolan* made enough money to warrant its being dusted off and remade for Garfield following

**Claude glares daggers at John Garfield. The young fellow wearing Chico Marx's hat is Billy Halop.**
*Courtesy Buddy Barnett*

his positive reception in *Four Daughters*. An unremarkable film, directed in a most atypical style by Busby Berkeley—the king of syncopated dance routines and overhead panoramas—*They Made Me a Criminal* nonetheless won its share of critical acclaim, with Berkeley's mundane, straightforward approach often singled out for its "punch." Objectively, however, even the artistry of the cinematographer, James Wong Howe, couldn't do much to distinguish the picture from any other of the dozen prizefighter epics released that same year.

Veteran viewers have come to regard *Criminal* as a blend of familiar, thematic plot contrivances, built around the skeleton of a story as old as Christ's parables; for the most part, that story unfolds pleasantly, if not a

little predictably. Less easy to take than the first-reel revelation that the champ is in fact a contemptible master of deceit, however, is the last-reel evidence that any growth or contrition we may have perceived on his part has been yet another exercise in duplicity. Although we've been led to believe that Johnnie has shed his scorn for his fellow man—much like a snake sheds his skin—he's both unpleasant and ungrateful in his reaction to Detective Phelan's magnanimity.

Phelan: "I was just thinkin' ... a smart guy like you ... if you hadn't laid yourself wide open for a dame and them kids, I'd never of found you. You're a terrible sucker."

Johnnie: "You're tellin' me? But I'd do it again, see?"

Phelan: "Well, I made a mistake in my life...."

Say, maybe I'm makin' another. Maybe I got the wrong guy! ... Go on, kid, beat it! Say, keep that kisser of yours out of the camera. You don't photograph good. So long, Johnnie!"
Johnnie: "So long ... sucker."

With that last word, playwrights Millhauser and Dix and scenarist Sig Herzig undermine any nobility which had thus far been accorded to Garfield. If believing that man is basically good and has the capacity to change for the better gets a person pegged for a sucker, then Johnnie Bradfield has hoofed it some 2000 miles to Arizona without having taken a single step toward being a more compassionate human being.

Rains hasn't much to do until the second part of the film, although that mistake of his—he had "railroaded the wrong guy to the hot seat"—keeps his character's name on plenty of tongues while the dramatic focus is still in New York. It's established early on that Phelan is sharp-eyed, but it takes a newspaper photo (somehow the candid of Johnnie taken out at the farm by Tommy's box camera has made its way into the New York dailies) to get him on the right train. Once in Arizona, the wily cop homes in on the boxer without any trouble, and Rains' few lines make it clear a) that it is the *policeman* who has had his eyes opened via love and sacrifice, and b) that the actor was as incapable of intentionally sounding like Dead End Kid Leo Gorcey as Gorcey would have been in trying to imitate Rains.

Perhaps had a bit more footage been devoted to Phelan's investigations, or had the character been allowed to interview some of those impressionable date farmers, Rains might have been able to give the flat, black and white role a bit of dimension and color. As can be inferred by the telegram quoted above, however, he was cast with an eye to giving Garfield the best support Warners' money could buy; Rains' opinions counted for little in the face of his studio contract. As written, adapted, and lensed, not even had Rains been firing all pistons could he have transformed Phelan—just another plot wrinkle in a story already heavily creased by

use—into some chain-smoking Javert, determined to hound the pugilistic Jean Valjean into tipping his deadly left hand.

Still, while he didn't just go through the motions, Rains might have tried harder to mute the air of half-hearted resignation which even to this day lingers about the picture.

***They Made Me a Criminal*** Warner Bros. Released January 28, 1939. 92 minutes.

John Garfield (Johnnie Bradfield); CLAUDE RAINS (Detective Phelan); Gloria Dickson (Peggy); May Robson (Grandma); Billy Halop (Tommy); Bobby Jordan (Angel); Leo Gorcey (Spit); Huntz Hall (Dippy); Gabriel Dell (T. B.), Ann Sheridan (Goldie); Robert Gleckler (Doc Ward); John Ridgely (Charles Magee); Barbara Pepper (Budgie); William Davidson (Ennis); Ward Bond (Lenihan); Robert Strange (Malvin); Louis Jean Heydt (Smith); Frank Riggi (Gaspar Rutchek); Cliff Clark (Manager); Dick Wessel (Collucci); Bernard Punsley (Milt); Irving Bacon (Speed); Sam Hayes (Fight Announcer)

Executive Producer: Hal B. Wallis; Associate Producer: Benjamin Glazer; Director: Busby Berkley; Assistant Director: Russ Saunders; Screenplay: Sig Herzig, based on the play, *Sucker*, by Bertram Millhauser and Beulah Marie Dix; Director of Photography: James Wong Howe; Art Director: Anton Grot; Editor: Jack Killifer; Gowns: Milo Anderson; Musical Score: Max Steiner; Musical Director: Leo F. Forbstein; Sound: Oliver S. Garretson

# *Sons of Liberty* (1939)

The colonies' independence isn't a fait accompli just because it has been so declared, and roving bands of patriots help George Washington (Montagu Love) and the Continental Army fight the British at every turn. One of these bands is the Sons of Liberty, led by Scot émigré Alexander MacDougal (Donald Crisp). MacDougal recommends Haym Salomon (Claude Rains), late of Poland but a fledgling American by disposition and philosophy, to the group. Salomon's lifelong quest for liberty impresses the men, and he is made welcome.

With New York in imminent danger of occupation under the British General Howe, the patriots set fire to the harbor and flee. Salomon is captured, questioned, and thrown into prison. Because he is a linguist, he is spared the gibbet and put to work interpreting for the British; within a short while, he becomes a spy for the patriots' cause and helps many American prisoners to escape. Back in prison a year later, he meets and comforts Nathan Hale before escaping himself and making for Philadelphia.

By 1781, Washington and his men have suffered three years of reverses, and are ragged and penniless. Colonel Tilgham rides to beg Salomon once again to help raise funds to underwrite the struggle for freedom. While wearing his prayer shawl, Salomon passionately addresses the congregation at his synagogue, and—taken together with the monies his own firm contributes— the appeal results in Washington getting the $400,000 needed to continue the fight. Everyone rejoices when General Cornwallis surrenders to Washington at Yorktown.

Salomon himself dies some four years later. He leaves his wife, Rachel (Gale Sondergaard), and his children without a hint of a fortune, but he bequeaths to them—and to all Americans—a legacy of freedom.

*Sons of Liberty* is Claude Rains' picture all the way, with few other characters (save for Montagu Love's eerily perfect George Washington) given much in the way of footage or dialogue. The 21-minute film won the Academy Award for Best Short Subject in 1939; it was the Warners' only Oscar in that apex year of American cinema. Jewish patriot Haym Salomon had been the object of executive scrutiny and discussion since 1937 when, says James C. Robertson, his name was linked with Paul Muni's and his story was under consideration for a feature-length presentation.[12] As the brothers Warner were doubtful whether Salomon was a big enough name (or a familiar enough story) to fill movie houses, the scope of the project dwindled as time passed.

Come 1939, however, there was a market for cries for liberty, no matter the size or scope. Adolf Hitler and the goons of the Third Reich were trampling life, liberty, and most of Europe under jackbooted foot, and the tale of Haym Salomon and another struggle for freedom became very timely indeed. Action ace Michael Curtiz—no slouch when it came to stirring the pot of passion and excitement—was assigned to direct the remnant of the story ex-silent film star Crane Wilbur had written and had intended to direct. Rains and Gale Sondergaard, who had played a married couple before (in 1936's *Anthony Adverse*) and who would do so later (in 1939's *Juarez*), were married again for this film, which was shot in Technicolor by veterans Sol Polito and Ray Rennahan. (Rennahan would go on to snag the Oscar as co-photographer of the year's big winner, *Gone with the Wind*.)

Playing the expatriate who became a patriot was a cinch for Rains, who only the year before had become a naturalized citizen of the United States. A veteran of World War I, Rains was aghast (as were most of Hollywood's British and Hungarian "colonies") at the Nazi juggernaut in Europe, and would soon be spending the greater part of his free time hawking war bonds and making personal appearances for the war effort.

Bearing all this in mind colors one's appreciation of Rains' delivery of his key speeches, none of which is long, but each of which is thus made extra memorable. Perhaps the best of the lot is the appeal Salomon makes right on the floor of the synagogue:

My friends, the struggle for our independence is in danger of being lost. General Washington has no money, food, or clothing for his ragged army. He has asked us to help him raise the $400,000 he so badly needs…. It isn't charity I ask; it's an offering to the cause of liberty, a cause sacred to us above all others because centuries of bitter persecution have taught us the value of liberty. If we want to continue to live as free men in a free land, if we want to bequeath to our children this priceless heritage, then we must give. It is not our duty to leave wealth to our children; it is our duty to leave them liberty.

**Apparently Haym Solomon had a *very* good year.** *The Wioskowski Collection*

Given the crucial nature of the message and the soul-stirring sentiments that underlay it, Rains avoids obvious theatricality and comes across as a simple man whose eloquence stems from the righteousness of his cause. His eyes fill with tears of pride as members of his congregation pledge the last of their belongings to outfit the men fighting in their name. The sequence starts marvelously, as Salomon asks Col. Tilgham to open the missive from Washington for him (thus making the general's emissary his *shabbas goy*), and closes on the warmest grin the motion picture camera would ever elicit from Claude Rains.

Rains looks dashing in his pony-tailed appliance and cocked hat, and wears the colonial-era costumes with a sartorial ease that is lacking in several other of his period

pieces. Although he's not given much chance in the abbreviated running time to add the layers of subtle characterization for which he was known, his depth of religious feeling is made clear when he quotes the 23rd Psalm to inspire Nathan Hale (Larry Williams).

Jessica Rains told the author that her father would occasionally wonder whether he did, in fact, have some Jewish blood; one can only speculate whether or how this may have affected his interpretation of the role.

*Sons of Liberty* was well intentioned, well regarded, and well received in its first run, and subsequently enjoyed a full theatrical reissue in 1948. Besides the recognition from the Academy, it also won the most unexpected of prizes for Michael Curtiz, who would never again make a two-reel film: a

$3,000 bonus, courtesy of Jack Warner, old deep pockets himself.

*Sons of Liberty* Warner Bros. Released April 1939. 21 minutes.

CLAUDE RAINS (Haym Salomon); Gale Sondergaard (Rachel Salomon); Donald Crisp (Alexander MacDougal); Montagu Love (George Washington); Henry O'Neill (Madison); James Stephenson (Colonel Tilgham); Larry Williams (Nathan Hale); Moroni Olsen (Robert Morris); Vladimir Sokoloff (Jacob)

Executive Producer: Jack L. Warner; Director: Michael Curtiz; Screenplay: Crane Wilbur; Director of Photography: Sol Polito, ASC, and Ray Rennahan, ASC; Costumes: Milo Anderson; Makeup: Perc Westmore; Musical Director: Leo F. Forbstein

## *Juarez* (1939)

Napoleon III (Claude Rains) and his empress, Eugenie (Gale Sondergaard), scheme to keep France's hold on Mexico. By arranging fraudulent "elections," they hope not only to establish a puppet monarchy with Maximilian of Hapsburg on the throne, but also to circumvent the Monroe Doctrine by claiming the monarchy to be the will of the people. Opposing the nouveau emperor are the followers of Benito Juarez (Paul Muni), elected president of the Mexican Republic.

Maximilian (Brian Aherne) soon discovers that there have been no "free elections," and, angry at having been duped by Napoleon, decides to abdicate. His wife Carlota (Bette Davis) counsels that he can be of greater service to the Mexican people by protecting them—as king—from the injustices imposed by the French. Convinced that a good king can accomplish what a good politician cannot, Maximilian agrees and offers Juarez the post of prime minister. The *presidente*, who has modeled his philosophy and his life upon Abraham Lincoln, cannot reconcile a monarchy with his belief in the power of the people and refuses.

Following the American Civil War, the United States sends word to Napoleon that France's presence in Mexico will not be tolerated under the Monroe Doctrine and that $50 million has been appropriated by Congress for weapons and munitions with which to arm the defenders of the Mexican Republic. Napoleon orders his armies to return home, destroying any chance Maximilian may have had at overthrowing his enemies and reuniting the country under his leadership, and effectively dooming Maximilian and his followers to death.

Carlota heads to Paris to lock horns with the French emperor over this betrayal, but suffers a mental collapse under the weight of her husband's hopeless situation and Napoleon's resolve to do nothing. In Mexico, Maximilian and his faithful generals are executed, and Juarez continues his fight to solidify the fledgling republic.

Legal wrangling over rights and attribution led screenwriters John Huston, Wolfgang Reinhardt, and Aeneas MacKenzie to draw upon both Franz Werfel's play, *Juarez and Maximilian,* and Bertita Harding's novel, *The Phantom Crown*, in adapting this aspect of the Juarez saga for popular consumption. As it was, the film saw its focal point shift radically in its journey from screenplay to screen. Pre-production trade ads referred to the project as *Maximilian and Carlota,* a title which keyed in on the presence of Bette Davis, Warners' reigning queen. When Davis was suspended over contractual disagreements, the part of Carlota was all but eliminated dramatically, and the narrative realigned to concentrate on the chasm which separated the ideals of the would-be emperor and the de facto president. After the flap had ended, Davis returned to above-the-title billing (shared with Paul Muni), but to a film which had been renamed and to a role which, save for its climactic "mad scenes," was really little more than window dressing.

Hal B. Wallis had convinced Jack Warner that this episode in Juarez's continuing fight for Mexican independence was worthy of

A *Juarez* costume test of Claude as Uradi, the role that ultimately went to Joseph Calleia. *The author's collection.*

extraordinary treatment, so the normally frugal production head (doubtless with an eye to making it all back and *mucho* more in lucrative Hispanic markets) pulled out most of the stops. A permanent pueblo set (designed by the quirky but brilliant Anton Grot) was constructed on the Warners' ranch, and the extensive locale not only lent the air of verisimilitude that the picture needed, but also returned its cost many times over in terms of the studio's own horse operas and leasing arrangements for the Westerns of others. With much of the story thus unfolding within, near, or atop these solid (but relatively cheap) adobe walls, corners could be cut elsewhere. The various salons of Napoleon's palace remain remarkably bare, and while most of the featured cast cavort in a sumptuous array of uniforms, gowns, and regalia, one has to admire—at least from a budgetary point of view—any film which can legitimately get away with clothing almost everyone else in a straw hat and frayed white pants.

As with most of the Warners' extravaganzas of the late thirties, *Juarez* showcases just about every character actor on the studio payroll. The mustache of the corrupt José de Montares underlines the prominent nose of Montagu Love, Pedro de Cordoba and Gilbert Roland add a bit of ethnic integrity, and everyone from Walter Kingsford and Vladimir Sokoloff to Louis Calhern and John Miljan are scurrying about like mice. Donald Crisp's stolid turn as Marechal Bazaine is more than acceptable, but it's a bit of a shock to catch John Garfield impersonating the fiery Porfirio Díaz. For one brief, shining moment, it seems that Joseph Calleia's Alejandro Uradi is finally on the side of the angels. Standing tall (amidst a bunch of scruffy patriots), he has us hoping that, just this once, he won't prove to be the type of oily weasel the Maltese actor made his own. No such luck.

As the Empress Eugenie, Gale Sondergaard is again married to Claude Rains, and she is as much advisor and soulmate to her husband as Carlota is to Maximilian. While neither empress has much screen time (and Eugenie has but a fraction of Carlota's), Sondergaard manages to imbue her character with enough dimension to make her a perverse parallel to Davis's idealistic queen.

Due to the circumstances mentioned above, Bette Davis wasn't given much opportunity to ... well, to be Bette Davis, and the few bits of eyelash fluttering, weeping, and introspection that she does bring off don't go very far in shifting the dramatic spotlight her way. Carlota's infertility is a *personal* problem, which pales alongside the weightier matters of liberty and democracy which the men are pondering, even when considered in light of the question of succession to the throne of Mexico.

Offsetting the images cast by the two empresses is a parallel between Brian Aherne's Maximilian von Hapsburg and Claude Rains' Napoleon, but the film's major thrust is the similarity between the gentle ideals of Maximilian and the tight-lipped declamations of Benito Juarez. Crucial to one's understanding of the picture is the awareness that both men share a passion for liberty and freedom from oppression; it is only in terms of how this is to be accomplished that they differ. (Maximilian's "Old World" coiffure and fondness for ermine robes contrasts sharply with the Lincolnesque attire and demeanor of the stoic Juarez, and visually reinforces this ideological rift.) The picture turns on the tragic fact that it is a word, "democracy," which separates the philosophies of the two men and, ultimately, makes them implacable foes.

An all but unrecognizable Claude Rains opens the film. With his trademark pompadour nowhere in evidence, and sporting a wig and facial appliance straight out of Gounod's *Faust*, it is his velvety voice that gives away the game. His Napoleon is a cigar-smoking bundle of nerves, whose moods swing wildly and often: one moment, a snarl of impotent anger at the news of an impending victory for the North in the American Civil War; the next, an appreciative purr at Eugenie's solution to the problem

John Bigelow (Hugh Sothern) infroms the emperor that the United States will enforce the Monroe Doctrine. The news doesn't sit well. *Courtesy Buddy Barnett*

of legitimizing the French presence in Mexico.

Like Maximilian, Napoleon is no soldier; having his picture painted while posing on an oversized hobby horse says more of his pretense at waging war than his fear of confrontation with the newly *re*-United States over the Monroe Doctrine. (Rains has his bantam emperor gag audibly on his cigar smoke, as Senator del Valle [Walter O. Stahl] reads him Ulysses S. Grant's riot act.) Both emperors follow the counsel of their wives, with the unhappy result that Napoleon ultimately faces financial and political hardship, while Maximilian faces the firing squad. Unlike his Austrian counterpart, though, the French monarch is not a man of honor; he is repeatedly depicted as a liar, an opportunist, and, in the words of the enraged Carlota, a murderer.

His comic-opera make-up (which, like every other aspect of the picture, was painstakingly researched) apart, Rains' Napoleon is no fool. Neither his bluster in the face of world opinion, nor his outrage at the unhappy results of a civil war an ocean away, betokens a lack of conviction within the man; rather, each is yet another nail in the coffin of European colonialism. Rains allows his character's skittishness to convey Napoleon's growing impotence, and the actor—always adept at portraying desperate men growing ever more so—turns his last close-up (with bizarre key-lighting changes by director Dieterle and cinematographer Tony Gaudio) into a metamorphosis: The frantic little emperor is transformed into a glowering Mephistopheles, thus triggering Carlota's flight from sanity.

Critical opinion of *Juarez* was uniformly tepid, as praise for individual performances was regrettably offset by dissatisfaction with the stolid nature of the narrative. Although many reviewers found Muni's work an excellent take on a rather one-note personality, they found Aherne's portrait more memorable. *The New York Times* said that "Juarez clearly is the hero of history, but Maximilian is the hero of the picture." *The Times'*

reviewer also felt burdened by the sheer number and portent of many of the movie's pronouncements and declarations, observing that

> Mr. Dieterle must answer the pained charge that he has taken advantage of the remarkable stage presence of the Messrs. Muni, Aherne, Garfield, and Rains to mount them, recurrently, on metaphoric soap boxes for purposes of declamation....
>
> April 26, 1939

Still, as time passed, perceptive reviewers began to appreciate the nuances they had bypassed in their condemnation of the production's straightforward presentation. Lawrence J. Quirk, author of *Fasten Your Seat Belts*—one of many book-length paeans to Bette Davis—noted:

> Rains' Napoleon is the best rendition ever of that upstart nephew of the original Napoleon, who began as a revolutionist, then became president of the French Republic, and finally the head of the Second Empire. Rains makes him proud, vain, crafty, elusive, and cowardly. His scenes are relatively few but Rains makes them vivid.[13]

With splendid performances up and down the line, *Juarez* clocks in at a long (but not overly so) 125 minutes. Isolated moments of lunacy (a poster proclaiming a "national plebiscite" on whether the people will vote for a "monarchial [sic] form of government" is torn down, presumably by one of the illiterate peons who made up 80 percent of the population) do nothing to detract from the sense of the historical moment. Accompanied by another of Erich Wolfgang Korngold's stirring musical scores, the film—which made another one of those *New York Times'* Ten Best lists—edifies as much as it entertains, and that's not such a bad thing, is it?

*Juarez* Warner Bros. Released June 10, 1939. 125 minutes.

Bette Davis (Carlota); Paul Muni (Benito Juarez); Brian Aherne (Maximilian von Hapsburg); CLAUDE RAINS (Napoleon III); John Garfield (Porfirio Díaz); Donald Crisp (Marechal

Bazaine); Joseph Calleia (Alejandro Uradi); Gale Sondergaard (Eugenie); Gilbert Roland (Col. Miguel López); Henry O'Neill (Miguel Miramón); Pedro de Cordoba (Riva Palacio); Montagu Love (José de Montares); Harry Davenport (Dr. Basch); Walter Fenner (Achille Fould); Alexander Leftwich (Drouyn de Lhuys); Georgia Caine (Countess Battenberg); Robert Warwick (Major Du Pont); Gennaro Curci (Señor de Leon); Bill Wilkerson (Tomas Mejia); John Miljan (Mariano Escobedo); Hugh Sothern (John Bigelow); Irving Pichel (Carbajal); Frank Reicher (Duc de Morny); Walter Kingsford (Prince Metternich); Holmes Herbert (Marshal Randon); Louis Calhern (LeMarc); Vladimir Sokoloff (Camilo); Manuel Díaz (Pepe)

Producer: Hal B. Wallis; Director: William Dieterle; Associate Producer: Henry Blanke; Dialogue Director: Irving Rapper; Assistant Directors: Jack Sullivan & John Prettyman; Screenplay: John Huston, Wolfgang Reinhardt, Aeneas MacKenzie, based on *Juarez and Maximilian*, by Franz Werfel, and *The Phantom Crown*, by Bertita Harding; Director of Photography: Tony Gaudio, ASC; Art Director: Anton Grot; Editor: Warren Low; Gowns: Orry-Kelly; Musical Score: Erich Wolfgang Korngold; Musical Director: Leo F. Forbstein; Orchestrations: Hugo Friedhofer & Milan Roder; Sound: C. A. Riggs and G. W. Alexander; Technical Advisor: Ernesto Romero; Makeup: Perc Westmore

While *Juarez* was in production, word reached the studio that an independent Spanish-language variation on the same theme was nearing completion, thus jeopardizing Warner Bros.' potential revenues from the Hispanic markets. When that film's producer went belly up, Jack Warner bought the picture out from under him, dubbed the footage into English, and had the English-speaking featured cast (among them: Lionel Atwill, Conrad Nagel, Jason Robards, and Gustav von Seyffertitz) rework their own parts. Released as *The Mad Empress* in mid-December, 1939, the film made back all costs, offered no competition to the big-budget Paul Muni/Bette Davis spectacular, and promptly disappeared from view.

## Daughters Courageous (1939)

Moments after she has announced her impending marriage to Sam Sloane (Donald Crisp), Nan Masters (Fay Bainter) is dismayed to discover that Jim Masters (Claude Rains), the man who had walked out on her and on their family some 20 years earlier, has suddenly come home. Jim's arrival is inopportune and the reception he receives from Nan and her four daughters (Tinka [Rosemary Lane], Linda [Lola Lane], Cora [Gale Page], and Buff [Priscilla Lane]) is quite chilly. Only housekeeper Penny (May Robson) still has a remote corner free in her heart for the prodigal father.

At first, even the girls' boyfriends are down on Jim, but, gradually, Jim's charm and understanding win them—and the girls—over to his side. This is extremely awkward for Sam, who finds his expected place as head of the household in imminent danger of being usurped. Nan is disturbed not only by her ex-husband's newly found popularity, but by the attention Buff has been paying to Gabriel López (John Garfield), the wastrel son of one of the local fishermen. Buff is drawn to Gabe because he has the same spirit of wanderlust and yearning for adventure that her father has, and Nan realizes that Buff is in very real danger of being abandoned by Gabe much as she, herself, had been abandoned by Jim two decades previously.

Sam appeals to Jim, asking that he leave once again; Sam knows his plodding, businessman ways can't compete with Jim's savoir-faire, and putting the girls in a position where they have to choose between two fathers would be intolerable. Nan, too, asks Jim to disappear, making him realize that his presence would change the face of every relationship in the house and would deny Cora and her fiancé George (Frank McHugh) the chance at happiness that only Sam can provide.

Jim sneaks out of the house the next day, just prior to Sam and Nan's wedding, and makes for the railroad station. There he's joined by Gabe, whom he had convinced not to elope with Buff. As the two board the train, bound for a life of travel and adventure, they slide effortlessly into a joint effort at separating a rich fellow passenger from his money. Back at the house, Mr. and Mrs. Sloane, together with their four daughters and potential sons-in-law, sit down to their first dinner as a family.

When *Four Daughters* made Warners a cool million dollars and gave a boost to the career of novelist Fannie Hurst, a sequel was in the works faster than you could say "Mickey Borden." *Four Wives* would be deemed an important enough project to merit the attention of both of the screen writing Epstein brothers, and while they were kept busy, crafting lines guaranteed to elicit empathy, regret, and warm-hearted appreciation, the studio cast about for some other vehicle into which the large and marvelous cast could be shoe-horned. It was felt that Dorothy Bennett and Irving White's play, *Fly Away Home*, was appropriate and the team set out to work that magic once again.

And, boy! Did they ever. Scarcely a critic could be found who didn't start his review by pegging *Daughters Courageous* as a sibling of *Four Daughters*, or end his review by liking the new arrival better. The similarities are readily apparent, the critics argued, but it is the differences that make the second picture the more memorable. Much of the focus of the drama is the difficulty that love presents even to those far from the first flowering of youth.

Fay Bainter is on the receiving end of much the same filial affection that Claude Rains had garnered as Adam Lemp, but she is also bedeviled by the romantic attentions of her two leading men. And Bainter is wonderful as Nan, probably the most precarious role of the film; she manages to reflect the gradual thaw of her girls toward their father and convey her own feelings and concerns about him, while never appearing to waiver from her devotion to Sam. In a medium

which normally equates romance with youth and sensible shoes with women above a certain age, the picture was all the more courageous for moving the middle-aged Mrs. Masters and her two swains into the spotlight for the better part of the running time.

Priscilla Lane's parallel romance with John Garfield is thus a double-duty plot device, keeping virtually everyone in the cast as closely as possible to his/her *Four Daughters* persona and priming the pump for the younger viewers. Lane's as cute as ever, but is a bit more precipitous in dumping Jeffrey Lynn this time around than she had been in the original; then again, Garfield's Gabriel López is marginally less acerbic than his Mickey Borden had been, so maybe the trade-off is to be expected.

A welcome surprise is Gabe's genuine fondness for Jim, which comes across at the railroad station. "I've appointed myself your guardian," the younger man informs his dubious partner. "When we get to Los Angeles, I'll make it legal." It's not that Gabe is *not* a loner, it's that even loners need companionship. "It's a great day for the tramps of the world," Jim chuckles; "we're getting new blood." Making Gabe a *Portuguese* flimflam man was hardly germane to the proceedings, but Garfield had just played Porfirio Díaz in Warners' *Juarez*, and his second go-round as a Latino was an elaborate in-joke, courtesy of the ever-witty Epsteins.

Rains steals *Daughters Courageous*, as it's impossible to concentrate on anyone else when he's on-screen. Even May Robson, whose own capacity for larceny has been noted elsewhere, can do little other than share the accumulated wealth during her several solo bits with him. Rid of Adam Lemp's fur and fuzz, Rains is free to laugh, smile, pout, wink, and otherwise maneuver his mobile face into any of a thousand and one expressions, all of which are captivating. At times, he's given more than enough help from director Curtiz: When Jim is cold-shouldered away from the fireplace and into a corner, a handy radio allows him his moment of triumph:

You know, when a father's neglected in certain sections of Malay, he collects a dozen human skulls and bangs on them with the jawbones of asses to attract attention to himself. I find turning on the radio much more sensible.

Exiled to the couch for the night, he revels in the concern his daughters show him when they blanket his shivering form and close the window. It's obviously the most puerile of devices, engineered by a father who never quite escaped his boyhood, but it succeeds twice. The third time is the charm, though, and Buff fixes his wagon by removing not only the quilt she's brought, but the other blankets—and his thin sheet—as well. A nice ironic touch has Jim helping Gale Page's Cora with her lines and showing her the ins and outs of upstaging the play's nominal star in her one brief scene; Rains' objective opinion on the practice would have been worth soliciting.

Frank S. Nugent of *The New York Times* also succumbed to Jim's silver tongue and engaging manner:

As Mr. Rains plays him, he is, in fact, a disarmingly attractive man, with an impudent humor and a facile tongue, very like the impertinent fisherman's son with whom his youngest daughter has fallen in love. Naturally that makes him still more menacing to the orderly routine of the tribe, especially when his charm has begun to take effect.

(June 24, 1939)

Nugent went on to crow that "Mr. Rains is best part of it," and the sentiment still stands a lifetime later. *Daughters Courageous* did not—despite near unanimity of praise among the trade and popular press—gross as much as *Four Daughters* had. Still, the film was profitable enough to warrant a remake several years later (*Always in My Heart*, 1942), and remains a cherished delight to fans of the series. And to fans of Claude Rains, Jim Masters will always be an unabashed study in pure charisma.

*Daughters Courageous* Warner Bros. Released July 22, 1939. 100 minutes.

John Garfield (Gabriel López); CLAUDE RAINS (Jim Masters); Jeffrey Lynn (Johnny Heming); Fay Bainter (Nan Masters); Donald Crisp (Sam Sloane); May Robson (Penny); Frank McHugh (George); Dick Foran (Eddie Moore); George Humbert (Manuel López); Berton Churchill (Judge Hornsby); Priscilla Lane (Buff Masters); Rosemary Lane (Tinka Masters); Lola Lane (Linda Masters); Gale Page (Cora Masters); Tom Dugan (Joe); Hobart Cavanaugh (Rich Sucker); Wilfred Lucas, Jack Mower (Conductors); Nat Carr (Court Clerk); George Cheseboro (Bar Owner); Jack Gardner (Tim)

Executive Producer: Hal B. Wallis; Director: Michael Curtiz; Associate Producer: Henry Blanke; Assistant Director: Sherry Shourds; Screenplay: Julius J. and Philip G. Epstein, based on the play, *Fly Away Home*, by Dorothy Bennett and Irving White; Directors of Photography: James Wong Howe and Ernest Haller; Art Director: John Hughes; Editor: Ralph Dawson; Gowns: Howard Shoup; Music: Max Steiner; Musical Director: Leo F. Forbstein; Orchestral Arrangements: Ray Heindorf; Sound: C. A. Riggs, Oliver S. Garretson; Makeup: Perc Westmore

# *Mr. Smith Goes to Washington* (1939)

Jefferson Smith (James Stewart), head of the state chapter of the Boy Rangers and political babe in the woods, is appointed to fill in the remainder of a vacated term in the U.S. Senate. This is just fine with boss Jim Taylor (Edward Arnold), Senator Joseph Paine (Claude Rains), and Governor Hopper (Guy Kibbee), all of whom have been looking for someone to take the fall for a new (and unnecessary) state dam, while they reap a fortune in real estate profits. At first, Smith is the object of ridicule, good for demonstrations of sign language and bird calls, and not much else. He finds himself embarrassed by the press and even his secretary, Saunders (Jean Arthur), thinks him incompetent.

Not anxious to have his patsy walk out just yet, Paine calms Smith and counsels him to work on legislation that would put a Boy Ranger campsite on state property. Saunders, falling in love with Smith in spite of herself, advises him that Jim Taylor's dam is set for just that property. Smith appeals to Paine, but the Senator explains how compromise is the watchword of the political world, and how one has to play ball if one is to get anything at all accomplished. Disappointed, Smith threatens to reveal the details of Taylor's land fraud, but Paine is ready for him; armed with forged documentation, he accuses Smith of plotting to make a killing by lobbying to situate the Boy Ranger camp on land that he, himself, owns.

Smith is stunned by the accusation, but, encouraged by Saunders, he returns to the Senate the next day, exposes Taylor and Paine's corrupt plans, and launches a filibuster, refusing to yield the floor until he has made his case. Taylor's political machine sees to it that no word of Smith's appeal reaches his home state newspapers or radio stations. The young man talks on for hours; just when it seems that he has reached the limit of his endurance, Paine—who has been cut to the quick by Smith's honesty and integrity—attempts suicide in the cloakroom. Prevented from doing so, he rushes back onto the Senate floor and confesses to everything, incriminating himself and his cronies, and exonerating Smith.

In 1933 Frank Capra's *Lady for a Day* garnered some very nice notices for the director, author Damon Runyon, and star May Robson. It was the following year, however, that the magic that would ultimately be hailed as "Capra-corn" exploded onto the scene, when *It Happened One Night*—a gem of a comedy which everyone (but *everyone*) had seriously underestimated—walked off with all five major Academy Awards. Neither Clark Gable nor Claudette Colbert had wanted to make the film, Columbia didn't spend a dime more than necessary to publicize it, and Louis B. Mayer must have kicked himself silly for weeks following Oscar night; *he* had exiled Gable to Harry Cohn's

world of horrors as a punishment, and MGM had had the first option on "Night Bus," the property upon which the film was based, but had passed due to concerns over how the heroine of the piece was portrayed.

Capra's knack for making heroes of the common clay was thus celebrated, and the director was off and running. The exotica of *Lost Horizon* (1937) and the lunacy of *You Can't Take It with You* (1938) separate his two most renowned paeans to the average Joe: *Mr. Deeds Goes to Town* (1936) and *Mr. Smith Goes to Washington*. Gary Cooper had essayed the title role in the earlier film and was supposed to reprise the part in the Washington adventure, which, of course, would have been renamed for the character. Coop was otherwise occupied, so Stewart got the nod. Both men exuded a "boy next door" type of wholesomeness, but only Cooper had enjoyed real stardom to that point. *Smith* did wonders for Stewart; he was nominated for the Oscar (and lost), but went on to appear with Dietrich in *Destry Rides Again* (1939), Margaret Sullavan (in *The Shop Around the Corner* and *The Mortal Storm*, both 1940), and Katharine Hepburn in *The Philadelphia Story* (also 1940), for which he *didn't* lose the Oscar. The presence of such stellar actresses not only reflected Stewart's rise to the top, but helped ensure it.

As events in the Beltway have demonstrated ad nauseam, it's nearly impossible to determine which politician is straight and which is acting according to a hidden agenda. Whom can you trust? Sadly, the goings-on in *Mr. Smith Goes to Washington* were prophetic small potatoes when compared with the intensity of the sundry scandals that came to light in the decades that followed the picture's D.C. premiere. Still, congressional outrage hadn't yet become commonplace when Kentucky Senator Alben Barkley (later FDR's VP) overreacted to Sidney Buchman's adaptation of Lewis R. Foster's "The Man from Montana." The venerable senator claimed that the film made him and the rest of that august body look like fools, unable to distinguish between integrity and duplicity. Possibly in reaction to this, but, more likely, in appreciation for a splendid plunge into unfamiliar waters, some heartfelt critical bravos were immediately awarded old cowpoke Harry Carey for his turn as the vice-president with an eye for honesty; at least the president of the Senate was perceived as being something more than a fool. Thankfully, most of the citizenry and at least a two-thirds majority of the critics could distinguish between the excesses of certain of the *dramatis personae* and the ways and means of their duly elected counterparts. Rains' debonair but staggeringly corrupt "Silver Knight" thus brought him to the Academy's attention for the first time; he lost to Thomas Mitchell, whose fondness for the bottle in *Stagecoach* copped him the statuette.

The scoundrels *are* a grand lot, though, with each bringing his own richly hued vocal nuance to the film: Guy Kibbee had very few rivals when it came to blending snarls and whimpers, and, together with portly Eugene Pallette—he of the bellow and the bombast—he stokes the fires that bring Jim Taylor's political machine to a full head of steam. Rains, more glib and oily than either of these lesser rascals, provides the necessary grease, while Edward Arnold, as the political boss, keeps the flow of corruption measured and unwavering. On the side of the angels, Jean Arthur transmogrifies majestically from the tough as nails Gal Friday who has seen everything to the tough as nails girlfriend who has finally found something worth keeping; the beauty and credibility of the conversion is as much due to the actress's style and substance as to the director's trademark smoothness. Thomas Mitchell's Diz Moore remains one of the most lovable of lushes in an era where drinking was admired and DUI was an infallible source of low comedy.

Senator Joseph Paine encompasses the best of all of Rains' gentlemen knaves. He is articulate and moneyed, affable and well connected, influential and Machiavellian.

Unlike them, however, he has somehow managed to convince himself that he has been acting altruistically for most of his lengthy career. Rains' other key roles—the grandees and emperors who preceded Paine—broke hearts, promises, and treaties, and all for personal satisfaction. (The Little Corporal may have claimed he was acting in France's best interest when he scotched brother Jerome's diddling Betsy Patterson, but, *mes amis*, Napoleon *was* France.) The Holleniuses, Grandisons, and Sebastians who would follow in the senator's wake knew in their hearts that it was blind ambition, titanic ego, or quiet desperation that fueled their schemes. Their goodness was but a charade, and their suave appearances were always deceiving.

Paine, however, genuinely believes that objective good ultimately flows from his shady dealings; he as much as says so to Smith and, like most cinematic villains, whatever else he may twist or pervert, he cannot lie about his modus vivendi:

> You've been living in a boy's world. This is a man's world.... You have to check your ideals outside the door like you do your rubbers. I've had to compromise, I've had to play ball.... That's how states and empires have been built since time began.

It takes Smith's collapse to make the senator see how much damage his lies and forgeries have done both to this one individual and to the democratic system at large. Taylor's many years of compromise are seen as just so much bargaining with the devil; his own wretchedness reflected in Smith's suffering, Paine tries to take his own life. The justice he takes into his own hands is to be biblical—an eye for an eye, as it were—and we at once see that the senator's name is no happy accident.

The Capitol is the very heart of America, of course, and it was felt that there could scarce be a traditional battleground subject to more scrutiny than either the House or the Senate. When Rains bursts onto the Senate floor, shouting that Smith had been

Mr. Smith (James Stewart) is taken with Susan Paine (Astrid Allwyn), but not nearly so much as he'll be taken by her father, the Silver Knight himself. *The author's collection*

truthful all along in his "every word about Taylor and me and graft and the rotten political corruption of my state," the catharsis can be cut with a knife. The maxim of that day seems to have been that recognition of America's ills is the first step to effecting America's cure.

Those were simpler times, however, and conscience was the only independent prosecutor needed.

*Mr. Smith Goes to Washington* Columbia. Released October 19, 1939. 126 minutes.

James Stewart (Jefferson Smith); Jean Arthur (Saunders); CLAUDE RAINS (Senator Joseph Paine); Edward Arnold (Jim Taylor); Guy Kibbee (Governor Hopper); Thomas Mitchell (Diz Moore); Eugene Pallette (Chick McGann); Beulah Bondi (Ma Smith); H. B. Warner (Senate Majority Leader); Harry Carey (Senate President); Astrid Allwyn (Susan Paine); Ruth Donnelly (Mrs. Hopper); Grant Mitchell (Senator MacPherson); Porter Hall (Senator Monroe); Pierre Watkin (Senate Minority Leader); Charles Lane (Nosey); Dick Elliott (Carl Cook); Jack Carson (Sweeney); Allan Cavan (Ragner); Lloyd Whitlock (Schultz); Maurice Costello (Diggs); Baby Dumpling, Billy, Delmar, Gary, and Harry Watson, John Russell (The Hopper Boys); with H. V. Kaltenborn

Producer and Director: Frank Capra; Screenplay: Sidney Buchman, based on the story, "The Man from Montana," by Lewis R. Foster; Director of Photography: Joseph Walker, ASC; Editors: Gene Havlick, Al Clark; Montage Effects: Slavko Vorkapich; Musical Score: Dmitri Tiomkin; Musical Director: M. W. Stoloff; Art Director: Lionel Banks; Assistant Director: Arthur S. Black; Gowns: Kolloch

## *Four Wives* (1939)

Called to her gynecologist's office, Emma Lemp Talbot (Gale Page) is disheartened to learn that she is barren, while Ann Lemp Borden (Priscilla Lane), found to be carrying the child of her late husband, Mickey (John Garfield), doesn't know *what* to think. Memories of Mickey's hard life and tragic death fill her days and nights, disconcerting her fiancé, composer Felix Deitz (Jeffrey Lynn), and prompting sister Kay (Rosemary Lane) to call in Dr. Clinton Forrest, Jr. (Eddie Albert) to help Ann sort through her confusion.

Seizing on Clinton's advice to forget the past and embrace the future, Ann elopes with Felix. At the surprise party thrown for the newlyweds at the Lemp home later, Felix offers to work on Mickey's unfinished symphony, and fourth sister Thea Lemp Crowley (Lola Lane) informs her family and friends that she and husband, Ben (Frank McHugh), are about to adopt a baby. Just after the adoption goes through, Thea discovers she is pregnant.

With the baby on the way, Felix doesn't want to go on an extended concert tour. Ann insists he leave, however. Frustrated at having to battle Mickey's ghost at every turn, the young composer boards his train for New York. Ann goes into premature labor, and her newborn daughter may die. Arriving at the hospital unbeknownst to his wife, Felix gives his blood to save the child, and then returns to his tour. On the radio, Ann hears her husband conduct Mickey's "Symphonie Moderne," which Felix had completed as promised. With Mickey finally getting a measure of the renown he deserved, Ann feels a sense of fulfillment and fully accepts her new husband, their daughter, and their life together.

Thea and Ben have twin girls, Emma and Ernest (Dick Foran) are given custody of the adopted young girl, and Kay and Clinton marry.

Conspicuously missing from the above synopsis are Claude Rains and May Robson.

Reprising their respective roles of Adam Lemp and Aunt Etta, the two are essentially window dressing in this well crafted tale of new beginnings: magnificent, eye-catching, highly enjoyable window dressing, perhaps, but window dressing nonetheless. Claude and May are kept out of harm's way with variations on their original shtick, while the rest of the cast—identical to that of the first film, down to Vera Lewis's omniscient Mrs. Ridgefield and old film clips of John Garfield as a disembodied Mickey Borden—carry the picture from subplot to subplot. As in *Four Daughters*, most of the heavy theatrics are left to Priscilla Lane, blondest and prettiest of her siblings; to her credit, the lovely young actress handles the pathos well and the viewer's experience is a pleasant one.

This is not to say that the old pros don't have their several grin-inducing moments. The picture opens with Adam and sundry of his daughters doing household chores in sync with the measured melodies of Beethoven: Dad is swiping ineffectually at the soap-covered window panes, and at least one of the stairs is receiving a cursory dusting from a young and curvy female Lemp. In a flash, Aunt Etta hijacks the Victrola and quickens the pace courtesy of the latest 78 by Benny Goodman. "That's just a cheap trick to speed up production," growls Briarwood's honorary Doctor of Music, but only after having unconsciously boogied his way through a few panes first.

Later, the old man manages to shift the attention and the sympathy to himself in the course of commenting on the delivery of yet another of Ernest's bouquets:

Adam: I suppose I'll have to wait until Father's
  Day before someone brings me some flowers.
Thea: Say, when *is* Father's Day?
Adam: *Last* Sunday.

Rains and the girls play the moment for its humor rather than its sentiment, and another syrupy interlude is neatly sidestepped.

Still later, while young Dr. Forrest is kept waiting at the door, Kay is primped by her sisters for maximum visual impact: They adjust her chair, correct her lighting, even provide her with something impressive to thumb through when her new fella is led onto the scene. Things don't go quite as planned, however, and it is Kay who must introduce her new beau to the assembled Lemp clan. When her turn comes, Aunt Etta is found deep in thought, nestled in what had been Kay's chair: "Yes, dear? Oh, we've met before. Excuse me, I was just reading this cookbook. It's *so* intellectual."

There are other bits—equally warm, equally droll—but nothing into which the two veteran performers can sink their teeth.

Reviews for *Four Wives* were generally good, although not on a par with the superlatives *Four Daughters* had earned. This time around, Philip Epstein joined his brother Julius (and Maurice Hanline) in taking up Fannie Hurst's gauntlet, and the end result proved a trifle more cinematic than its predecessor had been. Most of the critics found the cast capable and well-balanced, while lauding Priscilla Lane's winning battle with mawkishness. A disproportionate amount of attention was paid to the double-exposed clips of John Garfield, but it was that (and some uncredited camera work by James Wong Howe) that lent the picture its slight visual edge in the first place.

In a telephone conversation with the author, Jessica Rains recalled how her father's Warner Bros. contract allowed him to turn two features down before having to accede to a third. "They'd offer him a couple of totally unacceptable scripts," Ms. Rains said, "and then he'd end up in one of the Four Whatever things."

Adam Lemp may not have been the most challenging of roles or the weightiest of credentials, but there were far more unpleasant ways to earn $4000 a week.

*Four Wives* Warner Bros. Released December 25, 1939. 110 minutes.

Priscilla Lane (Ann Lemp Borden); Rosemary Lane (Kay Lemp); Lola Lane (Thea Lemp Crowley); Gale Page (Emma Lemp Talbot);

CLAUDE RAINS (Adam Lemp); Jeffrey Lynn (Felix Deitz); Eddie Albert (Dr. Clinton Forrest, Jr.); May Robson (Aunt Etta); Frank McHugh (Ben Crowley); Dick Foran (Ernest Talbot); Henry O'Neill (Dr. Clinton Forrest); Vera Lewis (Mrs. Ridgefield); John Qualen (Frank); John Garfield (Mickey Borden); Olin Howland (Joe); Pat West (Charlie); Ruth Tobey (Mathilde); Dennie Jackson (Boy Soprano); Wilfred Lucas (Conductor); George Reeves (Lab Technician)

Executive Producer: Hal B. Wallis; Associate Producer: Henry Blanke; Director: Michael Curtiz; Dialogue Director: Jo Graham; Screenplay: Julius J. Epstein, Philip G. Epstein, and Maurice Hanline, based on the story, "Sister Act," by Fannie Hurst; Director of Photography: Sol Polito, ASC; Art Director: John Hughes; Assistant Director: Sherry Shourds; Editor: Ralph Dawson; Gowns: Howard Shoup; Musical Director: Leo F. Forbstein; Musical Score: Max Steiner; Orchestral Arrangements: Hugh Friedhofer and Ray Heindorf; "Mickey Borden's Theme": Max Rabinowitsh; Sound: Oliver S. Garretson; Makeup: Perc Westmore

A Warner Bros./First National Picture

# *Saturday's Children* (1940)

Bobby Halevy (Anne Shirley), young daughter of bookkeeper Henry Halevy (Claude Rains), is anxious to start at the new job her father has obtained for her at Martin's, his own place of employment. At the office, Bobby takes notice of Rims Rosson (John Garfield), currently in the art department, and the two are soon dating—on Monday nights only. As time passes, Bobby and her family assume that there are wedding bells in the couple's future. When Rims announces he's taking a job in Manila—a company there is interested in looking at Rims' plans to turn hemp into silk—the young girl is distraught. Her sister Florrie (Lee Patrick) convinces Bobby to pretend that she's considering marriage with another suitor in order to make Rims come to his senses and pop the question himself.

The plan works, and Mr. and Mrs. Rosson are soon nestled in an apartment over a garage. Their fortunes take a downturn, however, when the war forces Mr. Norman (Berton Churchill) to lay Bobby off for the duration, and Rims is asked to take a cut in salary not long after. As they begin to squabble over money, the specter of Rims' opportunity in the Philippines hovers over Bobby's head. She discovers she is pregnant, but when her husband barks in frustration at the strain another mouth to feed would inflict on the family, Bobby refrains from telling him.

A letter informs the Rossons that Rims' job opportunity in Manila is still available, and the couple seems destined to part. When Rims admits to Mr. Halevy that he'd take Bobby along with him if only he had the money to do so, the older man attempts to kill himself for the insurance money. Thankfully, he is saved by the frantic actions of a night watchman, and escapes with nothing more than a few bruises.

Mr. Halevy's noble act convinces Rims that his marriage must be worth saving, if only because somebody else is willing to die for it. He announces that he's staying on, right there, with Bobby, and he's thrilled to learn that he's going to be a father.

If you confine yourself only to the tidbits included in the film's trailer, you might come to the conclusion that this adaptation of "Maxwell Anderson's Pulitzer Prize Winning Comedy" is funny instead of rather dark. Not that the picture doesn't try hard to balance every less-than-cheery vignette with a mildly amusing sequence or a semi-droll line. It's just that the constancy with which John Garfield and Anne Shirley are made to deal with frustration, lay-offs, the effects of war, disappointment, anxiety, second-guessing, anger, wage reductions, collection agencies, apathy, pessimism, separation pains, dead-end jobs, and attempted suicide doesn't leave time for much other than a chat or two with an uncomfortably drab and downtrodden Claude Rains. Garfield is even made to propose that he and Anne Shirley *celebrate*

each time they're kicked in the teeth by that old rascal, Life; had they stuck by that plan, it's doubtful whether even a single "Oh, boy" would have made the final cut.

Aimed at an audience which had weathered the Depression and was now faced with additional uncertainties and sacrifices, *Saturday's Children* is comedy, not because it occasionally brings a smile to the face (it does), but rather because—as per the classical definition of "New" comedy—it concerns everyday life. Maxwell Anderson's play had already been filmed twice—as a part-talkie in 1929 and as *Maybe It's Love* in 1935—and the Epstein brothers' rendition followed the former fairly closely. This was only the second feature credit for director Vincent Sherman (until *The Man Who Talked Too Much*, he had been busy writing screenplays with the Epsteins and others), and he had to wade through a sea of cast changes to do it. Per the AFI catalogue, Garfield was tapped only when Jimmy Stewart proved unavailable, and Anne Shirley was the last in a line of leading ladies which had included Jane Bryant, Olivia de Havilland, and Marilyn Merrick, in that order. Rains was the first (and only) choice for Shirley's father, but Sherman still went on record with misgivings—not about the actor's ability, but about his own inexperience:

While [Rains and I] were friends and I felt he respected me, I was nevertheless worried about how he might react to my directing him.... On the first day of shooting, he was on the set on time and was letter-perfect in his lines. Early that morning, we rehearsed a long and substantial scene, and after I finished explaining what I hoped to accomplish to the cast, I glanced over at Claude. He was smiling and gave me an imperceptible—to all but me—nod of approval. I shall always be grateful for that gesture. It gave me the courage and confidence I needed.[14]

*Saturday's Children* was fairly well received by the critics, but flopped at the box office. It contains elements (Rosson's clumsiness in the office, his scatterbrained inventions) which would earlier have been tailored for farceurs like Cary Grant or William

**Colleagues in more than a few pictures, John Garfield, James Wong Howe, and Claude share the wok at Howe's Chinese restaurant.** *Courtesy Rick Farmiloe*

Powell, but had the misfortune to arrive on the scene just after the demise of the screwball comedy. The shopping list of woes that confronts Rims and Bobby—attempted suicide apart, perhaps—is probably not out of line for the average marriage, but it does mitigate against the light-hearted air the trailer and the film's publicity campaign worked at establishing.

Anne Shirley is very pretty and rather good, and when her harping about tricking Rims into this, that, or the other thing begins to wear down the viewer's patience, it's really one of the rare errors in judgment made by those madcap Epsteins, and no fault of her own. "The Different" John Garfield (the trailer hedges at calling him

"The New" John Garfield) likewise isn't too bad, but his Rims Rosson falls just shy of the norm for both affability and eccentricity in lovable but inept husbands. Save for the Brooklynesque cartoons played by George Tobias and Dennie Moore, none of the other cast members are much more than faces in the crowd.

Except for Claude Rains, that is; but he has certainly looked far better elsewhere. Gone is the rakish wave of hair over the eye and the trick eyebrow; gone, too—or nearly so—is the eyebrow itself, as Perc Westmore pancaked the actor with enough light powder to render all but his most strenuous expressions invisible. With his hair parted in the middle, and a pair of wire-rimmed spectacles coming and going per the passion of the moment, Rains is the picture of insipid middle age. And well might he be; although Mr. Halevy is one of Rains' stable of understanding, lovable fathers, the wisdom he dispenses is heavily laced with self-pity and despair. "I guess what's happening to you is the final defeat for me," he whines to Bobby, who's looking for comfort now that things seem blackest:

Do you know when I stopped living? When I was 43. I realized then what the end of my life would be—exactly what it had been up to then: repetitious, dull, and completely worthless to anyone…. But at least there was one thing left to me; I could see to it that it didn't happen to you.

He even pauses to kvetch about having to wear "last year's model" eye-shade at the office.

Nor does he have much to offer at first about the virtues of matrimony:

Marriage is no love affair, my dear. It's a house, bills, dishpans, and family quarrels. That's the way the system beats you. They bait the wedding with romance, and hang a 300-pound landlord around your neck and drown you in grocery bills.

In his infinite wisdom, playwright Anderson had allowed Halevy to change his tune a few moments later (and the Epsteins seconded the motion), yet this sudden reversal doesn't ring true; it seems much more an accommodation to Bobby than an article of conviction. Cranky old Adam Lemp would never have been caught with *his* integrity down.

Desperate times call for desperate measures, but Rims and his pining for Manila are never sufficiently desperate—or credible—to dash the hopes of the most average of viewers for a happy ending. (That "Same Old" John Garfield might well have walked; this different version, never.) Nonetheless, in a moment of revelation wherein he stops just short of snapping his fingers, Halevy decides to do himself in. He fails, of course—this *is* a comedy—but his foolhardy attempt at suicide has made Rims realize that there's already

enough silk in the world without his depleting the stock of hemp, and that maybe Bobby and marriage aren't so bad after all.

Rains won some good notices—"Strong in the support as girl's plodding and sympathetically understanding father" admitted *Variety*—despite the part's being less well written than the scripters and source material might indicate. With much of his dialogue verging on unadulterated pessimism, it's tough to determine the source of all this talk of the character's "sympathetic nature." Unless, of course, the warmth of his smile and the essence of the "Same Old" Claude Rains transcended Perc Westmore's unflattering pall.

***Saturday's Children*** Warner Bros. Released May 4, 1940. 97 minutes.

John Garfield (Rims Rosson); Anne Shirley (Bobby Halevy); CLAUDE RAINS (Henry Halevy); Lee Patrick (Florrie Sands); George Tobias (Herbie Smith); Roscoe Karns (Willie Sands); Dennie Moore (Gertrude Mills); Elizabeth Risdon (Mrs. Halevy); Berton Churchill (Mr. Norman); Frank Faylen (Cab Driver); John Ridgely (Mr. MacReady); Margot Stevenson (Mrs. MacReady); Jack Mower (Mac); John Qualen, Tom Dugan (Carpenters); Creighton Hale (Mailman); Maris Wrixon, Lucille Fairbanks (Nurses)

Executive Producer: Hal B. Wallis; Associate Producer: Henry Blanke; Director: Vincent Sherman; Screenplay: Julius J. Epstein, Philip G. Epstein, based on the play, *Saturday's Children*, by Maxwell Anderson; Dialogue Director: Irving Rapper; Assistant Director: Elmer Decker; Director of Photography: James Wong Howe; Special Effects: Robert Burks; Art Director: Hugh Reticker; Editor: Owen Marks; Gowns: Milo Anderson; Musical Director: Leo F. Forbstein; Sound: C. A. Riggs; Makeup: Perc Westmore

A Warner Bros./First National Picture

*Saturday's Children* was presented on the *Lux Radio Theatre* on October 26, 1936, several years prior to Warners' feature-film presentation. Robert Taylor starred as Rims, Olivia de Havilland was Bobby (Harrington, not Halevy), Frederick Perry was her plodding and sympathetically understanding father, Mona Barrie was Florrie, and Chester Klute played Willie. On October 2, 1950, the work was adapted for television by the *Lux Video Theatre*.

## *The Sea Hawk* (1940)

Scheming to expand the Holy Roman Empire he heads, Spain's King Philip II (Montagu Love) sends Don José Álvarez de Córdoba (Claude Rains) to meet with Queen Elizabeth (Flora Robson). En route to the island, the galleon carrying Álvarez de Córdoba and his daughter, Doña María (Brenda Marshall), is attacked by Captain Geoffrey Thorpe (Errol Flynn), a buccaneer who robs from the rich and gives to the English crown. While the Spanish ambassador is thus occupied, Elizabeth is counseled by Sir John Burleson (Donald Crisp), who argues that only with a mighty navy can Britain ward off the advances of Philip II; and by Lord Wolfingham (Henry Daniell), who maintains that the Iberian king means the English no harm whatsoever.

Elizabeth, swayed in part by promises of monies from the plundering of other Spanish vessels in Panama, sides with Sir John and Captain Thorpe. Thorpe has meanwhile met Doña María and has fallen in love with her. In Panama, the buccaneer and his men—having been betrayed by Wolfingham—are captured and sentenced to life imprisonment as galley slaves. When Don Álvarez threatens Elizabeth with war if she does not dismantle the fleet her navy is building, Thorpe, who has discovered that the Spanish Armada is being readied for a surprise attack on Britain, leads a slave uprising, steals a ship, and arrives at the English court in time to warn the queen of Spain's treachery.

England is thus prepared (and thus saved), Thorpe and Doña María are reunited, and the ex-buccaneer is elevated to the rank of Knight of the Realm.

When Warner Bros. subsumed First National Pictures at the end of the twenties a good number of literary properties—rights and all—went along with the deal. One of these was Rafael Sabatini's *The Sea Hawk*, which First National had released to great acclaim and box-office back in 1924. A first-class production all the way—there had even been a spiffy Photoplay edition to commemorate the occasion—the picture had definitely been one of Milton Sills' most impressive credentials. More recently, Warners had tapped the Sabatini cache for *Captain Blood* (1935), a monumental success which first teamed the virginal Olivia de Havilland and the swashbuckling Errol Flynn, and it seemed about time for another adaptation. Hence, *The Sea Hawk*.

The *Sea Hawk* which made it to the screen, though, was a far cry from either the Milton Sills silent extravaganza or the novel on which it had been based; indeed, Rafael Sabatini could have pored over the credits crawl for weeks without spotting his name. The heroic narrative, which bore more than a passing resemblance to the saga of Sir Francis Drake, was attributed to Howard Koch and Seton I. Miller. Few doubted that Flynn would be the Sea Hawk (the scenario establishes a cadre of similarly tagged valiant English sea captains) despite early publicity blarney, and the rugged star turned in what is arguably his finest, most genuine performance, as Geoffrey Thorpe.

Warners went for the gold in order to film some of the most exciting sea battle footage ever and spent upwards of $1.75 million, much of which was earmarked for a brace of full-sized galleons and an enormous sound stage/deep-water tank in which the ships would frolic. In light of such awesome expenditures, other corners were trimmed: wardrobe, sets, and appointments from 1939's *The Private Lives of Elizabeth and Essex* were again pressed into service, and clips from the 1924 *Sea Hawk* (and both versions of *Captain Blood*) supplemented newly shot footage. The brass had to pass on Technicolor—the budget was already stretched taut—but Thorpe's debacle in Panama would be tinted sepia in consolation.

Flora Robson was approached to play the Virgin Queen; the British actress had already essayed the role in the British *Fire Over England* in 1937, and was considerably less expensive (and obstreperous) than Bette Davis, the studio's resident Elizabeth. Author James C. Robertson writes that Robson already had a theatrical commitment and almost demurred, but, between Michael Curtiz's cajoling and Errol Flynn's total cooperation, the actress was able to chalk up her second cinematic appearance as the Virgin Queen and still make her date at the theater.[15]

Henry Daniell takes Basil Rathbone's place for the obligatory last-reel sword fight with Errol Flynn, and their climactic duel is reasonably exciting, if somewhat familiar to Flynn fans; the candle business and shadow-play make it *deja vu* all over again. No viewer in his right mind feels his blood race when Daniell draws his rapier, but with Rains (a ghastly swordsman; ask Louis Hayward) out of the picture at this point, it's Daniell or no one. Sources indicate that Flynn was genuinely ill at the time the duel was to be photographed, with the result that it took cinematographer Sol Polito and Fred Cravens (the studio's fencing master, who doubled for both actors) eight days to wrap on the sequence.

Don José Álvarez de Córdoba marked Rains' second whack at a Spanish grandee (cf. Don Luis in *Anthony Adverse*) and the last of the actor's titled (and usually brocaded) noblemen; only an emperor (Caesar) and a king (Herod) would be left on his plate. As is befitting the cliché about the last and the best, Don Álvarez is the most purely political of the bunch. More arrogant than any of his cinematic predecessors (no mean feat for a man sporting that bizarre, Salvador Dali-esque coiffure), he is incredulous that his claims of (for want of a better phrase) diplomatic immunity have not dissuaded a Sea Hawk from sinking his ship, indignant when his remarks on English thievery draw retorts about Spanish incompetence, and indecorous in the manner whereby he informs

Queen Elizabeth of Thorpe's enslavement. He is deceit masquerading as outrage. He is a hypocrite who whines "Foul" while playing foul. He is Senator Joseph Paine in a cloak and velvet breeches.

Rains and corrupt politicos seemed to go together naturally during the thirties, no matter whether these were said to be acting under the aegis of their sovereigns, or in defense of some narrow view of justice. As Don Álvarez, Rains raises both of these flags, snarling from just this side of contempt at the Virgin Queen that Philip II (nicely played by Montagu Love, right down to the king's gouty leg) is growing impatient with continual English provocation. He is diverted—only momentarily—from scoring additional diplomatic points when he discovers his niece has been carrying a torch for the cutest of the Sea Hawks. "Your Grace," he admits to Elizabeth, "I would have spared her had I known." Nevertheless, he dashes Doña María's hopes again when he tells her that her beloved Thorpe is the one man in England he cannot and will not save.

Rains plays Don Álvarez as being more jingoistic than his king and less contemptible than Wolfingham (who is, after all, a traitor to England). Dramatic license has Philip II yearning for the Spanish flag to someday fly over Japan, but Don Álvarez, created from whole cloth, would doubtless queue up early for the chance of spitting in the eye of the shogun. Rains couches his character's lies in courtly eloquence, as if daring his audience to get past the medium for the message. For all this, he is miles more subtle and dangerous than Henry Daniell's treacherous lord, whose glacial demeanor is a window into an emotionless soul, and from whom the most innocuous of words emerge menacing and profane. For Daniell's villain, the sword is the logical end; for Rains', the sword is superfluous.

*The Sea Hawk* Warner Bros. Released August 31, 1940. 126 minutes.

Claude and Henry Daniell: This photo appears in *Webster's Unabridged Dictionary* near the entry "scheme." *Courtesy Buddy Barnett*

Errol Flynn (Captain Geoffrey Thorpe); Brenda Marshall (Doña María); CLAUDE RAINS (Don José Álvarez de Córdoba); Flora Robson (Elizabeth I); Alan Hale (Carl Pitt); Henry Daniell (Lord Wolfingham); Una O'Connor (Miss Latham); James Stephenson (Abbott); Gilbert Roland (Captain López); William Lundigan (Danny Logan); Julien Mitchell (Oliver Scott); Montagu Love (Philip II); J. M. Kerrigan (Eli Matson); David Bruce (Martin Burke); Clifford Brooke (William Tuttle); Clyde Cook (Walter Boggs); Fritz Leiber (Inquisitor); Ellis Irving (Monty Preston); Francis McDonald (Kroner); Pedro de Cordoba (Captain Mendoza); Ian Keith (Peralta)

Executive Producer: Hal B. Wallis; Associate Producer: Henry Blanke; Director: Michael Curtiz; Original Screenplay: Howard Koch, Seton I. Miller; Director of Photography: Sol Polito, ASC; Dialogue Director: Jo Graham; Editor: George Amy; Art Director: Anton Grot; Music: Erich Maria Korngold; Musical Director: Leo F. Forbstein; Orchestrations: Hugo Friedhofer, Milan Roder, Ray Heindorf, Simon Bucharoff; Sound: Francis J. Scheid; Assistant Director: Jack Sullivan; Costumes: Orry-Kelly; Makeup: Perc Westmore

A Warner Bros./First National Picture

# *Lady with Red Hair* (1940)

Chicago, 1899. Socialite Mrs. Caroline Carter (Miriam Hopkins) loses custody of her son Dudley (Johnnie Russell) in a well-publicized divorce hearing. Needing money to win him back legally, she heads to New York where she offers David Belasco (Claude Rains) a promise that his next play will be completely underwritten if she is its star. Pretending to accede to her wishes, the playwright is rid of her for a while; several months later, however, Mrs. Carter reappears and Belasco is taken with her persistence. She is given the lead in a new drama, which promptly flops, causing her to rethink her plan and to agree to marry Lou Payne (Richard Ainley), one of the actors residing at her boardinghouse.

Belasco convinces her not to give up, so,

bidding good-bye to Lou, Mrs. Carter heads for New York, stars in a new play, and receives the renown she has craved. Back in Chicago after more than a year on Broadway, the ex-socialite wins over the hostile audience with a tearful appeal, but discovers that in the interim her son has irrevocably grown apart from her. Hoping to deal with the pain through work, she becomes an international star, only to grow tired of constantly being "on"; she leaves Belasco and heads back to New York, where she marries Lou Payne.

Seeking to join forces once again with her mentor, Mrs. Carter is rebuffed by the irate Belasco; she determines to use her own money to finance her future theatrical successes. As her bank balances plummet, however, so does her reputation. Every play she produces fails miserably, while Belasco's string of hits continues unabated. Always quick-tempered, she now becomes unsure of her own talents, unable to draw upon the spirit she had manifested at the outset of her acting career.

On the night before *The Case of Mrs. Hartley* opens, Lou appeals to Belasco not to turn his back on the actress he had created. Within minutes of the cocky impresario's arrival at the theater, though, he and Mrs. Carter are having at it once again. Despite the fireworks, the play is a smash, and the winning combination of David Belasco and Caroline Carter appears to be heading for another sensational season.

During the mid to late thirties, Warner Bros. had made lots of money with Paul Muni and his gallery of famous personages. With *The Story of Louis Pasteur* (1935), *The Life of Emile Zola* (1937), and *Juarez* (1939), the studio had sown seeds in the chancy field of historical biography and had reaped both industry recognition and financial bliss. The filmed memoirs of Mrs. Leslie Carter—the Lady with Red Hair—were, however, less acclaimed than these stories of freedom fighters, microbe hunters, and founders of the naturalist movement in literature; they also hit the screen at a less advantageous time.

By the dawn of the forties, the public taste had taken a dramatic turn. War was raging in Europe, and yesterday's heroes lost a good deal of their relevance; perhaps it was no coincidence that Paul Muni's screen characters became less valorous as his screen appearances became less frequent. With Winston Churchill's cigar prodding him in the ribs, FDR was picking up the pace of American commitment. Even the most rabid isolationists empathized with their suffering British brethren, and the byword more and more became "action": President Roosevelt signed lend-lease into law barely three months after *Lady* was released. In this milieu, the story of the resolve of a divorcee of another era to win for herself fame and riches—no matter how good her underlying cause—hadn't much of a chance. Tagged "women's picture" by The New York Times (Variety categorized it as a "glamour stage story"), the film's box-office prospects were thought iffy right off the bat. The fact that not one person in a hundred was cognizant of Mrs. Carter (very few theater-goers still referred to her as "the American Sarah Bernhardt") as he/she was with Louis Pasteur didn't help things much, either.

For those who *were* conversant with Mrs. Carter's sufferings and peregrinations, the screenplay's liberties with the lady's published memoirs was disconcerting. Only in the picture did little Dudley Carter choose to stay on with his father; in real life, he went off with his Mum, and the old man scissored him out of the will. Nor did the actress reconcile so neatly with David Belasco; not only did they never rejoin forces professionally, not a word passed between them until Mrs. Carter corresponded with the fatally ill impresario some 20-odd years later. Still, the authenticity of the film's scenario was not so much the problem as was the timing of the film's production and release.

Like the character she's playing, Miriam Hopkins starts off rather shrilly and imperiously, only to calm and focus her energies once Claude Rains—he and his persona every inch more imperious than she and hers—storms onto the scene. Hopkins' courtroom outbursts, which do so much to alienate her from Chicago society and to lose the jury's collective sympathy, are as painful to watch as Mrs. Carter's initial strides toward becoming a great actress. Of course, this may have been a solid gold act of genius on the part of Kurt Bernhardt; the veteran director fled Germany in 1940, found a home at Warners, and spent the rest of the decade turning out (in the words of Ted Sennett) "a number of hard-breathing 'weepers' for female stars."[16] With a track record extending back to the early days of Germany's Ufa Studio, Bernhardt was certainly capable of stylistic subtlety.

Intertwined throughout the film (as well as in the more interesting sections of the actress's memoirs themselves), Belasco and Mrs. Carter are as spiritually conjoined as Svengali and Trilby, even as their ongoing professional relationship smacks of Henry Higgins and Eliza Doolittle. Missing from *Lady*, though, is a resolution of depth; there is neither the death of the two protagonists as in *Trilby*, nor the impending marriage which wraps up *Pygmalion*. *Lady with Red Hair* just ends, without bothering to establish whether Mrs. Carter is but a puppet to the masterful impresario; and neglecting to let us see what happen to the pair after *The Case of Mrs. Hartley* closes. The lady's last words on-screen are the nebulous "Thank you, David."

Rains has a few choice moments apart from Miss Hopkins, not the least of which is the "Bishop of Broadway's" harangue about meeting Mrs. Carter per the request of theater owner, Mr. Fairchild. His voice laced with fury, the clerically attired playwright storms about his office, clearly not to be trifled with; he is the very picture of righteous indignation.

Belasco: I haven't time to eat and he asks me to
    see society's stage hopefuls! I don't care if
    Fairchild owns this theater! I don't care if you

Miriam Hopkins as Mrs. Carter, the "Lady with Red Hair." Claude, as David Belasco, shouldn't wear a clerical collar if he's going to steal the picture. *Courtesy Susan Duic*

owe him nine years rent! Nothing in the world will make me see this woman!

Harper (in a woefully plaintive voice): David, please. For me?

Belasco: (in an instant) Aw, all right.

One of Rains' best bits comes when Belasco—beside himself at Mrs. Carter's inability to convey emotion—usurps her place at rehearsal. Reaching above his head, he grabs the leading man by the shoulders from the rear and clings to him desperately. "You loved me once," he caterwauls, launching and groping his way into a not-quite word-perfect rendition of the sort of tripe which epitomized dime novels and American popular theater at the turn of the century. The vignette gives Rains a chance to let down his curly hairpiece and to indulge in some genuinely funny theatrics. The tension builds again later as the impresario, anxiously pacing the theater back-alley, monitors the length of the ovation while recounting to Lou how "They'll applaud tonight and pan the show tomorrow. Sometimes I wish I'd never gone into this business." Apart from stomach-grinding moments such as this, though, Rains' impresario is every bit as egocentric as Shaw's Higgins, as in command as du Maurier's Svengali, and as condescending as, well ... as the real David Belasco.

While Hopkins is emoting for the balcony both on and off the stage, Rains steals another one; this time, however, he's got some competition. Helen Westley is an absolute card as Mrs. Frazier, the boardinghouse landlady who has seen them come and go; she's got a table-full of support from some of the finest character actors on the Warners lot: Victor Jory, Cecil Kellaway, Fritz Leiber, and an extremely young Cornel Wilde ham it up as they exchange news of recent triumphs and up-and-coming bookings. Only Richard Ainley's Lou Payne seems out of place; (what's a Brit doing hoping for a break with a Scranton stock company, anyhow?) An almost gratuitous—but

substantial and unfortunately necessary—annoyance is young Johnnie Russell as Mrs. Carter's beloved porker of a son, Dudley.

Variety's Walt wrote that Rains provided "a standout characterization," and added that the actor's David Belasco "will be tabbed as one of the season's best portrayals." The New York Times reviewer admitted that Rains "contributes an interesting character study," although "we had the feeling, perhaps unjustly, that this couldn't actually be Belasco." Both reviews (and others) singled out Helen Westley's performance as the "amusing and authoritative" Mrs. Frazier.

Not a bad picture—just not what the audiences of the moment were clamoring for—*Lady with Red Hair* is uneven (because of Richard Ainley and, to a lesser extent, Hopkins) but enjoyable (largely because of Rains, Helen Westley, and that crew at the boardinghouse). Mrs. Carter may be no Pasteur, Zola, or Juarez, but she's still worth a look.

*Lady with Red Hair* Warner Bros. Released November 30, 1940. 78 minutes

Miriam Hopkins (Mrs. Leslie [Caroline] Carter); CLAUDE RAINS (David Belasco); Richard Ainley (Lou Payne); Laura Hope Crews (Mrs. Dudley); Helen Westley (Mrs. Frazier); John Litel (Charles Bryant); Mona Barrie (Mrs. Brooks); Victor Jory (Mr. Clifton); Cecil Kellaway (Mr. Chapman); Cornel Wilde (Mr. Williams); Fritz Leiber (Mr. Foster); Johnnie Russell (Dudley Carter); Selmer Jackson (Henry DeMille)

Executive Producers: Jack L. Warner and Bryan Foy; Associate Producer: Edmond Grainger; Director: Kurt Bernhardt; Screenplay: Charles Kenyon and Milton Krims; story by N. Brewster Morse and Norbert Faulkner, based on the memoirs of Mrs. Leslie Carter; Dialogue Director: Hugh Cummings; Assistant Director: Art Lucker; Director of Photography: Arthur Edeson, ASC; Art Director: Max Parker; Editor: James Gibbon; Gowns: Milo Anderson; Music: H. Roemheld; Musical Director: Leo Forbstein; Sound: Oliver S. Garretson; Technical Advisor: Lou Payne; Makeup: Perc Westmore

A Warner Bros./First National Picture

## *Four Mothers* (1941)

Things are going well for the Lemp family, with financial security promised thanks to everyone's investment in Ocean Zephyrs, a Florida waterfront community masterminded by son-in-law, Ben Crowley (Frank McHugh). Most of the citizens of Briarwood have also invested, as the well-respected Adam Lemp (Claude Rains) is on the board of directors. But when Ocean Zephyrs is destroyed by a hurricane, those same townspeople turn on Adam, holding him responsible for their monetary loss.

Looking to repay his neighbors, Adam tries for a bank loan on his house, but is refused, and then is fired by the Briarwood Musical Foundation. Together with Ben, other sons-in-law, Felix (Jeffrey Lynn), Clint (Eddie Albert), and Ernest (Dick Foran), agree to put aside their own interests and work wholeheartedly to repaying the angry investors. Clint cannot bring himself to leave his research, however, and this—plus the inordinate amount of time his work has kept him away from her—prompts his wife, Kay (Rosemary Lane), to venture off to a singing job in Chicago.

When Adam discovers that the Ocean Zephyrs debt is driving a wedge into his family, he sells his house to Mr. Davis (Thurston Hall), who intends to raze it and build an apartment building on the lot. Adam and his sister, Etta (May Robson), move into an apartment themselves, and, just as things seem bleakest, a letter arrives stating that everyone in the family is happy and well, and that Ben is having wild success selling lots on "Lemp Acres"—some land that Adam had bought earlier and which he had thought worthless.

Adam is hired by the Beethoven Festival Committee to conduct the world-famous concert in Cincinnati, and, afterwards, he is given a hero's welcome by the citizens of Briarwood. To top things off, the old Lemp house has been moved in one piece to a choice lot on Lemp Acres, and Kay learns

she's pregnant, thus justifying the girls being "Four Mothers."

You have to squint slightly to see the debt *Four Mothers* owes to Fannie Hurst's "Sister Act," but this third segment in the Lemp saga is as long on pushing family values as *Four Daughters* had been, and that one had stood very comfortably in Hurst's substantial shadow. Little marital trauma is to be had this time around, so John Garfield's shade can rest in peace. (Garfield biographer James N. Beaver, Jr. avers that, following *Daughters Courageous*, Warners had put the actor on the first of many suspensions for flatly refusing to play any more roles like the "snotty fisherman" of the *Four Daughters* clone.)[17]

The picture even has the time to indulge in something of an in-joke for longtime Warner Bros. ticket-buyers. When Clint admits to Ann that he's been disappointed so often by dead-end experiments that he's thinking of giving up his research, the feistiest of the Lemps bristles, "Did Louis Pasteur ever quit? Did Ehrlich quit?" "I don't know," Cliff rejoins, a broad grin on his face. "I've been too busy to go to the movies lately."

With marital squabbles relegated to the back burner, there's not much for the Lane Sisters (and Gale Page) to do. The boys (Lynn, McHugh, Albert, and Foran) play first string in this one, behind Rains and May Robson, who had pretty much sat out the first two games of this triple-header. The earlier pictures had established that Adam and Etta were crotchety but lovable, possessed of that wisdom which age alone can bring, and good for a warm chuckle or a pleasant diversion from whatever momentary angst was being suffered by one of the Lane Sisters (or Gale Page). With it only a question of time before Clint and Kay discover that nobility and happiness need not be mutually exclusive, even the normally irrepressible Priscilla Lane looks a tad embarrassed as she kvetches that members of the family will actually have to (*gasp!*) go to work to redeem Adam's pledge to Briar-wood.

Having come within inches of being an insufferable bore on the subject of modern music and Beethoven for two entire pictures, Adam is vindicated philosophically (and financially) by being the only man capable of wielding the baton at the big concert. Whereas Rains had put an edge to his voice in the earlier films, he out-and-out barks and snarls at his (literally) fair-weather friends. Typical is the advice he gives to the community music foundation (which has just sacked him):

It has been the ambition of my life to see Briar-wood become a center for the development and the appreciation of good music, and I want you all to know, that if, at any time, under any circumstances, you need my help ... you can go to blazes and whistle for it!

The night before, having exited the drug-store after a first-rate curtain line ("The Briarwood Cry Baby Club! Hah!"), Adam remains in top form while counseling Ben as to how to break the news of the hurricane to Kay and the others:

Adam: You just gotta walk right in and let 'em have it, like a man!
Ben: Maybe you better walk in and let 'em have it for me, will you, Adam?
Adam (only slightly discomfited): Me? I'm afraid I might be too *tough* on 'em!

And sometimes the old musician can be ob-streperous just to keep in shape:

Adam: You know, Felix, after 30 years in the music business, I don't think much of it.
Felix: I'm afraid you're right, Adam.
Adam: Oh, is that so? If that's the way you feel about music, why don't you get out of it!?

While his lines are only marginally more cantankerous than those he's been used to, Rains jumps at the opportunity to widen his eyes and flare his nostrils in outrage; it's clear that, next to Beethoven, vituperation is Adam Lemp's greatest passion. Still, Dad

can be discombobulated in any of a dozen ways. Advised that his beloved family home will be torn down to make way for apart-ments, Adam is momentarily speechless; that tornado of a voice is cut to a near whis-per in the wind and those eyes widen in dis-belief, not anger, as he completes the sales pitch that will break his heart but uphold his honor.

May Robson, too, is given some of her choicest moments ever as Etta Lemp. Steven Morehouse Avery's original story may have fallen a bit short of the redoubtable Miss Hurst's heartwarming style, but much of his dialogue is every bit the equal of Hurst and/or the archly witty Epstein brothers. "You'd sell your own soul if it had any front footage," Etta growls at Ben, as she fights off the tears brought on by Adam's decision about the house. It's not just a clever line in itself; it's the *only* line for May Robson's Etta in circumstances such as these.

And in but one of several clever ex-changes between them, Etta and Adam go at it, tooth and nail, heart and soul:

Etta: If you weren't a stubborn, cantankerous old man, you'd go back to Briarwood where you belong!
Adam: The trouble with most old people is they spoil the taste of life by not knowing when they've swallowed it.
Etta: I wouldn't know. I'm not that old!

Nor can she content herself merely to watch proudly as her baby brother enjoys his mo-ment of triumph:

Etta: Ah! Look at his hair! Look at his tie!
Thea: It seems to make him greater somehow.
Etta: I suppose we have to be thankful his shirt-tail isn't hanging out.

The key to the relationship may be found in the post-concert rush of the newspaper-men. "Has Mr. Lemp always been a genius?" Etta is asked. "Well," she responds, pulling no punches, "he's always had a bad disposi-tion." With the girls evidently getting their tenacity, humor, drive, warmth, affection, and musical talent from their father's side of

**Surrounded by the Four Daughters/Wives—by the Lane Sisters (and Gale Page), May Robson, and Jeffrey Lynn. The end of *Four Mothers* is in sight and there will be no more sequels. Claude apears euphoric.** *Courtesy Susan Druic*

the family, their mother's contribution to the gene pool is pretty much left to guesswork.

*Four Mothers* was the last of the Lemp family adventures, and the last of the five pictures in which Rains and Robson appeared together. The grand old lady from Melbourne, Australia—who had been nominated at age 75 as Best Actress (for *Lady for a Day*, 1933)—would conclude her film career with *Joan of Paris* the following year.

*Four Mothers* Warner Bros. Released January 4, 1941. 85 minutes.

CLAUDE RAINS (Adam Lemp); Jeffrey Lynn (Felix Deitz); Eddie Albert (Clint Forrest); Frank McHugh (Ben Crowley); May Robson (Aunt Etta); Gale Page (Emma Lemp Talbot); Dick Foran (Ernest Talbot); Vera Lewis (Mrs. Ridgefield); Priscilla Lane (Ann Lemp Deitz); Rosemary Lane (Kay Lemp Forrest); Lola Lane (Thea Lemp Crowley); Thurston Hall (Mr. Davis)

Executive Producer: Hal B. Wallis; Associate Producer: Henry Blanke; Director: William Keighley; Screenplay: Avery; Original Story: Steven Morehouse Avery, suggested by the story, "Sister Act," by Fannie Hurst; Director of Photography: Charles Rusher; Editor: Ralph Dawson; Sound: Charles Lang; Musical Director: Leo F. Forbstein; Music: Heinz Roemheld; Song, "Moonlight and Tears," Music/Lyrics: Heinz Roemheld, Jack

Scholl; Orchestral Arrangements—Ray Heindorf; Art Director: Robert Haas; Gowns: Howard Shoup; Makeup: Perc Westmore

A Warner Bros./First National Picture

## *Here Comes Mr. Jordan* (1941)

Fighter Joe Pendleton (Robert Montgomery), the "Flying Pug," is snatched from this vale of tears when his plane crashes. Unfortunately, Messenger 7013 (Edward Everett Horton) has collected Joe some 50 years before his time. By the time Mr. Jordan (Claude Rains), the heavenly official in charge of transitions, has been informed of the error, Joe's body has been removed from the wreckage and cremated. The discorporate fighter finally selects as a replacement the body of Bruce Farnsworth, a dishonest businessman who has just been drowned in the bath by his wife Julia (Rita Johnson) and his treacherous personal secretary, Abbott (John Emery). As Farnsworth, Joe makes amends for some well-engineered larceny that had been attributed to the innocent father of Bette Logan (Evelyn Keyes), and Joe and Bette begin to fall in love.

Joe sends for his old fight manager, Max Corkle (James Gleason), and manages—with the help of his lucky saxophone—to explain to the incredulous Max what has transpired and that he is now occupying Farnsworth's body. Joe, who won't be denied his shot at the championship, has exercised Farnsworth's body into "the pink," and bankrolls Max to arrange with K.O. Murdock's manager, Lefty (Don Costello), for a match between K.O. and Farnsworth. Mr. Jordan advises Joe that he will indeed be champ, but not necessarily in his present identity. Aghast that their first attempt at murder has failed, Julia and Abbott strike again, shooting Joe/Farnsworth down in cold blood. After Joe and Mr. Jordan have gone off to resume their quest for another replacement, the conspirators hide the body they have killed again.

Joe/Farnsworth is reported missing by Max and, as the weeks pass, a police investigation under Inspector Williams (Donald McBride) picks up steam. Returning to the Farnsworth manse to pick up his lucky saxophone, Joe has Max turn the radio on for the Murdock-Gilbert fight, and everyone hears that Murdock has fallen without being hit. "He's been shot," Mr. Jordan tells Joe, who asks to be able to finish the fight in Murdock's body. He does, beats Gilbert decisively, and becomes the new champ. When Max turns up at the ring, he's able to locate Farnsworth's body for the cops, thanks to Mr. Jordan's omniscience on matters such as these, and is hired on by *Murdock* as his new manager, thanks to Mr. Jordan's having erased all of Joe's memories from the newly resuscitated boxer. In the hallway, Murdock bumps into Bette, each sees something familiar and loving in the other, and off they go, to a new and happy life together.

In 1978, Warren Beatty starred in (and produced and co-wrote) *Heaven Can Wait*, an updated adaptation of Harry Segall's eponymous play and a reworking of the 1941 Columbia smash. Beatty, pretty much known to that point for his irresistibility to the opposite sex and his flair for the off-beat, scored a direct hit with *Heaven*; the film was well-liked by the public and warmly greeted by the critics. Almost to a person, the reviewers mentioned how Beatty's handiwork was nearly as good as *Here Comes Mr. Jordan*.

Robert Montgomery, whose bland good looks had made him a favorite with distaff ticket-buyers since the late twenties, proved once again that he could do—and do extremely well—whatever he cared to do. He moved as easily from charming psychopaths (*Night Must Fall*, 1937, wherein, with his ubiquitous hatbox, he apparently had stolen a trick from Claude Rains' *The Man Who Reclaimed His Head*); to affected Brits (like Lord Peter Wimsey, in 1940's *Busman's Honeymoon*); to suave, bemused partners in love and crime, as in *Mr. and Mrs. Smith* (1941). (Oddly enough, the American actor was *not* the first choice for any of these roles except for the very British Wimsey.)

Montgomery is aces as Joe Pendleton; there's not a false note in the performance, if you choose to overlook the actor's wince-inducing saxophone work. Even with his sax under his arm or hanging from the ring post (and allowing for the requisite Hollywood wax job), Joe is no cartoon or caricature of a pug, despite his nickname. When apprised that he's defunct, he doesn't take on all comers, as mobster Eddie Kagle would do in Harry Segall's other tale of post-mortem mix-ups, *Angel on My Shoulder*, but neither does he go gently into that good night. He insists on his rights, badgers Messenger 7013 (a wonderful turn by Edward Everett Horton), and takes both heavenly toilers to the ropes to make good on their promises throughout the picture. Without so much as a change in hairstyle, voice, or mannerism, Montgomery *becomes* Bruce Farnsworth and K. O. Murdock quickly and effortlessly. And when Murdock raises his head from the canvas after Mr. Jordan has worked his wonders once again, it's hard not to be moved by the realization that it's *Montgomery* climbing to his feet; although we've been in on the game since the first reel, the dynamics of the picture are such that a miracle has seemingly taken place before our eyes.

*Here Comes Mr. Jordan* was one of Rains' favorite films, and, as has been written elsewhere, he relished the opportunity to appear with rail-thin James Gleason. Like Rains, Gleason had trod the boards since childhood (some sources say *infancy*); unlike Rains, the New York actor made no move to overcome the peculiarities of his speech. Virtually every role he played thus had more than just spiritual ties with the Big Apple, and virtually every line he uttered was couched in that distinct patois known as Brooklynese. Gleason's Max Corkle is priceless, and nowhere else in a career that spanned over 35 years and encompassed more than 100 pictures did he steal the thunder from two actors the caliber of Robert Montgomery and Claude Rains as he does in the revelation scene

(wherein he's made to swallow the truth about Joe, Farnsworth, and Mr. Jordan) and the investigation scene (wherein he drives the always apoplectic Donald McBride to bark out one of his trademark epithets: here, "Holy Cats!").

Flanked by Montgomery and Gleason, and buttressed by Horton and McBride—colorful actors, all, in colorfully written parts—Rains is left to make whatever impression he can as the calm Mr. Jordan. It's quite a challenge, and Rains opts to underplay the role. Smart move. The heavenly official has all the answers; save for the unique circumstance effected by 7013, he's never surprised, never taken aback, never at a loss for what to do. His is the gift of knowledge—not prophecy—so he has no trouble giving assurances to Joe's restless soul. Situated as he is, the cosmic scheme of things is an open book. As he finally reveals to Joe,

Remember how I told you you wouldn't be cheated? Nobody is, really. Eventually, all things work out. There's a design to everything. You were meant to be champion. You are. You and Murdock are one; you belong to each other. This is your destiny, Joe.

With a part such as this, Rains had no barns to storm or scenery to chew. His delightful exchange with Edward Everett Horton ("Overzealousness! Out for record collections! This happens right along with the inexperienced!") is as close as he's allowed to come even to raising his voice. A lesser actor might have succumbed to the dangers of such preternatural calm and turned the angelic Jordan into a droning and monotonous source of predictable feel-good pap. But, drawing on largely self-taught techniques which had been sharpened since his earliest theater days and which had been tested to the nth degree in Universal's *The Invisible Man*, Rains once again creates a memorable portrait chiefly from voice alone.

If Jack Griffin's features had been masked by gauze, Mr. Jordan's are almost a mask unto themselves. A look of supreme confidence is always to be found on his face, and a smile fashioned by omniscience is never far from his lips. Jordan's message—succinctly outlined above and essentially the disclosure that virtue *does* have other rewards—demands aplomb if it is to be believable and theatricality if it is to be interesting. Rains makes the character not just relevant, but subtly prepossessing.

*Here Comes Mr. Jordan* was—and remains—one of the most engaging, entertaining, and uplifting fantasies Hollywood ever produced.

*Here Comes Mr. Jordan* Columbia. Released August 21, 1941. 93 minutes.

Robert Montgomery (Joe Pendleton); Evelyn Keyes (Bette Logan); CLAUDE RAINS (Mr. Jordan); Rita Johnson (Julia Farnsworth); Edward Everett Horton (Messenger 7013); James Gleason (Max Corkle); John Emery (Tony Abbott); Donald MacBride (Inspector Williams); Don Costello (Lefty); Halliwell Hobbes (Sisk); Benny Rubin (Bugs)

Producer: Everett Riskin; Director: Alexander Hall; Screenplay: Sidney Buchman, Seton I. Miller, based on the play, *Heaven Can Wait*, by Harry Segall; Director of Photography: Joseph Walker, ASC; Editor: Viola Lawrence; Assistant Director: William Mull; Art Director: Lionel Banks; Music: Frederick Hollander; Musical Director: M. W. Stoloff; Gowns: Edith Head

# *The Wolf Man* (1941)

Following the death of his older brother, Larry Talbot (Lon Chaney) is welcomed back to his ancestral home in Llanwelly, Wales, by his father, Sir John (Claude Rains), and his boyhood chum, Paul Montford (Ralph Bellamy), now a police official.

While helping get a telescope in order, Larry catches sight of Gwen Conliffe (Evelyn Ankers), daughter of the owner of a local curio shop. Anxious to meet the lovely young woman, Larry buys a silver-headed cane bearing a pentagram from her; thus is he first acquainted with the lore of the werewolf. Although Gwen is engaged to groundskeeper Frank Andrews (Patric Knowles), she agrees to accompany Larry to the Gypsy fair that evening. At the fair, Gwen and Jenny Williams (Fay Helm) go to have their fortunes told; the morose Gypsy seer, Bela (Bela Lugosi), spying the pentagram in Jenny's palm, chases the frightened girl off into the night. Moments later, she is savaged by a wolf. In a futile effort to save the young girl's life, Larry clubs the animal to death with his silver cane; having been bitten during the struggle, he is brought back to Talbot Manor.

Come morning, his wound has vanished, and Larry is informed that in the confusion of the night before he must have killed the Gypsy Bela instead of the wolf. Larry is later told the truth of the matter by Maleva (Maria Ouspenskaya), the Gypsy's mother and guardian: her son had been a werewolf and now, by virtue of having survived the attack, so is young Talbot. Unable to withstand the baleful glow of the full moon, Larry changes form and slays a gravedigger.

With the village on the alert for a rogue wolf, traps are laid, and Sir John grows concerned over the changes which have occurred in his son. Once again a beast, Larry is snared by a trap on the moors. Maleva intones a Gypsy prayer and restores the wounded man to humanity; he escapes the trap before the villagers can come upon him.

The following night, the hunt is on in force. Hoping to prove to his son that his fears are merely the products of his feverish imagination, Sir John binds Larry to a chair and joins the other men on the moors. The rays of the moon transform Larry again. Breaking free of his bonds, he rushes out onto the moors, where he begins to stalk Gwen, who has been searching him out to tell him of her love for him. The wolf man attacks her, and her screams bring Sir John running. Hammering relentlessly at the snarling figure with the silver-headed cane, Sir John kills it and saves Gwen.

Maleva once more recites her mystical verse. Dumbfounded, Sir John looks on as the motionless horror metamorphoses into the form of his son, Larry.

Lon Chaney, Jr. had paid his thespic dues here, there, and everywhere throughout the thirties, and his successful turn as Dynamo Dan McCormick in Universal's *Man Made Monster* (1941) assured him of his place beneath the yak's hair in what promised to be *the* horror film of the decade for the studio. Sure enough, *The Wolf Man* was a box-office bonanza, and the title character developed into an icon as quickly as had Frankenstein's Monster and Count Dracula; this, in turn, assured the younger Chaney a place behind Karloff and Lugosi (and his own father) in the pantheon of interpreters of the grotesque.

Everyone went into the production anticipating great things, and producer/director George Waggner assembled a first-rate cast with uneven results. Beautiful Evelyn Ankers, on her way toward winning renown as the forties' greatest scream queen, was great, but handsome Patric Knowles couldn't make much of an impression in a nothing role. Ralph Bellamy, perennial second lead who almost never got the girl, and Warren William, whose days as a romantic figure were pretty much behind him, and who was moving into roles with an avuncular bent, were merely adequate. Bela Lugosi's presence, brief as it was, lent a legitimacy to this stylistic throwback to the Golden Age of horror films, and the Hungarian's talents made memorable a part which lesser actors might have dismissed as a bit.

Grand old Maria Ouspenskaya—she of the Stanislavsky School—would prove to be perfect as Maleva, Gypsy shaman and *deus ex machina*. Madame Ouspenskaya had stayed on in the United States following a mid-twenties' tour by the Moscow Art Theatre and had tackled the English language with the same genius (and tenacity) for which she had become famous; she soon was heralded as one of the brighter (if decidedly more peculiar) lights on Broadway. Complementing her own stage career by tutoring

others in the dramatic arts, she was summoned in 1936 to Hollywood where, for her film debut (reprising her Broadway role in Samuel Goldwyn's *Dodsworth*), she won an Academy Award nomination. (Like Rains, Mme. Ouspenskaya would receive more than one nomination, but would never take home the statuette.)

*The Wolf Man* was the occasion of Rains' return to Universal; he hadn't worked at the studio since *Mystery of Edwin Drood*, but had in the interim become a mainstay at Warners, where he demonstrated the kind of versatility a horror career under the Laemmles would have stifled. Although it was tailored expressly for Chaney, the werewolf picture neatly dovetailed into what could be considered Universal's established formula for Rains: top-billing in a tale of madness and murder. (Two years later, yet another such tale, *Phantom of the Opera*, would deviate from this norm only in terms of billing.) Still, *The Wolf Man* was the only one of Rains' Universal thrillers wherein the scripted madness wasn't his to manipulate. In fact, Sir John Talbot is virtually the embodiment of calm rationality; that he is also shown to be 100 percent *wrong* about lycanthropy is at the core of Curt Siodmak's screenplay.

A variation on the classic schizophrenic, *The Wolf Man* was originally conceived with the understanding that its myriad transformations would be purely subjective; i.e., visible only through the eyes of Talbot. Such subtleties were not part and parcel of the rip-snorting horror renaissance at Universal, and Siodmak was instructed to redirect the flow of his story in order to make the werewolf an objective reality. This he did to the satisfaction of George Waggner and others, but the wily scenarist managed to circumvent the stripping away of all doubt. At the final wrap, save for Maleva (who won't talk), Gwen (who wouldn't talk), and Sir John (who's speechless), no one with any firsthand knowledge of the horror that's been running rampant in the area has been left breathing. As they had earlier (when Larry

The old guard flank the rookie: Warren William *(left)* and Claude swap insights while Ralph Bellamy shows he's not bad at holding a pipe. *Courtesy Richard Bojarski*

had bludgeoned the lupine Bela with his silver cane), the local authorities chalk up the latest crushed skull to another bout of "confusion." Wolf Man? *What* Wolf Man?

Sir John, although relegated to the emotional sidelines for most of the picture—until the climactic confrontation, he doesn't seem much the sort who *could* break a sweat—is still very much cognizant of the pertinent superstitions. He's also letter perfect on the wolfbane ditty which spills from the lips of all Llanwellians at the slightest provocation:

Even a man who is pure of heart and says his prayers by night, may become a wolf when the wolfbane blooms, and the autumn moon is bright.

(Sequels would, of necessity, find the little verse modified slightly: the moon would be "full and bright" and left free to work its magic during any of the four seasons.)

This sort of thing is supposed to be balderdash, of course, and Sir John, who personifies stability and old money, is backed here by a Greek chorus composed of legal (Montford) and medical (Dr. Lloyd) types who couldn't be expected to think any other way.

While Lon Chaney's sundry metamorphoses lured thrill-seekers to the box-office, it is Claude Rains' transformation from skeptical, aristocratic commentator to incredulous, wide-eyed executioner—effected without need of Jack P. Pierce's wizardry or

*(From left)* **Maria Ouspenskaya, Lon Chaney, Evelyn Ankers, Claude Rains and Warren William, as seen by Swedish caricaturist Kroll.**

John P. Fulton's stop-motion camera lens — that closes out this study in duality. Diffused by the fog and reflected in his unbelieving eyes, the light of the moon has succeeded in changing forever Sir John's philosophy on life, death, and superstition. By inadvertently slaying his own son, Sir John has effectively undermined scientific dogma, legal integrity, and moral certainty; there is very little left on which to speculate with a stiff upper lip.

Sloughed off by most critics as an undisguised B, *The Wolf Man* made a fortune, spawned numerous sequels, and encouraged RKO Studios to engage Val Lewton, a brilliant young writer/producer whose string of psychological horror films would turn that genre on its ear. For Rains, it was over to Warners for murder and madness of different sorts.

*The Wolf Man* Universal. Released December 20, 1941. 71 minutes.

CLAUDE RAINS (Sir John Talbot); Warren William (Dr. Lloyd); Ralph Bellamy (Paul Montford); Patric Knowles (Frank Andrews); Bela Lugosi (Bela, the Gypsy); Lon Chaney (Lawrence Talbot); Evelyn Ankers (Gwen Conliffe); Maria Ouspenskaya (Maleva); Fay Helm (Jenny Williams); J. M. Kerrigan (Charles Conliffe); Forrester Harvey (Mr. Twiddle); Leyland Hodgson (Kendall); Doris Lloyd (Mrs. Williams); Harry Stubbs (Reverend Norman); Tom Stevenson (Richardson); Olaf Hytten, Gibson Gowland (Villagers); Eric Wilton (Talbot Chauffeur); Harry Cording (Wykes); Ottola Nesmith (Mrs.

Bally); Connie Leon (Mrs. Wykes); Jesse Arnold (Gypsy Woman); Ernie Stanton (Phillips)

Producer and Director: George Waggner; Screenplay: Curt Siodmak; Director of Photography: Joseph Valentine; Art Director: Jack Otterson; Associate Art Director: Robert Boyle; Editor: Ted Kent; Assistant Director: Vernon Keays; Set Decorator: Russell A. Gausman; Musical Director: Charles Previn; Musical Score: Charles Previn, Hans J. Salter, Frank Skinner; Sound Director: Bernard B. Brown; Technician: Joe Lapis; Special Photographic Effects: John P. Fulton; Makeup: Jack P. Pierce; Gowns: Vera West

# *King's Row* (1942)

Among the children living in turn-of-the-century King's Row are Parris Mitchell (Scotty Beckett); his best friends Drake McHugh (Douglas Croft) and Cassandra Tower (Mary Thomas); Randy Monoghan, a tomboy from the wrong side of town (Ann Todd); and Louise Gordon (Joan Duval), the stuck-up daughter of Dr. and Mrs. Henry Gordon (Charles Coburn and Judith Anderson). The apple cart is overturned when, for no apparent reason, Cassandra is suddenly removed from school—and from all social life—by her father, the cryptic Dr. Tower (Claude Rains).

Years pass, and, with the blessing of his beloved grandmother, Madame Von Eln (Maria Ouspenskaya), Parris (Robert Cummings) decides to take up medicine. Studying under Dr. Tower, Parris comes to like the man and to appreciate his brilliance, but is still perplexed as to Cassandra's (Betty Field) decidedly peculiar behavior. His pal, Drake (Ronald Reagan), can't offer advice, as he's upset that *his* long-time girl, Louise Gordon (Nancy Coleman), won't stand up to her tyrannical parents and marry him. Drake turns his attention elsewhere.

Finishing his studies with Dr. Tower, Parris heads to Vienna, where he studies psychiatry. He is informed by letter that his erstwhile medical mentor has killed himself and his daughter, and has left the Tower

estate to Parris. Later, the young man receives a note from Randy (Ann Sheridan), telling him that Drake, whose inheritance had been embezzled by a dishonest bank official, has had both his legs amputated following an accident at the train yard where he has been working. Despite Randy's love and encouragement, Drake seems hopelessly despondent.

Returning home, Parris discovers the reason for Dr. Tower's mysterious behavior and deadly actions. He also finds Louise—mad with jealousy at Randy's having married "her" Drake and totally consumed with hatred for her own father—very vocally maintaining that the now-deceased Dr. Gordon had cut off Drake's legs for no reason other than misguided revenge for the young man's "wildness" and supposed abandonment of his daughter. Receiving love and guidance from Elise Sandor (Kaaren Verne)—a Viennese émigré who, with her father, now lives in the home where Parris had grown up—the young psychiatrist gambles that Drake's being told of Dr. Gordon's vindictiveness will snap him out of his perennial self-pity. The desperate gamble works, and Drake and Randy (as well as Parris and Elise) face a bright tomorrow in King's Row.

Anticipating Grace Metalious' *Peyton Place* by years, Henry Bellamann's *King's Row* was another of those Small Town-America-cum-Hell best-sellers snapped up by readers and eagerly awaited by picture-goers. No one walking through the movie house doors was at all surprised that, while the welcoming placard to the community highlighted the words *good* and *town*, the vast majority of the local citizenry failed to live up to the advertising.

Underrated director Sam Wood, who two years earlier had helmed United Artists' version of Thornton Wilder's *Our Town*—a more benevolent, slightly saccharine exploration of similar themes—did a grand job massaging Bellamann's ponderous masterwork into shape. Although still overlong at 127 minutes, the film benefited from Casey

Robinson's sensitive adaptation; instances of homosexuality, nymphomania, euthanasia, and incest found in the novel (and deemed verboten by Hollywood censors) were eliminated, as was any mention of Cassie's pregnancy. Several of the crimes of violence requisite to the plot line were committed offscreen *and* made less sensational in the subsequent telling. In fact, Cassie's illicit sexual relationship with Parris was handled so subtly as actually to have escaped the notice of most of the ticket-buyers, who failed to understand either Drake's boyish and incredulous backslapping or the imagery of the dark and stormy night, wherein Wood's vision, James Wong Howe's cinematography, and Erich Wolfgang Korngold's tempestuous musical themes were as overwhelming as passionate embraces were to the doomed lovers.

Curiously, the filmed saga of the vast and rambling novel ended up as a 100 percent studio-bound picture. Producer Hal Wallis may have felt that William Cameron Menzies' genius at production and set design obviated the need for exterior shooting and—save for a couple of patently phony backgrounds—he was right. Wong Howe revealed that:

Everything, even the apple orchard, was done in the studio.... [Menzies] designed the sets and did the sketches for the shots; he'd tell you how high the camera should be. He'd even specify the kind of lens he wanted for a particular shot; the set was designed for one specific shot only, and if you varied your angle an inch you'd shoot over the top.[18]

The story is basically a three-parter, following the sundry adventures of five of the community's children as they grow and interact. With quirks and traits established at its outset, the film jumps forward, and the five young adults, for better or worse, become more firmly entrenched in their own particular behaviors. The give and take of their relationships with one another and with the King's Row establishment comprises the balance of the picture.

With the exception of *The New York*

*Times'* Bosley Crowther, who cared neither for the story nor its execution, almost all the critics found Ronald Reagan's work to be the best he had done to that point, Ann Sheridan's performance to be a pleasant and most gratifying surprise, and Robert Cummings' efforts to be rather lightweight and short of the mark. Betty Field—the not-quite-adult Cassandra—didn't really stick around long enough in the proceedings to merit consideration as one of the leads. Field was widely praised for her portrayal of Cassie though the character was long gone by the time the various dramatic threads trailing through the final third of the picture—Drake's soul-killing disability, Randy's providential reappearance as his soulmate from the other side of the tracks, Parris' winning both his shingle *and* the gal just in from left field—had been woven into a cathartic happy ending.

Unlike Maria Ouspenskaya's Mme. Von Eln, who seems no more wizened at the conclusion of the picture than at the beginning, Rains is allowed to age along with the rest of the populace. His initial appearance—during which he indulges in some brief, formal, and rather distant remarks to the child Parris—reinforces remarks made by Madame's maid, Anna (Ilka Gruning):

There's something weird about those Towers. A doctor who says he's a doctor and never has a patient, and his wife, who stays in an upstairs room all the time. Gives a person the creeps.

Tower and Charles Coburn's sadistic and unforgiving Dr. Gordon apparently share responsibilities for King's Row's medical needs, and the circumstance is not a happy one. Gordon's incompetencies and opinions leave a wake of victims who are worse off for the healing than for the disease, while the enigmatic Alexander Q. Tower is evidently regarded with suspicion by everyone other than Mme. Von Eln and the ever-saintly Parris.

It is developed, of course, that Rains' character is not so much a mad doctor as a fledgling psychiatrist, perhaps concerned more about a patient's psyche than about his or her physical symptoms. Nonetheless, his removing Cassie from school so that she is kept constantly in his presence (the only vestige of a more overtly incestuous situation in the Bellamann original)—together with a fleeting glimpse of the reclusive Mrs. Tower—does make Anna's facile opinion credible. It's only later, while he's "reading" medicine with the older man, that the adult Parris (and the audience) gradually come to peer behind the facade and to see the brilliant physician as a long-suffering victim and not as an insensitive jailer.

Rains hasn't much screen time in which to sculpt this multi-dimensional figure; he's a suicide before the picture is half over. Still, he so imbues his few lines and fewer speeches with what had become his trademark ardor, that when *Cummings* recounts some information from Tower's notes and observations ("Today I noticed the first sign in Cassandra; early maladjustments of dementia praecox"), one can't help but hear Rains' voice. And in order to truly appreciate Rains' astute reading of the role, one must view the picture *twice*, if only to see for oneself how the delivery of earlier, emblematic lines, like

A little loneliness won't hurt you to speak of. You get used to it.

    or

In this modern, complicated world, man breaks down under the strain, the bewilderment, disappointment, disillusionment; gets lost, goes crazy, commits suicide.

    or

Mankind's building up the biggest psychic bellyache in history.

must be reassessed in the light of that explanatory note.

Initially, Hal Wallis had cast James Stephenson as Dr. Tower, chiefly on the basis of the British actor's splendid work in

*The Letter* (1940). It was only after Stephenson succumbed to a heart attack while in the midst of his wardrobe tests that the call went out for Rains to replace him. In his autobiography, *Starmaker*, Hal Wallis groused to Charles Higham about Rains' subsequent reactions :

We called Rains at his home in Chester County, Pennsylvania, and he declined instantly. But we tried again, rushed him the book, and he finally agreed to break off his much-needed vacation and make the long train journey west. His refusal to fly meant a considerable delay in our schedule.[19]

Rains was given tremendous help in cultivating the tortured physician by cinematographer James Wong Howe, whose "melodramatic leanings" helped add dimension to the actor's already splendid portrayal:

Howe used Dr. Tower's house to mirror the mood of the piece and the emotions of the characters. In early scenes, the house takes on a dungeon-like appearance with ink-black shadows on dark wood walls and few highlights. The camera tracks backward with [Robert Cummings] to capture his fear as he moves cautiously throughout the house. When he meets [Rains], Rains is shot from low angle with shadows hiding his face and no backlight to keep him from blending into the darkness. The concept of Rains as a fearful, mysterious character is fulfilled. Cummings is shot from high angle, over Rains's shoulder, to establish the doctor's dominance. The low-angle shots up at Rains reveal dark ceilings which complete the ominous prison atmosphere. The house has, in fact, become a prison for Cassandra because Dr. Tower will not let her leave.

Later, after Cummings has befriended Rains, the house loses some of its oppressiveness. Middle grays replace fearful shadows, and the angles return to normal. Rains's face loses the characteristic shading, and he immediately becomes a likable character.[20]

It may have been that the town of King's Row just had too many problems for *The Times*' grouchy Mr. Crowther; or, perhaps he found the citizenry's usual stop-gap solution to those problems—a cup of coffee (pre-dating *Twin Peaks* by a half-century)— a tad facile and ineffective. Nevertheless, he did manage a begrudging *well done* to Rains,

ANN          ROBERT          RONALD          BETTY
# SHERIDAN CUMMINGS REAGAN FIELD

KINGS ROW

Presented by WARNER BROS. Pictures Inc.

Country of Origin U.S.A.

**Only the sensitive and well-intentioned Parris Mitchell (Robert Cummings) understands Dr. Tower's angst.**

maintaining that he was "an impressive victim of some strange mental malaise as Dr. Tower" (though what it is, one has to guess).

Following the Los Angeles opening, Edwin Schallert (of that city's *Times*) lauded the whole shebang, maintaining that "Coburn and Rains are at their most convincing." *Variety* felt the film was an "impressive, moving treatment" of the novel, which "should draw strong grosses," and wrote that Rains "achieves a shrewd blend of surface hardness and underlying warmth as the mysterious local physician." While the trade paper's comments about the actor were accurate, its predictions of a healthy box-office were not; despite the fact that the reviews were, for the most part, complimentary, the film was only moderately successful.

*King's Row* Warner Bros. Released April 18, 1942. 127 minutes.

Ann Sheridan (Randy Monoghan); Robert Cummings (Parris Mitchell); Ronald Reagan (Drake McHugh); Betty Field (Cassandra Tower); Charles Coburn (Dr. Henry Gordon); CLAUDE RAINS (Dr. Alexander Q. Tower); Judith Anderson (Mrs. Harriet Gordon); Nancy Coleman (Louise Gordon); Kaaren Verne (Elise Sandor); Henry Davenport (Col. Skeffington); Maria Ouspenskaya (Mme. Von Eln); Ernest Cossart (Pa Monoghan); Pat Moriarity (Tod Monoghan); Ilka Gruning (Anna); Minor Watson (Sam Winters); Ludwig Stossel (Dr. Berdoff); Erwin Kalser (Mr. Sandor); Egon Brecher (Dr. Candell); Ann Todd (Randy as a Child); Douglas Croft (Drake as a Child); Scotty Beckett (Parris as a Child); Mary Thomas (Cassandra as a Child); Joan Duval (Louise as a Child); Eden Gray (Mrs.

Tower); Danny Jackson (Benny Singer); Henry Blair (Willie); Leah Baird (Aunt Mamie); Julie Warren (Poppy Ross); Mary Scott (Ginny Ross)

Executive Producer: Hal B. Wallis; Associate Producer: David Lewis; Director: Sam Wood; Screenplay: Casey Robinson, based on the novel, *King's Row*, by Henry Bellamann; Director of Photography: James Wong Howe; Art Director: Carl Jules Weyl; Production Designer: William Cameron Menzies; Musical Score: Erich Wolfgang Korngold; Orchestral Arrangements: Hugo Friedhofer; Musical Director: Leo F. Forbstein; Special Effects: Robert Burks, ASC; Sound: Robert B. Lee; Editor: Ralph Dawson; Gowns: Orry-Kelly; Makeup: Perc Westmore

A First National Picture

## *Moontide* (1942)

The favorite juke joint of the San Pablo dock workers is "The Red Spot," and that's where Tiny (Thomas Mitchell) comes looking for his pal, Bobo (Jean Gabin). Tiny has found them both a job, but Bobo is more interested in dancing, drinking, and brawling than heading off to work. Come the dawn, Bobo comes to on a bait barge, where he overhears that elderly dock worker Pop Kelly (Arthur Aylesworth) had been robbed and strangled the night before. Bobo agrees to sell bait in exchange for his room and a couple of bucks, and then heads into town to find Tiny.

Since Bobo can't remember that all-important night, Tiny is purposefully cryptic and vaguely threatening. Bobo is befriended by Nutsy, a night watchman-cum-philosopher (Claude Rains), and is soon linked with Anna (Ida Lupino), a down-on-her-luck waitress whom he saves from suicide. Gradually, Anna and Bobo fall in love and decide to be married. This doesn't sit well with Tiny, who has been blackmailing Bobo over a violent incident years earlier, and wants Anna to disappear.

After the wedding, Bobo heads off to make a couple of bucks by repairing Dr. Brothers' (Jerome Cowan) inboard motor.

Tiny shows up at the barge. Anna comes to the conclusion that Tiny had strangled Pop Kelly, and is brutally hurt by Tiny when she threatens to tell Bobo. Anna is taken to the hospital by Dr. Brothers and Nutsy, and Bobo searches for Tiny. As he closes in on his erstwhile pal on the sea wall by the barge, the terrified Tiny falls into the surf and is swept away.

Anna is brought back to the newly painted and refurbished barge, and she and Bobo look forward to a long and happy life together.

*Moontide*, Willard Robertson's best-selling novel, was purchased by Fox as the vehicle by which France's reigning hunk, Jean Gabin, would be introduced to The American Woman. "Here He Comes, Ladies!" trumpeted the ad campaign, and the stocky Gaul's rugged masculinity was to prove as irresistible on this side of the Atlantic as it had elsewhere. To pique the interest of the *male* ticket-buyers, the actor was touted as the French Spencer Tracy; his performance as Bobo managed to curl the toes of enough gals, while entertaining (without threatening) enough of their dates to make for a profitable first picture in anybody's book. Gabin retreated to France after a follow-up (*The Imposter*, 1942), though, preferring to launch a truly international career from his European home-base, rather than become another charmingly accented novelty in the Tinseltown collection. Still, while in the States the actor pitched in and worked for the war effort alongside his stateside colleagues at the Hollywood Canteen.

Gabin appears completely at ease with Bobo's colloquialisms, his English, *magnifique*, although one suspects that—especially at this point in the scheme of things—he was just one hell of a nuanced actor who could give each word its due, each phrase its proper weight, even without a complete proficiency in the language. The Frenchman, who had started out his professional life with the *Folies Bergère* in the twenties, would charm the buttons off *les femmes* in any of four languages for some 45 years; like Chevalier, the septuagenarian Gabin demonstrated more joie de vivre and sex appeal than any of the granite-chinned pretty boys hired to handle the love interest in his last few films.

*Moontide* is essentially a one-set picture, notwithstanding the small chunks of characterization unearthed in "The Red Spot" and the moments spent on staircases and in hallways, so a trio of superlative performers pitches in to compensate Gabin for the lack of spectacle. Ida Lupino, the intense British-born beauty who would go on to direct powerful films noir, is splendid as Anna, once the screenplay gets her past her tiresome, tight-lipped phase. Lupino makes Anna's dream of an idyllic relationship on a gaily painted bait barge seem not only credible but desirable, and that's no mean feat. Thomas Mitchell, who had snatched the Oscar out of Rains' hands in 1939, plays another of his creepy hangers-on with a penchant for betrayal and cheap whiskey, and the role of Tiny calls for nothing more.

The Coca-Cola-swilling Nutsy is really superfluous to the action, but the old philosopher is the link that connects a couple of vignettes in the episodic screenplay, and acts as the voice of reason amidst all the argument and confusion. A free spirit—he apparently sleeps on the beach, showers in the Morro Castle flop-house (filmed in the presence of censors and causing Rains to comment that "In forty years of acting, I have never been so wet!"), and drinks soda pop at "The Red Spot"—he nonetheless has something which approximates a real job and a second (and more formal) suit of clothes. Nutsy is the tattered edge of genteel society, more akin to Ann than to Bobo, but crucial to Bobo if the dockworker is to make the jump from his wandering, chaotic past to some semblance of life as it is lived by others.

The role plays to Rains' casual side, there being not the slightest indication that anger, jealousy, or any other of the Seven Deadly Sins has ever once visited the even-tempered vagabond. Educated, private, and not a little enigmatic (Bosley Crowther said "Rains is

something mysterious as a philosophic prowler of the night"), Nutsy may very well be the closest Rains came to playing himself in his 56 films. Missing only is the tinge of hauteur the actor could exude at times, as Rains the man was never as much one to suffer fools as Rains the actor was required to in many of his pictures.

Renowned American novelist John O'Hara adapted Robertson's masterwork, and no-nonsense director Archie Mayo brought the screenplay to life. O'Hara, whose greatest fame stemmed from his tales of Gibbsville, USA (based on his vision of his Schuylkill County, Pennsylvania, hometown), worked mainly on recrafting others' accomplishments in the forties (*I Was an Adventuress*, *Strange Journey*, etc.), while several of his own (*Butterfield 8*, *From the Terrace*, *Pal Joey*) were filmed in the decades to follow. The best-selling author kept in touch with Rains, who journeyed from New Hampshire late in life to attend the wedding of O'Hara's daughter, Wiley, in Pottsville. Mayo joined forces with Rains only once more, in United Artists' *Angel on My Shoulder* (1946), the director's last major screen credit.

*Moontide* 20th Century–Fox. Released May 29, 1942. 94 minutes.

Jean Gabin (Bobo); Ida Lupino (Anna); Thomas Mitchell (Tiny); CLAUDE RAINS (Nutsy); Jerome Cowan (Dr. Brothers); Helene Reynolds (Woman on Boat); Ralph Byrd (Reverend Price); William Halligan (Bartender); Victor Sen Yung (Takeo); Chester Gan (Hirota); Robin Raymond (Mildred); Arthur Aylesworth (Pop Kelly); Arthur Hohl (Hotel Clerk); John Kelly (Mac); Tully Marshall (Mr. Simpson); Ralph Dunn (Policeman); Tom Dugan (First Waiter)

Producer: Mark Hellinger; Director: Archie Mayo; Screenplay: John O'Hara, based on the novel, *Moontide*, by Willard Robertson; Director of Photography: Charles Clarke, ASC; Editor: William Reynolds; Sound: Eugene Grossman, Roger Heman; Music: Cyril J. Mockridge, David Buttolph; Art Directors: James Basevi, Richard

**Two wanderers living on the edge of God's blue sea: Bobo (Jean Gabin) and Nutsy (Claude).** *Courtesy Susan Duic*

Day; Set Decorator: Thomas Little; Costumes: Gwen Wakeling; Makeup: Guy Pearce

## *Now, Voyager* (1942)

Lisa Vale (Ilka Chase) arranges for Dr. Jaquith (Claude Rains), America's foremost psychiatrist, to work at bringing the owlish and browbeaten Charlotte Vale (Bette Davis) out from under the domination of her mother (Gladys Cooper). Under Jaquith's care, Charlotte regains some degree of self-confidence, improves her appearance, and treats herself to an ocean voyage to the nethermost reaches of Brazil.

Onboard the ship, she meets and falls in love with Jerry Durrance (Paul Henreid).

Although he is married with two daughters, Jerry likewise becomes enamored of Charlotte, and the two reveal their problems to each other. (Jerry's younger daughter, Tina [Janice Wilson], feels as unwanted by her mother and is as insecure as Charlotte ever was.) Jerry and Charlotte have several romantic misadventures while in Rio de Janeiro. Although each feels true love for the first time ever, they part, and Charlotte returns to her Boston home.

The Vale family is astounded at the new Charlotte, and Mother, determined to keep her daughter guilty and beholden, purposely throws herself down the stairs. Nevertheless, buoyed by Jaquith's good counsel, Charlotte remains her own woman and soon finds herself being romanced by millionaire Elliot

Livingston (John Loder). A date is set, but the engagement is called off when Charlotte runs into Jerry by chance and realizes how much she still loves him. A subsequent argument leaves her Mother dead of a heart attack. Charlotte, feeling guilty in spite of herself, checks back in at Cascade, Jaquith's sanitarium.

At Cascade, Charlotte meets and befriends Jerry's daughter, Tina, in whom she sees her former self. Jaquith gives Charlotte permission to take the girl under her wing; thankfully, their relationship is filled with happiness and love, and Jerry allows Tina to move back to Boston with her new friend. Some time later, Jerry and Jaquith visit the Vale household, where Jerry announces that he cannot allow Charlotte to continue to keep Tina with her out of pity for the girl and/or for him. Charlotte responds that she has come to think of the girl as *their* child— hers and Jerry's—and she hopes that he will understand that she considers every facet of her life—her love, Tina, the home, the Vale wealth—to be theirs together.

*Now, Voyager* was the spiritual child of *Stella Dallas*, Olive Higgins Prouty's earlier (and twice filmed) sinus-clogging women's story, but both the best-selling novel and the splendid motion picture that evolved from it are head-and-tails superior in every way. The book was the third installment of what would become a four-part history of the Vales (along with *White Fawn* [1936], *Lisa Vale* [1938], and *Home Port* [1947]). Bette Davis was 33 years old when Warners bought the property. She was not, however, the studio's first choice for Prouty's ugly duckling. Edmund Goulding, who had originally been slated as director, had asked for Irene Dunne on a loan-out from Columbia. When Goulding fell ill, Michael Curtiz took over and the part was offered, in turn, to Norma Shearer and Ginger Rogers. Davis, meantime, had convinced producer Hal B. Wallis that she was the only viable choice for the role, so Curtiz bailed out—favoring yet another action/adventure project over

wrangling with Bette—and Irving Rapper stepped in.

Davis had a field day in *Now, Voyager*; she relished the transformation from hirsute frump to svelte and well-appointed beauty and personally worked on the screenplay.[21] The role remained a favorite of hers to the end of her life, the production was as angst-free as any production revolving around Bette Davis had a right to be, and Davis was nominated for her fifth Oscar in as many years. She lost. Gladys Cooper, positively detestable as the iron-willed Vale matriarch, was up for the Best Supporting Actress award; she, too, failed to cop the statuette. Davis was thrilled to work with Cooper, whom she personally adored, and also came to like and enjoy young Janis Wilson, who played Paul Henreid's troubled daughter, Tina. (Author Stine reports that Wilson was cast in *Watch on the Rhine* [1943] because of Davis's fondness for her.)

Paul Henreid made his Warner Bros. debut (on a loan-out from RKO) as Jerry Durrance, and despite initial misgivings over his character's appearance (which was changed; at first, "He wore a satin smoking jacket, his hair was brilliantined and he was covered in a pound of makeup"[22]), Henreid went on to make a wonderful impression on the studio and the public at large. Jerry is probably the most pleasantly animated of the several leads Henreid enacted opposite Davis and/or Rains, and Casey Robinson's screenplay can take most of the credit for that. In his autobiography, *Ladies' Man*, the Austrian émigré admitted a tendency to find fault with many of the parts thrown his way; by underplaying intensely, he could vent his frustration and irritation on-screen. His Victor Laszlo (in *Casablanca*) is the embodiment of virile patriotism and, as such, is not wholly genuine. As Karel Novak (*Deception*), he leaps between extreme passion and calm detachment without setting foot in that wide expanse of normalcy and realism which separates the two. Nonetheless, his Jerry Durrance is untouched by the actor's later dissatisfaction or ennui; in a justly famous scene, Henreid gets top marks for introducing sensuality into the normally pedestrian process of lighting cigarettes.

Dr. Jaquith is one of those characters who appears only once in a while—he *is* Johnny-on-the-spot at the outset and the wrap—yet who is quoted or referenced continuously during the action. Rains' presence is thus pervasive throughout the picture, although the actor himself is seen infrequently. Most of Jaquith's dialogue smacks of pop psychiatry:

People walk along a road. They come to a fork in the road. They're confused. They don't know which way to take. I just put up a signpost: Not that way; this way.

But Rains, whose voice could make the most preposterous claptrap sound symphonic, gives the lines substance and the occupation, integrity. Sigmund Freud had just died just three yers earlier, having examined the psyche, the id, and the ego for well over a half century, but most Americans viewed psychoanalysis askance. Gladys Cooper's scripted opinion of psychiatry was doubtless shared by many, so Jaquith had to have the stability and professionalism of a Claude Rains if the prevalent imagery of high wire fences and yowling inmates was to be dispelled.

When he was first approached to play the part, though, Rains was having none of it. As Hal B. Wallis recounted:

...He turned down the part, insisting it was too sketchy. Casey Robinson built up the role, and Rains agreed to do it for the then enormous salary of $5000 a week. I offered him $25,000 for six weeks but his agent Mike Levee was adamant and we went ahead with the required arrangement.[23]

Despite Levee's tenacity, Casey Robinson's tailoring, and its being crucial to the progression of the narrative, the role remained a brief one, and Rains was afforded only small—if positive—nods in the reviews.

Irving Rapper allowed the actor a bit of shtick with his pipe, and the resultant humorous touch ("Messy things, pipes. I like 'em!") humanizes Jaquith in everyone's eyes, save Mrs. Vale's. Rains *was* a pipe-smoker in real life and also enjoyed an occasional cigar. He did not smoke cigarettes, however, and never quite managed to deal with them on-screen in a casual or realistic fashion. Jessica Rains told the author how her father never could inhale cigarettes without gagging slightly, and thus much preferred to use them merely as hand props.

The film's title is taken from Walt Whitman and is brokered to the audience via a sort of prescription for self-confidence given by Jaquith to Charlotte just prior to her making her way into the world:

Untold want, by life and land near granted,
Now, Voyager, sail though forth to seek and find.

It's a lovely sentiment that ties in nicely with the shipboard motif, the romance at sea, the "small world"-type coincidences which pepper Charlotte's path, and her initial efforts at cruising through life incognito ("Forget you're a hide-bound New Englander," Jaquith counsels her), or as someone else (Camille Beauchance?) altogether.

As a matter of fact, almost everything ties in together in this film: Cole Porter's "Night and Day" is heard as Jerry and Charlotte are "reintroduced," and their dialogue strikes home on two levels. When the Vale parlor fireplace is lit for the first time within anybody's memory, the audience is nearly bludgeoned senseless by light, energy, and conflict symbolism. Later, Charlotte must literally cross a bridge at Cascade to assume a new role in Jaquith's eyes and Tina's life. Even Max Steiner's music—he won in *his* Oscar category—didn't so much fit the mood as it created it; with Kim Gannon's lyrics about uncertainty under the starry skies, the lush and captivating "Charlotte's Theme" soon became the pop hit, "It Can't Be Wrong."

Still, the reason Charlotte can caution Jerry against asking for the moon when they already have the stars is that Rains' Dr.

**Bette Davis felt this scene foreshadowed Charlotte Vale's marriage to Dr. Jaquith!**

Jaquith has laid the groundwork for all their heavenly bliss. In an *American Classic Screen* magazine interview with film historian Anne Etheridge, however, Davis confessed that, per her own interpretation of subsequent events,

Charlotte finally married Jaquith because he was strong and she had become strong. Jerry would never have been strong enough for her. Anyone who had any intuition at all felt that Charlotte married Jaquith. That scene where they were planning the new wing together, brother! It was so obvious!

The critics were mixed, but the popular vote was unanimous: *Now, Voyager* was a tremendous hit. Casey Robinson, Irving Rapper, and the first-string cast toyed expertly with the audiences' emotions; there were even gleeful reports of spontaneous applause when Gladys Cooper expired in her chair.

*Now, Voyager* Warner Bros. Released October 31, 1942. 117 minutes.

Bette Davis (Charlotte Vale); Paul Henreid (Jerry Durrance); CLAUDE RAINS (Dr. Jaquith); Gladys Cooper (Mrs. Henry Windle Vale); Bonita Granville (June Vale); Ilka Chase (Lisa Vale); John Loder (Elliot Livingston); Lee Patrick (Deb McIntyre); Franklin Pangborn (Mr. Thompson); Katherine Alexander (Miss Trask); James Rennie (Frank McIntyre); Mary Wickes (Dora Pickford); Janis Wilson (Tina); Michael Ames (Tod Andrews); Charles Drake (Leslie Trotter); Frank Puglia (Giuseppe [aka Manuel]); David Clyde (William); Lester Matthews (Captain); Ian Wolfe (Lloyd); Claire du Brey (Hilda)

Producer: Hal B. Wallis; Director: Irving Rapper; Screenplay: Casey Robinson, based on the novel, *Now, Voyager*, by Olive Higgins Prouty; Director of Photography: Sol Polito, ASC; Art Director: Robert Haas; Sound: Robert B. Lee; Editor: Warren Low; Dialogue Director: Edward Blatt; Set Decorator: Fred M. MacLean; Montages: Don Siegel; Special Effects: Willard Van Enger, ASC; Musical Score: Max Steiner; Musical Director: Leo F. Forbstein; Orchestral Arrangements: Hugo Friedhofer; Gowns: Orry-Kelly; Makeup: Perc Westmore

A Warner Bros./First National Picture

*Now, Voyager* was broadcast twice on Lux Radio on NBC. The first program was aired on May 10, 1943, and featured Ida Lupino as Charlotte, Dame May Whitty as Mrs. Vale, Mary Lou Harrington as Tina, and Rains' dear friend, Albert Dekker, as Dr. Jaquith; Paul Henreid reprised his role from the motion picture. Lux's second version was aired on February 11, 1946, and the drama was later televised by the *Lux Video Theatre*.

# *Casablanca* (1943)

Everybody comes to the Café Americain, Casablanca's busiest night spot, but when beautiful Ilsa Lund (Ingrid Bergman) walks in one evening, owner Rick Blaine (Humphrey Bogart) is beside himself. He and Ilsa had been lovers, briefly, in Paris, just before the Nazi occupation. Although they had planned to flee the country together, a last-minute farewell letter had left Rick confused and bitter at the railway station.

Some time has passed since then, and the big news at Rick's is that two German couriers have been found murdered, their letters of transit—unimpeachable documents assuring safe passage to the bearers—stolen. The news doesn't faze the cynical Rick, and amuses Captain Louis Renault (Claude Rains), Vichy police chief and frequenter of the café. Louis is certain that Victor Laszlo (Paul Henreid), renowned anti-Nazi freedom-fighter, is hoping to use those letters of transit to escape from Casablanca.

Also aware of Laszlo's intentions is Gestapo Major Heinrich Strasser (Conrad Veidt), whose sudden arrival can only mean that Laszlo is not to leave Casablanca alive. Fearing this, Ilsa appeals to Rick to help her get her hands on the letters; she confesses to the stunned American that Victor Laszlo is her husband. She had run away from Rick in Paris only because she had received word that Laszlo, whom she had thought a victim of the Nazis, was still alive. In exchange for his help, Ilsa will remain in Casablanca with her ex-lover.

Cognizant of Rick's peculiar loyalties, Major Strasser has Renault turn up the heat officially; professing outrage at the discovery of illegal gambling on the premises, Louis orders the café closed down. If anything, this only brings things to a head more quickly. Arranging to sell his place to Signor Ferrari (Sydney Greenstreet), a black-market entrepreneur, Rick offers the documents to the Laszlos and takes them to a waiting plane.

When Major Strasser storms onto the airfield and attempts to detain the couple, he is shot by Rick. A carload of Gestapo goons and Vichy policemen pulls up almost immediately, but after a tense moment, Louis chooses to side with the angels and sends the Axis agents scurrying off in the wrong direction. Laszlo and Ilsa head for the freedom of Lisbon, and Rick and Louis stroll together into an uncertain future.

In the half-century-plus since its initial release, Warner Brothers' *Casablanca* has received the kind of intense scrutiny and study to which only a handful of pictures has ever been subjected, and has earned for itself both overwhelming popularity and universal recognition. It has been the topic of countless articles and essays, has inspired several books and two TV series, and has become a part of American pop culture. Adept movie buffs still regard its stars as icons of a braver, nobler age, and still relish passages from its archly brilliant screenplay.

It's tough, however, to find a ticket-buyer under the age of 20 who is well acquainted with the film, but this is eminently understandable; *Casablanca* is not now, nor has it ever been, a movie for kids. The basic thrust of its narrative embraces the qualities of love, loyalty, honor, and human dignity; all unfold and interact against the background of a war which—due to the passage of time and the dulling of sensibilities—has lost its immediacy. Even when the picture was new, its charms didn't work their magic on the younger set; any and all lessons to be learned were aimed at the adults who were living with personal sacrifice and international chaos, and who were praying for the kind of resolution Humphrey Bogart had effected: quick, clean, and with the good guys victorious. *Casablanca* demands rapt attention from the viewer, and, to an audience reared on blinding pyrotechnics, for whom noise and light and bloodied prosthetics have supplanted wit and subtlety and interpretation, this may be too much to ask. The saga of Ilsa and Rick might just have to wait until the current crop of moviegoers grows into it.

Although it's a tapestry of interweaving relationships, the picture *has* had a tendency to cook down to just that: the saga of Ilsa and Rick. Love surviving the rigors of war is, was, and will always be a classic theme—especially when the notion that all is fair in either one has been drummed constantly into the collective consciousness—and this mother of all themes detracts from the pivotal role that Rick Blaine plays in the larger drama. Virtually everyone who passes Arthur Edeson's lens stands before the café owner literally or figuratively; relationships between or among the other characters are peripheral to the action of the film. From Strasser to Ferrari; from Carl the waiter (S. Z. "Cuddles" Sakall) to Ugarte the parasite (Peter Lorre); from Yvonne (Madeleine Le Beau), who wants in, to the Brandels (Joy Page and Helmut Dantine), who want out: everyone comes to Rick. The relationship between the expatriate American and Ilsa Lund, of course, is the most obvious; the relationship between him and Louis Renault, however, is the most gratifying.

Of his 56 feature films, including those in which he played the eponymous hero or was billed above the title, *Casablanca* remains the most renowned of Claude Rains' features, and Louis Renault, arguably, his most celebrated character. The suave yet feisty little official is almost the antithesis of Rains' usual cadre of cultured cads, whose wry remarks mask the stirrings of true villainy from the eyes of others. In fact, many of the picture's most quotable lines are either bons mots from Renault which can stand up quite well on their own (the immortal "Round up the usual suspects," for example), or witty exchanges wherein his sparring with Rick raises world-weary cynicism to an art form:

Louis: "I've often speculated on why you don't return to America. Did you run off with a senator's wife? Did you abscond with the church funds? I'd like to think you killed a man; that's the romantic in me."
Rick: "It's a combination of all three."
Louis: "What in heaven's name brought you to Casablanca?"
Rick: "My health. I came to Casablanca for the waters."
Louis: "The waters? What waters? We're in the desert."
Rick: "I was misinformed."

An unproduced play (*Everybody Comes to Rick's*, by Murray Burnett and Joan Alison) was the source for Julius Epstein's, Philip Epstein's, and Howard Koch's Academy Award-winning screenplay. Determined to avoid grinding out yet another trite and featureless vignette of wartime intrigue, the brothers Epstein and Mr. Koch likewise avoided the play's facile characterizations. Hence, Rick was transformed from an adulterous attorney to Bogart's tight-lipped saloon keeper with a shadowy past and a penchant for honor; that noble Norwegian, Ilsa Lund, rose gloriously from the ashes of Lois Meredith, American trollop; and Luis Rinaldo, satyr-cum-Nazi sympathizer, gave way to the dapper, derisive, and delightful Louis Renault.

Rains is magnificent in the role which many fans regard as an extension of his own personality: aloof, mildly condescending, subtly mocking. At a casual glance, Louis *is* just another "poor, corrupt official," whom

**Buy this ice cream or you'll never see an exit visa.**

we view skimming a piece of the casino action and whom we suspect (but do not view; Joe Breen and the Production Code made sure of that) exchanges exit visas for sexual favors. Despite his basking in the "prevailing wind" from Vichy, he is fond enough of Rick to warn him not to interfere in the matters of Ugarte's arrest, Laszlos' mission, and Strasser's intentions. He may be quick to accommodate the Gestapo officer, but he's equally quick to derail with whimsy the Nazi's pointed interrogation of his friend.

Yet, as depicted by Rains, Renault's knee-jerk accession to Strasser's every impulse somehow manages to intimate that the policeman is merely going through the motions, biding his time. Behind those twinkling eyes will be found the same spirit of loyalty and integrity which gallons of booze and years of bitterness have not erased from Rick. Like Rick, Louie needs to be shaken from his complacency; and like Rick, Louie finds his salvation in Laszlo and Ilsa Lund. The saloon-keeper and the Vichy policeman offer alternate takes on the same theme, and the exchanges between them, as well as a good number of the self-revealing comments each makes apart from the other, serve to point this out.

Their climactic stroll into the night underscores their shared passion for freedom, but, in fact, Rains and Bogart accentuate their characters' similarity through stylistic counterpoint from their very first scene together: Rains molds his magnificent voice into the very model of the policeman's professional parry and thrust; his eyes dart about, always probing, always searching for the truth in (or behind) the statement. Bogart's flat delivery reflects Rick's rote response to the chaos about him, and his cool, assessing gaze takes in truth and deceit, detects fidelity and betrayal, with unfailing calm.

Except to first-time viewers, or to those who have been conditioned by recent cinematic trends to expect the ultimate triumph of evil over goodness, Ilsa's boarding the plane at the denouement is never in doubt. In fact, it may be said with confidence that Mrs. Laszlo is the only person, on or off the screen, to be surprised at Rick's noble decision. Throughout the picture the American has exhibited the kind of selfless wisdom (under the guise of cynical disinterest) which makes his choice for the greater good a foregone conclusion.

Not so with Louis. Despite his admiration for Rick and his acting in larcenous synergy to keep the Café Americain profitable (and his own pockets comfortably lined), Renault is not quite so predictable. We've had flashes of the uncertainties which roil beneath his otherwise blasé surface, but his being made of the same, stern stuff as the American isn't assured until the final scene, where we witness the emergence of Louis the man from the recesses of Louis the puppet. It is, in fact, this moral ambiguity which makes Louis so interesting and—dare one say?—endearing. Nothing could be more tempting, or easier, for him than to continue his cushy sycophancy (albeit now with Signor Ferrari) by fingering Rick to the Nazis. Nor could any words be more cathartic than "Major Strasser has been shot; round up the usual suspects." Nor any action so joyously symbolic than his tossing the Vichy water into the trash.

During a film career that spanned 30 years, Rains seldom got to walk into the sunset with the girl. In *Casablanca*, he gets to walk into the fog with a man, and nothing could be more stirring, reassuring, fulfilling, moral, or natural.

*Casablanca* Warner Bros. Released January 23, 1943. 102 minutes.

Humphrey Bogart (Rick Blaine); Ingrid Bergman (Ilsa Lund); Paul Henreid (Victor Laszlo); CLAUDE RAINS (Captain Louis Renault); Conrad Veidt (Major Heinrich Strasser); Peter Lorre (Ugarte); Sydney Greenstreet (Signor Ferrari); S. Z. Sakall (Carl); Dooley Wilson (Sam); Madeleine Le Beau (Yvonne); John Qualen (Berger); Joy Page (Annina Brandel); Helmut Dantine (Jan Brandel); Marcel Dalio (Croupier); Leonid Kinskey (Sascha); Corinna Mura (Singer); Ludwig Stossel (Herr Leuchtag); Ilka Gruning (Frau Leuchtag); Frank Puglia (Arab Vendor); Dan Seymour (Abdul); Richard Ryan (Heinz); Gregory Gay (German Banker); Curt Bois

Producer: Hal B. Wallis; Director: Michael Curtiz; Screenplay: Julius Epstein, Philip Epstein, Howard Koch, based on the unproduced play, *Everybody Comes to Rick's*, by Murray Bennett and Joan Alison; Director of Photography: Arthur Edeson, ASC; Art Director: Carl Jules Weyl; Montages: Don Siegel, James Leicester; Musical Director: Leo Forbstein; Musical Score: Max Steiner; Songs "Knock on Wood" "Muse's Call" and "That's What Noah Done": M. K. Jerome

and Jack Scholl; Song "As Time Goes By": Herman Hupfield; Orchestral Arrangements: Hugo Friedhofer; Editor: Owen Marks; Special Effects: Lawrence Butler (Director) & Willard Van Enger, ASC; Dialogue Director: Hugh MacMullan; Sound: Francis J. Sheid; Set Decorator: George James Hopkins; Makeup: Perc Westmore; Wardrobe: Orry-Kelly

## *Forever and a Day* (1943)

Made with the cooperation of virtually every Hollywood studio, featuring almost every British expatriate actor and actress working in Southern California at the time, helmed by no fewer than seven directors (of whom the majority worked at their craft full time), and in the works from first until last for well over a year, RKO's *Forever and a Day* inspired contemporary English audiences to remain brave beneath Nazi bombs, and contrived to have contemporary American audiences applaud them for doing so. The film lauded sacrifice, dedication, perseverance, and love, while deploring cowardice, deceit, avarice, and exploitation. It also netted a financial windfall for both the British War Effort and the National (U.S.) Foundation for Infantile Paralysis.

For 1943 picture-goers, desperately desiring entertainment, peace of mind, and moral support, *Forever and a Day* was a star-studded paean to the "indomitable British spirit." Nearly 60 years later, it is a picturesque curiosity. Both helped and hindered by its episodic nature and venerable framing device, the film is uneven, dated, and strangely inconclusive; for the right audiences, however, it is still a moving and enjoyable experience.

The story concerns a manor house—built from the ground up in 1804 by Eustace Trimble (C. Aubrey Smith), of late, retired from the admiralty—and its myriad occupants over the ensuing 140 years. Rains is Ambrose Pomfret, a moneyed ne'er-do-well who is the legal guardian of Susan Treachard (Anna Neagle) until the day she's married.

Ready to propose after a few hours of casual acquaintance is Billy Trimble (Ray Milland), dashing young son of Eustace. For some unexplained reason, Billy's falling into marriage so precipitously irritates Pomfret, but no effort is made to halt the wedding. During the reception, Billy is called up to help Lord Nelson battle Napoleon Bonaparte. Off he goes.

Months later, Billy and Susan's son is born, and Eustace rejoices in the marvelous coincidence which has his grandson and the announcement of Nelson's defeat of the French fleet crossing the Trimble House threshold together. Arriving moments after both of these is the news that Billy has been killed in action; drawing upon his wellspring of resolve and jutting out his granite-like chin, Eustace climbs the grand staircase to welcome his grandson and to celebrate the inexorable progress of life.

Time passes. Susan and her young son are preparing to leave the family manse, when who should turn up as new owner of Trimble manor but Ambrose Pomfret. Susan is aghast and predicts that her erstwhile guardian will never know a moment's peace in the house:

A house is more than bricks and mortar. It's all the people who lived in it; it's their lives, their joys, and their sorrows. It's love, friendship, decency—all the things you have never known. That's why this house doesn't want you.

It is not long after that Pomfret, sodden with drink and trembling with rage and terror, hears Eustace Trimble's ghostly voice issue forth the patriarch's portrait over the mantelpiece:

It's no good, Pomfret. This is not your house, and nothing you can do will make it yours. It is the Trimbles' house, and it will always be the Trimbles' house!

Pomfret has a seizure and falls to the floor, breaking his neck. So begins the long history of friction between the Pomfrets and the Trimbles.

This vignette and those which follow are told within the framework of a World War II German bombing raid on London. An American Pomfret (Kent Smith) has come to purchase the old house from a Trimble (Ruth Warrick). When he admits he sees no point in paying cash for a structure that could be reduced to rubble at any moment, she launches into the house's history, which is but a microcosm of England's own glorious past.

Other flashbacks show the families intermarrying, branching out to America, making inroads in up-and-coming technology, adapting to make ends meet during the most difficult of times, and at once celebrating the bravery of England's youth and mourning its loss because of the world's tyranny and injustice.

Virtually everyone involved in the production donated his/her services to the project, and many of the huge cast contented themselves with the smallest of bits just so they could participate in the statement the picture was making. Ennobled by the fact that there was a war on, few people grumbled that the charity President Roosevelt had selected for the American portion of the box-office windfall struck closer to *his* home than to those of the majority of the citizenry.

The scope of the project had originally included France and sundry instances of its national esprit, but when that government signed the armistice with Hitler, the Brits decided to go it alone. *Let the Rafters Ring*, an historic/patriotic huzzah by Robert Stevenson, was to be the pivot on which all the dramatics turned, but this was later whittled to a nub, elaborated upon by the efforts of some 21 writers and renamed *This Changing World*. Pre-production began back in May of 1941, but the vagaries of war constantly interrupted the shooting schedule, and some 18 months passed before the picture was wrapped. Despite numerous pleas for cooperation, stars would absent themselves from the studio on their appointed days in order to visit hospitals, entertain wounded troops, provide a bit of moral boost to frightened and bewildered civilians, and, in several cases, join the armed forces themselves.

Contemporary reviews were mixed, a situation which disturbed RKO Pictures and disconcerted concerned American and British authorities. Some were indubitably superlative:

The talent is so brilliant that it makes the new Rivoli offering an absorbing and moving show. (*New York Herald Tribune*, March 13, 1943)

One of the outstanding box-office pictures of the year. (*Harrison's Reports*, January 23, 1943)

Other reviews showed reservations and chose to separate the film's undeniably praiseworthy motivation from its technical and/or artistic merit. Still, efforts were taken to cut slack wherever possible and even the normally dyspeptic Bosley Crowther managed to skirt the line between flagrant honesty and sis-boom-bah.

Under [unwieldy] circumstances, it is surprising that the film was actually made and also that it should be as agreeable as it is. For, in spite of its very strong flavor of sentimentality and its way of loving England for its upper classes alone, "Forever and a Day" does have some amusing and affecting passages. (*The New York Times*, March 13, 1943)

With 78 "top-flight players" on the roster of a 104 minute film, only a handful received anything more than a few seconds screen time, and fewer still were shown off to their best advantage. Crusty old C. Aubrey Smith got to shoulder most of the weight of the British Empire on his shoulders; lovely Gladys Cooper, her *lower* lip quivering in the firelight, gave a splendid example to British moms who mourned the loss of their sons; Ida Lupino showed that spunk might well be more important than beauty in the long run; and, to a lesser extent, Edward Everett Horton, Roland Young, Charles Laughton, Merle Oberon, Robert Cummings, Cedric Hardwicke, and

Buster Keaton (!) made more of an impression than their colleagues.

The opening segment succeeded in setting the tone: No one exemplified the stalwart soul of the Englishman more than Smith, and neither the passage of time nor the best efforts of the Hun would ever displace his spirit (or his portrait) from his home, his rock, his England. Rains and the others of the piece are rather closer to being people than symbols, and so don't weather the compacted time frame nearly so well as the patriarch. Everything that happens does so at an alarming pace: Ray Milland and Anna Neagle apparently marry the day after they first meet, Rains' Machiavellian influence over her is somehow foiled, the baby is born, Napoleon is defeated, Milland is killed, the baby is grown, Anna Neagle is again on the march, and Rains is back, as detestable as ever despite his decade-long absence. Within a heartbeat, Rains is depressed, drunk, dead. No one ever explains why he was such a rotter, and that includes the 78 actors, the 21 writers, and the seven directors.

"Claude Rains ... does not impress as the menace," sniffed *Variety*.

Some days it doesn't pay to get out of bed.

*Forever and a Day* RKO. Released March 26, 1943. 104 minutes.

Brian Aherne, Ida Lupino, Merle Oberon, C. Aubrey Smith, Robert Cummings, Ruth Warrick, Kent Smith, Roland Young, Gladys Cooper, Ray Milland, Anna Neagle, CLAUDE RAINS, Charles Laughton, Dame May Witty, Una O'Connor, Edward Everett Horton, Cedric Hardwicke, Buster Keaton, Jessie Matthews, Herbert Marshall, Robert Coote, Ian Hunter, Nigel Bruce, Reginald Gardiner, Arthur Treacher, Edmund Gwenn, Halliwell Hobbes, Patric Knowles, Montagu Love, Victor McLaglen, Richard Haydn, Clyde Cook, Elsa Lanchester, Gene Lockhart, Reginald Owen, Donald Crisp, George Kirby, Billy Bevan, Aubrey Mather, Walter Kingsford, Ivan Simpson, Eric Blore, Wendy Barrie, Ethel Griffies, June Lockhart, Lumsden Hare, et al ("Many others offered their services but did not eventually appear due to no fault of their own."—Voice under the credits)

Producers/Directors: Rene Clair, Edmond Goulding, Cedric Hardwicke, Frank Lloyd, Victor Saville, Robert Stevenson, Herbert Wilcox, based on a story contributed to by Charles Bennett, C. S. Forrester, Lawrence Hazard, Michael Hogan, W. P. Lipscomb, Alice Duer Miller, John Van Druten, Alan Campbell, Peter Godfrey, S. M. Herzig, Christopher Isherwood, Gene Lockhart, R. C. Sherriff, Claudine West, Norman Corwin, Jack Hartfield, James Hilton, Emmet Lavery, Frederick Lonsdale, Donald Ogden Stewart, Keith Winter; Directors of Photography: Robert De Grasse, Lee Garmes, Russell Metty, Nicholas Musuraca; Editors: Elmo J. Williams, George Crone

RKO provided all production technical services; the studio's in-house technicians went uncredited in the final film.

## *Phantom of the Opera* (1943)

**Claude as Ambrose Pomfret. The Trimbles don't care much for him. Maybe it's the hat.**

Paris Opera first violinist Erique Claudin (Claude Rains) is dismissed from his position after decades of service, but his only concern is how to get enough money to continue to pay for singing lessons for Christine DuBois (Susanna Foster). When Claudin comes to believe that the musical publisher Pleyel (Miles Mander) has stolen his piano concerto, he throttles the suspected thief and is himself driven into madness and the Paris sewer system by a pan of acid hurled into his face.

Sometime thereafter, Mlle. DuBois is found to have not only two beaux—Anatole Garron (Nelson Eddy), the principal baritone at the opera, and Raoul Daubert (Edgar Barrier), a captain of the Sûreté—but something of a guardian angel as well. One of the resident divas, Mme. Biancarolli (Jane Ferrar), is mysteriously drugged at the outset of a performance, and Christine is quickly rushed in to cover. The young woman is a smash, so the feisty Biancarolli demands that her understudy be permanently demoted to the chorus, but the prima donna's spite—and her life—are cut short by a fatal visit from Christine's masked patron.

When the opera house management shows more gumption than common sense—casting Mme. Lorenzi (Nicki Andre) rather than Christine as lead in the next opera—disaster strikes. Timing his hacksaw strokes to coincide with the louder sections of Lorenzi's entrance music and aria, Claudin sends the massive crystal chandelier crashing down onto the horrified spectators below. In the midst of the melee, the confused Christine is led down to the cellars far below the opera house.

Exhorting Franz Liszt (Fritz Leiber) to play Claudin's concerto from the stage, Garron and Daubert make their way into the subterranean passages in search of the crazed composer and the soprano. They are guided by Claudin himself, hammering away at the piece's staccato chords on his piano as Liszt does the same far above his head. The frantic men find the underground lair just as Christine tears the mask from the phantom's face. The disfigured Claudin snatches up a convenient saber, but the reverberations from Raoul's pistol-shot cause the already crumbling walls to collapse, burying the madman and ending his reign of misguided terror for all time.

A spectacular musical entertainment—opulent, tasteful, and so finely wrought as to garner five Academy Award nominations and two Oscars—but no great shakes as a horror film, 1943's *Phantom of the Opera* has traditionally settled into second place behind the Lon Chaney original in the estimation of most genre buffs. Nonetheless, while Erik—the 1925 phantom—was in all ways and everywhere more exotic, grotesque, and diabolic than his war-years counterpart, quite a few fans have come to find the silent picture on the whole less satisfying than the Technicolor remake.

Many of the admirers of Rupert Julian's silent classic overlook the fact that (Chaney's indisputable genius apart) the film's most notable feature—lots of phantom, little opera—was the happy result of the lack of sound technology in 1925. Footage of tutu-clad ballerinas and cape-swirling extras—mouths in motion—was all that was needed then to indicate the heady musical world in which the piece was grounded. In the silent-film milieu, opera could be *suggested* and still satisfy purists, but any sophisticated sound treatment would have to devote some serious time to the art form in order to please latter-day opera lovers.

Hence, methods and formulae which had worked wonders and had drawn capacity crowds a decade or two earlier were now relegated to the junk heap as passé and untenable. In addition, wartime restrictions on spending and construction resulted in careful budgetary study taking the place of artistic impulsiveness. When it came to the Leroux remake, it was determined that a certain part of the audience would be there for the phantom, another part (women, mostly) for the boy-girl/love interest business, and a decent number would pay just to hear the

music and gape at the spectacle. Thus, the structure of the silent version—65 percent opera ghost, 25 percent Christine and Raoul, 10 percent ersatz opera nonsense—was no longer practical. When one recalls that, save for Abbott and Costello, Universal's premier movie attraction of the early forties was soprano Deanna Durbin, one realizes how the screen time Chaney's Erik had enjoyed in the mid-twenties was just no longer feasible.

More than that, the studio brass had invested a ton of money in the picture (some $1.75 million, a *fortune* for Universal), and a disproportionate part of that had been allocated to the leasing of phenomenally expensive Technicolor equipment. If there were going to be any ominous shadows in *this* version, they would be couched along lines arrived at by committee: cinematographer, director, art director, wardrobe designer, and Natalie Kalmus, the contractual Technicolor consultant. The thought of spending megabucks on something which would in essence differ little from most of the studio's slick, black and white horror programmers also mitigated against stacking the dramatic chips in favor of the guy in the mask and the cape. If 85 percent of the audience would be induced to part with the price of admission by lush melodies, spectacular visuals, and a period variation on boy meets girl/boy loses girl/boy wins girl, the Phantom would have to make the absolute most of the fraction remaining to him to make any impact at all.

Contemporary Phantom fans were titillated by rumors that the Opera Ghost was to be impersonated (variously) by Broderick Crawford, Lon Chaney, Jr., or Charles Laughton. The only given was the presence of Miss Durbin, and when the lovely young warbler bailed, director Henry Koster went along for the walk. Arthur Lubin cheerfully took over following Koster's defection; as he indicated to John and Michael Brunas and Tom Weaver in *Universal Horrors*, he immediately lobbied for Claude Rains as his phantom of choice. Jumping headfirst into the role, Rains spent weeks practicing violin-fingering exercises prior to filming and didn't stint on suggesting how he might more clearly depict his motivations, improve his performance, and contribute to the integrity of the production, either. Lubin admitted:

...He was very difficult to direct. But he was worth listening to; most of his suggestions were very valuable. I would say to him, "Well, Claude, I don't agree with you, but we'll shoot it your way, then we'll shoot it my way and see." He forgot that the director in those days had the final cut![24]

Over the years, Rains' performance has been denigrated by those who prefer to discount the actor's talent and concentrate on his height. To harp about this is absurd given the forcefulness of, say, Alan Ladd and James Cagney, and ignores the menacing power of such diminutive bogies as Edward G. Robinson, Peter Lorre, and, well ... Bogie. Chaney, himself several inches under that requisite six feet, did away with fewer individuals in the course of the 1925 original than Rains did in the remake.

With the flamboyantly bizarre elements to be kept to an absolute minimum—gone was any mention of Devil's Island, the Black Arts, or feasting one's soul on accursed ugliness—Rains and Lubin had to strive mightily to produce a memorable Phantom. This was itself an uphill battle, as Rains was billed *below* Susanna Foster—a teenage coloratura from the American West—and Nelson Eddy, Hollywood's famed "singing capon." Ample screen time (too much, said many) was spent in setting up the "origins" of the title character; since this version didn't start *in medias res* (as had Chaney's), however, the exposition was necessary. Few would argue that the resultant Erique Claudin was one of Paris's (if not life's) great nebbishes, but that miscalculation was due to the screenplay and not to the actor.

It goes without saying that Claude Rains' makeup falls far short of the face devised by the Man of a Thousand Faces. Chaney's Erik bore the scars of dissolution and perversion,

arranged unforgettably on a death's-head palette. Rains' character, though, donned his mask to hide the effects of a dousing with acid. Even so, the tepid treatment on which Jack Pierce and the actor settled (there had been numerous experiments) didn't merit the overdone reaction proffered by Miss Foster. Pierce and Lubin later sought to blame Rains for the makeup's ineffective nature. While the proud actor probably had balked at the thought of anything remotely approaching the level or complexity of the Chaney treatment—after all, this *was* a sound film, Rains' voice was a magnificent instrument, and Chaney's landmark facial appliances had made even the simplest speech impossible—Pierce could at least have made sure that his paint, putty, and collodion spanned the entire facial surface covered by the stylish mask he, himself, had designed.

Neither of Universal's two versions of *Phantom* is the classic rendition it could have been, and each has undeniable strengths and deplorable weaknesses. For all its supposed relationship to the world of classical music, the Leroux story is vividly and primarily visual. The power (and the charm) of the 1925 melodrama is centered in Lon Chaney. The 1943 retelling offers an aural dimension denied its predecessor, and while for some viewers *any* opera is too much opera, the balance between the Phantom and his musical world could definitely have been skewed differently. Still, given the overhauling given to the original for all the reasons mentioned above, Claude Rains' splendid portrayal stands out amid a production of great beauty but failed promise.

***Phantom of the Opera*** Universal. Released August 27, 1943. 92 minutes.

Nelson Eddy (Anatole Garron); Susanna Foster (Christine DuBois); CLAUDE RAINS (Erique Claudin); Edgar Barrier (Raoul Daubert); Leo Carrillo (Signor Ferretti); Jane Farrar (Mme. Biancarolli); Fritz Feld (Lecours); J. Edward Bromberg (Amiot); Steven Geray (Vercheres); Frank Puglia (Villeneuve); Hume Cronyn

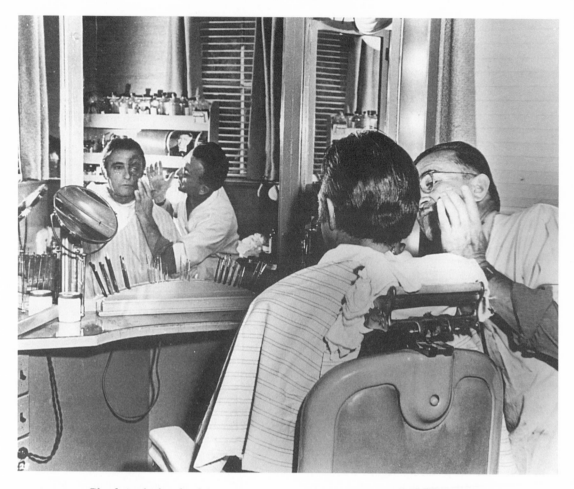

Claude in the hands of the master: Universal's Jack P. Pierce. *Courtesy Richard Bojarski*

(Gerard); Barbara Everest (Christine's Aunt); Fritz Leiber (Franz Liszt); Nicki Andre (Mme. Lorenzi); Gladys Blake (Jeanne); Elvira Curci (Yvette); Hans Herbert (Marcel); Kate Lawson (Landlady); Miles Mander (Pleyel); Rosina Galli (Celeste); Walter Stahl (Le Fort); Paul Marion (Desjardines); Beatrice Roberts (Nurse); Muni Seroff, Dick Bartell, Jim Mitchell, Wheaton Chambers (Reporters); Belle Mitchell (Ferretti's Maid); Ernest Golm (Office Manager); Renee Carson (Georgette); Lane Chandler, Stanley Blystone (Gendarmes); Cyril Delevanti (Bookkeeper); John Walsh (Office Boy); Alphonse Martell (Policeman); Edward Clark (Usher); William Desmond, Hank Mann (Stagehands)

Producer: George Waggner; Executive Producer: Jack Gross; Director: Arthur Lubin; Screenplay: Eric Taylor and Samuel Hoffenstein, based on the novel, *The Phantom of the Opera* by Gaston Leroux; Adaptation by John Jacoby; Directors of Photography: Hal Mohr, W. Howard Greene; Art Directors: John B. Goodman, Alexander Golitzen; Technicolor Consultant: Natalie Kalmus; Editor: Russell Schoengarth; Assistant Director: Charles Gould; Set Decorators: Russell A. Gausman, Ira S. Webb; Dialogue Director: Joan Hathaway; Sound Director: Bernard B. Brown; Technician: Joe Lapis; Musical Score and Direction: Edward Ward; Opera Sequences: William Von Wymetal, Lester Horton; Choral Director: William Tyroler; Orchestrations: Harold Zweifel, Arthur Schutt; Makeup: Jack P. Pierce; Hair Stylist: Emily Moore; Costumes: Vera West

*Phantom of the Opera* had originally been scheduled for a later (mid–October) release, and its September 13, 1943, appearance on *The Lux Radio Theatre* was to have whet the audience's appetite for Universal's Technicolor extravaganza. Rains couldn't make the broadcast and was replaced by Basil Rathbone. Cf. *Radio*

## *Passage to Marseilles* (1944)

Intending to write a series of stories on the Free French Air Squadron, American journalist Manning (John Loder) is taken by the peculiar face of one of the airmen, Jean Matrac (Humphrey Bogart). Captain Freycinet (Claude Rains) tells how he had met Matrec.

At the beginning of the war, Freycinet was recalled from New Caledonia and was traveling to Marseilles on the *Ville de Nancy*, an armed French freighter. They came upon a canoe carrying five half-dead men, and Captain Malo (Victor Francen) ordered the men brought aboard. Major Duval (Sydney Greenstreet) suspected the men were fugitives from Devil's Island, and the men confided to Freycinet that they were. Renault (Philip Dorn) had deserted from the French Army at 16 years of age; Marius (Peter Lorre) was a Parisian pickpocket; Garou (Helmut Dantine) had killed his girlfriend in a lovers' quarrel; Petit (George Tobias) had slain a petty official in a fit of anger. Matrac, their leader, had been an anti-Fascist newspaper publisher; he had ended up in Cayenne after being framed for murder. The escape had been masterminded by Grandpere (Vladimir Sokoloff), an elderly prisoner who had the men promise to fight to liberate France when they returned home. The weight of so many men had threatened to swamp the canoe, so Grandpere had stayed behind on Devil's Island.

As the *Ville de Nancy* steamed across the Atlantic, Captain Malo received word that France had signed an armistice with Hitler. The Fascist-leaning Duval was overjoyed at the news; Malo secretly changed course,

intending to take his ship to England. When Duval learned of this, he instigated a mutiny, but the convicts and the loyal French sailors restored Malo to command. Jourdain, the wireless operator and also a Fascist, broadcast their location, and the ship was attacked by a German bomber. Seizing a machine gun, Matrac brought the plane down, but not before Marius was killed. When the convicts reached Britain, they joined the Free French Air Squadron, and Matrec became their top gun.

Freycinet explains how, after every mission, Matrac flies over a little farm in Romilly and drops a message to his wife and child. As he speaks, the Flying Fortresses return to the base, but Matrac has not survived. Freycinet promises that his message will be delivered.

It's sad that for every few dozen *Casablanca* groupies, there are only a couple of movie buffs who have sat through *Passage to Marseilles*. The picture may not be one of Bogart's top ten (or even top twenty), but it moves along at an appreciable clip, has loads of action, and doesn't dwell overlong on the requisite romantic element. It really doesn't deserve its present "also ran" status. Perhaps the Casablancans feel that, with largely the same cast once again pitting those Vichy devils against the French patriots, it's just more—but less—of the same. Then again...

Back in 1939, as Warners was preparing a fictionalized exposé of Devil's Island, the French government began to foam at *la bouche*. High dudgeon, outrage, and threats of the loss of a lucrative overseas market prompted the studio to deep-six the project, but despite its acquiescence, France boycotted the Warner product for a couple of months. In 1942, *Casablanca* came, saw and conquered, and the team of Charles B. Nordhoff and James N. Hall—the novelists who had brought the world *Mutiny on the Bounty* and *The Hurricane*—unveiled *Men Without Country*. A tale of French honor even in the face of French oppression, the story was bought outright by Warners even before it was published, and was assigned to veteran screenwriters Casey Robinson and Jack Moffitt. In light of the success of *Casablanca*, no one cared much that the Vichy regime was offended and the Free French movement was tickled to death that the scenario had *Vive la France!* on the lips of everyone save for the most transparent of villains.

While the story outline was simplicity itself, the body of the screenplay was couched in the flashback mode and, at times, employed flashbacks within flashbacks. This latter device was used to relate Bogie's tale of woe and to establish his bond with Michelle Morgan and the son he has never seen. Unless you were keeping score, the awkwardness of the whole thing pretty much escaped notice in Michael Curtiz's capable hands. Wartime restrictions on Hollywood-studio spending and construction resulted in the extensive use of glass paintings and miniatures, and Jack R. Cosgrove and Edwin DuPar were called in for the model work; unfortunately, due to lighting deficiencies, much of this remains pretty obvious to him who has eyes to see. James Wong Howe fared better with the principal photography (and *its* attendant lighting) for the set-bound production.

Rains is the picture of French pluck and resolve, and he cuts a dashing figure in his spiffy uniforms and an eye-patch. His Captain Freycinet had been a hero in World War I and, albeit gently deprecating his role before Manning ("I'm getting along, blind in one eye; I'm nothing but a liaison officer"), he is now the hub of the hidden air base populated by his Vichy-intolerant countrymen. Modesty apart, though, his audience with the American reporter *is* nothing more than a springboard from which he launches into the body of the film, which is yet another demonstration of the untypical but eminently marketable toughness of Humphrey Bogart.

Both Manning's unsolicited observation of the man ("I've never seen a stronger face, or a stranger one") and Freycinet's repeated insistence that Matrac is probably the greatest patriot of them all are difficult to fathom except in the light of the billing: this is a Humphrey Bogart picture, and if anyone's going to be strong or strange (even when merely quietly asking a favor), or to become obsessively jingoistic, it's going to be Humphrey Bogart. Each of Bogie's *Casablanca* cronies does receive his moment in the spotlight, though, with Peter Lorre getting an extra helping of pathos as he expires with a little wave to Bogie. The fact that Bogie waves back with about as much emotion as a mechanic would show while tuning an engine can only reinforce his shipmates' scripted admiration for Matrac, the quintessential strong silent type.

Rains' gabby Freycinet is hardly the silent type, but his part in the onboard fracas makes it bloody clear that he didn't survive the Great War on luck alone. Because of those flashbacks within flashbacks, he is more an omniscient narrator than would normally be realistic or acceptable; still, the captain's ability to recount the most intimate of words and the most personal of reactions doesn't detract much from the integrity of the exposition. Those various bits of business between Bogie and Michele Morgan are crucial if audiences are to recall Bogie and Bergman, and it's likely that, caught up in the dynamics of the escape, the mechanics of the rescue, or the regularity with which the *Ville de Nancy* is host to melee or subject to attack, few people would notice Freycinet's impossible attention to detail, anyhow.

One thing most people did notice was that Rains quietly stole every scene in which he appeared. *Variety* didn't split any hairs:

The best job of all is done by Rains. Not only does he have the biggest part in the picture, but he practically captures all the acting honors in a film filled with good acting.
                              (February 16, 1944)

As if the largest role weren't enough, he's even given the opportunity to showcase his persuasive tones at the picture's climax,

During a break in the shooting, Claude regales Hal Wallis *(second from left)*, Victor Francen *(standing)*, and a couple of genuine fighting men with a story from his personal catalogue. *Courtesy Jessica Rains*

wherein he reads over Bogart's grave the poignant and philosophic letter that never made it to the Matrac heir. Whether the Matrac boy (despite his having his father's eyes and spirit) or any other six-year-old on the face of the earth could have puzzled out just what in hell his dad was going on about behind all that flowery hoopla is inconsequential. 'Tis a poetic scene, supercharged with the idealism, the patriotism, and the optimistic shortsightedness that are to be found in virtually every Second World Wartime motion picture dedicated to man's ongoing fight for liberty over tyranny. Bogart's screed is not a personal credo, for all its "I's" and "we's"; it's a public declaration,

crafted in high-flying sentiments and soul-stirring phrases and intended to edify as it inspires. Full of noble sound and righteous fury, it really doesn't signify anything other than an uplifting bridge from *this* story of love and war to the one set to open in theaters everywhere the week after next.

And it may well be that this similarity to so many like soapboxes in so many other movies, rather than its resemblance to the more superficial aspects of *Casablanca*, is what relegates *Passage to Marseilles* to the second-class citizenship it bears today.

*Passage to Marseilles* Warner Bros. Released March 11, 1944. 110 minutes.

Humphrey Bogart (Jean Matrac); CLAUDE RAINS (Captain Freycinet); Michele Morgan (Paula); Sydney Greenstreet (Major Duval); Philip Dorn (Renault); Helmut Dantine (Garou); Peter Lorre (Marius); George Tobias (Petit); John Loder (Manning); Vladimir Sokoloff (Grandpere); Eduardo Cianelli (Chief Engineer); Victor Francen (Captain Malo); Konstantin Shayne (First Mate); Louis Mercier (2nd Engineer); Monte Blue (2nd Mate); Stephen Richards (Lieutenant Hastings); Hans Conreid (Jourdain); Frederick Brunn (Bijou); Billy Roy (Mess Boy); Charles LaTorre (Lieutenant Lenoir)

Producer: Hal B. Wallis; Director: Michael Curtiz; Screenplay: Casey Robinson, Jack Moffitt, based on a novel by Charles Nordhoff & James N. Hall; Director of Photography: James Wong Howe, ASC; Special Effects: Jack R. Cosgrove (Director) & Edwin DuPar, ASC; Dialogue Director: Herschel Daugherty; Editor: Owen Marks; Art Director: Carl Jules Weyl; Set Decorator: George James Hopkins; Montage: James Leicester; Musical Score: Max Steiner; Orchestral Arrangements: Leonid Raab; Musical Director: Leo F. Forbstein; Technical Advisor: Sylvain Robert; Sound: Everett A. Brown; Assistant Director: Frank Heath; Gowns: Leah Rhodes; Makeup: Perc Westmore

A Warner Bros./First National Picture

## *Mr. Skeffington* (1944)

Every eligible bachelor in 1914 New York is mad for Fanny Trellis (Bette Davis), whose great beauty and flirtatious manner make her the recipient of adulation, proposals of marriage, and countless floral arrangements. Trouble brews when it's discovered that her brother Trippy (Richard Waring) has defrauded his employer, millionaire stockbroker Job Skeffington (Claude Rains), of $24,000. Fanny finds that Skeffington is also an admirer of hers and marries him to protect her brother. Angered and ashamed, Trippy runs off to fight in the Great War, joining the Lafayette Escadrille.

Skeffington finds that marriage is no deterrent to Fanny's scandalous behavior, but, like his Biblical namesake, he is a patient man. Finding herself pregnant with Job's child, Fanny insists traveling to California with her cousin George (Walter Abel) and bearing the child there, so that she will not be have to be gawked at by her friends and beaux while in her "puffy" state.

Little Fanny is but a year old when America enters the war, and both Job and George are commissioned as officers. They are home on leave a year or so later when Fanny receives news that Trippy has been killed in action. As far as Fanny's concerned, her husband is to blame for her beloved brother's death. "If it hadn't been for Job," she sobs to George, "Trippy wouldn't have gone to war and all."

Armistice is declared, but even this can't keep Fanny at home; little Fanny grows through her toddler and early childhood years doted on by her father and all but ignored by her mother.

Time passes, and fashions (and suitors) change. Fanny sues Job for divorce, citing his dalliances with his secretaries, but, feeling that custody of a child would put a crimp in her style, she allows Job to take their daughter off to Europe with him. More years pass, and little Fanny—now 18 and nearly all grown up—appears at the doorstep in New York. Sent home from Berlin as protection from the Nazis, the girl (Marjorie Riordan) is immediately attracted to her mother's latest (and youngest) beau, Johnnie Mitchell (Charles Drake), and he to her.

Fanny is stricken with diphtheria and although she survives the onslaught of the disease, her hair turns gray and her beauty fades. At the advice of a psychoanalyst (George Coulouris), she invites her old suitors to a dinner party, where, garishly made-up and bewigged, she watches them politely recoil from her. Young Fanny then announces that she and Johnny Mitchell are to be married and will be moving out of state. As all seems darkest, George arrives and reveals that Job has returned from Germany, penniless and nearly unrecognizable. Fanny discovers that her husband has been blinded in a concentration camp and cannot see that her beauty is gone. Finally touched to the point of caring for someone other than herself, she brings Job back into their home and welcomes him into her heart.

Obviously, nothing made it past the Warners' front gate without the imprimatur of Jack L. Warner. *Mr. Skeffington* was already adjudged a winner by its proud production crew when it was delivered to the Burbank projection room for Warner's private screening.[25] The official nod was the only hurdle to be jumped before the film went into general release. As was frequently the case, the boss's reaction was most interesting:

At one point when Bette Davis was on screen Warner asked for [the film] to come to a halt. The projector was stopped. The lights were switched on. Jack looked around him. "People," he said, "are saying 'Fanny' too much." [Producer] Julius Epstein looked at him incredulously. "But it's her name, you know."

As with most Bette Davis vehicles of the mid-thirties to the mid-forties, *Mr. Skeffington*'s on-screen theatrics paled beside the drama that unfolded behind the cameras. The picture had first been announced late in 1940, with Edmund Goulding slated to direct. Then, Davis had taken umbrage at the thought of playing a middle-aged harridan. Film historian Rudy Behlmer rescued from oblivion the note the 32-year-old actress fired off to Warner:

It is physically impossible for me to play this woman of fifty—I am not old enough in face or figure, and I have worked too hard to do something that I know I would never be convincing in. If your action in these matters is suspension ... I would appreciate knowing as soon as possible so I can open my house in New Hampshire.[26]

The source novel had been published in England only the year before by "Elizabeth" (Mary Annette Beauchamp Russell), became a household word thanks to the Book-of-the-Month Club, and was instantly snapped up by Paramount. Rumored to have been inspired by the sexual adventures of American actress Fanny Ward in pre-war London, the story went nowhere at Paramount, nor did it find legs subsequently over at Warners. Charles Higham (*Bette: The Life of Bette Davis*) reports that the studio was actively (but unsuccessfully) pushing to unload the property on someone else when, "in desperation," the Epstein twins—late of *The Man Who Came to Dinner* and *Casablanca*—were hired to rewrite and produce it.

Hence, interest in the project was rekindled in 1943, when Davis was won over by the twins' gift of clever gab, and when Paul Henreid was offered the title role. Henreid, however, was sore at the shabby treatment he had received from Warner since *Casablanca* had wowed America; unwilling to pay the expensive Austrian's tab for just *any* run-of-the-mill release, the frugal studio chief had eased him toward suspension by offering him roles no leading man could possibly accept. There was gold amidst the dross, however, and Henreid may have erred in turning down *Watch on the Rhine* (1943), which brought the Oscar to Paul Lukas, and *Mr. Skeffington*, for which Claude Rains received his third Academy Award nomination. (Some accounts say Rains didn't get the part on the first rebound, but was approached only after Lukas and John Loder had been tested.)

Tragically, as costume and makeup tests were getting underway, Davis' husband Farney (Arthur Farnsworth) collapsed on Hollywood Boulevard and died a day later. Uncharacteristically sensitive, Jack Warner told the distraught actress to take as much time as she needed to recover from her loss; ever the trouper, she was back on the lot in just over a week, but the strain did nothing to help her impersonate Fanny Trellis, the outstanding American beauty of her day. Still, the resolve with which Davis took command of her emotions was admired by her coworkers and appreciated by the studio brass.

The speed with which she took command of the production, however, was another thing entirely. She refused to do retakes

**This unretouched studio portrait clearly reveals Claude's nearly useless right eye.**

ordered by director Vincent Sherman, kvetched about several of Perc Westmore's more arduous make-ups, and battled over color schemes with Technicolor consultant Natalie Kalmus. (The picture was ultimately filmed in black and white.) When Jack Warner queried as to why the film was so behind schedule, the Epsteins' memo pulled no punches: "Bette Davis is a slow director."

Sherman may have thrown up his hands over Davis' peccadilloes, but he was at one with the actress where Rains was concerned. "We both knew Claude's work," wrote the director in a marvelous essay, "[and] we fought to have him on the picture."[27] Rains was touched by his colleagues' support and reveled in the role; he especially enjoyed the Epsteins' witty dialogue, which appreciably lightened what could very well have been a five handkerchief experience. In fact, the brothers wisely closed the film with a reprise of the running gag about Fanny's broken dates with Janie Clarkson, thus sparing audiences diabetic shock.

Almost anyone could have crafted a competent Job Skeffington from the Epsteins' clever lines, but Rains milks them for their every irony, while avoiding the bathos they continually skirt. Job's Jewish faith, a matter which so worried the Office of War Information that it specifically warned the studio about playing into the hands of the Nazi propagandists, is downplayed that its importance to the underlying drama is almost forgotten. When it resurfaces, during a crucial scene in which Skeffington is apparently bent on talking his beloved daughter *out* of leaving her mother's care, Rains underplays where others might have opened the sluice gates, and the audience *feels* the extent to which this good man would go to protect those he loves.

In a piece for *American Classic Screen* magazine, Anne Etheridge disclosed how the bond between little Fanny and Job touched a nerve in the actor. The relationship, Etheridge wrote, marked "the only time Rains forgot his character and let his personal feelings interfere with his delivery." Citing the scene wherein Job and Fanny discuss custody of their daughter, Bette Davis agreed:

Without knowing it, he wasn't going to be talked to that way even as Skeffington. He forgot his character and I sat there in absolute shock. My great friend, whom I would have done anything on God's earth for in a scene, turned on me personally. I shook all over. I was so frightened of him in that scene, it was unbelievable.... He was not going to have it, even though that was the way the scene was written.

Job, of course, is not always ruled by heady emotion, and Rains is delightful when recounting Trippy's excesses in dishonesty ("He created everything but Rhode Island," he informs an incredulous Fanny) or clutching his little girl to his uniform jacket. Vignettes like these give Skeffington a realistic edge that most of the others lack; actually, except for Walter Abel's level-headed George Trellis and George Coulouris's wonderful, no-nonsense Dr. Byles, Rains' Job is the only

Claude, Bette Davis, and little Gigi Perreau take a stroll for Frances Rains' camera. Note the light reflectors on the roof of the facade in the background. *Courtesy Jessica Rains*

human being in a scenario populated by character *types*.

Rains' superlative performance found critical unanimity, making his loss on Oscar night all the more difficult to understand. Even Bosley Crowther, normally given to liking nothing in his chosen field of study, admitted: "Claude Rains plays with honor and dignity in the plainly subordinate title role, but it is hard to conceive why he never gives his wife a light chip on the jaw." (*The New York Times*, May 26, 1944)

He might have cracked all that Max Factor.

*Mr. Skeffington* Warner Bros. Released August 12, 1944. 146 minutes.

Bette Davis (Fanny Trellis); CLAUDE RAINS (Job Skeffington); Walter Abel (George Trellis); Richard Waring (Trippy Trellis); George Coulouris (Dr. Byles); Marjorie Riordan (Young Fanny); Robert Shayne (MacMahon); John Alexander (Jim Conderley); Jerome Cowan (Edward Morrison); Charles Drake (Johnny Mitchell); Peter Whitney (Chester Forbish); Dorothy Peterson (Manby); Bill Kennedy (Thatcher); Tom Stevenson (Rev. Hyslup); Walter Kingsford (Dr. Melton); Halliwell Hobbes (Soames); Gigi Perreau (Fanny at age 2); Bunny Sunshine (Fanny at age 5); Sylvia Arslan (Fanny at age 10); Dolores Gray (Singer); Ann Doran (Marie); Erskine Sanford (Dr. Fawcette); Molly Lamont (Miss Morris); William Forrest (Clinton); Cyril Ring (Perry Lanks); Bess Flowers (Mrs. Thatcher)

Producers and Screenwriters: Julius J. Epstein, Philip G. Epstein; Director: Vincent Sherman; Based on the novel, *Mr. Skeffington*, by "Elizabeth"; Director of Photography: Ernest Haller, ASC; Musical Score: Franz Waxman; Orchestral Arrangements: Leonid Raab; Musical Director: Leo F. Forbstein; Art Director: Robert Haas; Set Decorator: Fred M. McLean; Sound: Robert B. Lee; Editor: Ralph Dawson; Montage: James Leicester; Gowns: Orry-Kelly; Makeup: Perc Westmore

A Warner Bros./First National Picture

Adapted for NBC's *The Lux Radio Theatre*, *Mr. Skeffington* was broadcast on October 1, 1945. The noted film director, William Keighley, was the guest host, and the principal cast featured Bette Davis and Marjorie Riordan (repeating their movie roles), Paul Henreid (Job Skeffington), Jack Edwards, Jr. (Trippy), and Joe Kearns (George).

## *Strange Holiday* (1945)

John Stevenson (Claude Rains) and Sam Morgan (Milton Kibbee) are returning from a vacation in the isolated north woods when their plane makes a forced landing in a farm field. After an hour's wait on the strangely desolate main highway, Stevenson gets a lift into town, while Morgan stays with the plane. In town, Stevenson finds the streets all but deserted, a women's store salesgirl in a despondent trance, and his office locked. He heads home, after being urged to do so by the dispirited office building manager, and finds that his wife, Jean (Gloria Holden), and his three young children are missing.

Stevenson is accosted in his own house by two men, who sap him and cart him off to a sort of jail. When he cries out for a lawyer and demands his rights, he is brought before an examiner (Martin Kosleck) who informs him that America has been all but taken over by Nazi-like forces, via an insidious master plan of innuendo and propaganda, compounded by American apathy. Suspecting his prisoner of being a spy, the examiner mercilessly beats Stevenson with a rubber hose.

Half-dead, Stevenson comes to on the cell floor, where he realizes that the horrific takeover would never have been possible had Americans like himself been aware that liberty is not a gift, but a victory. Thankfully, the entire incident turns out to be a dream.

With apologies to Sir William Gilbert, *Strange Holiday* is a thing of shreds and patches.

In December 1941, the American people were appalled by Japan's sneak attack on

Pearl Harbor, and citizens opting for isolationism in the face of such outrage were as scarce as Yankee fans at Ebbetts Field. Within a year, however, attitudes began to broaden, and folks who gave their all for the war effort would come to loggerheads with those who felt that their own individual actions were either inconsequential or superfluous. While still in the process of retooling for the war, General Motors was actively concerned about the perils of sloth and/or indifference in a populace accustomed to a liberty that seemed assured—at least in part—by the wide expanse of the Atlantic Ocean.

GM vice-president Paul Garrett went on record with the company stance on the dangers of inaction and inattentiveness in wartime:

Every one must realize that this war is no pushover.... It is a war of ideas and ideals as much as a clash of arms, and we never will be free or happy again until the horrible forces loosed by a madman in Berlin are crushed forever.
(*International Photographer* magazine, November 1942; p. 5)

In light of these sentiments, General Motors had earlier approached radio wizard Arch Oboler and had arranged for his prize radio play, *This Precious Freedom* (1940), to be filmed as an important ideological statement and targeted at GM war workers and their families. It remains unclear whether the film was originally two or four reels in length, but, some time after the film had been screened in cities where GM war plants were located, MGM acquired—and shelved—the short.

In February 1944, the *Hollywood Reporter* announced that the short was to be extended to feature length, with new scenes (which would reflect recent events) shot by the Elite Pictures Corporation, co-owned by Oboler and B-film producers A. W. Hackel, Edward Finney, and Max King. Elite registered the picture, now six reels in length, with the Library of Congress on September 20, 1945, and *Strange Holiday* went into general release a month later.

Due to its tatterdamalion nature and untimely release date, the film was not a success. The previous May had witnessed VE (Victory in Europe) Day, and the 2nd of September had marked the surrender of the Japanese Empire after the atomic strikes against Hiroshima and Nagasaki. As *Variety* noted (in its October 24 review):

Typical comment from a sailor, overheard at the Rialto after the show caught, bears out the author's thesis: "I just came back from winning the war—I don't want to see this kind of stuff after that."

Nor, apparently, did most war-weary Americans, who left Oboler's message about complacency floating in the air like a hanging curve ball. The warning about apathy fell on deaf ears.

This irony apart, had *Strange Holiday* been helmed by someone with more visual acumen than the radio-oriented Oboler, it might have drawn larger crowds. Both the original GM footage and the later additions were shot on a shoestring, and although stock shots of jackbooted goons on the march and atomic explosions, claustrophobic sets, and familiar backlot streets (devoid—thanks to the exigencies of the screenplay—even of inexpensive extras) were painted with the widest palette of angle and light that photographer Robert Surtees could wield, their obvious artificiality and cheapness worked against everyone's best efforts. At one point, Rains opens and enters the same room (from opposite ends) a half-dozen times. He's *supposed* to be wandering through his house, searching out his family members, but not even the repeated change of paintings on the wall behind him makes the illusion successful.

Working with editor Fred Feitshans, Oboler tried valiantly to offset the more preachy aspects of the screenplay with a succession of abrupt cuts, fades, and flashbacks; *anything* to keep the picture moving. The results, though, are never less than unfortunate, with audiences frantic for catharsis left

**The original one-sheet poster from *Strange Holiday*, a strange motion picture.** *Courtesy Alan Levine*

wondering whether Stevenson's waking from his nap the second time around signified a cyclical format (meaning that the outcome was inevitable), or if there was still time for a happy resolution.

Rains fights an uphill battle to keep the viewer's interest from waning in a script awash with deep thoughts and portentous words. Repetition in the delivery of dialogue may be a potent tool in the arsenal of radio; in films, however, there is always the danger that it will be (as it is here) more of an irritant to the audience than an effective dramatic device. "Don't you know?" is proffered almost antiphonally as a zombie-like response to Rains' puzzled queries, and one is desperate for a more realistic, logical exchange between more true-to-life people. When Kosleck finally does spill the beans, the hows and whys of the whole situation still remain dreadfully cryptic.

Not unexpectedly, Oboler did a more competent job on the aural dimension of the film. The array of offscreen voices and sound effects punch up the episodic visuals. Occasionally, however, the sound mix is off, and bits of Rains' introspective monologue are lost in a confusing wall of declamation and noise. Of course, that confusion may have been purposeful, meant to reinforce for the audience Stevenson's pain and bewilderment. It's the wealth of *other* confusion that helps undermine the picture.

Long on sermonizing, the film was woefully short on logic. Just how long did Stevenson and his pal spend getting on each other's nerves up there in God-knows-where? Conflicting snippets of dialogue indicate anywhere from two to four weeks, and while either is too ludicrously brief to cover the total corruption of a nation, the trashing of its laws and customs, and the subjugation of its populace, both are entirely too *long* vis-à-vis a normal "vacation" away from one's loving wife and three young children.

Why would the new powers-that-be forbid merchants to sell their wares? What possible good could come from overthrowing the *economy*? With the streets deserted—the citizens supposedly cowering in their homes or languishing (between beatings) in shadowy jail cells—why would paperless newsboy Tommy risk a whipping just to stand on his corner? Would Miss Simms (Helen Mack) venture forth to the women's shop (when no business can be conducted) just for girl talk with the listless zombie of a saleswoman? How can one of John Stevenson's sons be John Junior, and the other, *Woodrow* Junior? Per the shadows on the wall, has America been subverted by the Nazis (the swastika) or the fascists (the fasces) or both? Are there no distinctions to be drawn—no matter how facile—between the two?

The film was viewed as a curiosity when it premiered in its new, longer format. *The New York Times* found it

…a succession of sadistic sequences which smack of having been contrived for their shock effect. If this be a new form of cinematic impressionism, then give us back the old days of simple, straightforward story telling, for "Strange Holiday" only adds to confusion of thought on a serious matter. (October 20, 1945)

The reviewer felt that neither Rains nor his colleagues were "able to do much toward making this film comprehensible." The "Bible of Show Business," on the other hand, wrote that the actor "practically carries the plot and does a fine job." (*Variety*, October 24, 1945)

Business was middling at best, and the picture quickly was withdrawn from circulation. Come mid–1946, Rains was enjoying good press, both for his stellar performance in Hitchcock's *Notorious* and his notorious $1+ million salary (for *Caesar and Cleopatra*); the value of his name, even when connected with Oboler's uncomfortable study of an unpopular theme, was just too potent to ignore. *Holiday* was edited from 61 minutes to 55 and handed over to PRC (Producers Releasing Corporation), one of the more active of the poverty-stricken independent studios mired in Hollywood's "Gower Gulch."

The picture made about as much sense and impact the second time around as it had the first. Gone was its brief epilogue, wherein FDR's voice had declaimed the Four Freedoms over a montage of scenes of America at her most bountiful; in its place, a narrator offset a shot of clouds in the heavens by paraphrasing one of Rains' choicest lines:

This is a story that never happened and that will never happen as long as we remember that freedom is never a gift but a victory, which each of us must guard with heart and mind.

Redundant, perhaps, but terribly necessary. When Elite had first opened the picture, audiences exited the theaters still wondering if it had all been a dream; Roosevelt's patriotic summation had inspired, but not enlightened, them.

Even in the reworked PRC release, however, the poor editing left the viewer uncertain as to whether a last-reel picnic scene was a flashback to happier times, a bit of wishful thinking on Stevenson's part, or the denouement. When the scene faded, Rains was back in his cell, leaving audiences frustrated and confused.

The September 4, 1946, issue of *The Motion Picture Exhibitor* allowed how "Rains is capable, and does the best job that he could" [sic], while admitting that PRC had unleashed an "unusual meller" with "limited appeal." *Variety* gave the film another glance (on November 6), but concurred with the trade paper: "[*Strange Holiday*] is a strange offering for regular theaters, and will turn only slight profit for PRC." Reviewer "Brog" also noted that the "Heavy and lengthy dialog that falls to Rains keeps general pace slow with little interest around."

The picture's provocative theme was ultimately undone by Arch Oboler's inability to reshape for the screen a work first created for the airwaves. Rains carried his own weight, but even assisted by Robert Surtees' ambitious lens and Gordon Jenkins' appropriate musical score, he couldn't shoulder the world.

*Strange Holiday* Elite Pictures Corporation. Released October 19, 1945. 61 minutes. PRC Released September 2, 1946. 55 minutes.

CLAUDE RAINS (John Stevenson); Bobbie Stebbins (John, Jr.); Barbara Bates (Peggy Lee); Paul Hilton (Woodrow, Jr.); Gloria Holden (Jean Stevenson); Milton Kibbee (Sam Morgan); Walter White, Jr. (Farmer); Wally Maher (Truck Driver); Martin Kosleck (Examiner); Priscilla Lyons (Betty); David Bradford (Boyfriend); Tommy Cook (Newsboy); Griff Barnett (Regan); Ed Max (First Detective); Paul Dubov (Second Detective); Helen Mack (Miss Simms, Secretary); Charles McAvoy (Guard)

Producers: A. W. Hackel, Edward Finney, Max King; Director and Screenwriter: Arch Oboler; Director of Photography: Robert Surtees; Music: Gordon Jenkins; Editor: Fred Feitshans, Jr.; Art Director: Bernard Herzbrun; Special Effects: Howard Anderson, Ray Mercer; Assistant Director: Sam Nelson; Sound: W. H. Wilmarth

# *This Love of Ours* (1945)

Rich and famous Dr. Michel Touzac (Charles Korvin) is off for a medical convention in Chicago, leaving behind his young daughter, Susette (Sue England), who adores him and who worships the memory of her (presumably) dead mother. In a café in Chicago, Michel comes upon his wife, Karin (Merle Oberon). Now calling herself Florence, she provides piano accompaniment to caricaturist Joseph Targel (Claude Rains). After meeting briefly with Michel, Karin attempts suicide, but her husband operates and saves her life with his own innovative surgical techniques. While reading through his wife's diary, Michel begins to realize how much suffering the woman has endured due to his anger, jealousy, and misunderstanding. Some years earlier, during their young daughter's second birthday party, Michel had leapt to some unfortunate conclusions about Karin's fidelity, and had left Paris for America, with Susette in tow.

After recuperating in a sanitarium, Karin agrees to go home with Michel, and there to be reacquainted with her daughter, all the while posing as Michel's second wife, Florence. Susette resents the woman's presence, however, and refuses to address her as "Mother." Distraught and on the verge of leaving forever, Karin throws Susette another birthday party, and both Targel and Uncle Bob (Carl Esmond) show up. Bob fills "Florence" in on the pain Michel has been living with since he left Paris, and she forgives him at once; her love for him is likewise rekindled. Targel presents Susette with a portrait of her mother, drawn solely from the young girl's flowery descriptions. When she recognizes the woman in the drawing as Florence, the light dawns, and she calls out for her mother to stay.

A common perception running through the sundry reviews of *This Love of Ours* concerned the knack of director William Dieterle for keeping this renegade Pirandello piece from scampering like a good little women's picture down the old treacle highway. Critical comments such as this, together with the general awareness most men had that Merle Oberon was not at all unpleasant to look at, helped fill seats with ticket-buyers of both sexes and gave Universal a tidy little return on its $2 million investment. With wartime spending restrictions somewhat eased as of VE Day, studios everywhere constructed long overdue new indoor and outdoor sets and amortized the costs via the budgets of the features to be shot in, on, around, or anywhere near the new builds.

No matter whether you split hairs over Dieterle's touch, Oberon's sex appeal, or Charles Korvin's talent for manly suffering, *This Love of Ours* is quality treacle, pure and simple. Nevertheless, there are some highly enjoyable moments in the picture, and almost all belong to Claude Rains. Playing a role which presages his Alexander Hollenius in *Deception* (the artist who takes in and keeps someone else's honey warm until that someone else walks back in, unannounced, to reclaim her), Rains soft-pedals the angst and allows Oberon and Korvin (and young Sue

England) to coax the tears. Unlike his Hollenius, Rains' Targel is not a self-absorbed egomaniac, but a genuinely good man whose basic philosophy ("Life is funny, and people are even funnier") is damn near the first statement anyone makes to the adolescent Suzette without misting over.

Everyone can live with the status quo until Oberon stops playing the piano and shoots herself. That crucial operation utilizing Korvin's radical procedures follows, and not only are the assembled medicos impressed, but Oberon is wrestled back from the Stygian darkness without disturbing her hair or makeup. With a little rest, she'll be able to get back to hating Korvin again in no time. Since soap opera convention demands that emotion or circumstance prevent the principals in any given idiocy from speaking openly to one another, this would go on indefinitely were it not for the intercession of Targel and a convenient *deus ex machina*, Uncle Bob (Carl Esmond). Esmond, whose character has never—indeed, *could* never—hate anyone in his whole life, not even when he's blind and Korvin is choking the bejesus out of him at the Steinway, is clearly an angelic force of restoration. During his big dramatic moment—when the sound of her voice and the pressure of her fingers reveals Karen and Frances to be one and the same—he almost glows, thanks in part to clever lighting and soft-focus photography.

Targel can laugh at himself as well as at others. His elfin grins and chortles during the redemptive birthday party are delightful tonics to the oppressively heavy atmosphere the Touzacs have been breathing to that point. His talent at drawing gives him a natural "in" with Susette, for whom images speak more loudly and with greater honesty than words. And the artwork, of course, sets up that touching moment when the young woman's eyes are opened by Targel's portrait of her mother.

Still, watching Targel work as a caricaturist at Hinky Joe's café, one senses an underlying touch of sadism in the artist's personality. His audience's laughter is triggered

**Claude as Joseph Targel, a kind-hearted caricaturist who works best when someone pounds on the piano.** *Courtesy Jessica Rains*

both by his wry observations and the reactions of the subjects he sketches; because more patrons seem disconcerted than pleased with his work, this is dangerous territory. It is only later, while he's drawing Susette, that one understands that Targel's humor and art are intertwined with his refusal to take life, or himself, too somberly. Although the caricaturist most definitely has his serious side, at the denouement—as Hans Salter's weepy music envelopes the Touzac manse and the principals are huddled together moistly— Rains uncorks his widest and most winning grin; happiness has been restored.

Claude Rains as a philosophizing café caricaturist is altogether delightful and contributes some mildly amusing moments to an otherwise doggedly tragic drama.
>     (*The New York Times*, November 1, 1945)

Amen.

All this happiness was decidedly un-

Pirandello-ish, but it satisfied enough customers and turned enough of a profit to warrant a remake, so Universal-International released *Never Say Goodbye* in 1956, with Rock Hudson and German actress Cornell Borchers doing the loving/hating; George Sanders took over at the sketch-pad for Rains. Director Jerry Hopper was no William Dieterle, however, and there was not nearly enough audience sniffling to satisfy the studio accountants.

*This Love of Ours* Universal. November 2, 1945. 90 minutes.

Merle Oberon (Karin [Florence] Touzac); CLAUDE RAINS (Joseph Targel); Charles Korvin (Michel Touzac); Carl Esmond (Uncle Bob); Sue England (Susette Touzac); Jess Barker (Chadwick); Harry Davenport (Dr. Jerry Wilkerson); Ralph Morgan (Dr. Lane); Fritz Leiber (Dr. Bailey); Helen Thimig (Tucker); Leon Tyler (Ross); Ferike Boros (Housekeeper); Andre Charlot (Flambertin); Dave Wilcock (Dr. David Dailey); Barbara Bates (Mrs. Dailey); Howard Freeman (Dr. Barnes); Selmer Jackson (Dr. Melnik); Joanie Bell (Susette as a Small Child); Maris Wrixon (Evelyn); Ann Codee (Anna); Doris Merrick (Vivian); Cora Witherspoon (Woman)

Producer: Howard Benedict; Director: William Dieterle; Screenplay: Bruce Manning, John Klorer, Leonard Lee, based on the play, *Come Prima Meglio de Prima* ("Like Before Better Than Before"), by Luigi Pirandello; Director of Photography: Lucien Ballard; Music: Hans J. Salter; Editor: Frank Gross; Art Directors: John B. Goodman, Robert Clatworthy, Eugene Lourie; Set Decorators: Russell A. Gausman, Oliver Emert; Gowns: Vera West; Merle Oberon's Costumes: Travis Banton; Director of Sound: Bernard B. Brown; Technician: Charles Carroll; Assistant Director: Fred Frank; Hair Stylist: Carmen Dirigo; Dialogue Director: Victor Stoloff; Associate Producer: Edward Dodds; Makeup: Jack P. Pierce

The film's working title was *As It Was Before!*

# *Caesar and Cleopatra* (1946)

Pompey the Great, one third of the Triumvirate which includes Marcus Crassus and Julius Caesar, begins a civil war in Rome and then flees to Egypt. He is pursued there by Caesar (Claude Rains), who is angered to find that Pompey has been slain by the soldiers of the child pharaoh, Ptolemy. Caesar comes upon Cleopatra (Vivien Leigh), a young and beautiful girl who is Ptolemy's sister and his rival for the throne. Very shortly, Caesar has her on the road to womanhood and even her formidable nurse, Ftatateeta (Flora Robson), is pleased with her progress.

The Egyptians are not pleased with Caesar, however. Using Pothinus (Francis L. Sullivan) as their spokesman, General Achillas (Anthony Eustrel), head of the Egyptian army *and* the Roman army of occupation; Theodotus (Ernest Thesiger), a sage; and Lucius Septimius (Raymond Lovell), the military Tribune, urge the Roman emperor to withdraw from their land before he and his 3000 men are annihilated. Egypt for the Egyptians! With the help of Britannus, Caesar's slave (Cecil Parker); Rufio, his second in command (Basil Sydney), and Sicilian merchant Apollodorus (Stewart Granger), Caesar holds Cleopatra's palace against the whole of Egypt's armed forces.

Cleopatra begins to scheme to have Caesar return to Rome. Not only is she anxious to rule Egypt without him, she has made him promise to send Marc Antony—with whom she was infatuated as a child—to marry her. Pothinus tries to warn Caesar of Cleopatra's plans, and the furious young queen orders Ftatateeta to assassinate him. Caesar is disgusted by this treachery, but Lucius Septimius, taken with the emperor's integrity, pledges his allegiance and reveals that General Mithridates and the Roman legions are about to fight the armies of Ptolemy in Memphis. As Caesar and his men leave to join their allies in battle, Rufio kills Ftatateeta, believing her to be untrustworthy and dangerous.

Caesar and the Romans are victorious, and Egypt is placed in the trust of Rufio, whom the emperor has named Roman governor. As he departs, Caesar agrees once again to send Marc Antony back to the beautiful Cleopatra.

Had they turned the cameras on the *making* of *Caesar and Cleopatra*, they might very well have ended up with a picture that was both epic and unforgettable; they didn't, however, and the result, while still enjoyable, is uneven and a little tedious. Lots of money was spent—figures run anywhere between £1.2 million and £1.5 million sterling—but wartime restrictions and artistic excesses conspired to bog production down for months on end. Extant reports and interviews indicate that director Gabriel Pascal managed to alienate everyone, including Rains (who, per Sir John Gielgud, referred to Pascal as "the Hungarian horse-thief"), Leigh, and even George Bernard Shaw. Bernard F. Dukore reports that things got so bad that

Once production ended and before the movie opened, the film's technicians called a union meeting and passed a resolution never to work with Pascal again.[28]

Pascal had wanted to sire an epic, something as immortal as *Gone with the Wind*, with the scope of an *Intolerance*, and the weighty respectability of *Ben-Hur*. Numerous sets—some massive in every sense of the word—were built in England, only to be transported to Egypt for location shooting when World War II and English weather interfered. The sets *are* Technicolor-ful but they look just like movie sets, while the picture's premier optical effect, the burning of the library of Alexandria, is amateurish and unconvincing. For all the money spent and effort expended, "*Caesar and Cleopatra* is not a visually spectacular film. It merely has large settings and crowds."[29]

Shaw had always been popular in the United Kingdom (*Major Barbara* and

*Pygmalion* were in perfect sync with the heart of the British working class), and he regarded *Caesar and Cleopatra* as one of his most inherently cinematic plays. Unfortunately, for all its cleverness, the play could not muster sufficient numbers to keep the London productions open long enough to meet the notes. How could the filmmakers hope to push the picture—geared optimistically for international release—into the black? As with the stage play, the film lacked appeal for the masses.

It may be Shaw's screenplay, it may be Pascal's direction, it may be contributory negligence; whither goest the ultimate blame, the viewer is left to feel that every line is worthy of being etched in stone. Granted, the dialogue as filmed is the end result of meticulous honing by a wordsmith who was second to none, but the principals sound altogether too quotably clever by half, and anyone with a bit of exposition to add delivers it as if it were the pivot on which the entire plot turns. Much of the time, the viewer senses the actors battling the urge to declaim, rather than converse, and entirely too much energy is spent couching arch and precious rejoinders—suitable for samplers, every one—in smirks, wry sidelong glances, or stock facial expressions of triumph. Making matters worse, dialogue exchanges are often prosaically photographed, thus rendering the few genuinely witty and/or powerful pronouncements awkward and unsatisfying. In the charming first-reel Sphinx scene, for example, Rains is made to deliver lines while either poorly lit or shot from behind, and at least once the camera holds on Vivien Leigh too long, transforming her from expressive speaker to immobile reactor, and undermining the visual element of the conversational give-and-take.

If sacred is the text, profane is the inattention to detail; what is *not* said often leads to confusion. Classical historians or specialists in the antiquities may not raise an eyebrow over the apparent disloyalty to Caesar of the Roman army that occupies Egypt, but few others can explain why one British-cadenced, armor-clad soldier is at sword's point with another. Or what Caesar hopes to accomplish by isolating his men on the lighthouse of Pharos. Or why this most canny of military plotters fails to consider an attack by water. Or how Caesar and a handful of followers "have held the palace against the whole of Egypt's armed forces" for six months.

The film cries out for a lusty action sequence or two to engage the eye and relieve the ear, but the word, not the sword, was Shaw's forte. Still, dialogue which had been bright and witty in 1901 seemed a trifle dull and slow-moving to this new generation's ears (the nonagenarian playwright had allowed no one other than himself to alter the script), while the Hungarian director—a Shavian specialist himself—was too cowed by Shaw and too inexpert at moving large numbers of extras to infuse the picture with the visual energy needed to counteract the pace of the text. Apart from some tepid last-reel battle footage featuring 12 zillion extras in papier-mâché armor, only Ftatateeta and Apollodorus get to mix it up with anyone, and they take turns picking on the same inept Roman foot-soldier.

Vivien Leigh's performance was widely praised by American critics (the Brits were a tad less impressed). To be sure, in her early, "girlish" scenes she is delectable and magnificent. Later in her maturation, however, she seems drawn and angular, and her role also seems to shrink during the latter half of the picture. (No one misses little whiny Ptolemy by then, and the welcome news that Mithridates is about to engage the boy king's armies at Memphis merely reminds one that the kid hasn't been counted out yet; it does nothing for audience adrenaline.) Cleopatra is still around, of course, first glaring daggers at Pothinus, then unleashing Ftatateeta on him, all the while pining for Marc Antony (while ignoring a hale and half-naked Apollodorus). But she no longer seems to have any particular relevance to the Roman game plan. In repeatedly depicting her as preoccupied with an event which does not occur within the film's running time (the arrival of Marc Antony), the screenplay trivializes Cleopatra's role in the disaster which leads up to it: The total subjugation of her country by Rome. This, in turn, makes a mockery of the ongoing "training program" the bemused-but-sincere Caesar has been conducting with her for the body of the film, or of Caesar's presumed integrity. Either way, when the smoke clears, Rufio is in charge of the whole shooting match. Cleopatra's just *there*.

Virtually every short biographical sketch of Rains mentions that he was personally chosen by Bernard Shaw for *Caesar and Cleopatra*, and that he earned in excess of $1 million for the honor; few accounts get into much detail thereafter. Regarding the first item: Shaw had envisaged Johnston Forbes-Robertson as Caesar when he was writing the play, and John Gielgud as the emperor when he was adapting same for the screen. By the early forties, Forbes-Robertson was deceased and Gielgud, far from enthusiastically seizing the opportunity, had passed on it. In a letter to the author, Sir John confirmed this:

It is quite true. Shaw did come to see a matinee of *Love for Love* in which I played Valentine and also directed it. I stupidly did not keep his letter but I did turn down his suggestion for me for Caesar. I [had] met Pascal a couple of times and disliked him so much that I refused the part.

It was only then that Rains was approached by GBS; technically, the actor won the role on the second bounce.

As for the cash, Rains signed on for a flat $50,000 for 12 weeks, with up to an additional $50,000 payable if the production were extended for any length of time, for any reason. As an American citizen on a British work permit, Rains was subject to abominably high income taxes should he still be working in England even a day beyond the allotted six months. As was mentioned above, the frustrations associated with the war; the vagaries of the wretched English climate during fall, winter, and spring; and

the subsequent move of the company to Egypt kept him under contract—and thus liable for those taxes—for quite some while. Thankfully, his contractual terms obligated the J. Arthur Rank organization to pay the taxes (some $1.3 million) directly to the British government; only the $100,000 in stipulated fees ever saw its way back to Rains' Pennsylvania bank. Billing-wise, Leigh was to have the top spot in publicity materials and the picture's opening credits; Rains was to head the cast scrawl at the end.

Whether clad in laurel wreath and toga, or girded in armor, Rains is charming, sagacious, and avuncular: every inch the perfect Shavian Caesar. But he is *not* physically formidable, nor is one completely convinced of his warrior's prowess in battle: again, dead on, per GBS. Apart from his dive from the Pharos wall (done by a double) and his subsequent swim to the nearby ship (during which he was towed on a trolley-like raft), Rains' most strenuous assignment was to find a foothold from which to climb up the not-so-great Sphinx at the picture's outset. Shaw's is a Caesar given more to vocal chess than physical gymnastics—the array of aphorism, argument, observation, and pronouncement with which the scenario is rife is his most potent weapon—and Rains both appreciates and accommodates the distinction.

As had happened in Vivien Leigh's case, Rains was showered with superlatives by the American critics, while many British reviewers found him wan and wanting. To be completely honest, most British walked into the film with a chip on their collective shoulder: few fans of film, theater, Shaw, Leigh, or Rains could reconcile what they considered immorally excessive spending on a *movie* while the country was rationing itself silly in order to win the war. They also grumbled over the casting of the principals, the disposition of the characters (viewers were outraged that Britannus opted to remain Caesar's slave rather than return to his country a free man), and the perceived ridicule to which the ruling classes were subjected.

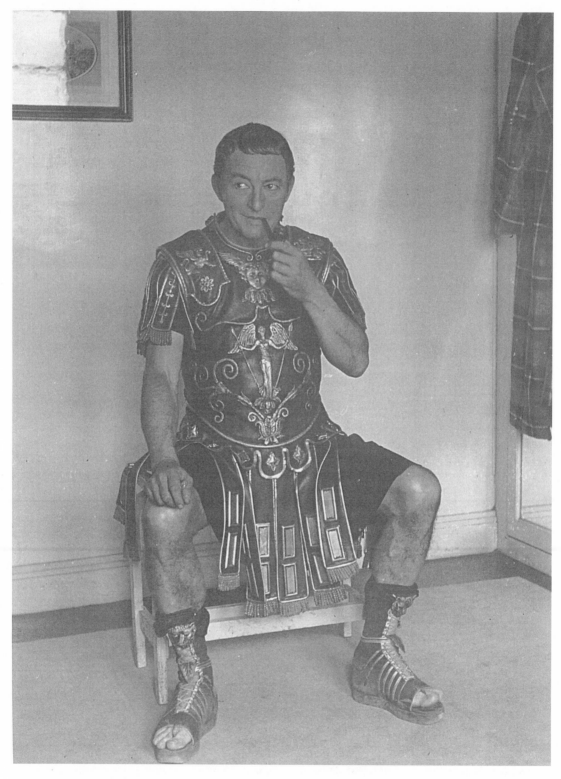

Claude enjoys a pipe before Caesar is off to join Mithridates in Memphis. *Courtesy Jessica Rains*

In the USA, the film received a mixed critical reception. Some naysayers complained that the sheer volume of dialogue accentuated the paucity of action. Others, having eyed a succession of posters featuring Leigh diaphanously clad in the classic Egyptian fashion, griped about the lack of love interest and the "sexlessness" of one of history's most famous femme fatales. Of those who viewed the picture in a more positive light, Bosley Crowther of *The New York Times,* a lover of wordy scripts, was in his element:

Mr. Pascal has fashioned an elegant spectacle around a play which is essentially conversational and pitched to the intellect. He has gathered a wise and witty discourse within a fancy and fluid frame and has directed for its exposition a remarkably entertaining cast. If the discourse does wax slightly tedious at times in the course of two hours, and if some of the matters of discussion seem a bit disconnected and vague, you can blame Mr. Shaw, the script writer, who chose not to tamper with his play.

(September 6, 1946)

Rains had been something of a Shavian virtuoso during his stay at London's *Everyman Theatre* in the twenties, and he was honored to return to the fold while at the height of his powers. He felt *Caesar and Cleopatra* was a mixed blessing, however. He loved the role and thought that the picture had captured Caesar's wit and wisdom, but regretted that this had apparently been accomplished by playing down the man's fire. He was invigorated by the quality aspects of the production, then disappointed that the film lost some $3 million when released. Working with old chums Flora Robson and Basil Sydney was a delight; dealing with Vivien Leigh's moods was not. Most difficult, however, was his extended separation from Frances, Jennifer, and Stock Grange.

*Caesar and Cleopatra* The Rank Organisation/Distributed by Eagle-Lion. Released January 1946. 138 minutes. Distributed in the United States by United Artists

CLAUDE RAINS (Julius Caesar); Vivien Leigh (Cleopatra; courtesy of David O. Selznick); Stewart Granger (Apollodorus); Flora Robson (Ftatateeta); Francis L. Sullivan (Pothinus); Basil Sydney (Rufio); Cecil Parker (Britannus); Ernest Thesiger (Theodotus); Raymond Lovell (Lucius Septimius); Anthony Eustrel (Achillas); Anthony Harvey (Ptolemy); Robert Adams (Nubian Slave); Michael Rennie (First Centurion); James McKechnie (Second Centurion); Olga Edwards, Harda Swanhilde (Cleopatra's Lady Attendants); Esme Percy (Major Domo); Stanley Holloway (Belzanor); Leo Genn (Bel Affris); Alan Wheatley (Persian); Anthony Holles (Boatman); Charles Victor (First Porter); Ronald Shiner (Second Porter); John Bryning (Sentinel); John Laurie, Charles Rolfe (Auxiliary Sentinels); Felix Aylmer, Ivor Barnard (Noblemen); Valentine Dyall, Charles Deane (Guardsmen); Jean Simmons (Harpist)

Producer and Director: Gabriel Pascal; Scenario and Dialogue: George Bernard Shaw; General Manager of Production: Tom White; Script Editor: Marjorie Deans; Decor and Costumes: Oliver Messel; Art Director: John Bryan (courtesy Gainsborough Pictures Limited); Music: Georges Auric; Conductor: Muir Matheson, with the National Symphony Orchestra; Director of Photography: F. A. Young, FRPS, Jack Hildyard, Robert Krasker, Jack Cardiff; Camera Operator: Ted Scaife; Sound Recording: John Dennis; Editor: Frederick Wilson; Dubbing: Desmond Dew; Matte Shots: Percy Day; Chief of Color Control Department: Natalie Kalmus; Assistant: Joan Bridge

# *Notorious* (1946)

When Alicia Huberman (Ingrid Bergman) learns her father has been sentenced to 20 years' imprisonment for treason, she goes off on a bender, during which she meets with Devlin (Cary Grant), an American intelligence agent. Devlin is aware that Alicia's loyalty was to the Allied cause and he proposes she work for him by taking a job with the Rio de Janeiro office of I. G. Farben, a German chemical firm suspected of preparing to strike a blow for the erstwhile Nazi cause.

Although Alicia and Devlin fall in love,

he remains somewhat cool to her and actually goes along with her decision to marry Alexander Sebastian (Claude Rains), the CEO of Farben. Marriage is the perfect cover for the ongoing investigation, to which Sebastian is oblivious despite the suspicions of his mother (Leopoldine Konstantin) and the concerns of many of the Farben executives, ex-Nazis all. Alicia and Devlin discover that uranium, a key ingredient of the atomic bomb, is being secreted in Sebastian's wine cellar. Unfortunately, her new husband deduces that Alicia is an American spy when he comes upon a broken wine bottle.

Acting on his mother's advice—and with her assistance—Sebastian begins to slowly poison Alicia. The Farben chief is careful to avoid having any of this come to the attention of the others in his circle, as his foolhardy actions would doubtless result in his own liquidation. Devlin turns up at the doorstep himself, however, some five days after Alicia has failed to make contact with him, and physically carries the woman to safety. Sebastian is powerless to do anything other than object weakly, and his comrades, cognizant that their leader has somehow endangered their mission, close in for the kill at the doorway of the mansion.

*Notorious* is a big-budget, big-name, tale of intrigue. Cary Grant, who had been merely big back in 1935 (cf. *The Last Outpost*), was *huge* at this point. Ingrid Bergman had enjoyed one hit after another (and had nabbed the Oscar for *Gaslight* in 1944) since boarding that plane with Paul Henreid at the close of *Casablanca,* and Alfred Hitchcock was basking in the well-deserved glow of worldwide adulation. The Third Reich had been obliterated the year before but, now more than ever, Nazis were the movie villains of choice. The mad scramble to attribute to them everything from the atom bomb to the coming of the anti-Christ fueled numerous feature films.

Film scholars have dissected *Notorious* for decades. As long as there are retrospectives, revival houses, or nostalgia channels on cable it's unlikely that this attention will cease. Grant's no-first-name Devlin and his relationship with Alicia have provided the basis for much of this prose, which usually centers on how these particular Cary Grant and Ingrid Bergman characters differ essentially from every other Cary Grant and Ingrid Bergman character we've come to know. The studies run the gamut from the droll to the deranged, and it fell to Hitchcock himself to explain the fundamental difference:

> The story of *Notorious* is the old conflict between love and duty. Cary Grant's job—and it's a rather ironic situation—is to push Ingrid Bergman into Claude Rains' bed. One can hardly blame him for feeling bitter throughout the story, whereas Claude Rains is a rather appealing figure, both because his confidence is being betrayed and because his love for Ingrid Bergman is probably deeper than Cary Grant's.[30]

Even granting Hitchcock's phenomenally meticulous attention to imagery, symbolism, and detail, and allowing this unique filmmaker the integrity of his vision, neither of the romantic leads treads too far afield from his/her more usual turf. Ben Hecht's script (which closely followed an original story by Hitchcock) differs most notably from the usual Grant scenario in that it offers little of the glib wit for which the actor had become popular.

It *is* a bit novel to see Ingrid Bergman try her hand at portraying indecisiveness; the Swedish beauty had already fashioned a reputation for knowing her own mind (and not being reticent about giving others a piece of it), and her romantic link to Italian director Roberto Rossellini—a brazen move that would raise the adjective *notorious* a notch or two—was only a couple of years off. Nevertheless, she was no stranger to the role of the irresistible beauty caught up in an intrigue of international proportion.

Claude Rains, then, is the only one of the principal players to flex unfamiliar thespic muscles in *Notorious*. His Alexander Sebastian might almost be two separate people: the coolly competent industrial giant whose energies are secretly devoted to the resurrection

It's early in the proceedings, and Alicia Huberman has not yet come between Alexander Sebastian and his mother (Leopoldine Konstantin). *Courtesy Susan Duic*

of the Master Race, and the little boy, sexually insecure (an Internet review of the film uses the splendid phrase "precariously heterosexual") and dominated by the mother upon whose advice he depends and for whose approval he is willing to commit murder. (In light of this, Hitchcock had originally wanted the decidedly effeminate Clifton Webb for Sebastian.) Never before had one of Rains' scoundrels been so appallingly dependent upon someone other than the object of his lust, and the actor was nominated for his fourth Academy Award for the novel portrayal. (Neither he nor nominee Ben Hecht won.)

Hitchcock was fond of having the mama's boy as part of his stable of recurrent charac-

ters, and if Anthony Perkins' Norman Bates remains the most outrageous of the crowd, Rains' Alexander Sebastian is the most pathetic. Continually cowed by his mother (Leopoldine Konstantin—late of the Deutsches Theater under Max Reinhardt—was the sternest female presence Hitchcock could find after Ethel Barrymore passed on the part), he is smaller in stature than the "bride" who tantalizes him without extending so much as the possibility of sexual fulfillment. In this milieu, the roles of mother and lover appear to be interchangeable: Alexander addresses both women as "Madame," and heads to the bedroom—his mother's—to break the joyous news of his marriage and to broach the dangerous subject of his wife's betrayal. As the Farben chief gets little satisfaction in the bed of either woman, his remarks about Paul Prescott and Devlin's good looks intimate that he might very well be capable of turning down yet another path. Later, as Alicia struggles to clear her head after a dose of the poisoned demitasse, Alexander's shadow seems to blend with that of Mme. Sebastian; the two conspirators almost meld into one entity. Even Rains' trademark pompadour is clipped close to the sides, causing the actor to look more like a young boy fresh from the barber than a sophisticated, middle aged businessman.

When all is said and done, *Notorious* really hasn't much to do with Nazis and uranium; the wine bottle in the basement is just another of Hitchcock's MacGuffins, a mere plot device. The film tells a dark and unsettling love story preoccupied with the need for mutual trust and the lengths to which some people need go to attain it. No fan of Grant or Bergman was fooled by the wisps of intrigue which Hitchcock blew past Ted Tetzlaff's lens; for them, it was boy-meets-girl, boy-loses-girl, boy-gets-girl all the way, and it was a certainty that He'd get Her off the tracks before the train came roaring past.

Although Rains was proud of his multifaceted performance and honored to work with Hitchcock, he was under no delusion that the picture was anything other than an off-kilter romance, wherein his coming in a distant second went with the territory. "I am not Van Gable Rains," he joked with columnist Philip K. Scheuer:

I lost Cleopatra to Mark Antony in "Caesar," Miss Davis to Paul Henreid in "Deception," and Miss Bergman to Cary Grant in "Notorious."

His height, he went on to explain, conspired with his less than chiseled profile to work against him in matters such as these:

All the years in the theater I used to pray at night that I would wake up with about three inches added to my height. The films have been more satisfactory but I'll tell you a little secret. For "Notorious" I had to step up on a ramp to be near

Miss Bergman. Every time the ramp was moved in Mr. Hitchcock would say, "There goes the shame of Rains."
Los Angeles Times (October 20, 1940)

Shame or no, Rains won his just share of superlatives. Bosley Crowther crowed that, as the pathetic Nazi, he had rendered "a smooth and morbific performance," thus flattering and flabbergasting Rains at the same time. In his full-length review of the film for *The New York Times*, Crowther elaborated:

Mr. Grant, who is exceptionally solid, is matched for acting honors in the cast by Claude Rains as the Nazi big-wig.... Mr. Rains' shrewd and tense performance of this invidious character is responsible for much of the anguish that the situation creates.
(August 19, 1946)

While praise for the cast members was universal, the vote on the film's ultimate worth was split. For a Hitchcock picture it was straightforward of plot and visually restrained (although there's a pip of a crane shot which begins at the top of the grand staircase in the Sebastian foyer and which, after a lengthy and marvelously smooth downward flight, culminates in a dramatic closeup on the key Alicia is clutching in her hand). Some critics decried the film's lack of invention, and others found fault with its pace. As celebrated as the film is today, it generated more than one yawn among those in the critical circle of the time. That *Notorious* grossed some $9 million domestically in its first release, however, indicates that even those who were inclined to nod off paid for the privilege with the price of admission.

*Notorious* RKO Radio Pictures. Released September 6, 1946. 101 minutes.

Cary Grant (Devlin); Ingrid Bergman (Alicia Huberman); CLAUDE RAINS (Alexander Sebastian); Louis Calhern (Paul Prescott); Leopoldine Konstantin (Madame Sebastian); Reinhold Schunzel (Dr. Anderson); Moroni Olsen (Walter Beardsley); Ivan Triesault (Eric Mathis); Alex Minotis (Joseph); Wally Brown (Mr. Hopkins);

Gavin Gordon (Ernest Weylin); Charles Mendl (Commodore); Ricardo Costa (Dr. Barbosa); Eberhard Krumschmidt (Hupka); Fay Baker (Ethel); Antonio Moreno (Señor Ortiza); Frederick Ledebor (Knerr); Luis Serrano (Dr. Silva); William Gordon (Adams); Charles D. Brown (Judge); Peter Von Zerneck (Rossner); Fred Nurney (Huberman)

Producer and Director: Alfred Hitchcock; Assistant Producer: Barbara Keon; First Assistant Director: William Dortman; Screenplay: Ben Hecht, based on an original story by Alfred Hitchcock; Director of Photography: Ted Tetzlaff; Special Effects: Vernon L. Walker, Paul Eagler; Editor: Theron Warth; Musical Score: Roy Webb; Musical Director: C. Bakaleinikoff; Sound: John E. Tribby, Terry Kellum; Set Decorators: Darrell Silvera, Claude Carpenter; Art Directors: Albert S. D'Agostino, Carroll Clark; Costumes: Edith Head

*Notorious* received the *Lux Radio Theatre* treatment on January 26, 1948, but only Ingrid Bergman was on hand to reprise her film role. Joseph Cotton stood in for Cary Grant, and Joseph Kearns took over Claude Rains' role of Sebastian. Others in the cast included Gerald Mohr (Prescott), Jack Kruschen (Joseph), and Janet Scott (Mme. Sebastian).

## *Angel on My Shoulder* (1946)

Newly released from prison, gangster Eddie Kagle (Paul Muni) is shot down by his ex-henchman, Smiley Williams (Hardie Albright).

Eddie comes around in a hot, sulfurous wasteland, which, as he gradually realizes, is Hell. Attempts to overpower the "screws" in order to escape do him no good, and he soon finds himself in "the fire room, in the 55th circle of darkness." Eddie's passion for revenge—as well as his being a dead ringer for the forthright Judge Frederick Parker—gains the attention of Mephistopheles (Claude Rains), who passes himself off as Nick, a "trustee," and helps the determined gangster make it back to life and the surface.

Nick offers Eddie the chance to get even

with Smiley, if Eddie will return the favor; he is to possess Judge Parker's body and, through a series of intentional crimes and circumstances, drive the judge—and all the good he stands for—into ruin. When Parker passes out during a trial, Eddie moves in, and the judge's resultant abnormal behavior is, for the most part, chalked off as being due his fainting spell and "illness." Parker's secretary and fiancée, Barbara (Anne Baxter), is advised by Dr. Higgins (Onslow Stevens), a psychiatrist, to humor the injured man and to avoid antagonizing him.

To Nick's consternation, Eddie fouls up every carefully formulated attempt to discredit the judge—if anything, Parker has now become a veritable shoo-in as governor of the state. When he begins to understand that the judge has the love of a wonderful woman, the admiration of the children, and the respect of the citizenry, Eddie realizes how decent life *can* be. Overhearing some telling words in a sermon, he informs the Devil that he is no longer under his infernal control.

With one last ace up his sleeve, Nick arranges for Eddie to confront Smiley Williams in the judge's apartment. Although given every chance to shoot down Smiley in cold blood, Eddie demurs, and the ex-henchman plunges to his death accidentally. Cognizant that his remaining on earth makes it impossible for Barbara to be joined with her rightful mate, Eddie bids the tearful woman farewell. The judge comes around—once again, his old self—and Eddie and Nick head back to the blazing pit. Eddie, too, is *his* old self, and he blackmails the Devil into making him a Hellish "trustee" in return for his silence.

The upshot of most "Bargain with the Devil" stories is that turnabout is fair play, and classic examples of the literature include wry wrap-ups wherein his Nibs somehow gets the short end of the stick. *Angel on My Shoulder* not only turns on one of these traditional reversals—in return for agreeing to accompany him back to Gehenna and keeping mum about the sorry display of infernal managerial skills, Eddie extracts a promise that Nick will never again go near Barbara and the Judge—it is itself an example of a classic turnabout.

The screenplay (by Harry Segall and Roland Kibbee) was based on Segall's original story, which owed a great deal to that "Beat the Devil" sub-genre and not a little to *Here Comes Mr. Jordan*, an earlier fantasy dealing with angelic types—on shoulders, behind backs, and in your face—also written by Mr. Segall. (Fans of the 1941 Columbia motion picture [or purchasers of this book who have chosen to follow a chronological sequence when dealing with Mr. Rains' cinematic career] are already well aware that Robert Montgomery was put through *his* body-snatching paces by Rains back then.) Mindful of the rule on turnabout—and with the jingling of *Jordan*'s cash register still in his ear—Segall juggled those same elements and came up a winner once again.

For Paul Muni, it was the smell of *sulfur* that promised good fortune. One of the great character actors of the previous decade—and a true leading man by virtue of his box-office draw, if not his looks and sex appeal—Muni had felt his motion picture momentum shudder during the few years prior to *Angel*. The frenetic rhythm of the forties had relegated slow-moving historical biographies to the back-burner, and the infamous Muni temperament, which reportedly targeted Archie Mayo during production here, did nothing to slow the feeling that the master impersonator had become a luxury too costly to be affordable.

Nevertheless, while *Angel on His Shoulder* wasn't in the same league as most of Muni's earlier triumphs, neither could it be considered a comedown. It was (and remains) a good-spirited take on a popular theme and a sharp example of Muni's own propensity to lose his personality while "getting into" his roles. His performance as the bewildered gangster, albeit light years from his deadly serious Tony Camonte in *Scarface* (1932), is certainly as effective and is infinitely more animated.

In addition to appearing twice in motion pictures with Rains, Muni had supplanted his British colleague in the role of Wang Lung (which Rains had undertaken for the Theatre Guild back in 1932) in MGM's prestigious version of *The Good Earth* (1937). Rains, apparently, was never even up for consideration in the role he had created, but per the AFI Film Catalogue, Charles Boyer *was*. Go figure.

If Muni received the greater quantity of the witty script's beneficence, Rains still fell heir to many amusing situations and most of the quality lines. His Beelzebub is ever mindful that humanity's occasional opting for the good means additional hardship in the Pit. Explaining why the temperature has "fallen" to a chilly 180 degrees, the warden (Kurt Katch) informs his boss,

It's a labor shortage, Sire. Especially the boiler room personnel. There's been a fearful drop. We're operating at 73 percent of normal.

Wry humor is in evidence everywhere, and even when reveling in James Van Trees' atmospheric key lighting, Rains' Lucifer is no dour demon. He chortles at Eddie's desperate struggles against the overseers, is quick to grin maliciously at the least sign of triumph, and is quicker yet to atone for that grinning when the additional deceit suits him. *Variety* opined that "Rains shines as the Devil, shading the character with a likable puckishness good for both sympathy and chuckles."

Rains' Prince of Darkness is nothing if not compelling. Delivered in those persuasive tones of his, the requisite temptations sound as they should: logical, desirable, and totally satisfying. Before breaking free of his grasp, Eddie admits to Nick:

You got a way of puttin' things which makes sense, although inside me I know that I shouldn't follow your advice. But it's like you said: I'm only doing Barbara a favor, protecting her....

"Now you're beginning," Nick strokes, "to see straight and think clearly."

Smiley Williams just went out the window on his own. Eddie Kagle (Paul Muni) is innocent and there's not a damn thing the devilish Nick (Claude) can do about it. *Courtesy Richard Bojarski*

Later, Rains is given a little passage which is less colloquial and more along the lines of Boito's *Mefistofele*, or of Milton's Lucifer (or even of King David's query in Psalm 8), as he addresses his Adversary:

Must I run afoul of You again? Am I doomed forever to be vanquished? What has this sub-human creature, incubated and reeking of foulness, done to become Your favorite?

We're only given the one, quick peek at the eternal frustration and weariness of the Father of Lies, and Rains' delivery—done without benefit of the inspirational music which accompanies the others in *their* moments of truth—gives the Devil more than his due.

The film's title is derived from the sermon that Erskine Sanford's minister is concocting from Scripture and bits of personal inspiration. Like so many other messages of comfort or importance that find their way into pictures such as these, the reverend's is just what the doctor ordered. Referring to the Temptor as Mephistopheles (a name Rains' character had used in making his introductions with Eddie Kagle), the little minister counsels: "When he whispers in your ear, turn away your head and listen instead to the angel on your shoulder."

With Muni flirting with (but never quite succumbing to) caricature as the Damon Runyanesque mobster, Rains' Devil is all the more realistically human. While this is in part a testimony to the actor's acumen and talent, it's also due to a literary tradition which, in the sum total of its myriad forms, spans recorded history: for his unmitigated evil, the figure of Lucifer has always inspired fear in man; yet, at the same time, he has frequently evoked profound sympathy for his irrevocable loss of proximity to God. Playwrights, poets, novelists, filmmakers—and even some theologians—have cut the Dark One a little bit of dramatic slack.

Some years ago, novelist Jean Kerr titled one of her books of humorous stories after a comment made by one of her children. When her son came home from school one day, a bit depressed because he had been chosen to play Adam in the grammar school play about the Garden of Eden, the disconcerted Mrs. Kerr asked him point blank: "Why are you so sad? You have the lead." "I may have the lead," answered her son, "but the snake has all the lines."

*Angel on My Shoulder* United Artists. September 20, 1946. 95 minutes.

Paul Muni (Eddie Kagle); Anne Baxter (Barbara Foster); CLAUDE RAINS (Nick); Onslow Stevens (Dr. Higgins); George Cleveland (Albert); Hardie Albright (Smiley Williams); James Flavin (Bellamy); Erskine Sanford (Minister); Marion Martin (Rosie [Mrs. Bentley]); Jonathan Hale (Chairman); Murray Alper (Jim); Joan Blair (Brazen Girl); Fritz Leiber (Scientist); Kurt Katch (Warden); Sarah Padden (Agatha); Addison Richards (Big Harry); Ben Welden (Shaggsy); George Meeker (Mr. Bentley); Lee Shumway (Bailiff); Russ Whiteman (Intern); James Dundee, Mike Lally, Saul Gores, Duke Taylor (Gangsters); Chester Clute (Kramer); Edward Keane (Prison Yard Captain)

Producer: Charles R. Rogers; Director: Archie Mayo; Screenplay: Harry Segall and Roland Kibbee, based on an original story by Harry Segall; Director of Photography: James Van Trees; Musical Score: Dmitri Tiomkin; Editor: Asa Clark; Editing Supervisor: George Arthur; Art Director: Bernard Herzbrun; Special Effects: Harry Redmond, Jr.; Production Managers: David Sussman and William J. Fender; Associate Producer: David W. Siegel; Set Dresser: Edward G. Boyle; Sound: Frank Webster; Gowns: Maria Donovan; Men's Wardrobe: Robert Martien; Photographic Effects: Howard Anderson; Makeup: Ern Westmore

## *Deception* (1946)

Pianist Christine Radcliffe (Bette Davis) is ecstatic to learn that her erstwhile lover, cellist Karel Novak (Paul Henreid), had not succumbed to the ravages of World War II, but is performing right in New York City. Reunited at her apartment, both are anxious to resume their passionate relationship, but Karel is suspicious of the plush flat, its many expensive objets d'art, and the furs hanging in the closet. How could a poor music teacher afford to live in so luxurious a fashion?

Christine admits to having a rich patron, the renowned composer, Alexander Hollenius (Claude Rains), who, she claims, treats her as he does all his friends: extravagantly, yet arrogantly. Anxious to divert Karel from continuing this line of questioning, Christine proposes they be married at once. They are, but the festive air following the wedding is chilled by Hollenius' sudden arrival; he is clearly displeased by this turn of events. Visiting him the next morning, Christine begs him not to reveal their former romantic liaisons to Karel, whom she truly loves. Amused at this display of emotion, Hollenius agrees, and soon asks Karel to be the soloist at the world premiere of a newly composed cello concerto.

All is not well, however. Playing upon Karel's nerves, Hollenius soon renders him nearly incapable of performing well. Christine discovers that cellist Bertram Gribble (John Abbott) has been retained, and fears that the composer is prepared to replace Karel at the premiere. Visiting Hollenius just before the concert, she is told that he has decided to let her husband play the piece and then revel in his newfound celebrity for a few hours; shortly thereafter, some inkling of Christine's former relationship with the composer will "accidentally" slip into the conversation. Aghast, Christine shoots Hollenius and runs off to the concert hall.

After the performance, Christine reveals everything to Karel, who maintains that he will stand by his wife in her future tribulation.

While on the set of *Deception*, Claude was told there was something under the windshield of his new car. Horrified (he had just totaled his *old* car), the actor and director, Irving Rapper, were relieved—and apparently amused—by a practical joke. *Courtesy of the Jerry Fitzpatrick Collection*

If one counts his appearances in the British productions of *Daniel* (1921) and *The Love Habit* (1923), then Claude Rains was no stranger to the dramatic works of Louis Verneuil. Nor, in fact, was the French playwright a stranger to America. His play, *Jealousy*, had been adapted for the screen by Paramount in 1929, and had given Jeanne Eagels and Fredric March yet another good credit. Come 1946, the play was back again. Twice. As *Deception*, it had been hand-tailored for the screen and painstakingly reconfigured to fit Bette Davis. As *Obsession*, it had received a new translation and an updating, and was packing them in on Broadway.

The real challenge to screenwriters John Collier and Joseph Than was to take what was essentially a two-person play, expand the cast without losing the dynamic of the original, and still come up with a showcase for Davis. Because the egotistical Hollenius never appeared during the stage production, the character had to be fabricated from existing dialogue and the writers' fecund imagination. No one dreamt that the tyrannical composer, whose physical presence in the play was deemed superfluous to the drama's action, would become—in Claude Rains' hands—the most overwhelming persona in this wildly popular movie.

Paul Henreid was cast as Davis's husband,

and the actor's propensity to stare glumly when called upon to do anything other than laugh or cry may have facilitated the ease with which he was pushed into the dramatic shadows. An Austrian émigré, Henreid arrived in Hollywood via Britain in the early forties. His brand of cool, understated thesping won him an array of romantic leads while most of Tinseltown's heroic types were fighting the war. For many, the actor's underplaying indicated a narrow range, and his supposed ability to display a spectrum of subtle emotions with one, Sphinx-like glance smacked of the emperor's new clothes. Critic Richard Winnington spoke for the multitudes when, in reviewing 1946's *Of Human Bondage*, he observed that Henreid "looks as though his idea of fun would be to find a nice cold damp grave and sit in it."

Bette Davis was all for Henreid as her costar. For one thing, the couple, who had shown some real chemistry earlier in *Now, Voyager*, had become fast friends; for another, Henreid was the sort of actor Davis could eat alive if and when the opportunity presented itself. The actress was also initially thrilled with the project. She had always idolized Jeanne Eagels, so an opportunity to walk in her shoes would be a hoot. The pleasure didn't come easily, however. The actress was injured in a car crash during the first week of production, and was to feel the effects of the accident for years to come.[32] Pregnant, she was terrified that the impact might have in some way harmed the child she was carrying. Always the perfectionist, she was concerned also that a visible pregnancy would make the scripted melodramatics more tawdry to censor Joe Breen's eyes, or, worse, risible in the eyes of the audience. Arguments with Jack Warner over impending roles were followed at home by battles with Sherry (William Grant Sherry, her third husband, one of the few men in her life whom she could not dominate), and this, too, served to wear her down. Going 46 days over schedule, *Deception* was "a nightmare" for Bette Davis, "relieved only by Claude Rains' brilliantly exaggerated playing of the composer." Exaggerated?

With Joe Breen dyspeptic over the inconsistency of most plot details with the Production Code (Jeanne Eagels' steamy take on all this had been released the year before the Code became "law"), director Irving Rapper had his actors wring the requisite vice more from their delivery than from their dialogue. Pauses had to be more than pregnant and looks impossibly arch, if the meaning behind them was to be conveyed. (In her review in *PM* magazine, Cecilia Auger would gush, "It's like grand opera, only the people are thinner.") With the exception of Henreid, whose few excursions into heady emotion made one recall Dr. Jekyll's transformation into Mr. Hyde, the others of the triumvirate rose to the challenge and did their best to mine the craftily constructed script for its hidden wealth. This sort of thing was old hat to Davis; besides, having Verneuil's work reworked to highlight and reinforce *her* character's nature (to the total exclusion of her husband's) gave her an edge up even before shooting started. But Rains, saddled with a character just in from left field, had to pull out all the stops to hold his own.

In light of this, Davis' confession to biographer Whitney Stine reveals that Rains did more than just distract her from her "nightmare":

Claude Rains rightfully stole the picture. It was up to him to work against the dialogue and to make the audience understand, through his jealousy, that they had been having a hot affair, and that he was not just her piano teacher. He worked like ten men on that movie.[33]

Nor was Davis alone in her assessment of her old partner's theft. Bosley Crowther gave his *New York Times* readers a bit of background, before lowering the boom:

In the play, the man who is bumped off never appears on the stage. Miss Davis might have wished that in the film, too, he were kept more discreetly concealed. For the mephistophelian performance of Claude Rains in this villainous role makes her look completely childish and, from the viewpoint of logic, absurd. As a famous and worldly composer

**Director Irving Rapper is at Claude's arm, and Bette Davis is at his knee: Christine Radcliffe sup-
plicates herself before Alexander Hollenius.** *Courtesy Richard Bojarski*

with some vicious attachment to a dame, he fills
out a fascinating portrait of a titanic egoist. And
all of the cynical analysis which he so expres-
sively speaks on the subject of female behavior
strips Miss Davis' character of appeal.

(*The New York Times*, October 19, 1946)

Archer Winsten, in the same day's number of *New York Post*, also clucked in admiration:

Claude Rains, it must be admitted, goes to town
with his characterization of the high-living composer and genius. If you wish to call his flam-
boyant measures hammy, you must add that they
have quality, flavor and the so-called inner flame.

Had Rains' performance been judged
solely on the merits of his cocked eyebrow
and steely gaze, or of his running the gamut

from bitchy to bitchier, he might very well
been accused of playing not Alexander Hollenius but *Bette Davis*. In going his costars
one better, however, and creating a character of seamless cloth where before there had
been none, he had to bypass the traditional
actor's tricks and conjure up a monster whose
arrogance was rooted in genius, and whose
life's breath was drawn from the sighs and
whimpers of those around him. As steeped
in megalomania as the Invisible Man, as
vengeful a spirit of music as the Phantom of
the Opera, Hollenius is the third and, perhaps, the most terrifying of Rains' three
great grotesques. To throw Christine's world
into unimaginable chaos, to ring the chandelier down on the insecure Karel, the
scorned composer has only to tell the truth.
His flair for bedeviling each of his prey with

half- and near-truths, swaddled always in the wryest of expressions or the most dismissive of gestures, won for Rains superlative reviews.

The actor was especially proud of his work in the film's restaurant scene, as it required him to do more than merely give an edge to Collier and Than's lines:

> It was a scene involving innumerable nuances and innuendoes, delicate shading, subtleties, the whole made more difficult by the many "hand props" required—wine glasses, wine lists, a cigarette case, napkins. The principal burden was on Rains, in close-up, for six and one-half minutes and eight pages of virtual monologue…. Rains did it to perfection, in one take … the crewmen actually cheered. Bette kissed him, Rapper and Henreid pumped his hand.[34]

*Deception* was the final film of Rains' long-term contract with Warners. The picture has weathered the years well, primarily because it is so much larger than life that it defies being pigeon-holed into any one time frame. Even caught up in the drama, one still has a sense that the principals will shortly begin to posture and *sing* of love, honor, and betrayal to the Puccini-ish melodies of Erich Maria Korngold's sweeping score. It's that kind of picture. As film historian Clive Hirschhorn said—echoing the judgments of almost all the critics and commentators who preceded him—"It was Rains' film all the way."

*Deception* Warner Bros. Released October 26, 1946. 111 minutes.

Bette Davis (Christine Radcliffe); Paul Henreid (Karel Novak); CLAUDE RAINS (Alexander Hollenius); John Abbott (Bertram Gribble); Benson Fong (Jimmy, the Manservant); Louise Austin (Norma); Kenneth Hunter (Manager); Jean DeBriac (Andre); Philo McCullough, Gertrude Carr, Bess Flowers (Wedding Guests)

Producer: Henry Blanke; Director: Irving Rapper; Screenplay: John Collier, Joseph Than, based on the play, *Jealousy*, by Louis Verneuil; Director of Photography: Ernest Haller, ASC; Musical Score and Hollenius' Cello Concerto: Erich Maria Korngold; Music Director: Leo F. Forbstein;

Editor: Alan Crosland, Jr.; Sound: Dolph Thomas; Dialogue Director: Jack Daniels; Wardrobe: Bernard Newman; Director of Special Effects: William McGann; Special Effects: Edwin DuPar, ASC; Makeup: Perc Westmore

## *The Unsuspected* (1947)

While on the phone with Althea Keane (Audrey Totter), Roslyn Wright (Barbara Woodell), the secretary of Victor Grandison (Claude Rains), is strangled by her employer and left hanging above her desk; the physical evidence is carefully rearranged to suggest suicide. It is resolved that Roslyn had been much too curious about how Grandison, the writer and raconteur of a radio program of murder mysteries, had been tapping into the fortune of Matilda Frazier (Joan Caulfield), his ward, who had recently been lost at sea.

Arriving at the estate with bag and baggage is Steven Francis Howard (Michael North), who claims to be Matilda's husband. Although viewed with suspicion by Grandison, detective Richard Donovan (Fred Clark), and gal Friday, Jane Moynihan (Constance Bennett), North is allowed to stay on, especially after it is learned that Matilda has miraculously survived her catastrophe at sea and is, at that moment, on her way home.

Reunited with the members of the household (including Althea, who is Grandison's niece, and her husband Oliver Keane [Hurd Hatfield], who had once been Matilda's intended), Matilda is aghast over Roslyn's murder and bewildered over Howard's claims.

Matilda discovers that the mysterious young man had been *Roslyn's* fiancé, and that he is determined to bring Grandison—whom he suspects of the murder—to justice. Sensing that he's being maneuvered into a corner, Grandison shoots Althea, frames Oliver as the killer, and then disposes of him by cutting through the brake cables of the car he's using. Gradually, Howard wins Jane and Raymond Donovan to his side, and the three conspire to stop Grandison once and for all.

The murder expert has a few more aces to play, however. He instructs a thug to sap Howard and toss him into a trunk; the trunk is carted off to a junkyard, where it is to be burned. Under the pretense that she is helping him construct his latest script, Grandison has Matilda write a suicide note; moments later, he has drugged her champagne, planted the note next to her unconscious body, and left for his broadcast. The young woman is saved by the arrival of Donovan and the police, who bring her to her senses and then manage to free Howard from his makeshift coffin moments before it is set afire.

The group converges on the radio station, where Grandison, aware that his schemes have been uncovered, reveals to his listeners that he, himself, has been a murderer.

The three sets of hands that crafted *The Unsuspected* belonged to Charlotte Armstrong, who had penned the original story; Bess Meredyth, who adapted it for the screen; and Ranald MacDougall, who added dialogue and helped with the scenario. Nowhere is any debt to Otto Preminger's *Laura* (1944) acknowledged, but most ticket-buyers and virtually all the critics gave Otto his well-deserved thumbs-up. Easily as convoluted as any of the burgeoning number of films noir it accompanied to the theaters, *The Unsuspected* is probably more entertaining than most for the stylistic touches of Michael Curtiz and the suave underplaying of Claude Rains.

Rains flows along at his cool and calculating best, even when let down by puzzling inconsistencies in the screenplay. Very few other actors could have had their Victor Grandison—"renowned writer, art collector, and teller of strange tales" that he is—credibly evince an air of haughty self-assurance while simultaneously displaying an occupational incompetence that has the mystery fans in the audience shaking their heads in disbelief. Revealed as Roslyn's murderer right off the bat, Rains sustains his aura of superciliousness even when his exquisitely poor timing—he chokes the bejesus out of the supposed suicide while she's in mid-phone call—has those same viewers wincing. The cosmopolitan criminal is caught napping again later, as he stands unaware in front of an all-important clock in a photograph of the crime scene. Taken together with a distressing tendency to demonstrate his incriminating recording machine to just about every interested party, and his foolish leaving of Matilda on the divan, *underpoisoned*, these lapses might very well have necessitated the picture's being renamed *The Unsuited*, had anyone other than Rains played the killer.

Most of the major characters in the screenplay are painted with a roller, rather than a detail brush. (Exception: Fred Clark, doing a damn fine job in his movie debut.) Canny veteran Constance Cummings is given little room in which to convincingly bring her Jane Moynihan about a full 180 degrees; a photo and a couple of "What ifs?" are all it takes for her to bail out on the boss she has adored for years. Hurd Hatfield's Oliver may or may not have been a hopeless drunk before meeting Althea, but his one-note characterization adds nothing save a minor plot detail, and quickly grows tiresome.

Michael North, the recipient of an "And introducing..." billing up front, had been *Ed North* prior to *The Unsuspected* and disappeared, no matter what his name, soon after. His Steven Francis Howard is one grating son of a bitch, evidently unable to alter his tone, fully open his mouth, or display something other than a smarmy half-grin on his face. Althea will naturally make a play for him, as he wears trousers (Oliver: "I have no claims on Althea; she belongs to mankind"), but only the dreariest, most predictable of romantic traditions leads Matilda into his arms. Joan Caulfield, a victim of the derivative script, enacts Matilda as such a wide-eyed innocent that she might well have stumbled into the proceedings while en route to the set of *Rebecca of Sunnybrook Farm*.

Rains and Audrey Totter, too, are almost too broad to be real, but they differ from the others in that they are mirror images, and each complements and fills out the other. Totter had come to find a comfortable niche in noirish thrillers, where her gold-digging propensities and eye-popping figure usually led some poor schnook straight to perdition. Here, her motives are always and everywhere transparent, while Rains, of course, is the unsuspected. The shapely actress is always lit well, her assets (and her actions) solid, seductive, and readily apparent; the actor is frequently a shadow or a reflection during his more reprehensible moments. Totter is the flesh, Rains is the spirit; together, they are one, with identical goals (if disparate methods) Rains' several tête-à-têtes with Totter are the highlights of the film, and the interplay between the two leaves little doubt as to the genetic tie between uncle and niece. Only an overriding drive for self-preservation forces Victor to pull the trigger on dear Althea.

Victor: You and I were enjoying Matilda's money, weren't we? Now that she's come back, what do you suppose is going to happen to you?
Althea: You'll take care of me, Victor. You must have money hidden away; money Matilda could never trace.
Victor: You and Roslyn had one trait in common. You were both much too inquisitive.

Michael Curtiz had originally selected *The Unsuspected* back in 1945 as the first picture for his own production company. Per author James C. Robertson (*The Casablanca Man*), Orson Welles was Curtiz's first choice for Victor Grandison; only after the actor was declared unavailable, and both Jennifer Jones and Joan Fontaine took a bye on Matilda, did Rains and Joan Caulfield step into their shoes. The picture was Curtiz's first noir, and much of its success (some $875,000 in the black) was due to the director's capable hand, Anton Grot's splendid

sets, and Woody Bredell's rich photography. Still, the film has never been viewed as one of the great noirs, and, as quoted by Robertson, Curtiz apologized, stating "It looks as though I tried to make a great picture out of a story that wasn't basically a great story."[35]

*The Unsuspected* Warner Bros. Released October 11, 1947. 103 minutes.

Joan Caulfield (Matilda Frazier); CLAUDE RAINS (Victor Grandison); Audrey Totter (Althea Keane); Constance Bennett (Jane Moynihan); Hurd Hatfield (Oliver Keane); Michael North (Steven Francis Howard); Fred Clark (Richard Donovan); Jack Lambert (Press); Harry Lewis (Max); Ray Walker (Donovan's Assistant); Nana Bryant (Mrs. White); Walter Baldwin (Justice of the Peace); Barbara Woodell (Roslyn); Douglas Kennedy (Bill); Ross Ford (Irving); Art Gilmore (Announcer); David Leonard (Dr. Edelman)

Producer: Charles Hoffman; Director: Michael Curtiz; Screenplay: Bess Meredyth, Ranald MacDougall, based on *The Unsuspected* by Charlotte Armstrong; Director of Photography: Elwood Bredell, ASC; Musical Score: Franz Waxman; Musical Director: Leo F. Forbstein; Special Effects Photography: Robert Burks; Special Effects: David C. Kertesz (Curtiz), Harry Barndollar; Art Director: Anton Grot; Set Decorator: Howard Winterbottom; Costumes: Milo Anderson; Makeup: Perc Westmore

A Michael Curtiz Production

## *The Passionate Friends* (1949)

Mary Justin (Ann Todd) has married international banker Howard Justin (Claude Rains), but her heart is, and always has been, promised to Steven Stratton (Trevor Howard), a university biology instructor. While on holiday in Switzerland, Mary dreams of the week-long idyll that she and Steven had had some nine years earlier, unaware that, by chance, Steven is occupying the room adjoining her own.

During that fateful week, nearly a decade previously, Mary and Steven had met repeatedly in Howard's absence, and had come to the decision that she would seek a divorce. Neither of the passionate friends had counted on Howard's tenacity, however, and it was Steven who had departed the scene, while Mary had stayed on in the role of dutiful wife.

They meet accidentally over breakfast at the Swiss hotel, and each tells the other that he/she is now far happier than they had been in the past. Steven is in fact married, with two small children. He and Mary enjoy a speedboat jaunt around the lake, and then ride the cable car to the mountaintop, where they have lunch and reaffirm that life has been good to them both. Their return to the hotel is witnessed by Howard, who has arrived early from a business trip. The kiss the two friends share upon Steven's departure, the fact that they had had adjoining rooms, even the tears in Mary's eyes: Everything conspires to convince Howard that his wife has been unfaithful, and he sues for divorce.

Frantically, Mary tries to locate Steven, to inform him of the proceedings and to put his mind at ease. She discovers that he is arriving at Victoria Station, but is unable to communicate with him, as his wife is on hand. To Mary's horror, a solicitor serves Steven with the divorce papers, which name him as a correspondent; it is all the professor can do to calm his hysterical wife. The friends finally meet and say their goodbyes to each other. When her impromptu conversation with Howard sends him into a rage, Mary heads into the underground station, intending to throw herself under a train.

At the last moment, however, she is restrained by her husband, who, in love with her despite all, gently invites her back home with him.

*The Passionate Friends* had to be re-titled *One Woman's Story* before it could be considered fit for American consumption, but one can sit through the entire film—edified by its gentility, chagrined by its dramatic irony—without so much as once spying anything that remotely resembles passion. Rains' wry observation about the British being *sooo* very British was never so on-target as it is here. Ann Todd and Trevor Howard are *sooo* postured, *sooo* controlled, *sooo* understated, that when Rains occasionally raises his voice to bark "Get out!" to one or the other, it's unsettling and almost boorish. Flashbacks and flashbacks-within-flashbacks (Shades of *Passage to Marseilles*) add up to very little. A few kisses and a clinch or two make it through all the verbiage, but, somehow, one senses that they've been included in the proceedings only because one ought not to have a love story without them; they are demonstrations of acting technique, not moments of frenzied desire, and never are they for an instant credible. It ought not to be forgotten that when women in British movies goad their menfolk into "making love" to them, they're asking for words—not actions—and lots of clever, well-formulated words, at that. Presumably, at some point, these "friends" must have played house, but it's nearly impossible to envision them shutting up long enough to be caught in *flagrante delicto*.

Director David Lean thought so much of Ann Todd that he divorced his wife to marry her. (By 1954—alas!—the bloom was off the rose and they separated, to divorce three years later.) Regarded as the "British Garbo," the reserved blonde actress had joined the *Passionate Friends* cast right after having completed *The Paradine Case* for Alfred Hitchcock, whose own inclination toward reserved blond actresses has become the stuff of legend. It's tough, though, sitting through her wooden performance in *The Passionate Friends*, to discern the irresistible spark that bewitched David Lean, or the fascination which both Rains' and Trevor Howard's characters were supposed to have felt. Todd spends most of the picture staring wistfully off into space, straining for words that were never spoken, or recalling trysts that were really too dull for words[36]; save for the briefest of scenes on the Swiss hotel patio, her most animated expression is captured in a photo of her atop a piano.

**The one-sheet poster from the picture's original British release.**

In his later years, Trevor Howard acquired the sort of craggy face which had obviously weathered a lifetime, cried out character and maturity, and was not at all unpleasant to look at. During the early to mid-forties, however, he was as physically plain as a man could be yet still ended up time and again as the object of on-screen affection for the cream of Britain's beauties. This was most likely due either to the war, or to the lure of Hollywood, since both left the English cinema so bereft of romantic leads that nearly anyone who could wear an ascot with panache or quote obscure Romantic poets with conviction sooner or later found himself playing opposite Margaret Lockwood, Sally Grey, or Googie Withers (or Ann Todd).

One might argue that, despite all appearances to the contrary, Mary is not so superficial as to be attracted only by Steven's *(ahem)* virile good looks, but is drawn more to his (I don't know; I'm stumbling badly here) mind, or perhaps to his jolly good sense of humor – maybe to the way in which he prepares chicken for lunch or remembers even the salad dressing on Alpine picnics. It might just be their perfect chemistries; two supposed lovers wouldn't again indulge themselves in so much ponderous existential dialogue until Woody Allen and Diane Keaton in 1976's *Love and Death*. The problem is that, while English audiences at the end of the forties may have had little difficulty in looking between the lines to discover the passion these friends share, the contemporary viewer is overwhelmed by the sheer volume of those lines, and this might very well lead on to conclude that the driving desire underlying the relationship is for clever conversation.

In contrast to the two chatty lovebirds, whose flitting about thither and yon is meant to depict genuine human emotion, Rains' Howard Justin is supposed to strike one as less of an authentic person for being a businessman. He may be able to caress those English vowels as meticulously as Steven, but his vocation involves the making of money, not the study of life (Stratton is a biology teacher), so his philosophy might be just the slightest bit misguided and selfish. For most of the film, Howard *acts* only in the pursuit of his business interests; when confronted by emotional issues, he *reacts*, and his reactions give the picture the only real passion it has.

Rains has two grand scenes, each of which is head and shoulders above the dithering nonsense which brackets it, and both of which are the most memorable vignettes in the movie. In the first, he has discovered that Mary and Steven did not go to the theater as they had said, but—presumably—had sneaked off to indulge in some sort of forbidden behavior. When they return to the Justin house and Steven is invited in for a drink, Mary notices a program from the play they had not seen, lying in plain view on the coffee table. She now knows that Howard knows that they weren't at the theater, and she is forced to own up to the deception in order to end Howard's game of cat-and-mouse. Howard is clearly in control here, playing mind games and reveling in moral one-upmanship, and Rains keeps it arch and cool, almost purring "All sorts of strange ideas come into your head; you even think of killing," before thundering the first of those startling "Get outs!" Kevin Brownlow's biography of the director devotes a chapter to *The Passionate Friends* and reveals how David Lean worked with Rains at milking the scene for all its uncomfortable worth.[37]

The second scene is more of a brief tour-de-force, as Mary returns to plead for Steven with her husband. The mention of Stratton's name is a mistake, and Rains takes a step backward, as if physically struck, before hurling the vitriol:

I didn't expect love from you, or even great affection. I'd have been well satisfied with kindness and loyalty. You gave me love, kindness, loyalty.... But it was the love you'd give a dog, and the kindness you'd give a beggar, and the loyalty of a bad servant!... You were my wife and you made me hate and despise myself, and I don't want you anymore. Now get out!

The speech is powerful, if a tad too perfectly constructed and glib to be spontaneous, and Rains' delivery serves to open Todd's eyes past half-mast for one of the few times in the picture.

Crafted in the image of 1945's *Brief Encounter*, another tale of a couple's being more civilized than amorous, *Friends* suffered from lesser native wit; Noel Coward's *Still Life* had ignited the earlier picture, whereas H. G. Wells—never among the drollest or earthiest of writers—provided the source material here. Wells' novel was not easily tailored to the screen (as Maurice Elvey had discovered when directing Leslie Howard Gordon's adaptation for Stoll back in 1922), but the path was a little less thorny this time around,

as the screenwriters (Lean, Eric Ambler, and Stanley Haynes) opted to forego the book's extensive discourse on the Boer War. Nonetheless, there were all sorts of pre-production problems: Lean, who had signed on as producer, was forced to switch places with Ronald Neame, the original director; sets were budgeted, built, and razed; locations were scouted and found wanting. Brownlow's account of these difficulties in his biography of Lean makes for a much more enjoyable time than does a screening of *The Passionate Friends*.

Because times and mores have changed, this woman's story will try your patience rather than hold your attention. Of the three principals, only Howard Justin's behavior, perceptions, and reactions have kept their realistic edge in the half century that has passed since the film's initial release, and this is due, at least in part, to Claude Rains' having enacted the role with passion.

*The Passionate Friends* Pinewood/Cineguild. January 20, 1949. 91 minutes. US title: *One Woman's Story*; released by Universal-International in May 1949.

Ann Todd (Mary Justin); CLAUDE RAINS (Howard Justin); Trevor Howard (Steven Stratton); Isabel Dean (Pat); Betty Ann Davies (Miss Layton); Arthur Howard (Servant); Guido Lorraine (Hotel Manager); Marcel Poncin (Hall Porter); Wilfrid Hyde-White (Solicitor); Natasha Sokolova (Chambermaid); Helen Burls (Flowerwoman); Frances Waring (Charwoman); Wanda Rogerson (Bridge Guest); Jean Serrett (Emigration Official)

Producer: Ronald Neame; Director: David Lean; Screenplay: Eric Ambler; Adapted by David Lean, Stanley Haynes, based on the novel, *The Passionate Friends*, by H. G. Wells; Director of Photography: Guy Green; Camera Operator: Oswald Morris; Sets Designer: John Bryan; Editor: Geoffrey Foot; Costume Designer: Margaret Furse; Assistant Director: George Pollock; Associate Producer: Norman Spencer; Sound Recordists: Stanley Lambourne, Gordon K. McCallum; Dubbing Editor: Winston Ryder; Continuity: Margaret Sibley; Hair Dresser: Biddy Chrystal; Music: Richard Addinsell; Music

**While not quite *The Lady or the Tiger*, Ann Todd's choice of Trevor Howard is frankly mystifying.**
*The author's collection*

Played by the Philharmonica Orchestra of London, Conducted by Muir Matheson

Exterior Scenes photographed at Lac d'Annecy, Haute-Savoie, and the Chamonix-Mont Blanc districts of France.

A J. Arthur Rank Presentation

Distributed in the U.K. by General Film Distributors, Ltd.

## *Rope of Sand* (1949)

News that Mike Davis (Burt Lancaster) has returned to Diamantstad, South Africa, travels fast and pleases both police commandant Paul Vogel (Paul Henreid) and Colonial Diamond Company supervisor Fred Martingale (Claude Rains). Davis had

been caught and severely beaten by Vogel two years earlier, after a hunter Davis had been guiding had breached the company's posted "Prohibited Area." The hunter had died, but had first discovered a cache of diamonds; Davis had claimed that he had no knowledge of the gems' whereabouts. Since that time, he has been unable to find a job or leave the area, courtesy of Martingale's wide-ranging influence.

Martingale's standing offer—a normal life in exchange for the return of the diamonds—is tendered and refused. Vogel is all for beating it out of Davis; Martingale is more insidious and employs Suzanne Renaud (Corinne Calvet), a saucy number with a head for larceny, to seduce the ex-guide into leaking the gems' location. Davis is immune to Renaud's charms; Vogel is not, though, and falls hard for the working girl, going so far as to propose to her. Suzanne turns the commandant down, having meanwhile fallen hard for the seemingly oblivious Davis. Through subterfuge, Davis overpowers Vogel, steals a halftrack, and recovers the diamonds, leaving the commandant to his fate in the desert. Vogel is spotted near a police observation post and brought back to Diamantstad.

Infuriated, Vogel threatens to try both Dr. Hunter (Sam Jaffe), who had earlier treated Davis, and Suzanne. When he's taunted by Suzanne, Vogel lashes out and Hunter is accidentally killed; the evidence is arranged to frame Suzanne for the doctor's death. Safe in Angola, Davis is informed of Hunter's demise and Suzanne's peril by Toady (Peter Lorre), a philosophic drunkard. Davis returns to make Martingale a proposition: the girl for the diamonds. Martingale agrees and types out a letter exonerating Suzanne of Hunter's death; Vogel is made to sign the document at gunpoint. Surreptitiously, the mine executive slips a pistol to Vogel, but cries out in warning to Davis; Vogel is shot dead. Davis and Suzanne leave via steamboat the next day, love in their eyes and one of Martingale's jumbo diamonds— a going-away present—in their hands.

An interesting but overlong (at 104 minutes) programmer, *Rope of Sand* is hampered by some mediocre writing, a ghastly performance by Corinne Calvet, and a complete waste of the unique and always welcome Peter Lorre. The film's plusses include some splendid photography (the combined efforts of three crackerjack technicians), another moody score by Franz Waxman, Paul Henreid's sadistic Vogel—by turns, a stallion and a gelding—and one of the richest roles Claude Rains ever fell into in the latter part of his film career.

Nominal star Burt Lancaster is all right, but most of the awkward and/or impossible lines are thrown his way, and stuff like "If you ever tried to leave me, I'd follow you until I wore the earth smooth!" was made for silent movie title cards, anyway. Lancaster's knock down/drag out with Henreid is a highlight, nonetheless, and his overcoming the cowardly commandant's streetfighting tactics—Vogel tries everything from boots in the groin to sand in the eyes and then takes a run at the poor bastard with the halftrack—must have had the audiences on their feet more than once.

Paramount's tale of diamonds and deserts marked Corinne Calvet's American movie debut, and it was fortunate that *la jeune fille* was as statuesque as she was. Granted, she was hacking her way through some not very classic dialogue in a second language, but there are moments when—given both her pronounced accent and her nasal delivery— she sounds remarkably like Madeline Kahn as Lili Von Shtupp in Mel Brooks' *Blazing Saddles* (1974). Calvet's superstructure saw her through a string of decent enough films, mainly in the fifties, when aerodynamically impressive starlets were "introduced" and then shoveled under in record numbers.

Peter Lorre followed up *Rope of Sand* with about two dozen more film appearances, most of which were lengthier and less forgettable than this one. Part philosopher, part con man, part drunk, his Toady is all unnecessary contrivance, and there's very little doubt that the role was written expressly to add the Lorre name to the already potent marquee value.

This was Paul Henreid's fourth picture with Rains, and the veteran Austrian was at last out of Bette Davis' shadow, Humphrey Bogart's shadow, and ... well, Claude Rains' shadow, and allowed to be a genuine, 14-karat SOB in his own right. Commandant Vogel is a sadist, a coward, a woman beater, a dirty fighter, a liar, a cheater at cards, and a hell of an interior decorator. It's implied that he's an ex–Nazi: He has profited by the suffering of war victims and brags of the unfortunate circumstances which befell the elderly French (read: Jewish) owner of the antique vase he now holds. He does his best work in front of a gaggle of police goons or behind a gun, and yet, for all the volume of

BURT LANCASTER
·
PAUL HENREID
·
CLAUDE RAINS
·
PETER LORRE

in HAL WALLIS' Production **ROPE of SAND**

· SAM JAFFE   *and introducing* **CORINNE CALVET** · Directed by WILLIAM DIETERLE · Story and Screenplay by Walter Doniger · Additional Dialogue by John Paxton · A Paramount Picture

If looks could kill, Paul Henreid wouldn't need that gun. Corinne Calvet is in the clinches with Burt Lancaster, and Claude—standing on a least *three* boxes—finds the whole thing droll.

characterization, Vogel isn't given a single memorable thing to say that isn't countered, ignored, or topped by someone else. Be that as it may, the police commandant is quite a departure from the strong, silent, victimized types Henreid had made his own during and just after the war.

For Rains, the Fred Martingale role must have been as impishly delightful as is the experience of *watching* Fred Martingale; Rains' eyebrow hadn't been kept so busy in years. The mining company executive is a well-situated cad for whom honesty and deceit are cards to be carefully played if the game is to remain amusing. He takes Suzanne onboard—considering her brazen ploy to extort money from him as a successful job interview—at a promised £500 merely to get a certain man to answer a certain question:

"'Michael, darling, where are the diamonds?' In your own sweet way, of course."

Rather than a mere hypocrite, Martingale is a creature of contrasts. He is at once amused and annoyed by Davis's return. He speaks up for Vogel, urges others at the club to vote him membership, and then blackballs the commandant himself. Asked by the headwaiter to entertain Mlle. Renaud in a colleague's absence, he rejoins "Jacques, I'm indebted to you … or I may never forgive you." He sneaks Vogel a pistol one moment, while yelling a warning to Davis the next. Martingale is never so happy as when Vogel or Davis is thrown off balance by the latest turn of events. "You know," he grins to Suzanne, "my fondest hope was that you'd find the diamonds. But this? Set each of them against the other? The memory of it will warm me in my old age."

Martingale clearly enjoys the power plays he and Suzanne engineer, and one finds facets of other of Rains' heavies in him. He is tempter (a la *Angel on My Shoulder*), throwing woman in the path of man so as to complicate the game. He is industrial executive, mindful of the whims of his peers and superiors (a la *Notorious*). He is international rapscallion, given to spreading his web locally and across adjacent borders (presaging *Lisbon*). He revels in his authority, and smirks at the idea of a challenge to it, yet still cuts off at the knees any serious attempt to undermine it. When Vogel takes a notion to complain about Martingale's obstruction of his every move, the company point man spits venom:

Vogel: If you don't stop your constant interference, I'll take the whole story to your directors…

Martingale: If [Davis]'s not released in five minutes, I'll have a story of my own to tell in every club in South Africa. A story of how a Capetown trollop made such a complete and utter fool of our poor Vogel that he proposed to her and was rejected. A French tramp, who looked like a lady…

Director William Dieterle has Charles Lang shoot most of Rains' exchanges in two-shots or close-ups, aware that talking heads sequences would capture every subtle move of the actor's expressive face. Afforded equal screen space with the romantic principals much of the time and even relegated frequently to the foreground, Rains is thus given carte blanche to steal every camera set-up from Lancaster, Calvet, and/or Henreid, and steal them he does. Never has a Rains scoundrel smiled so often or so winningly. Honesty couldn't find a smoother surface from which to slip, yet Martingale is the first to confess disappointment in his fellow man: "I never know what to think anymore; I'm being completely disillusioned. Has money completely lost its power? Is everyone motivated now by love?"

Rains won considerable praise for his "artfully sinister" director, and the role has to

be numbered among the very best of his lesser known appearances. *Rope of Sand* is uneven, but much of its drive and stability comes from the "nifty performance of the effete head of the syndicate" (*Variety*'s words) of Claude Rains.

**Rope of Sand** Paramount. Released September 23, 1949. 104 minutes.

Burt Lancaster (Mike Davis); Paul Henreid (Paul Vogel); CLAUDE RAINS (Arthur Martingale); Corinne Calvet (Suzanne Renaud); Peter Lorre (Toady); Sam Jaffe (Dr. Francis Hunter); John Bromfield (Thompson); Mike Mazurki (Pierson); Kenny Washington (John); Edmund Breon (Chairman); Hayden Rorke (Ingram); David Hoffman (Waiter); Georges Renavent (Jacques, the Headwaiter); David Thursby (Henry, the Bartender); James R. Scott (Clerk); Josef Marais and Miranda (Specialty Singers)

Producer: Hal B. Wallis; Director: William Dieterle; Screenplay and Original Story: Walter Doniger; Additional Dialogue: John Paxton; Director of Photography: Charles B. Lang, ASC; Special Effects: Gordon Jennings, ASC; Process Photography: Farciot Eduoart, ASC; Editorial Supervisor: Warren Low; Sound Recording: Harold Lewis, Walter Oberst; Music: Franz Waxman; Music and Lyrics to "The Zulu Warrior" and "The Crickets": Josef Marais; Art Directors: Hans Dreier, Franz Bachelin; Set Decorators: Sam Comer, Grace Gregory; Assistant Director: Richard McWhorter; Costumes: Edith Head; Makeup: Wally Westmore

# *Song of Surrender* (1949)

Somewhere in 1906 New England, village elder Elisha Hunt (Claude Rains) is curator of the General Tyler Winthrop museum. Hunt's child wife Abigail (Wanda Hendrix) is content with their rather simple existence until New York lawyer, Bruce Eldridge (Macdonald Carey), a gramophone, and a fistful of Enrico Caruso 78s intrude into her life. Abigail is captivated by the music and attracted to Bruce.

Eldridge and his fiancée, Phyllis Cantwell (Andrea King), have bought Elisha's old family home, and are making a less than good impression on the locals with their raucous, big city ways. What's more, Elisha, Deacon Perry (Henry Hull), and just about everyone in town regards music as the devil's tool. Told to dispose of the gramophone, Abigail hides it in a nearby cave and plays the records at night when Elisha is off at meetings. When her husband is out of town for an extended spell, Abigail heads off for a night on the town with Bruce—going so far as to don a borrowed ball gown and enjoy a glass of wine.

When Bruce returns to New York, Abigail settles down again with Elisha, whom she has persuaded not to destroy the "music box." A parcel from Bruce arrives, containing a copy of Caruso's *O Sole Mio*, a replacement for the record he has accidentally broken. Confronted by Elisha, Abigail confesses to playing the gramophone, meeting with Eldridge, and dancing in a place where there was music. The next day, after Elisha denounces her from the church pulpit, Abigail heads to New York and Bruce's arms.

Bruce insists they return to New England to make a formal break with Elisha, but when they do, they find that he has fallen victim to a stroke. Abigail stays on with her husband, and the couple enjoys a certain happiness together despite his infirmity. Come spring, Elisha dies suddenly, and, soon thereafter, the valley is filled with music once again, as Bruce (and gramophone) come back to claim Abigail.

From the number of composers, singers, and arias cited in the credits, you would think that *Song of Surrender* was a musical revolving around the life of Enrico Caruso, rather than the tale of a backward young girl finding fulfillment as a woman, armed only with a Victrola and selections from the standard tenor repertoire. (Don't complain: what would you have made of *Abigail, Dear Heart*, the film's working title?) Of course, the night air is also filled with romantic blather, but you've heard that sort of thing before, and you've heard it better, too. More disappointing

than the dreary predictability of the love triangle at hand is the realization that the music is only incidental to the tale. A few bars from each of those 78s and a couple of brief snatches of background melody, and that's all she wrote, unless you count Buddy Clark's crooning his way through the sappy title song; the rest of the movie hasn't so much as a chirping bird or a lowing cow to offset long stretches of total silence.

Special effects director Gordon Jennings might well have conjured up a grand old northeaster, replete with thunderheads and howling winds, to bolster Rains' condemnation of his wife and to shake his little church to its foundations in righteous indignation. He didn't. Hell's bells, Claude could have snarled that, with God's own music sounding throughout the valley, there was no need for any lesser kind; viewers with a taste for overt symbolism would doubtless have broken into a sweat. They didn't. As it stands, the soundtrack is absolutely lousy with silence; not the kind of silence that makes you feel for Miss Hendrix and her desperate need for a little *joie de vivre* in her otherwise dreary existence, but the kind that makes you look at your watch and wonder what you should do for dinner.

*Song of Surrender* is not only grounded in another era, it feels as if it had been *made* in another era—back during those several awkward years which bridged silent films and "100 percent talkies," perhaps. Like the part sound features of the late twenties, the picture is totally studio-bound, and not because of any inherent difficulties with embryonic sound technology (although it certainly plays as if synchronized recording was still problematic). Rather, because this is a little black-and-white programmer, meant to fill some space on a women's double-bill, and the choice between going with standing sets and springing for location shooting is an economic no-brainer.

*Variety* felt that director Mitchell Leisen drew "bright bits of business for supporting players," but, apart from Art Smith's Mr. Willis and Ray Walker's nameless auctioneer, the whole town and everyone in it wallows in shadow and gloom. Well, not quite everyone; Henry Hull, whose Deacon Parry is supposed to be the village poster boy for obstinacy and garrulousness, instead comes across as a cute old cuss, his "Ehh-yupps" puncturing the solemnity in which just about every event thereabouts is draped.

If the community is straight out of Nathaniel Hawthorne (and it is), is Abigail just another Hester Prynne knock-off, made to wear a scarlet RCA on her bodice? How in blazes did she end up with this gaggle of antique puritans to begin with? Almost everyone she consorts with is either over 60 years old, under 12, or has the personality of a plague out of Exodus; no wonder she's enticed away from the aches and pains of virtue by a drip like Bruce Eldridge, who, siren-like, lures her onto the rocks of beauty and the good life via some rather pedestrian translations of opera libretti.

Both Macdonald Carey and Wanda Hendrix enjoyed lengthy careers in undistinguished B films, and Carey—who was said to have grown sexier as he grew older—ended up in a couple of TV series in the fifties before becoming a fixture on the long-running soap, *The Days of Our Lives*; he died late in 1997. Gruff old Henry Hull appeared on-screen in everything from Charles Dickens to Eugene O'Neill, and in support of everyone from Valerie Hobson to Jayne Mansfield. He does admirably as Parry, sculpting through performance alone a dimension to the character that doesn't exist in the screenplay. Hull is Rains' only rival for the acting honors, and watching the old thesps chew up the scripted dross and spit out gold is one of the picture's very few pleasures. Only God knows what Eva Gabor is doing putzing around as the "Countess" Marina.

Rains is properly austere throughout the film, drawing his mouth into an immobile slit which speaks volumes, and exuding a coldness with his eyes that rivals the chilliest look Alexander Hollenius gave Charlotte Radcliffe at any point in *Deception*. Ad-

mittedly, the role is one dimensional; Elisha is elderly (but not so elderly as to fail to comment on Abigail's sudden frigidity) and fixated (on history, God, and General Tyler Winthrop, all of which appear to be interchangeable). He displays little humor, evinces less tolerance, and, ultimately, shows no compassion for his wife or her needs. Still, Rains is given a couple of shots at being a sport, wherein he gets to reveal that the forbidding old curator *does* have a heart, even if you have to blast for it.

Apart from his long-term Warner Bros. contract, Rains spent most of his career in film free-lancing, picking and choosing among projects which interested him artistically, or, on rare occasion, moved him financially. In the course of some 30 plus years, he had ventured onto the Paramount lot infrequently, much as he had over at Universal or RKO. *Song of Surrender* had little to offer artistically or financially, but it meant work for the aging actor, and work was Claude Rains' life's blood. Most reviews were casual—the film eliciting a response as mild as its drama—and it's doubtful whether Rains received another offer as a direct consequence of his appearance here. Suffice it to say, Paramount did not call again.

*Song of Surrender* Paramount. October 28, 1949. 93 minutes.

Wanda Hendrix (Abigail Hunt); CLAUDE RAINS (Elisha Hunt); Macdonald Carey (Bruce Eldridge); Andrea King (Phyliss Cantwell); Henry Hull (Deacon Parry); Elizabeth Patterson (Mrs. Beecham); Art Smith (Mr. Willis); Eva Gabor (Countess Marina); John Beal (Dubois); Dan Tobin (Clyde Atherton); Nicholas Joy (General Seckle); Peter Miles (Simon Beecham); Ray Walker (Auctioneer); Gigi Perreau (Faith Beecham); Ray Bennett (Mr. Beecham); Clancy Cooper (Mr. Torrance); Georgia Backus (Mrs. Parry)

Producer: Richard Maibaum; Director: Mitchell Leisen; Screenplay: Richard Maibaum, based on a story by Ruth McKenney and Richard Bransten; Director of Photography: Daniel L. Fapp, ASC; Art Directors: Hans Dreier, Henry

**If you don't laugh, you'll cry.** Claude in a gag shot which spoofs his role, the film's title, and its underlying theme. *Courtesy Jessica Rains*

Bumstead; Dialogue Director: Phyllis Loughton; Editor: Alma Macrorie; Assistant Director: John Coonan; Special Photographic Effects: Gordon Jennings, ASC; Process Photography: Farquot Edouart, ASC; Makeup Supervisor: Wally Westmore; Sound Recording: John McKay, John Cope; Song (*Song of Surrender*): Music: Victor Young, Lyrics: Jay Livingston, Ray Evans; Sung by Buddy Clark; *Serenade* by Schubert: Sung by Richard Tucker; *Una Furtiva Lagrima, O Sole Mio, O Paradiso, La Donna É Mobile*: from the Enrico Caruso recordings of RCA Victor; Music Score: Victor Young; Costumes: Mary Kay Dodson

A Mitchell Leisen Production

## *The White Tower* (1950)

Some time after her father had been killed attempting to climb the White Tower—a "virgin" peak in the Swiss Alps—Carla Alton (Alida Valli) returns to the village of Kandermatt to try her hand at it. After the occupants of the inn give the matter some thought, Carla is joined by Nicholas Radcliffe (Sir Cedric Hardwicke), Herr Hein (Lloyd Bridges), Paul Delambre (Claude Rains), and Martin Ordway (Glenn Ford). The group will be led by Andreas (Oscar Homolka), a local guide.

As they make their way up the mountainside, each person realizes that the climb has personal meaning. Hein, an ex-Nazi officer, is determined to prove that his still is the Master Race, and that the Germans are born conquerors. Radcliffe feels the need to prove to himself that he is not too old to appreciate the beauties and trials of nature. Delambre, a heavy drinker and a failed writer, sees this as the impetus to have him finish his book and thus win some sort of approval from his overly critical spouse, who scarcely bothers to look up from her knitting to spit in his eye. Carla, of course, must conquer the mountain to vindicate her father's death, and Ordway, an easygoing American, initially agrees to go along to get to know the beauteous Carla.

Less than halfway up, Radcliffe finds himself too weary to continue and camps out, waiting for everyone's return from the top. Soon Delambre, aware that he, too, cannot go on further, polishes off a liter of brandy and bids the others climb on without him. As the rest of the party ascends into a snowstorm, the Frenchman finishes his book (along with another bottle of brandy) and, inadvertently setting his tent afire, wanders off into the storm and oblivion.

Because Andreas continually climbs and descends the White Tower in an effort to keep track of the stragglers, Hein becomes impatient and makes for the top on his own. Carla, knowing that the freshly fallen snow is treacherous, warns Martin to wait another day, but the American, goaded by the ex-Nazi's taunts, follows Hein's footsteps upward. Near the summit, the German and American confront each other and Hein, too proud to accept the help that is offered, plunges to his death. Martin, now snowblind, is rescued by Andreas and Carla, who has come to realize that her feelings for Martin are much more important than her personal quest to beat the White Tower.

*The White Tower* was meant to be a topshelf production all the way for RKO, the smallest of the majors, but a monkey wrench or two managed to insinuate itself into the works. The assignment initially fell to producer Adrian Scott and director Edward Dmytryk, and this was a plus; the men had scored notable successes as a team with *Murder My Sweet* (1944) and *Crossfire* (1947), and, as individuals, hadn't done too shabbily, either. Unfortunately, both fell victim to Joe McCarthy's anti-Communist witch-hunt, and Sid Rogell and Ted Tetzlaff were eased into their empty shoes. Undeniably experienced, efficient, and prolific, neither replacement could muster the skills of his predecessors, and the production suffered.

Then, too, while James Ramsey Ullman's eponymous bestseller had successfully blended exciting action sequences with penetrating insights into the principals' hearts and minds,

Paul Jarrico's screenplay is undone by background plates, studio inserts, and at least one bona fide, dyed in the wool stereotype. For all their supposed nobility, the mountaineers' philosophies, values, and ideals are strictly black and white. Life's circuitous paths and the White Tower's treacherous crags may be mastered by keeping your nose clean, staying in shape, and trusting in your fellow man; fail to do so, and you're lucky not to end up on the wrong side of the snow. In the finished film, virtue is its own reward, and only the palpably inconsequential or villainous fail to make it to the wrap. Bridges' Hein (rhymes with swine) is overwhelmed by nature at her purest (all that wonderful white imagery), despite his *Übermensch* arrogance and enviable physique. Rains' Delambre is such a milquetoast that his wife's reaction to his presumed demise goes unfilmed; more tellingly, it goes unmissed.

Problems extended even to the casting of one of the available Alps as the White Tower; few of the peaks on the Swiss side of the property could be considered unspoiled. In fact, Switzerland had gone so far as to file a formal complaint that the legions of mountain climbers who were constantly roaming the ranges were fouling them with abandoned equipment, refuse, and human excrement. Mont Blanc in the *French* Alps filled in nicely for the virgin expanse, while most of the lower-lying natural wonders—and the mountainous panoramas—were lensed on Swiss acreage. Professional climbers may be seen in the long shots, stunt persons in the medium shots, and the actors themselves in the inserts.

Even with the best laid plans going agley, *The White Tower* is a fine entertainment, full of splendid location photography and well crafted performances of less-well-written roles. Lovely Alida Valli, who had made her cinematic debut in the Italian *I Due Sergenti* (*The Two Sergeants*) when she was only 15 years old, is still as wholesomely beautiful a gal as gosh-o'-golly American Glenn Ford could ask for. The Canadian-born Ford

positively glows, he's so personable throughout the film; this is a far cry from the cranky determination he would personify later in his career. Bridges, of course, was to show off his manly frame every week on TV's *Sea Hunt* in the latter part of the decade, and would go on to be so popular with audiences, would be considered so forthright, honest, and sincere, that the idea of casting him as a heavy became nearly as sacrilegious as the idea of having Jimmy Stewart take the fall in any of *his* pictures.

This was the first of the three films Rains committed to at RKO, and while he had more on his plate here than he would have in *Where Danger Lives*, he was probably still hungry after his scenes were finished. Apart from taking part in some brief introductions—over and done with before Valli can even doff her tam—Rains' ground-level footage pretty much boils down to his waxing philosophically about writers' block while sucking on a bottle of Jägermeister. While en route to the mountaintop (or the mountain middle, or however far he makes it, precisely), he grouses with Cedric Hardwicke (the two being perceived by the other climbers *and* the audience as being of a sufficient vintage as to preclude the successful completion of any physical activity), mouths a couple of fairly ambiguous (but supposedly profound) dicta, and ingests a king-size bottle of brandy.

As the climbers are supposed to be a microcosm of post-war Europe (we're lacking only a few minutes detour into the *Italian* Alps to account for everybody), Rains gets to be the Frenchman, although Paul Jarrico's screenplay doesn't move the idea much past the name Delambre. Also shoddily handled and left hanging like so many inept rappellers is the dubious relationship enjoyed by Rains and June Clayworth (as Mme. Astrid Delambre, emasculator of men and powerhouse knitter). Delambre's motivation for making the climb is likewise uncertain; he might just as well be anxious to get the hell away from Astrid as he is to be off in search of peace and fulfillment. Rains crams world-weary resignation into every one of his lines, but, without some kind of solid exposition giving them support, the lines don't mean much. Nor is there any resolution: In the picture's rush to put Ford and Valli on the train to happiness, nary a word nor a frame is squandered on determining whether the nouveau widow might actually be aggrieved enough to drop a stitch.

An unnecessary scripted slight has Valli refer to Rains as "the little man with the whiskers," the first disparaging cinematic reference to the actor's height in well over a decade.

The critics were pretty much satisfied that *The White Tower* wasn't the absolute worst way imaginable to spend an evening, and audiences—drawn as much by Technicolor wizardry as by drama—spent enough money to satisfy Howard Hughes' bean-counters. Bosley Crowther, who never much liked anything, didn't much like this, either, but he *did* give the three younger principals a clean bill of health. As for the veterans,

Claude Rains, as a garrulous weakling, is something of a bore, Sir Cedric Hardwicke, as another, is pathetic and Oscar Homolka, as the guide, is staunch.

(*The New York Times*, July 3, 1950)

Can't get much better than that, can you?

*The White Tower* RKO Released June 24, 1950. 98 minutes.

Glenn Ford (Martin Ordway); [Alida] Valli (Carla Alton); CLAUDE RAINS (Paul Delambre); Oscar Homolka (Andreas); Sir Cedric Hardwicke (Nicholas Radcliffe); Lloyd Bridges (Hein); June Clayworth (Astrid Delambre); Lotte Stein (Frau Andreas); Fred Essler (Knubel); Edit Angold (Frau Knubel)

Producer: Sid Rogell; Director: Ted Tetzlaff; Screenplay: Paul Jarrico, based on the novel, *The White Tower*, by James Ramsay Ullman; Director of Photography: Ray Rennahan, ASC; Associate Photographer: Tony Braun; Technicolor Color Consultant: Morgan Padelford; Special Effects: Harold Wellman; Music: Roy Webb; Musical Director: Constantine Bakaleinikoff; Film Editor:

The writer Delambre, dismissed by his wife and bereft of inspiration. The White Tower brings sweet oblivion.

Samuel E. Beetley; Sound: Roland Van Hessen, Clem Portman; Set Decorators: Darrell Silvera, Harley Miller; Art Directors: Albert S. D'Agostino, Ralph Berger; Hair Styles: Larry Germain

## *Where Danger Lives* (1950)

Enchanted by Margo Lannington's beauty and slightly in his cups, Dr. Jeff Cameron (Robert Mitchum) seeks out Mr. Lannington (Claude Rains) and asks for his daughter's hand in marriage. Jeff discovers that Margo (Faith Domergue) is the old man's wife, not his daughter, but the row that follows prevents his heeding Lannington's warning: There is something wrong with Margo. The fight leaves Lannington dead and Jeff dazed and injured; rather than call the police, the couple flee.

Assuming they will be charged with murder, Jeff and Margo drive to Mexico. Jeff is in considerable pain and drifts in and out of consciousness; he realizes that he has suffered a concussion and may fall into a coma. Still, he does most of the diving, both before and after they have traded Margo's high-profile car for an old truck. Jeff collides with a car whose driver turns out to be drunk; Jeff pays him off and he and Margo resume their journey, having learned via a radio that Lannington's body has been found and that they are wanted.

While in Postville, Arizona, Jeff and Margo are taken into custody for not participating in a local charitable celebration, and they look to avoid paying the $25 fine (Jeff gave most of their cash to the drunk driver) by claiming they're saving their money to be married. The townspeople insist that they marry that evening and provide the ceremony and a bridal suite. Margo (not Jeff) listens to a radio report which reveals that she has been undergoing considerable psychiatric treatment for mental illness. Margo had killed Lannington, smothering him with a pillow while Jeff had tended to his own wounds in the bathroom.

At Nogales, Margo pawns a diamond bracelet to buy their way into Mexico. Jeff, feeling the onset of paralysis, refuses to accompany Margo when she tells him that she has stashed thousands of dollars of Lannington's money in a Mexico City bank for just this sort of emergency. Jeff falls unconscious, and Margo smothers him with a pillow before joining the van for the trip across the border. Somehow, Jeff recovers and, although semi-paralyzed, makes it to the border-crossing point where a panicked Margo shoots him; Margo is then shot by the police, and her dying confession absolves Jeff. Later, while recovering in the hospital, Jeff asks to send a white rose to his old flame, Julie (Margaret O'Sullivan), but discovers that she is already in the building ready to care for him.

Somewhere between constructing the Spruce Goose and degenerating into the surreally picturesque hermit who would live out his days in a germ-free penthouse-cocoon high atop Las Vegas, Howard Hughes entertained a passion for Faith Domergue, a dark sultry actress as achingly beautiful as she was talentless. Hughes, who from 1948 to 1953 would buy, control, divest, and reacquire financial control of RKO Pictures, determined that her playing opposite he-man Robert Mitchum in a trendy yet inexpensive film noir would be just the ticket to propel the shapely starlet—being actively groomed as the "new Jane Russell"—into the cinematic stratosphere. Adding name value and weight to the whole shebang would be Claude Rains, just recently signed to a three picture contract with the troubled studio. (Part two of the Domergue campaign included releasing *Vendetta*, a period drama made by Hughes' production team prior to his snatching up controlling interests in RKO, while the furor over *Where Danger Lives* was at its height.)

Alas, there was no furor. Few moviegoers shared Hughes' enthusiasm for the lovely Ms. Domergue, and, with the screen awash with comely, statuesque young damsels, the hoped-for deluge of slavering male ticket-buyers never materialized. When Hughes finally departed the studio in 1953, Domergue went likewise, her last RKO feature, *This Is My Love*—a soap opera enlivened by the presence of Linda Darnell, as ravishing as Domergue and thrice as capable—hitting neighborhood screens early the following year.

*Where Danger Lives* had started life as Leo Rosten's novella, *White Rose for Julie*, and it took an appreciable amount of interference on Howard Hughes' part to relegate Julie and roses to a lower shelf. The film fit perfectly into the path Mitchum's career was then following, though. The big guy had first appeared in *Hoppy Serves a Writ* back in 1943, and a spate of westerns was followed by an equally concentrated series of war films. Noirs picked up the slack after the war was won, and these, released in tandem with a full spectrum of adventure films, kept the actor busy and his fans ecstatic. In spite of the brouhaha over Hughes' latest female discovery, *Where Danger Lives* was just another job to Mitchum, whose on-screen personas normally mirrored his off-screen personality: easygoing, open to anything, and not a little cynical. To his credit, the sleepy-eyed leading man does more than Faith Domergue to keep Margo appear intriguing, while avoiding the easy refuge of somnambulism with regard to his own character.

This was the second of the three pictures Rains contracted to appear in for RKO, and by far the least. Lannington barely lasts six minutes before Margo dispatches him (off screen) with her pillow, and Rains is given no time and less material with which to work to afford the cuckolded husband anything more than one dimension. His only scene bears more than a casual resemblance to similar circumstances found in *The Passionate Friends*, and his talking *around* Margo's fatal flaw ("You want her? You can have her, only first I think you should know what you're getting.")—alluding to without once articulating it—makes more for melodrama than for realism. Any of RKO's contract players (and there weren't many of them at this point, given the studio's Hughes-sanctioned tendency to purchase films for release, rather than to produce them in-house) could have filled the undemanding bill as well as the veteran character man. What Rains' brief presence brought, however, was an aura of legitimacy to the picture and a name that could be relied upon to lure patrons into the theater. He confessed to the *Los Angeles Times* (June 18, 1950) that "I wasn't ready to accept that engagement at the outset, but John Farrow persuaded me that the role could be adjusted satisfactorily."

Bosley Crowther observed that "Claude Rains throws a quick sneer as [the] husband before he is thoroughly done in," and none of the other mainstream critics could find much fuel for their fires. The scant mention the film receives nowadays almost inevitably comes in conjunction with the revelation that director Farrow was both husband to Maureen O'Sullivan and father to Mia.

**Mr. Lannington means business.** *Courtesy Susan Duic*

*Where Danger Lives* RKO. July 8, 1950. 82 minutes.

Robert Mitchum (Dr. Jeff Cameron); Faith Domergue (Margo Lannington); CLAUDE RAINS (Frederick Lannington); Maureen O'Sullivan (Julie); Charles Kemper (Police Chief); Ralph Dumke (Klauber); Billy House (Mr. Bogardus); Harry Shannon (Dr. Maynard); Philip Van Zandt (Milo DeLong); Jack Kelly (Dr. Mullenbach); Lillian West (Mrs. Bogardus); Ruth Lewis (Nurse Collins); Julia Faye (Nurse Seymour); Dorothy Abbott (Nurse Clark); Lester Dorr (Asst. Police Chief); Art Depuis (Intern)

Producer: Irving Cummings, Jr.; Director: John Farrow; Screenplay: Charles Bennett, based on the Story, "White Rose for Julie," by Leo Rosten; Director of Photography: Nicholas Musuraca; Music Score: Roy Webb; Musical Director: Constantine Bakaleinikoff; Editor: Eda Warren; Art Directors: Albert S. D'Agostino, Ralph Berger; Set Decorators: Darrell Silvera, John Sturtevant; Costumes: Michael Woulfe; Makeup: Mel Berns

# *Sealed Cargo* (1951)

Following the shelling by Nazi U-boats of a Danish schooner off the coast of Newfoundland, fishing captain Pat Bannon (Dana Andrews) boards the ship to investigate. Accompanied by two Danish members of his crew, Conrad (Philip Dorn) and Holger (Eric Feldary), Pat comes upon the wounded Captain Skalder (Claude Rains), who says that *his* crew had fled during the shelling and that his ship, *The Gaunt Woman*, is carrying barrels of rum from Trinidad. The schooner is towed into the little port of Trebor by Pat's fishing boat, the *Daniel Webster*.

Pat and Conrad remain suspicious, however, and board *The Gaunt Woman* secretly. They find a secret hold, where enough torpedoes and explosives "to blow up half the ships at sea" are stored. Pat figures that Skalder and his crew—whom he is sure will turn up shortly—are Nazis, and that they are planning to arm the German submarine fleet from the Newfoundland port. With the U-boats certain to start arriving at any time, the fishermen plot to destroy the schooner without blowing Trebor up as well.

It takes the combined efforts of Margaret McLean (Carla Balenda), her father (Onslow Stevens), the fishermen, and most of the townspeople to do so, but the Nazi crewmen are killed and *The Gaunt Woman* is destroyed, along with three German submarines which have surfaced alongside her. The American and Canadian civilians have done their part to help win the war.

*Sealed Cargo* is based on Edmund Gilligan's novel, *The Gaunt Woman*, and both the straightforward screenplay and Alfred Werker's muscular direction do justice to the nuance-free action tale. With the memory of World War II still fresh in 1951, no footage was wasted on delineating the deceitful, bloodthirsty Huns or the ingenious, resourceful North Americans. *Who* was no problem, and with Nazis a given, *why* was

superfluous, so Dana Andrews devoted 90 minutes of Yankee ingenuity to solving the *how* of the villains' plans. By concentrating on strategies and motivations, expensive sea battles could be supplanted by astute mixtures of fog machines, miniatures (an area in which RKO, home to *King Kong*, had long excelled), and rear projection screens, without anyone really feeling cheated. If nothing else, the picture would demonstrate how even a simple, freedom-loving fisherman could see through the nefarious schemes of an oppressive enemy.

And those schemes are beauts; it takes some heavy brow-furrowing on Dana Andrews' part before comes the dawn. By the time his Pat Bannon has unraveled every twisted thread, in fact, you begin to wonder whether you've really been sitting through your typical fishermen-and-Nazis saga, or you've accidentally wandered into the convoluted world of Raymond Chandler, and Mr. Andrews is impersonating Philip Marlowe in a slicker. You've already conceded that the below-decks torpedo arsenal—easily the length of a football field—could in no way, shape, or form share hold space in that schooner with a few hundred-odd barrels of rum and (presumably) the crew. But, hey … this is an espionage story, so nothing is what it appears to be. With Nazis who speak Danish, Danes who won't deign to do likewise, and Claude Rains, who plays a German impersonating a Dane who speaks English with a British accent (like all the truly great cinematic Nazi officers), what do you expect?

Director Alfred Werker had made a specialty out of visually oriented pictures, wherein the gist of simply delineated tales of good vs. evil was captured more by the physical interplay of representative types than by debate over at-odds ideologies or deep analysis of personalities. One need only glance at the best of his prolific output—1934's *The House of Rothschild*, for example, or his two Basil Rathbone yarns (*The Hound of the Baskervilles*, *The Adventures of Sherlock Holmes*) from 1939—to note that the man's strengths lay in providing a backdrop for the inevitable struggles of traditional enemies; explaining the *whys* and *wherefores* of fanaticism, prejudice, ignorance, arrogance, and such was best left to more cerebral filmmakers. Armed with a screenplay and a knack for setting the battlefield at hand, Werker would unleash his actors, trusting as much in their professionalism and fidelity to the spirit of the story as in his own vision.

Thus, Rains is as comfortable as an old shoe in a role which, a decade or so earlier, would most likely have fallen to Conrad Veidt, whose cultured Berlin tones consistently rendered him the major exception to the British/Nazi rule. Captain Skalder may be a loyal son of the Third Reich—the haughty disregard he has for Bannon and his men in the last reel would have done Hermann Göring proud—but he is also an *actor*. Although loath to reveal prematurely that he is an officer of the German Navy, Skalder is quick to forget that he is not in uniform, but in *costume*. His bloodied, dazed condition is really a charade, and the shelling of his schooner a carefully arranged stage effect. One would presume that he would bristle angrily if reminded that, in times of war, soldiers clad in mufti are not so much actors as they are *spies*, and where is the honor in that?

The brief foreword to the picture puts the whole thing into perspective. "Often forgotten," it lectures, "are the small victories—the acts of great personal courage by little people." The act of collective heroism on the part of the patriotic Trebor populace was a story worth telling and, thankfully, a story that could be told on a small budget.

*Sealed Cargo* marked the end of Rains' three-picture deal with RKO. The programmer was another notch on his belt ("Claude Rains clicks in his characterization of the German officer, getting across his menacing aspect underneath his quiet, cultured front"), but nothing of real import. The actor wouldn't make another feature film on a Hollywood soundstage until 1959.

*Sealed Cargo* RKO. Released May 19, 1951. 90 minutes.

Dana Andrews (Pat Bannon); Carla Balenda (Margaret McLean); CLAUDE RAINS (Captain Skalder); Philip Dorn (Conrad); Onslow Stevens (McLean); Skip Homeier (Steve); Eric Feldary (Holger); J. M. Kerrigan (Skipper Ben); Arthur Shields (Dolan); Morgan Farley (Caleb); Dave Thursby (Ambrose); Henry Rowland (Anderson); Charles A. Browne (Smitty); Don Dillaway (Owen); Al Hill (Tom); Lee MacGregor (Lt. Cameron); William Andrews (Holtz); Richard Norris (2nd Mate); Whit Bissell (Schuster); Kathleen Ellis, Karen Norris, Harry Mancke (Villagers)

Executive Producer: Samuel Bischoff; Producer: William Duff; Director: Alfred Werker; Screenplay: Dale Van Every, Oliver H. P. Garrett, Roy Huggins, based on the novel, *The Gaunt Woman*, by Edmund Gilligan; Director of Photography: George Diskant; Editor: Ralph Dawson; Music Director: C. Balakeinikoff; Art Director: Albert S. D'Agostino

An RKO Radio Picture

## The Man Who Watched Trains Go By (1953)

Kees Popinga (Claude Rains), chief clerk at the Groningen firm of De Koster and Son, is informed by Parisian detective Lucas (Marius Goring) that Dutch money has been making its way onto the French black market. Although relieved that his books pass inspection, Popinga is horrified to discover that Mr. De Koster (Herbert Lom) has systematically been looting his own firm and is preparing to disappear, leaving indications that he has committed suicide. Finding that the remainder of the firm's cash is about to disappear as well, the clerk struggles with his employer, who accidentally falls into one of the city's canals and drowns. Popinga snatches up De Koster's money bag and train ticket, and makes for Paris, hoping to join Michelle (Marta Toren), the mysterious and beautiful woman who has led the Dutch exporter to his ruin.

On the train, however, Popinga shares a compartment with Lucas, who knows of De

Koster's suicide, yet who cannot detain the clerk on any formal charge. Popinga flees from the train and catches up with Michelle, who convinces him to stay at a garage owned by her lover and partner in crime, Louis (Ferdy Mayne). Following a night on the town, Michelle uses her beauty to entice Popinga into promising to reveal the whereabouts of the money, which he has hidden in an abandoned automobile. When too much champagne and the exertions of the day cause the old man to drift off to sleep, Michelle runs to the junkyard to look for the money. Lucas has found the cache, however, and warns the young woman that she is playing a dangerous game; feeling betrayed, Popinga may try to kill her.

Once again, Popinga eludes Lucas and heads for the garage, where he forces Louis at knifepoint to instruct Michelle to come right over. She does, and the old man confronts her angrily. When she begins to belittle him, the enraged clerk stabs her and runs off into the adjacent train yard. Lucas follows his man onto the tracks and discovers that the events of the last few nights have robbed Popinga of his wits.

Georges Simenon's renown among English-speaking readers lies chiefly in his lengthy series of adventures of Inspector Maigret, the French detective whose ability to penetrate the criminal psyche inevitably allows the ultimate triumph of justice. Nonetheless, Maigret was not the author's only accomplishment; Simenon wrote more than 200 varied crime stories, and *The Man Who Watched the Trains Go By* was typical of this output in that it refused to dog any one formula. Nor, save for the characters' names and the broadest of underlying plot threads, did it resemble the screenplay crafted from its pages. There's no way that Rains' Kees Popinga would find himself tagged "The Gray Ghoul" like his literary counterpart.

In Harold French's scenario, Lucas the policeman is also very much an odd duck. Every bit as intuitive as Maigret, he reads Popinga like a book, yet still fails to act in a timely fashion to avert the homicide he predicts. Awakened by a phone call from the fugitive Dutchman, he has the call successfully traced (by his nightgown-clad wife, on an extension!), and then fails to follow up on the information. Perceptive enough to look into Popinga's mind, he is incapable of recognizing the little clerk's face in a small gathering at a flower seller's outside the local church.

Such character flaws cannot be ascribed to Marius Goring, however. The British actor, still slim and dapper at this point in his career, very nearly succeeds in making Lucas seem infallible, omniscient, or anything other than the herky-jerky mediocrity delineated by director/screenwriter Harold French. But, had Goring snagged Rains right there in the train *couchette*, it would have made for a very brief motion picture; a small dose of obtuse behavior was required if the drama was to live to a ripe, old 83 minutes.

Swedish Marta Toren, whose Michelle is a transparent, conniving bitch right out of *A Child's First Book of Stereotypes*, and Herbert Lom, whose self-righteous De Koster, Jr. turns out to be—*surprise!*—a thieving hypocrite, likewise do what they can to make their one-note characters vivid, while keeping the not-quite-clever plot at speed. Toren trades solely on her beauty and her power over men ("He'll give [the money] to me. He'll give it to me himself. He'll beg me to take it."); she is the quintessential vamp. Lom is given a prop with which to work: Gibb McLaughlin as De Koster, Sr. Moviegoers who like their symbolism weighty and unmistakable may regard the elder De Koster as a visual metaphor for the family firm; to the casual glance, functional, but in reality a lifeless husk, devoid of substance or spirit.

It's arguable whether Rains' Erique Claudin (from 1943's *Phantom of the Opera*) is as pathetic as his Kees Popinga, but that the latter role owes a good deal to the former is evident in one viewing of *Trains*. In both cases, oddball May-December relationships

**The chess motif, crucial to the picture. Herbert Lom, Claude, and Marius Goring.** *Courtesy Susan Duic*

underscore the dramatic action, madness comes to the fore, and theft of the protagonist's livelihood causes the worm to turn. (And, with *le bon Dieu*'s knack for irony, Rains goes for the throat of Herbert Lom, whose own *The Phantom of the Opera* [1962] would be scripted as a bigger loser than Claudin.) French's nebbish may have the edge on the French nebbish, though; one may squirm uncomfortably at the various sufferings of the Paris Opera violinist, but overhearing Popinga admonish Michelle for laughing at him by citing the dignity that membership in the chess club brings makes one fervently wish the Dutchman an immediate and painful death.

Still, unlike the other, etched-in-concrete principals, Popinga has the capacity to change,

and as quickly and dramatically as his circumstances. The clerk is discomfited by De Koster and Michelle at the Groningen railroad station—a myriad of emotions washes over Rains' immobile face—but he remains passive. At the chess club, he takes an active part in the ongoing deceit by keeping still as his employer lies. A bout of soul-searching at home just increases his sense of unease, and De Koster's confessions of embezzlement and lust, taken with his suicide ploy, lead to the unfortunate struggle by the canal. Popinga rapidly metamorphoses from opportunistic schlemiel to schizophrenic knife-wielder in the hours that follow.

Growing ever more uncertain of himself and gradually losing his grip on reality, the little clerk, whose dreams of freedom and adventure have always been intertwined with the romance and excitement of the international trains, becomes alternatively passive and aggressive. "I don't want to quarrel with you, sir," he growls at an elderly fly in Michelle's seductive web, "but if it becomes necessary to stick this [knife] into your heart, I shall!" Personality reversal, whether slow and deliberate, or near instantaneous, was one of the aces in Rains' hand, and few other of the movies' top-echelon character men (Charles Laughton, perhaps) could have moved so quickly, so convincingly from abject pathos to homicidal schizophrenia.

Harold French introduces the chess gambit early on, and the imagery grows subtler as the action becomes more physical. On the verge of losing a match to Lucas, De Koster agrees that Popinga take over his pieces; the detective cries "Checkmate" within a few moves. "Don't look so crestfallen, Mr. Popinga," Lucas consoles cannily. "Your boss made a wrong move." Later, while sharing a compartment on the Paris express, the policeman and the clerk battle over a portable chess set—and the whole De Koster affair—simultaneously. It is within this move/counter move framework that other disparities concerning Lucas—such as his being sufficiently clairvoyant to locate the hidden swagger without the slightest of clues, yet always and everywhere else a step behind or a moment too late to seize Popinga himself—must be viewed.

As the little clerk moves ever closer toward dementia, the chessboard is forgotten and the battlefield grows to encompass all of Paris. Popinga is the besieged king; he moves frantically, but with limited capabilities, hither and yon, looking to take any pieces that threaten his vague dreams of happiness with Michelle. Some, like the elderly patron of the nightclub or the children playing in the abandoned car where the money has been concealed, are but pawns, removed with drama but with no real effort. Others, like Louis, are more dangerous pieces, capable of greater harm because of their greater mobility and power. Lucas and Michelle, of course, are the opposing royals. While Michelle's queen moves easily and fluidly throughout Paris, Lucas is forced more frequently to react than to take the initiative; his strategies are dictated by everyone else's movements. Despite her undeniable power over him, Michelle's queen is taken by Popinga's king, before, once again, Lucas calls checkmate in the train yard.

*The Man Who Watched Trains Go By* was released in the United States as *The Paris Express*, the renaming an attempt to keep American audiences from thinking the picture concerned model-railroad hobbyists. Bosley Crowther derailed *Express*, finding that "The picture lacks quality, character, sympathy and suspense—and when the man goes mad at the finish, he's not the only one in the house." (*The New York Times*, June 6, 1953). Reviewing the film under its British title, *Variety* (December 31, 1952) opined that the picture was "strong enough to merit some wide and popular showing in the U.S." and that Rains "may not be ideally cast but does well with the role."

At 63 years of age, Rains really wasn't equal to the task of providing the physical edge to an otherwise predictable and talkative story. Without his character's pathetic fumblings with violence and frustrated sexuality, though, the film is all Marta Toren's supposedly irresistible charm and Marius Goring's knowing looks. Had Popinga been a tad less a country bumpkin (Lucas's phrase) and a bit more cosmopolitan, his lapses into lust, homicide, and madness would have had more of an ironic edge. But then, of course, he wouldn't have been the sort of man who watches trains go by.

*The Man Who Watched Trains Go By* Eros. Released February 1953. 82 minutes. (U.S. release, as *The Paris Express*, on June 5, 1953)

CLAUDE RAINS (Kees Popinga); Marta Toren (Michelle); Marius Goring (Inspector Lucas); Anouk Aimee (Jeanne); Herbert Lom (Julius De Koster); Lucie Mannheim (Mrs. Popinga); Felix Aylmer (Merkemans); Ferdy Mayne (Louis); Eric Pohlman (Goin); Gibb McLaughlin (De Koster);

**Driven mad with lust, greed, and fear, Popinga (Claude) threatens to dispatch Louis (Ferdy Mayne) unless the garage man sets up Michelle.** *Courtesy Susan Duic*

Mary Mackenzie (Mrs. Lucas); Robin Alaouf (Karl Popinga); Joan St. Clair (Frida Popinga); Roy Purcell (Plainclothesman); Michael Alain (Train Conductor)

Producers: Raymond Stross, Josef Shaftel; Director: Henry French; Screenplay: Henry French, based on the novel, *The Man Who Watched the Trains Go By*, by Georges Simenon; Music Composed and Conducted by Benjamin Frankel; Production Manager: Ernest Holding; Art Director: Paul Sherrif; Editor: Vera Campbell; Assembling Editor: Peter Hunt; Assistant Director: Adrian Pryce-Jones; Camera Operator: Gus Drisse; Location Manager: Teddy Joseph; Sound Editor: Len Trumm; Sound Recording: W. Lindop; Makeup: Stuart Freeborn; Technicolor Colour Consultant: Joan Bridge; Associate Producer: David Berman

# *Lisbon* (1956)

Suave crime lord Aristides Mavros (Claude Rains) agrees to snatch the aged husband of Sylvia Merrill (Maureen O'Hara) from behind the Iron Curtain for a substantial fee. Mavros then sub-contracts the escape to Captain Robert John Evans (Ray Milland), an expatriate American boat owner with larcenous tendencies of his own; each time Evans' boat, *Orca*, touches a Lisbon dock it is searched by Inspector Fonseca (Jay Novello) and his men.

While arrangements for Mr. Merrill's release are being finalized, Evans finds himself on the receiving end of some amorous advances from Sylvia. More to his liking, however, is young Maria Magdalena Masanet

(Yvonne Furneaux), one of Mavros' "secretaries," who is also attracted to the American. This does not sit well with Serafim (Francis Lederer), Mavros' jealous strong-arm man; he warns the young woman and threatens Evans in her presence.

In a moment of candor, Sylvia tells Evans that she wants her husband back, dead. Without proof of his death, she'll have to wait seven years to collect his $25 million estate. "And I don't want to wait seven years." When she proposes that the two of them marry after the whole business has been wrapped up, the captain is appalled. Rebuffed, Sylvia goes to Mavros and agrees that only the *body* of Mr. Merrill (Percy Marmont) should make it back to Lisbon.

Maria Magdalena overhears Mavros and Serafim plot the murders of Mr. Merrill and Evans, and she runs to warn the man she loves. After the sickly Merrill has been transferred to from a gunboat to *Orca*, Serafim gets down to work. Evans, however, manages to fire his flare-gun into the killer, who falls overboard and is lost at sea. Sylvia's plans are thwarted when her husband is brought safe and sound to Mavros' mansion, and Inspector Fonseca relieves Mavros of his passport, thus setting into motion deportation proceedings. Evans and Maria Magdalena take off together in search of happiness and adventure.

Shot on location, *Lisbon* is an unapologetic little B, with a so-so story and a slightly embarrassing need to suspend belief, but a wonderful cast.

Ray Milland pulled triple duty, producing and directing, as well as taking acceptable care of the heroics. The Welsh-born actor handled his production chores well, too, with major plusses in Nelson Riddle's melodic score and Jack Marta's photography of the Portuguese vistas. Milland opted to spring for Trucolor and Naturama—the poor man's CinemaScope—rightly feeling that the expense would increase the marketability of the Republic release. The widescreen process highlighted one of his deficiencies

as a director, though; more times than not, flat (i.e. adapted non-widescreen) prints of *Lisbon* captured only the *noses* of people engaged in conversation. Looking to make the most of Naturama, Milland had usually parked his actors on the extreme opposite ends of the frame.

Not as disconcerting, but equally noticeable, is the discrepancy in age between the slightly jowly hero and the women who are putty in his not-so-callused hands. The actor had passed the half-century mark before principal photography had gotten underway; in contrast, the chic Maureen O'Hara was not yet 36 years old, while Yvonne Furneaux had just turned 28. A couple of other semi-centenarians, Jay Novello and Francis Lederer, were likewise on display, but as the former was introduced as married and the latter was the heavy of the piece, Milland became the only port in the storm by default. (In his enjoyable if coy autobiography, Milland alluded vaguely to an actor he called "Hot Rocks Herbie," a libidinous presence who, although he fulfilled his contract, is difficult to spot or even guess at in the finished film.)[38]

Furneaux would make her deepest impressions later, in the horror film market, appearing to acclaim in both Hammer Films' *The Mummy* (1959), and Roman Polanski's *Repulsion* (1965), while O'Hara's movie credits would come to span five decades and countless genres. Probably neither woman regarded *Lisbon* as anything other than a paycheck, and being required to find the grandfatherly Milland irresistible must have been something of a daunting assignment.

Rains considered his work for Ray Milland as a paid holiday to the Iberian Peninsula, and in a letter to Norman MacDermott, former impresario of the *Everyman Theatre* and Rains' friend until death, wrote of Aristides Mavros as "an enlightened rapscallion who went to school wherever his father happened to be stealing."[39] The sort of urbane, gentlemanly cad one normally associates with the diminutive actor, Mavros comes by his disreputable vocation honestly.

**Aristides Mavros (Claude) comes to an understanding with Sylvia Merrill (Maureen O'Hara). Claude had briefly been considered to star opposite O'Hara in the 1939 *Hunchback of Notre Dame*.**

"We have been thieves for six generations," he explains to Mrs. Merrill, "very successful thieves."

The role allows Rains to display some of the puckish humor in which his scoundrels occasionally indulged; a good bit of that aforementioned "twinkle" can be seen in his eye, even when—as his act of charity to a thrush on his windowsill turns into an act of providing for his cat with an abrupt blow of a handy tennis racquet—his eyes are mere slits in a beaming face. *Variety* found the action "hard to take and completely unnecessary to set the Rains character," missing the point entirely. What Mavros does to the songbird, he plots to do to Evans. Within his circle of influence, Mavros dictates the pecking order; some must die so that others may live, and survival, as in nature, goes to the fittest. Evans is enticed into the Greek's

presence—$10,000 being *his* birdseed—and Serafim is to be the instrument whereby the captain is sacrificed to Mavros' insatiable greed.

A good looking film—only a featureless black background doubling for the sea and a cheesy interior set for the *Orca*'s cabin ruin the overall illusion—*Lisbon* would still have been pretty much indistinguishable from a contemporary gaggle of semi-travelogues-cum-adventure sagas were it not for the presence of that top-notch cast. Milland's days as a credible love interest were numbered, though, and his career would soon veer off towards his own TV series, *Markham* (1959), low- to medium-budget horror films, and second leads in made-for-television movies. The year 1956 would see Rains involved in a few TV projects of his own, and a very brief run in Arch Oboler's convoluted science-fiction drama, *Night of the Auk*. More wearing than any of these, thought, would be the actor's divorce from Frances Propper.

*Lisbon* Republic Studios. August 17, 1956. 90 minutes.

Ray Milland (Captain Robert John Evans); Maureen O'Hara (Sylvia Merrill); CLAUDE RAINS (Aristides Mavros); Yvonne Furneaux (Maria Magdalena Masanet); Francis Lederer (Serafim); Percy Marmont (Lloyd Merrill); Jay Novello (Inspector Joao Casimiro Fonseca); Edward Chapman (Edgar Selwyn); Harold Jamison (Philip Norworth); Humberto Madeira (Tio Rabio)

Producer and Director: Ray Milland; Screenplay: John Tucker Battle, based on a story by Martin Racklin; Director of Photography: Jack Marta, in Naturama and Trucolor; Music: Nelson Riddle; Editor: Richard L. Van Enger; Art Director: Frank Arrigo

Filmed on location and with the facilities of Amateau Lds. Tobis Studios, in Lisbon, Portugal.

# *This Earth Is Mine* (1959)

Having made her way from England to her family's estates and vineyards in California's Napa Valley, Elizabeth Rambeau (Jean Simmons) meets for the first time her grandfather, Phillipe Rambeau (Claude Rains), her Aunt Martha and Uncle Francis Fairon (Dorothy Maguire and Kent Smith), and her "half-a-cousin," John Rambeau (Rock Hudson). She soon discovers that Prohibition has driven a wedge between John and his grandfather; the young man wants to sell the family's grapes to bootleggers, while Phillipe plows under the best the vines offer so as to ready the soil for the time when wine can again be made and sold legally. Elizabeth also learns she is expected to marry neighboring vintner, Andre Swann (Francis Bethancourt), so that his lands will become part of the Rambeau holdings.

Smitten by Elizabeth, but before he learns that she has fallen in love with him as well, John impetuously drives off into the night with Buz Dietrick (Cindy Robbins), the lovely young daughter of one of the local growers. While John is away in Chicago—he has convinced many of the smaller growers to allow him to broker the sale of their grapes to a "syndicate"—the pregnant Buz and her father extort hush money from Phillipe. Buz then tells vintner Luigi Griffanti (Ken Scott) that the baby is his; Luigi is overjoyed, and the couple are married shortly thereafter.

When John returns to the valley, he is greeted coldly by Martha and Elizabeth, and dismissed angrily by his grandfather. Thoughtlessly tossing a cigarette into some dry grasses, John tears over to the Griffanti arbor, where he angrily demands that Buz confess to Elizabeth that they had never been intimate. Believing himself a cuckold, Luigi brawls with John and then shoots the young Rambeau as he drives off. Elizabeth learns the truth about Buz, but the mountain vineyards are devastated by the fire, and John is left with a leg paralyzed by Luigi's bullet.

The newspapers report that the states have begun to vote to revoke Prohibition. Along with his family and friends, Phillipe is thrilled by the news, but, sickened by the developments of recent months, doesn't live to see the 18th amendment repealed. In his will, the patriarch bequeaths to John "that which he had destroyed," the mountain vineyards. Together with Elizabeth, John works to revive the vines and to restore the sacred earth.

One of the last of the Technicolor extravaganzas of the fifties, *This Earth Is Mine* didn't do nearly as well as the brass at Universal-International would have hoped, despite numerous plusses. Alice Tisdale Hobart's source novel, *The Cup and the Sword*, had had its day in the sun and should have induced more of its sizable readership into theaters. Academy Award-winning art director Alexander Golitzen—together with the technical wizardry of CinemaScope—should have conspired to render irresistible all of the substantial charm of California's wine country. Veteran director Henry King's longtime association with Americana should have made his vision of this tale of life, love, and injustice unforgettable. The presence of kittenish Jean Simmons for the men, and Rock Hudson—1959's Number One Box-Office Sensation—for the women, should have guaranteed record turnovers of red- (and hot-) blooded American ticket-buyers in movie palaces everywhere.

Unfortunately, save for some eye-catching interior design and California's natural bounty, none of these assets translated well to the screen. King's prior efforts at recreating the spirit of America—*I'd Climb the Highest Mountain* (1951) and *Wait Till the Sun Shines, Nellie* (1952)—had been mounted on skeletons of romanticized nostalgia, while *Carousel* (1956) turned on an element of fantasy. Despite its setting in the days of Prohibition, *Earth* was essentially a story of passion and grit in the here-and-now, a milieu which had never been King's forte.

As for the sensuality of Simmons and Hudson, that—and the talents of Rains and Dorothy Maguire—evaporated in the wealth of ill-developed themes found in Casey Robinson's screenplay. In attempting to condense Miss Hobart's sprawling novel into two hours of entertainment and edification, Robinson cooked up a subplot-heavy slumgullion which never really cohered. For example, although the Napa vineyards have been cultivated for a half-century by Phillipe and his émigré European neighbors, for no fathomable reason they remain hotbeds of anti–Italian and anti–Semitic sentiment. The whitebread members of that Chicago syndicate of bootleggers run ethnic types Yankowitz (Ben Astar) and Petrucci (Alberto Morin) ragged, yet old Chu (Peter Chong), representing the Chinese faction that had almost never escaped persecution and bigotry during its assimilation into California society, hovers unmolested in the background and inherits a pile at Phillipe's passing. Ultimately, none of this means a hill of grapes.

Then, too, John Rambeau apparently has his way with Buz Dietrick, and her pregnancy and subsequent hasty marriage to Luigi Griffanti shift the light from ethnic intolerance to infidelity. When it becomes clear that Luigi really *is* the father of Buz's child, however—thus rendering unfair Phillipe, Martha, and Elizabeth's condemnations of young John—the audience resents its having been led down the primrose path purely for the hell of it. With the roguish Rambeau in reality as innocent as a schoolboy, and Elizabeth limned unattractively as uncertain, secretive, and moody, both Hudson and Simmons found themselves effectively disarmed of their most potent weapons, their sex appeal.

Less convoluted and needlessly abstruse than either of these, Phillipe Rambeau is supposed to be the one, immutable force in a sea of change. Instead, as delineated by the script, Rains' character is an out-of-date visionary, given to ruminating or pontificating endlessly on the quasi-divine nature of the grape and the sacredness of the earth. In both the novel and the film, Phillipe is merely an ennobling factor, on hand to lend a sense of honor and dimension to what many regard as just another business. Rains gives his sundry little speeches on love and God and grapes the pious tone they deserve, and does manage to sound more like a man of deep conviction than an Orson Welles-ish industry spokesman. Yet, despite Robinson's ear for dialogue and Rains' ability to massage a line, *The New York Times'* Howard Thompson was on target when he observed that all those "sacred earth" conversations really boiled down to discussions of *money*.

Rains looks wonderfully well as Phillipe Rambeau. Trim and dapper in a gray Van Dyke, the actor appears energetic and full of vim, even when relegated to his sickbed. Phillipe remains so vital, in fact, that his sudden death (off-screen) comes as a shock to the *dramatis personae*; to the savvy viewer, it's a foregone conclusion, dramatically. After a desperate spate of action (the fire, the brawl, the shooting, and a car wreck) much

**At the wrap party: Rock Hudson, Jean Simmons, Director Henry King, Dorothy McGuire, Claude.**

too late in the picture, there can be no forward motion other than the divvying up of
Phillipe's chattels and the scrutinizing of the
heirs' faces. Still, had Rains been given a few
minutes to wax eloquently in a deathbed
scene, it would have gone a long way to
counteracting the incessant and repetitious
prattle he had been forced to mouth earlier.

Contemporary critics were almost unanimous in perceiving the film as talk and more
talk, with a great deal of it dismissed as
"high-flown" and "conventional." The picture's lack of focus was deplored everywhere.
April 17, 1959, *Variety* wrote that "Claude
Rains fares best. His role is not explored in
any depth, but it has the merit of being easily recognizable and consistent." Over at *The
Times*, Mr. Thompson felt

Miss Maguire's sleek witch is the most impressive; Mr. Rains and Miss Simmons do their professional best; and Mr. Hudson seems a bit boyish for a stalwart family rebel.
                              (June 27, 1959)

Sammy Cahn and Jimmy Van Heusen's
title song, bellowed under the credits by Don
Cornell, took a whack at setting the film's
ideological stage; whether anyone was paying attention is another matter altogether.
Henry King's fragmented slice of Americana
may not have followed its source novel onto
any "Best" lists, but it did offer a different
view of Prohibition to audiences used to
TV's *The Untouchables*, and allowed Rains
to bask in the critical glow once again.

*This Earth Is Mine* Universal-International. Released June 26, 1959. (New York opening). 126 minutes.

Rock Hudson (John Rambeau); Jean Simmons (Elizabeth Rambeau); Dorothy Maguire (Martha Fairon); CLAUDE RAINS (Phillipe Rambeau); Kent Smith (Francis Fairon); Anna Lee (Charlotte Rambeau); Cindy Robbins (Buz); Ken Scott (Luigi Griffanti); Francis Bethancourt (Andre Swann); Stacey Graham (Monica); Augusta Merighi (Mama Griffanti); Peter Chong (Chu); Jack Mather (Derek); Ben Astar (Yakowitz); Alberto Morin (Petucci); Penny Santon (Mrs. Petucci); Emory Parnell (Berke); Lionel Ames (Nate Forster); Dan White (Judge Gruber); Geraldine Wall (Maria); Lawrence Ung (David)

Executive Producer: Edward Muhl; Producers: Casey Robinson, Claude Heilman; Director: Henry King; Screenplay: Casey Robinson, based on the novel, *The Cup and the Sword*, by Alice Tisdale Hobart; Directors of Photography: Winton C. Hoch, ASC and Russell Metty, ASC; Art Directors: Alexander Golitzen, George W. Davis, Eric Orbom; Set Decorators: Russell A. Gausman, Ruby R. Levitt, Oliver Emert; Sound: Leslie I. Carey, Vernon W. Kramer; Editor: Ted Kent, ACE; Gowns: Bill Thomas; Hair Stylist: Larry Germain; Makeup: Bud Westmore; Assistant Director: Joseph Behn; Musical Score: Hugo Friedhofer; Musical Supervisor: Joseph Gershenson; Song "This Earth Is Mine" by Sammy Cahn and Jimmy Van Heusen; Sung by Don Cornell; Special Photography: Clifford Stine, ASC

Technicolor, CinemaScope

# *The Lost World* (1960)

Just in from the Amazon, Professor George Edward Challenger (Claude Rains) repairs to the British Zoological Institute in order to raise enough money to go right back. His claims of having discovered a "Lost World" are pooh-poohed by Professor Summerlee, (Richard Haydn) who nonetheless agrees to accompany Challenger back to the unknown land if sufficient money can be raised and two additional qualified persons will volunteer to go as well. News reporter Ed Malone

(David Hedison) and playboy-adventurer Lord John Roxton (Michael Rennie) fill the bill; the news service for which Malone works underwrites the expedition even though Jennifer Holmes (Jill St. John), daughter of its owner, is denied permission to go along by Challenger.

Once at the Amazon River, the group is joined by helicopter pilot Manuel Gomez (Fernando Lamas) and Señor Costa (Jay Novello), in charge of their supplies. An unwelcome surprise for the professors is the presence of Miss Holmes and her brother, David (Ray Stricklyn). The next morning, they fly up onto a high plateau—Challenger's lost world—where, come nightfall, they are routed by the approach of a dinosaur, which then proceeds to destroy the helicopter.

In the course of making their way down the plateau, the group is imperiled by strangling vines, giant spiders, man-eating plants, rivers of molten lava, and more dinosaurs. They discover that another group of explorers under the leadership of Burton White had tried to conquer the Lost World three years earlier, but had ultimately been left to its fate by the irresponsible Roxton. They capture a beautiful native girl, who, along with the help of an aged, blind Burton White (Ian Wolfe), comes to aid them in their escape from her irate tribesmen and the volcanic action of the plateau.

Costa and Gomez perish in the course of the adventures, but Roxton manages to escape with plenty of diamonds for everyone, and Challenger looks forward to astonishing London with the Tyrannosaurus rex hatchling he has captured.

If one were to segregate Claude Rains' fantasy, horror, and science fiction output from the larger body of his work, *The Lost World* would rank up there with *The Invisible Man* and *Phantom of the Opera* as the most renowned titles in the lot. *Titles*, that is; the end product is way down there on the list.

*The Lost World* was Sir Arthur Conan

Doyle's best-known novel (save for *The Hound of the Baskervilles* and *The Valley of Fear*), and First National pulled out all the stops when, in 1925, it hired stop-motion animation wizard Willis O'Brien to bring a healthy assortment of genuine Jurassic beasties to the screen. Bluff and bearded Wallace Beery was Challenger back then, with Arthur Hoyt as Summerlee, Lloyd Hughes as Ed Malone, and Lewis Stone as Roxton. Bessie Love went along as the damsel in distress, an authentic brontosaurus came back to London with the group's survivors, and the whole epic was standard screen format, black and white, and—of course—silent. It was sensational.

Thirty-five years later, Irwin Allen, apparently encouraged by the success of Fox's *Journey to the Center of the Earth* (1959), pulled out what, for him, were all the stops; the remake became his own pet project. Allen co-wrote the screenplay and looked to inject gripping human interest in the few moments left untouched by optical or mechanical effects. As producer, he went for the gold, hiring veteran effects-meister O'Brien, who had not only astounded those 1925 audiences, but had floored the free world in 1933 with *King Kong*. Allen signed a slew of the decade's most popular B-list stars whom he directed in what he maintained would be "the adventure of a lifetime." The studio again went for CinemaScope and color (by DeLuxe), and the final budget was reportedly well over $1 million.

It was embarrassing.

The picture all but cloned *Journey to the Center of the Earth* in terms of visual design. Both pictures are big into rocks, lava, plants, and varmints, done up in garish primary colors and verging, at times, on iridescence. Each bright but cheesy item is neatly confined to its own little area, as if apportioned a meticulously measured plot in the backyard of some psychedelic gardener. In a stab at creating tension, both films' adventurers gingerly inch their way up, down, and across torturous yet picturesque *pathways* in this mostly virgin territory. *The Lost World* adds

a crowd of subterranean cannibals with Day-Glo war paint and stockpiles of golf-ball-sized crude diamonds within spitting distance of a reservoir of molten rock and an ever-vigilant water dragon.

Allen and Charles Bennett's screenplay effectively *halved* both the novel and the 1925 epic by eliminating the foolhardy but exhilarating introduction of the dinosaur into civilization. In order to pad what was now excess running time, the number of females (and their inevitable romantic yearnings) was doubled, the lizard choreography was extended (one despaired that the unexciting and interminable grand "battle of the dinosaurs" would end only with the both species going extinct), and the Burton White expedition subplot was expanded to encompass not only Burton playing *deus ex machina*, but some Roxton/Gomez melodrama and the unsettling revelation (via locket) that there had been *two* Fernando Lamases.

One Fernando Lamas was quite enough, thank you.

No one but *no one* acquits himself well in *The Lost World*. The cast runs the gamut from vapid (St. John) to near comatose (Rennie). Richard Haydn, who built a career out of impersonating character actor Franklin Pangborn, is so prissy here as to induce toothache. Señor Lamas spends most of his time with a guitar in his hand, a cigarillo in his teeth, and an enigmatic smile on his lips, while Ian Wolfe, notching up his zillionth film role, really hasn't much to do other than hand out directions and guns, and roll his eyes up into his head for his big close-up. Vitina Marcus is lithe and gorgeous and ... that's why she's here. Only David Hedison gets as close as anyone hereabouts ever comes to normalcy.

"Claude Rains, transformed by a somewhat pinkish hairdo and beard, is a caricature of the dedicated, belligerent zoologist." (*The New York Times*, July 14, 1960)

Admittedly, Rains' Professor Challenger is a bundle of the theatrical excesses eschewed by the actor while still a young man, enveloped in the slowing reactions and aging physique of the actor as mature artist: a match made in purgatory, definitely, but a caricature? Equipped with the traditional Challenger hair appliances (really more on the order of orange than pink), and brandishing a standard-issue British bumbershoot (with which to gesture dramatically), Rains elects to go overboard and play the cocksure scientist/adventurer as an insufferable, foot-dragging pain in the ass. Challenger is vain, argumentative, arrogant, eccentric, and potentially violent: before the film is five minutes old, he has assaulted poor Ed Malone with his brolly, and has cussed up one side and down the other everyone else on the airport tarmac. There is no place for nuance or finesse in such a person; subtlety is achieved via low-volume ranting and a quiescent umbrella.

Undoubtedly familiar with the Conan Doyle original, Rains may have felt that he had no choice but to go loud and ludicrous when presented with a script filled with blatant and indefensible errors, prostheticwearing lizards, French poodles, and pink Capri pants. From a performance point of view, his character has but one major defining speech (which suffers in comparison with the tightened version heard in the film's *trailer*), no quotable lines, few displays of knowledge or wit, and only a smattering of true dialogue exchange. So ... how better to deal with mediocre writing than to spew it or snarl it or bellow it? How better to handle middling dramatics than to turn up the juice and overact like mad? Choosing as he did to operate on one level while his colleagues chose variously and otherwise, Rains is out of sync with the other performances. Nevertheless, in a brief 1998 interview David Hedison admitted that he, too, was less than taken with the picture's scope and direction.

I hated the style of the thing. Dramatically, nothing in it was real. It was summed up for me with Jill St. John running around in pink tights with that silly little poodle.... But, then again, there were some positive aspects to it. Claude Rains

The movie wasn't worth much, but Claude thought enough of this portrait of himself as Prof. Challenger to squirrel it away. *Courtesy Jessica Rains*

was such a good actor and it was a pleasure to meet him and be in the same film with him. I'm such a fan of all those films he made at Warner Brothers.

*Filmfax* (Aug.-Sept. 1998)

*The Lost World* is neither the best of the catalogue (by a long shot) nor as abjectly awful as facile criticism might lead one to believe. Rains' turn as George Edward Challenger may have earned him a solid round of *tsk-tsk*ing from the less perceptive out there, but the wily old veteran exudes more energy glaring daggers and spewing venom than the entire complement of torpid lizards, luscious ladies, or Fernando Lamases.

*The Lost World* 20th Century–Fox. June 27, 1960. 97 minutes.

Michael Rennie (Lord John Roxton); Jill St. John (Jennifer Holmes); David Hedison (Ed Malone); CLAUDE RAINS (Professor George Edward Challenger); Fernando Lamas (Manuel

Gomez); Richard Haydn (Professor Summerlee); Ray Stricklyn (David Holmes); Jay Novello (Costa); Vitina Marcus (Native Girl); Ian Wolfe (Burton White); John Graham (Stuart Holmes); Colin Campbell (Professor Waldron)

Producer and Director: Irwin Allen; Screenplay: Irwin Allen, Charles Bennett, based on the novel, *The Lost World*, by Sir Arthur Conan Doyle; Director of Photography: Winton Hoch, ASC; Art Directors: Duncan Cramer, Walter M. Simonds; Set Decorators: Walter M. Scott, Joseph Kish, John Sturtevant; Music: Bert Shefter, Paul Sawtell; Orchestrations: Howard Jackson, Sid Cutner; Special Effects Photography: L. B. Abbott, Emil Kosa, James B. Gordon; Effects Technician: Willis O'Brien; Sound: E. Clinton Ward, Harry M. Leonard; Production Illustrator: Maurice Zuberano; Art Director: Ad Schaumer; Editor: Hugh S. Fowler, ASC; Costume Designer: Pal Zastupnevich; Makeup: Ben Nye; Hair Styles: Helen Turpin, CHS

# *Battle of the Worlds* (1960/63)

Sometime in the indeterminate future, Mars is home to a military force under Earth's "High Command." A planet which Professor Benson (Claude Rains) has dubbed the "Outsider" appears to be on a collision course with Earth. Making matters worse, a squadron of flying saucers from the rogue planet attacks and destroys any spaceships sent into its vicinity.

Prof. Benson calculates that there will be no collision, but that the Outsider will pass within 95,000 miles of Earth. Eve Barnett (Maya Brent), one of Benson's scientific cadre, informs him that the Outsider has stopped its forward motion and has begun to orbit the planet. Apoplectic, Benson announces that the Outsider must be destroyed immediately, otherwise the human race has only 840 hours until doomsday!

Another scientist (and Eve's sometime boyfriend), Fred Steel (Bill Carter), accompanies Commander Bob Cole (Umberto Orsini) and his wife, Cathy (Jacqueline Derval), as they attempt to shoot down the saucers. With the saucers impervious to

Earth weapons, Fred orders Bob to fly right up to one; the shock waves cause the saucer to spin out of control and to crash land on Earth. Using the saucer's control cylinder (which he calls "the cypher"), Benson manages to decipher the "language" of the Outsider; now, he announces, he can order the saucers to self-destruct. This is done in two shakes, and the High Command has the military ready "The Plan," which will result in the total destruction of the Outsider.

Benson, however, pleads for some time to explore beneath the surface of the planet, and he's given three hours. Guided by a homing device to the underground entrance, he, the Coles, Eve, and Fred find extraterrestrial cadavers. The professor goes on alone, searching for the electronic brain which has guided the planet's actions despite its programmers having been dead for eons. A series of cave-ins ("The Outsider is defending itself!") has everyone other than Benson beating a path for the exit. His discovery of the "immortal formulas" of the dead race and Cole's spaceship's reaching the safety zone above the planet are in a dead heat with the impact of the missiles fired by Earth's glassy-eyed military leaders. Earth is saved, but Professor Benson has died in the cause of science.

Altogether one of the least of Rains' pictures despite his top billing, *Battle of the Worlds* is definitely the toughest to document. Released in the states in 1963 by Topaz Films, it's a partially dubbed and edited version of *Il Pianeta degli Uomini Spenti* (*The Planet of the Lifeless Men*, 1960), which had clocked in originally at 95 minutes. *Battle* is one of a series of low-budget science-fiction clones by a team of canny and basically competent Italian filmmakers—frequently under the leadership of Anthony Dawson—which crossed the Atlantic in the early to mid-sixties on the backs of their faded American stars.

"Anthony Dawson" was a nom de guerre of prolific hack director Antonio Margheriti, whose name (in one form or another)

popped up on the credits scroll of well over a dozen low-budget space operas (like *Assignment Outer Space*), horror flicks *(Castle of Blood)*, and James Bond knock-offs *(Lightning Bolt)* which splayed across second-tier movie screens throughout the decade. As he did in most of his science-fiction pictures, Margheriti went through *Battle* like a dose of salts, indulging (along with Raffaello Masciocchi, his director of photography) in an array of colored filters, swirling lights, and camera maneuvers which encompassed almost every angle known to man. This frantic dash at bringing some kind of visual excitement to a screenplay bogged down with third-rate writing and fourth-rate logic is not, however, without its admirers. In *The Encyclopedia of Science Fiction Movies*, editor Phil Hardy (whose elicited opinions therein range from conservative orthodoxy to near lunacy) leans toward this latter extreme as he hallucinates:

The film is an object lesson in how to let cinema triumph over both script and acting, allowing visual style and imagination to carry their corrosively fascinating meanings. The result is an astonishing piece of cinema which dwarfs all pseudo-philosophic moralizing about Mankind and the World.[40]

Apart from a picturesque opening sequence which affords glimpses of the Sicilian coast, Eve and Fred's relationship, and actress Carol Danell's butt cheeks, the film is totally studio-bound. The spaceships are outfitted with gadget-less control *tables*, and Benson's den is awash with huge plants, but virtually all other interiors are crammed with shiny chrome tubes and scads of scientific-looking do-hickeys meant to remind the slower among us that—by jingo!—we're in the future. A neat touch—due in equal parts to Margheriti's budget *and* philosophy of design—has the members of the High Command merely images on a series of non-matching, black and white TV screens. Still, this is less a case of cinema "triumphing" over style and acting as it is the director's creative desperation leading to his casting furniture as actors.

Credits mavens have their work cut out for them: Annoying discrepancies pop up between the scrolls on the American release version and its pressbook, and the few and invariably brief notices the picture received in it initial run do nothing but compound the confusion. Depending upon the source consulted, one is hard-pressed to find evidence of any Italian involved in the production other than Umberto Orsini, who (in the pressbook, at least) is the only person to be accorded all the vowels due him. This mystifying insistence on anglicizing everyone's name is hardly helped by the jumble of typos and misspellings which pepper the few written commentaries on the picture.

Although most of the cast speak English in the film, all (save Rains) have been dubbed anyhow, and most of the near-misses in looping have viewers reaching for their bifocals. Changes of nomenclature between *Pianeta* and *Battle* can be bewildering: The rogue planet is the "Intruder" in the original and the "Outsider" in the import. Doubtless, too, those 11 minutes left on an Italian cutting room floor would have accounted for more (if not for more *important*) exposition: Why, for example, is Mrs. Collins referred to as the "Black Widow," and, what, if anything, does she add to the story other than the occasional pot of coffee?

The special effects run the gamut from A to B (apologies to Dorothy Parker), with rudimentary animation providing the graphics while spaceships and discs [sic] from the Outsider have it out. Stock footage takeoffs meld uncomfortably with adequate (though overlit) plastic models in space, but none of this matches Bob Cole's command ship when it at last sets down on the alien graveyard. Once Benson has "composed the music" to discombobulate the discs, a scene of space-suited types fingering what very much resemble metal car radios undoes whatever dramatic momentum has been building.

Mario Migliardi's score is quite eclectic: jazz riffs mingle with nondescript, all-purpose melodies; dirge-like tremolos vie with

**As Prof. Benson, Claude questioned the very foundations of the universe. Better he should have asked: Why is there no glass in this helmet?** *The author's collection*

overwrought fanfares; and snatches of electronic tone poems accompany the flashiest of the props. There's even a brief vocal piece dedicated to the Outsider under the closing credits. For all this, most of the sound and fury signifies close to zilch; themes match visuals only sporadically, and the whole is very much less the sum of the pieces. Once in a while, a dissonant blast will cause your eyes to water or your fillings to ache; other than that, unless you're listening for it with a critical ear, Migliardi's ragtag score trundles along innocuously in the background.

Rains' near participation in such SF classics as *The Day the Earth Stood Still* and *The Time Machine* did nothing to prepare him for the role of the testy professor here, but faint glimmers of *Forbidden Planet* and *When Worlds Collide* do flesh out Vassily Petron's derivative screenplay. (In fact, Margheriti and Petron needn't have looked much beyond their own *Assignment Outer Space—Pianeta*'s spiritual brother—for the nuts and bolts of their second "Planet on the Loose" concoction.) Still, Rains had enacted enough cranky eccentrics during his three decades of film work to play Benson in his sleep.

It's to his credit that Rains keeps his eyes open and his wits about him. Feisty and supercilious, yet somehow lovable (a clue that, perhaps, in the longer Italian original, Mrs. Collins made more than just coffee), it's his genius at calculus which gives him the edge on his colleagues, most of whom stand around wincing painfully, when not toying with buttons and switches on none-too-impressive looking machinery. The "Old Man" (almost every member of the first cast has a colorful sobriquet) never declaims when pontificating will do and tosses off his fateful numbers with a smug flair for the dramatic. Light-years ahead of both underlings and the "High Command," Benson's intellect finds no fulfillment until he milks the Outsider's electronic brain, and his panache remains undiminished until the planet itself begins to implode. With Rains running on all pistons from the get-go, the most dynamic of his co-players (and a vigorous debate could be had identifying *that* individual) is as pale and two-dimensional as the cartoonish rays emanating from the warring spaceships.

In another's hands, the character might have become little more than a mishmash of the stereotypical myopic scientist, foxy grandfather, and grouchy old bastard. As if to counteract that, Rains breathes fire into the mixture; even his most over-the-top lines verge on plausibility when snarled in that world-famous voice. He uses, rather than succumbs to, the recurrent shtick allotted him by the screenplay—chewing on ghastly looking cigar butts, growling at his subordinates—and any departures from the norm (his waxing unctuously while meeting

Bob and Cathy Cole, for example) are handled with what passes for a smile and the proper mix of smarmy insincerity and complete disregard for anyone's feelings. Without Rains, *Battle of the Worlds* would vanish completely into the black hole of early-sixties science-fiction dreck.

*Battle of the Worlds* U.S. release/Topaz Films, 1963. 84 minutes.

CLAUDE RAINS (Professor Benjamin Benson); Bill Carter (Fred Steel); Maya Brent (Eve Barnett); Umberto Orsini (Commander Bob Cole); Jacqueline Derval (Cathy Cole); Renzo Palmer (General Varrick); Carol Danell (Mrs. Collins); with Maria Mustari, Giuliano Gemma, Jim Dolen, John Stacey, Massimo Righi, Joseph Pollini, Aldo D'Ambrosio

Director: Anthony Dawson (Antonio Margheriti); Writer and Director, English Dialogue: George Higgins III; Screenplay: Vassily Petron; Director of Photography: Raffaello Masciocchi; Production Supervisor: Tommaso Sagone; Production Assistants: Averoe Stefani, Nino Masini, Cosmo Dies; Sound: Giovanni Rossi; Editor: Jorge Serrallonga; Camera Operator: Cesare Allione; Camera Assistant: Danilo Desidero; Music: Mario Migliardi; Assistant Director: Renzo Ragazzi; Script Girl: Tersicore Koloson

Produced as *Il Pianeta degli Uomini Spenti* by Ultra Films/Sicilia Cinematografica, 1960.

# *Lawrence of Arabia* (1962)

At the request of Mr. Dryden (Claude Rains), civilian head of Great Britain's Arab Bureau, Lieutenant T. E. Lawrence (Peter O'Toole) is assigned to assess the Bedouin uprising against the Turkish empire. As the Turks have allied themselves with the Kaiser's Germany, it is in Britain's best interests to support the rebellious desert tribesmen. Lawrence meets Prince Faisal (Alec Guinness), who provides him with the 50 men he needs to carry out his bold attack of the port city of Agaba. Risking his life to rescue an Arab who had fallen from his camel in the Nefud Desert, Lawrence wins the admiration of the nomads and the respect of Sherif Ali (Omar Sharif); Lawrence is soon outfitted in native dress.

The surprise attack on Agaba from the desert succeeds in part because Lawrence has convinced Auda Abu Tayi (Anthony Quinn) and his Howitat tribesmen to join him, Sherif Ali, and the Harith soldiers in the enterprise. It is Lawrence's dream to see the Arabs unite. Returning briefly to Cairo, "El Orans" advises General Allenby (Jack Hawkins) that, in return for gold and armaments, he and his Arabs will sabotage the Turkish railway system, effectively bringing the Turkish empire to its knees. This comes to pass, and Lawrence of Arabia is soon world famous.

Disgusted with Britain's jockeying for Arabian colonies, alarmed at his own bloodthirstiness, and still suffering from his torture at the hands of the Turks, Lawrence wants no part of Allenby's subsequent "big push" to Damascus. He soon realizes, however, that unless the Arabs reach Damascus first, the British will be in Arabia to stay. Under his command, the Bedouin forces capture the city and slaughter the ragtag Turkish soldiers seeking to flee. Arriving after the victory, the British Army finds the city under the control of the Arab Council. It isn't long before the ages-old suspicions of the tribesmen cause the council to collapse, and the Arabs leave Damascus in a body. Dryden and Allenby play at politics with Faisal, as Lawrence of Arabia rides off to the boat which will return him to England.

Scads of literature—historical, promotional, critical—greeted David Lean's *Lawrence of Arabia* when in opened in December of 1962, and little good can be done to paraphrase it here. The picture spelled stardom for Peter O'Toole, hunk-dom (and *Doctor Zhivago*) for Omar Sharif, and was regarded as yet another flawed masterpiece by director David Lean. Reviewers outdid themselves, deploring how the true image of Lawrence, the Mystical Poet, had been obfuscated by the spurious portrait of Lawrence,

With *(from left)* Anthony Quayle and Jack Hawkins. *Lawrence of Arabia* marked Claude's last professional trip abroad. *Courtesy Jessica Rains*

the Desert Warrior, and posturing as if filming *The Seven Pillars of Wisdom* would have made more sense to the common man than had the newspapers' accounts of English expansionism and Bedouin bravery.

Rains' role is a small one in *Lawrence of Arabia*: His Mr. Dryden pops up now and again in brief, albeit telling, scenes. The glib chief of the Arab Bureau does get the ball rolling, though, and he's still on tap at the end, when none other than Prince Faisal heralds him as the brains behind the intercultural compromises. "Me, Your highness?" queries Rains, in his curtain line. "On the whole, I wish I'd stayed in Tunbridge Wells."

Dryden is a political prototype, not necessarily British, nor inevitably corrupt. He's an amoral referee, guided less by the measurable suffering of any one group than by the likelihood of one hypothetical possibility over another. He and his ilk note the daily tolls of the battlefields and plot strategy accordingly, while Lawrence, Sherif Ali, and Auda Abu Tayi gallop across those same battlefields without being privy to any of the underlying motivations or hidden agendas. Lawrence progresses through the ranks—moving quickly from lieutenant to major to colonel with each subsequent instance of bravery/foolhardiness—but remains unable (or unwilling) to comprehend the scope of the larger picture.

Lawrence: I've told [the Bedouin] we have no ambitions in Arabia.
Allenby: Have we any ambitions in Arabia, Dryden?
Dryden: Difficult to say, sir.

To Lawrence, no words should be difficult to say, just as no actions should be impossible to perform. Lawrence is guileless, but his spiritual side, once given to quoting Thomistocles and the Koran, is gradually supplanted by egotism and the smell of blood. Dryden *has* no ego—it is the government which speaks when he opens his mouth—and gives no clue as to whether soldiering had played any part in his youth. He is not so much guileful as wily, and that is the mark of the consummate politician. As American journalist Jackson Bentley admits to Sharif Ali, politics is the art of answering without saying anything. Dryden makes this abundantly clear to Lawrence when pressed as to the terms of an English-French agreement to divvy up the Turkish empire (and Arabia) after the war:

Let's have no displays of indignation. You may not have known, but you certainly had suspicions. If we've told lies, you've told half-lies, and a man who tells lies, like me, merely hides the truth. But a man who tells half-lies has forgotten where he put it.

Following the Arab victory at Damascus and the subsequent exodus from the city, the tidying up is left to Allenby, Faisal, and Dryden. The unfailingly diplomatic prince advises Lawrence that battle has taken them as far as battle can: "There's nothing further here for a warrior. We drive bargains, old men's work." Newly promoted to colonel ("You'll have a cabin to yourself on the boat home"), Lawrence heads back to England. Neither Allenby nor Dryden offers any argument when Prince Faisal observes that "Orans is a sword with two edges. We are equally glad to be rid of him, are we not?"

Dryden's few exchanges, as clever as they are on paper, are rendered infernally profound (or, perhaps, profoundly infernal) when purred, whispered, or snarled by Rains. If judged purely by appearances—he is shorter than his colleagues, is deferential to everyone, and is usually the only suit in a room full of uniforms—he is the pettiest of bureaucrats. Appearances, however, like governments, are deceiving.

At 71 years of age, the actor was still spry enough to nose about locations and explore local sites while between scenes. "He just seems to materialize," marveled the script clerk to a local reporter. "He moves so quickly I scarcely see him coming."

Shot in the Moorish recesses of Spain, *Lawrence of Arabia* was Rains' last work abroad.

*Lawrence of Arabia* Columbia. Released December 16, 1962. 222 minutes.

Peter O'Toole (T. E. Lawrence); Alec Guinness (Prince Faisal); Anthony Quinn (Auda Abu Tayi); Jack Hawkins (General Allenby); José Ferrer (Turkish Bey); Anthony Quayle (Col. Brighton); CLAUDE RAINS (Mr. Dryden); Arthur Kennedy (Jackson Bentley); Donald Wolfit (General Murray); Omar Sharif (Sherif Ali); I. S. Johar (Gasim); Gamil Ratib (Majid); Michel Ray (Farraj); Zia Mohyeddin (Tafas); John Dimech (Daud); Howard Marion Crawford (Medical Officer); Jack Gwillam (Club Secretary); Hugh Miller (R.A.M.C. Colonel); Kenneth Fortescue (Allenby's Aide); John Ruddock (Harith Elder); Henry Oscar (Reciter); Fernando Sancho (Turkish Sergeant); Stuart Saunders (Regimental Sergeant-Major)

Producers: Sam Spiegel, David Lean; Director: David Lean; 2nd Unit Directors: Andre Smagghe, Noel Howard; Screenplay: Robert Bolt, Michael Wilson (uncredited); Director of Photography: F. A. Young; 2nd Unit Photography: Skeets Kelly, Nicholas Roeg, Peter Newbrook; Camera Operator: Ernest Day; Art Director: John Stoll; Assistant Art Directors: Roy Rossotti, George Richardson, Terence Marsh, Tony Rimmington; Set Dresser: Dario Simoni; Editor: Anne V. Coates; Production Designer: John Box; Music: Maurice Jarre; Musical Arrangements: Gerard Schurmann; Musical Coordinator: Morris Stoloff; Played by London Philharmonic Orchestra; Conducted by Adrian Boult; Sound: Winston Ryder, John Cox; Sound Recording: Paddy Cunningham; Assistant Director: Roy Stevens; Production Manager: John Palmer; Continuity: Barbara Cole; Wardrobe: John Wilson Apperson; Makeup: Charles Parker; Hairstyles: A. G. Scott

Technicolor and Super-Panavision (70mm)

# *Twilight of Honor* (1963)

Ben Brown (Nick Adams), a young drifter, is to stand trial for killing Cole Clinton (Pat Buttram), one of Durango, New Mexico's most popular citizens. Special Prosecutor Norris Bixby (James Gregory) sees Brown's conviction as a stepping-stone to the governor's mansion, and his case is strengthened by the fact that the entire town has prejudged the accused. Brown's wife, Laura Mae (Joey Heatherton), a sexpot and sometime prostitute, turned her husband over to the police herself, in order to collect the $10,000 reward.

Judge Tucker (Edgar Stehli) appoints David Mitchell (Richard Chamberlain) to defend Brown, and Mitchell seeks out the guidance of Art Harper (Claude Rains), his old law mentor. Art and David believe that Brown had killed Clinton when the older man had been found in bed with Laura Mae; this is a legitimate defense in New Mexico. Bixby sets out to prove that Brown connived to have his wife sleep with Clinton, thus invalidating the defense.

Buoyed by the love of Art's daughter, Susan (Joan Blackman), David convinces the Durango jury that Brown had killed Clinton in a fit of passion while defending his wife, and the young man is acquitted. Bixby's political momentum is halted, and David and Susan consider marriage.

Hoping for some crossover magic (much rarer in 1963 than it is nowadays), MGM constructed *Twilight of Honor* around Richard Chamberlain, the enormously popular star of the studio's weekly TV series, *Dr. Kildare*. With Chamberlain for the young ladies, curvy Joey Heatherton (daughter of Ray, daytime television's wholesome "Merry Mailman") for their dates, and Claude Rains, James Gregory, Pat Buttram, and Jeanette Nolan lending their old, familiar faces for the more mature viewers, the acting bases were covered. Al Dewlen's eponymous novel may have been derivative, but its egregious lifting of the best parts of Rains' early *They Won't Forget* was unknown to some and forgiven by the rest. Boris Sagal, who, like Chamberlain, would find his greatest successes in the hybrid realm of made-for-TV movies, was tapped to direct, and Henry Denker, a dramatist in his own right (he translated and adapted the Italian original of Rains' last play, *So Much of Earth, So Much of*

*Heaven*), reconfigured Dewlen's book for the screen.

Alas! So much sound, so much fury … and nothing gained but tepid box office performance. For Richard Chamberlain, who would carry on as the small-screen physician with the heart (and face) of gold until 1966, later efforts (like *The Music Lovers* [as Tchaikovsky, 1970] and *Lady Caroline Lamb* [1972]) made little real impact, and it remained for the "TV mini-series" genre (*Shogun* [1980], *The Thorn Birds* [1983]) to reinvent the actor's persona.

Nonetheless, while Chamberlain's noble attorney may fall short, James Gregory's special prosecutor is properly despicable—a quality which the actor parlayed into an extensive career—as is Edgar Stehli's Judge Tucker, who ignores the niceties of law in favor of sustaining the more ludicrous of prosecutorial objections. Joan Blackman's Susan Harper has "love interest" written all over her from her first on-screen moment (Chamberlain, we discover, has been a widower these past few years), but this is strictly formulaic; it wouldn't do for young Dr. Kildare to take up with a trollop like Laura Mae, the only other female of his own generation in Durango. Heatherton acts to her strength more than does Miss Blackman, and her provocative movements recall starlet Yvette Vickers' similar gyrations in *Attack of the 50-Foot Woman* and other films a decade earlier.

Rains is a wily old lawyer, partially incapacitated and completely on the wagon. He hasn't much to do, other than make the odd suggestion, chortle occasionally, or proffer the expected reaction, but his best moment has him describing how he gets a glow on. Urging his young colleague to swallow mouthfuls of forbidden liquor, Rains rejoices in each gulp. "This is how I have to drink nowadays," he admits to his co-star; "…vicariously. I get someone plastered, and then I stagger up to bed and sleep it off." The vignette is amusing enough, and both Rains and Chamberlain pitch in to wring it dry of its humor. With David all but moving his bed into the Harper household, however, the viewer awaits their collaboration to produce some ingenious masterstroke which will drive Bixby and his infernal forces back into the darkness. The jury is apparently swayed by David's sincere and pure-hearted final statement, so the moment never arises, and one comes away feeling cheated.

We know that Art is wheeled into the courtroom purely for effect—the lawyer says as much in an aside to David—but, dramatically, this is like priming the last cannon on the battlement and then leaving it unloaded. The cry of "Not Guilty" and the ensuing brouhaha is frankly TV-like, and quite insufficient. Movies of the day needed more than this, and more was something this screenplay was incapable of giving.

There are some nice visual touches, though. Filming in Panavision, Sagal and cinematographer Philip Lathrop conspire to introduce the many flashbacks alongside (or amidst) the character(s) recalling the occurrence for the court. The device is both highly effective, bridging the teller and the tale, and unusual; it certainly hasn't been worn down by overuse in the ensuing decades. Lathrop's black-and-white palette gives many of the scenes a noirish look, and the montage of grainy photos under the titles lends a documentary feel that certainly doesn't hurt.

*Twilight of Honor* was the last feature film on which Claude Rains worked. Although *The Greatest Story Ever Told* was released in 1965, Rains had enacted Herod the Great under David Lean's direction in May/June, 1963.

*Twilight of Honor* MGM. Released October 16, 1963. 104 minutes.

Richard Chamberlain (David Mitchell); Joey Heatherton (Laura Mae Brown); Nick Adams (Ben Brown); CLAUDE RAINS (Art Harper); Joan Blackman (Susan Harper); James Gregory (Norris Bixby); Pat Buttram (Cole Clinton); Jeanette Nolan (Amy Clinton); Edgar Stehli (Judge James Tucker); James Bell (Charles Crispin); George Mitchell (Paul Farish); Donald Barry (Judd Elliott); Bert Freed (Sheriff Buck

Veteran lawyer Claude Rains advises Richard Chamberlain that he will have done his best no matter what the verdict is.

Metro-Goldwyn-Mayer presents **"TWILIGHT OF HONOR"** in PANAVISION

**Neither Claude's magic nor Joan Blackman's beauty could rescue TV actor Richard Chamberlain from the Curse of Dr. Kildare, or the inadequacies of the film's script.**

Wheeler); Robin Raymond (Therese Braden); June Dayton (Vera Driscoll); Vaughn Taylor (Ballentine); Linda Evans (Alice Clinton); Arch Johnson (McWade); with Burt Mustin

Producers: William Perlberg, George Seaton; Director: Boris Sagal; Screenplay: Henry Denker, based on the novel, *Twilight of Honor*, by Al Dewlen; Director of Photography: Philip Lathrop; Camera Operator: Joe Jackman; Art Directors: George W. Davis, Paul Groesse; Set Decorators: Henry Grace, Hugh Hunt; Editor: Hugh S. Fowler; Music Composed and Conducted by John Green; Recording Supervisor: Franklin Milton; Mixer: Larry Jost; Assistant Directors: Donald Roberts, Al Shenberg, Richard Lang; Makeup Supervisor: William Tuttle; Makeup: Ron Berkeley, Agnes Flanagan; Hairstyles: Mary Keats

# The Greatest Story Ever Told (1965)

While assessing John Huston's *The Bible ... in the Beginning* (1966) in one of her collections of arch (but perceptive) movie reviews, Pauline Kael paused to put her finger on the problem which confronts most celluloid biographies of Jesus:

The stories of Genesis are, of course, free of that wretched masochistic piety that makes movies about Christ so sickly. Pasolini's *The Gospel According to Saint Matthew* was so static that I could hardly wait for that loathsome prissy young man to get crucified. Why do movie-makers think that's such a good story, anyway? The only thing that gives it plausibility is, psychologically, not very attractive. And whether it's told the DeMille way, loaded with hypocritic sanctity, or the Pasolini way, drabness supposedly guaranteeing purity and truth, it's got a bad ending that doesn't make sense after all those neat miracles.

The myriad adventures of Jesus (whether extra-biblical or according to Matthew, Mark, Luke, or John) were guaranteed box-office gold during the silent era, provided that the public could detect that reverence was displayed not only in the unfolding of the real or imagined events, but also in the personification of the Messiah. What passed for reverence in those days, however, occasionally got a little ripe. Once in his makeup as Jesus for Cecil B. DeMille's *The King of Kings* (1927), the venerable H. B. Warner was deferred to worshipfully by cast and crew alike, but was ordered to eat his lunch, alone, in his dressing room; apparently, to witness the ersatz Christ gobble a tuna fish sandwich would have been sacrilege.

When *King of Kings* was remade in color and with a cast of zillions in 1961, the mature look was out, and the role of the Lord was relegated to blue-eyed hunk, Jeffrey Hunter. On the whole, the rest of his colleagues displayed enough reverence to get this most familiar of balls rolling, but Hunter was deemed too lightweight for the part. The film failed to touch any save the pre-edified, was soon dubbed *I Was a Teenage Jesus* by the wags, and faded quickly to its present footnote-status in books on general movie history.

The speed of this fade is nowhere more evident than in the reviews which greeted George Stevens' *The Greatest Story Ever Told* some four years later; there is nary a comparison with nor scarcely a mention of its misguided predecessor to be found in the usual major sources. Instead, the critics were effusive in their regard for Stevens' broadly faithful narrative (although they did not ignore the film's weaknesses).

Demonstrably *not* one of these is Claude Rains' brief appearance as Herod the Great. As keen, deceitful, and merciless in life as any of Rains' villains of the early thirties, Herod climbed the ranks from governor of Galilee to king of all Jews via skillful toadyism to his Roman conquerors and cold-blooded murder of his Semitic brethren. The historian Josephus has him doing away with enough family members to rival Caligula's record, and here, at the outset of the tale of the Christ, he can still work himself into a lather over this supposed Messiah's daring to show his face during the current regime. Obviously on his last legs (*The Jewish Antiquities* has him dead by 4 B.C.), the crafty old king suckers in the Magi ("If you find this child, bring me word that I, too, might worship him") and then—taking no chances—has them followed.

With the Gospels failing to give many other quotable lines to Herod, Rains relied upon Stevens' and James Lee Barrett's well intentioned screenplay for further exposition. The scenarists drew upon the *spirit* of the tale and furnished the elderly actor with a pip of a vignette, wherein the wily old monarch discloses his religious hypocrisy, his contempt for prophecy, and his fear of opportunism:

God? Hmmmph! Where is God? Or the child of God, except in man's most dangerous imagination? The child of imagination is the child I fear.

Such fear leads to the slaughter of the innocents, and Herod no sooner smiles with pleasure at the news when he topples over dead on his throne. Wisely, David Lean had the fall photographed in long shot;[42] Rains' toothy-grin-cum-death-mask might have bordered on the ludicrous in close-up.

Most of the actor-oriented criticism of the film slapped the back of Max Von Sydow's Christ—reverently, of course. At the time, the Swedish actor was best known for his roles in Ingmar Bergman's artsy studies, and *Story* greased his way into the consciousness of the less eclectic moviegoer, for whom *Bergman* inevitably meant *Ingrid*. Von Sydow was praised for portraying a hale and hearty Jesus, and for struggling to deliver the Lord's very words as if they were being spoken for the first time. Stevens, in turn,

The inscription on the photograph reads, "To Dear Claude, who flew to my rescue. Your affection-ate friend, David Lean." *Courtesy Jessica Rains*

was lauded for his choice of Von Sydow, his ability to blend the profound humanity of the story with the awesome scope of the technology (Ultra Panavision 70 and Technicolor-Cinerama), and his efforts at keeping this greatest story from grating on the likes of Pauline Kael. The only minor *harrumphs* were over the picture's 225 minute length, Charlton Heston's "Tarzan-like" John the Baptist, John Wayne's take on a Roman spear-carrier, and Ed Wynn's portrayal of Ed Wynn.

Rains was named in several reviews (as were many of the plethora of renowned character actors dropped into the action like manna from heaven) and was hailed in all of these (unlike many of the plethora). *Variety* (February 17, 1965), for example, termed him "a standout." (While mention was made by individual critics of his/her own favorite personality, virtually every review I consulted for this essay unfailingly cited only two actors: Von Sydow as Christ, and the Duke as the centurion at the foot of the cross—and for drastically different reasons.) *The New Republic*'s Stanley Kauffmann simplified matters tremendously, stating point-blank that Rains and Max Von Sydow were the only exceptions to the appalling bad acting.

*The Greatest Story Ever Told* was Claude Rains' last feature film (in order of release), and the actor was every bit as breathless and weary as his on-screen character. The role didn't keep him long from his garden in Sandwich, New Hampshire, but, nevertheless, Herod was a plum, and Rains used his 30-odd years of screen experience to embody a man for whom fear of God and impending death was less threatening than a "child of imagination."

*The Greatest Story Ever Told* United Artists. February 9, 1965. 225 minutes.

Max Von Sydow (Jesus); Dorothy McGuire (Mary); Robert Loggia (Joseph); CLAUDE RAINS (Herod the Great); José Ferrer (Herod Antipas); Marian Seldes (Herodias); John Abbott (Aben); Rodolfo Acosta (Captain of Lancers); Philip Coolidge (Chuza); Michael Ansara (Herod's Commander); Joe Perry (Archelaus); Charlton Heston (John the Baptist); Donald Pleasance (The Dark Hermit); David McCallum (Judas Iscariot); Roddy McDowall (Matthew); Michael Anderson, Jr. (James the Younger); David Sheiner (James the Elder); Gary Raymond (Peter); Robert Blake (Simon the Zealot); Burt Brinckerhoff (Andrew); John Considine (John); Jamie Farr (Thaddeus); David Hedison (Philip); Peter Mann (Nathaniel); Tom Reese (Thomas); Telly Savalas (Pilate); Angela Lansbury (Claudia); Paul Stewart (Questor); Harold J. Stone (General Varus); Cyril Delevanti (Melchior); Mark Lenard (Balthazar); Frank Silvera (Caspar); Joanna Dunham (Mary Magdalene); Janet Margolin (Mary of Bethany); Ina Balin (Martha of Bethany); Pat Boone (Man at Tomb); Michael Tolan (Lazarus); Carroll Baker (Veronica); Sal Mineo (Uriah); Van Heflin (Bar Amand); Ed Wynn (Old Aram); Shelley Winters (Woman with No Name); Chet Stratton (Theophilus); Ron Whelan (Annas); Abraham Sofaer (Joseph of Arimathaea); John Lupton (Speaker of Capernaum); Russell Johnson (Scribe); Martin Landau (Caiaphas); Nehemiah Persoff (Shemiah); Joseph Schildkraut (Nicodemus); Victor Buono (Sorak); Robert Busch (Emissary); John Crawford (Alexander); John Wayne (Roman Captain); Sidney Poitier (Simon of Cyrene); Joseph Sirola (Dumah); Richard Conte (Barabbas); Frank De Kova (Tormentor)

Producer and Director: George Stevens; Screenplay: George Stevens and James Lee Barrett; Executive Producer: Frank I. Davis; Associate Producers: George Stevens, Jr. and Antonio Vellani; Director of Photography: William C. Mellor, Loyal Griggs; Sound: Franklin Milton, William Steinkamp, Charles Wallace; Editors: Harold F. Kress, Argyle Nelson, Frank O'Neill; Set Designer: David Hall; Art Director: Richard Day, William Creber; Costumes: Vittorio Nino Novarese, Marjorie Best; Second Unit Directors: Richard Talmadge, William Hale; Choral Supervisor: Ken Darby; Special Visual Effects: J. McMillan Johnson, Clarence Slifen, A. Arnold Gillespie, Robert R. Hoag; Music Score Composed and Conducted by Alfred Newman

In Creative Association with Carl Sandburg

# Theater and Concerts

*Claude Rains' theatrical career was quite extensive—the proscenium arch was both the Alpha and Omega of his public life—and despite our checking and rechecking myriad sources, the following is doubtless incomplete. This body of work deserves a book-length treatment of its own.*

## 1900

***Sweet Nell of Old Drury*** (*Theatre Royal, Haymarket*, August 30) Rains' theatrical debut (at 10 years old) reputedly found him *singing*. Unbilled, he was a voice in the

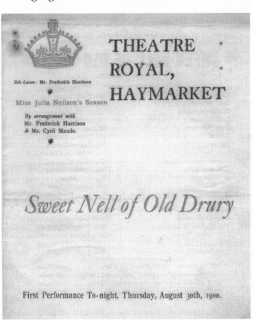

THEATRE ROYAL, HAYMARKET

*Sole Lessee:* Mr. Frederick Harrison

Miss Julia Neilson's Season

*By arrangement with* Mr. Frederick Harrison & Mr. Cyril Maude.

*Sweet Nell of Old Drury*

First Performance To-night, Thursday, August 30th, 1900.

**It's unclear whether Claude just milled around or actually sang, but this job was the first of what would be a remarkable career.** *Courtesy Susan Duic*

crowd—not yet a face—in Paul Kester's sappy four-act entertainment, which starred Julia Neilson as Nell Gwyn.

## 1901–1910

Young Claude worked behind scenes as page-boy and call-boy at the *Duke of York's Theatre*. Per Jane S. McIlvaine (*Farmer Rains On Stage Again, The Philadelphia Inquirer*, September 5, 1950), he "was fired when the manager caught him dipping into the leading man's pocket for carfare." Soon, he was call-boy at *His Majesty's Theatre*, under Sir Herbert Beerbohm-Tree, who doted on the lad, occasionally giving him money with which to buy books. From call-boy, Rains was promoted first to prompter and then to assistant stage manager.

***The Last of the Dandies*** (*His Majesty's Theatre*, May 30) "Winkles" may be the earliest featured role for the fledgling actor, who was billed as "Master Claude Rains." Clyde Fitch's four-act drama, which also featured Tree as (Count D'Orsay), Eugen Mayeur, and Dawson Milward, lasted but eight performances.

In his overview of the world of Edwardian theater, *Carriages at Eleven*, Walter MacQueen-Pope gives an amusing view of Tree, Rains' mentor at the time:

One of Tree's failings was a liability to forget his lines.... Cecil King, one of his great stage managers, learnt all his Chief's parts and would go on with the crowd to give him a quiet prompt and reminder. Once, however, this was not possible. The elusive lines occurred when Tree was on with only one other character, and at a moment when he was furthest from the corner. So, a brilliant idea occurred to the stage management. They would write the lines very large on a board, the call boy should go down into the orchestra pit, out of sight of the audience, hold up the board and Tree could glance down and read them off. Tree approved highly. The next performance the boy was duly in the pit with the board. The moment came, Tree dried up. He strolled down to the foot-lights, gazed idly into the pit, stared, smiled, stared again, shrugged his shoulders and then walked to the prompt corner. "What's the line?" he hissed. "But, Chief," whispered Stanley Bell, "the boy's down in the pit with it all written on a board." "I know, I know," replied Tree *sotto voce*, "but he's holding it upside down." And that call boy was Claude Rains, now a great star himself.[43]

Rains was assistant stage manager for Tree's near-mythic production of Shakespeare's *Henry VIII*, which began rehearsals at *Her Majesty's Theatre* on June 21, 1910. The play—all three and a half hours of it—opened on September 1 and made money every night of its 254-night run, before finally closing on April 9, 1911. In February, the 2000-foot filmed version opened in London, with Tree as Cardinal Wolsey, Arthur Bourchier as Henry, Reginald Owen as Cromwell, and Basil Gill as the Duke of Buckingham. There is no record that Rains was involved with the motion picture.

## 1911

*The God of the Mountain* (by Irish dramatist Lord Dunsany [Edward John Moreton Drax Plunkett]; *Haymarket Theatre*, June 28); back on-stage, Rains appeared as Slag, a beggar; he served as assistant stage manager here, too.

## 1911–1912

Rains toured Melbourne and Sydney, Australia, with Sir Harley Granville-Barker's company. He was stage manager for Maurice Maeterlinck's *The Blue Bird* and appeared in Bernard Shaw's *You Never Can Tell* (as Bohun). Back in London, Rains continued on as assistant stage manager at *Queen's The-*

*atre* for *The Blue Bird* from December 26 until February 3, 1912.

## 1912

When Stanley Houghton's *The Younger Generation* transferred from the *Haymarket* to *The Duke of York's Theatre* on February 10, Rains was hired on as assistant stage manager; the three-act play starred Nigel Playfair and ran until March 8.

Rains next documented appearance was as a spy (a mute role) in *The Golden Doom*, by Lord Dunsany and Norman O'Neill (music), which opened on November 19 at the *Haymarket Theatre*. The play lasted for 28 performances, with Ewan Brook, Henry Hargreaves, E. Lyall Swete, and Frank Ridley among the others in the cast.

That one did better than G. J. Hamien's *The Waldies*, which opened on December 8 at the *Haymarket* and closed the following day. Stage manager Rains was then at liberty, along with stars Norman McKeown and Cathleen Nesbitt.

At some point this year, Rains married actress Isabel Jeans.

## 1913

Rains appeared in Arthur Schnitzler's one-act "grotesque," *The Green Cockatoo* (*Aldwych Theatre*, March 9), as Grasset, a philosopher; also on the bill was *Contesse Mitzi*, another one-act Schnitzler piece. Like *Cockatoo*, it lasted for only two performances; Rains managed the stage for both plays.

Prior to that, on February 13, he was again the *Haymarket's* assistant stage manager for a fair run (35 performances) of Henrik Ibsen's historic drama, *Kongsemnerne*, which William Archer had translated and overhauled as *The Pretenders*. Starring was Montagu Love, with whom Rains would appear a number of times at Warner Bros.

In Frederick Harrison's production of *Typhoon* (*Haymarket*, April 2), the actor was seen as Omayi, Doctor of Laws, a member of the Japanese colony in Paris. Based on Melchior Lengvel's *Taifun*, the four-act play also featured Robin Shiells (Baron Yoshikawa), Arthur Stanley (Amamari), and Allan Jeayes (Marchland), among others. (Simpler times: it was thought imperative that the a notice in the program explain that

It will be noted that in the scenes where the Japanese are conversing with each other, and therefore supposed to be speaking their own language, they use no accent, though pitch and intonation have a certain national peculiarity. But in the scenes where they are conversing with Europeans, and are therefore supposed to be speaking a foreign language, a strong accent will be marked.)

Rains served as assistant stage manager for *Typhoon*.

Job security beckoned with a position as assistant stage manager when the *Haymarket* hosted Bayard Veiller's ***Within the Law*** on May 24. Actually, what was presented was an adaptation by Frederick Fenn and Arthur Wimperis, but the production ran 426 performances (until May 9, 1914) anyhow. Lightning strikes twice! While managing ***Within the Law***, Rains alternated playing Takejiro (with Douglas Gordon and George Owen) in a one-act curtain-raiser, *A Dear Little Wife*. Leon M. Lion and Nellie Dale rounded out the cast in Gerald Dunn's little comedy, which opened on June 6 and closed when Tree's extravagant production of the Veiller four-act drama did.

## 1914–1915

… Granville Barker sent for [Rains]. "I'd like you to take my company of *Fanny's First Play* to America," said Barker. "You'll act as my representative till I get there. All you have to do is watch the production, make sure that everything is all right on the stage. Clock the audience as it comes in, in order to check the box office, handle finances—ah—make speeches about Mr. Shaw and me before different clubs and organizations— I'd like you to see to it that the publicity is good, too—and, oh, yes—I nearly forgot," he added, "you'll play a small part."

(Katharine Roberts. *The Plow and the Star*, in *Colliers*, November 19, 1938)

In addition to his responsibilities as general manager of the troupe, Rains appeared in Shaw's *Androcles and the Lion* (as Spintho) and in Euripides' *Iphigenia in Taurus* (in New Haven, Connecticut; May) as the Herdsman. Reporting on the May 15 performance at the Yale Bowl, *The New York Times* found that

Of the two messenger speeches, Mr. Rains did rather better with his than Mr. [Philip] Merivale. Mr. Rains bounced a good deal, but the real fire was there. Mr. Merivale was apparently unstrung by the effect of his costume on the audience.

(May 16, 1915)

The Euripides piece was also performed at the stadium of the College of the City of New York on May 31 and June 5, 1915, and *The Times* commented on the May performance, too.

Claude Rains seems to have modified somewhat the sheer physical vigor of his performance as the herdsman, but it remains an exceedingly effective contribution to the play, so good, in fact, that many must regret that during the long Barker season at Wallack's [theater], he did all his work behind the scenes.

(June 1, 1915)

## 1919

Following wartime service, 1915–1919, Rains played Mears in Douglas Murray's comedy, ***Uncle Ned*** (*Lyceum Theatre*, Sheffield, March 24), and Ivan Petrovich in ***Reparation*** (*St. James' Theatre*, September 26). Based on a translation and adaptation of Leo Tolstoy's *The Live Corpse*, the three-act drama was produced and directed by Stanley Bell. Also featured in the cast were Agnes Thomas (Anna Pavlovna), Ion Swinley (Victor Karenin), Henry Ainley (Fedya), and Alice Moffat (Masha), among others. Besides acting, Rains was stage manager for ***Reparation***.

## 1920

Rains was stage manager and appeared as Casca in Shakespeare's ***Julius Caesar*** (*St.*

*James*, January 9; Clifton Boyne was the doomed emperor and Henry Ainley the eloquent Marcus Antonius). Sticking by Ainley for the reprise of *Uncle Ned*, he was once again Mears (and stage manager)—Ainley was Edward Graham—when the comedy opened at the *St. James* on March 27. Several weeks later, he was seen as Ivan Alexandrovich Klestakoff in *The Government Inspector* (based on Nikolay Gogol's *Revizor*, aka *The Inspector General*; *The Duke of York's Theatre*, April 13), and before being promoted to Cassius for the provincial tour of *Julius Caesar*. Giannetto in Luigi Pirandello's *The Jest* followed in August at the *Wimbledon*. (Per Jeanne Stein's recap of Rains' career for the November 1963 *Films in Review*, "In '20 he fell in love with, married, and divorced, an actress named Marie Hemingway.")

## 1921

Having forsworn stage management for acting, Rains was the title character, Daniel Arnault, in Sybil Harris's adaptation of Louis Verneuil's *Daniel* (*St. James*, January 15); Lyn Harding, C. Aubrey Smith, and Edith Evans were among the other players. *The Times* felt Rains was a "brilliant success" as the corpse-like invalid, and said that he made

… a haunting thing of it—an utter wreck, but a picturesque, romantic wreck, a choice curio shattered, the irretrievable ruin of something comely and precious.

He stayed put for George Middleton and Guy Bolton's *Polly with a Past* (which opened on March 2; Rains was "The Stranger," Edith Evans showed up again, and Noel Coward headed the cast list). He then appeared as Hilary Fairfield in Clemence Dane's *A Bill of Divorcement* (*St. Martin's Theatre*, March 14), and played Laurent, le Marquis de Mortain, in *Legion of Honour* (at the *Aldwych*, August 24).

On November 17, Rains (as Kit Marlowe)

and The Reandean Company opened in Miss Dane's *Will Shakespeare*, an "Invention in Four Acts," at the *Shaftsbury*; Basil Dean directed. With Philip Merivale (Will Shakespeare), Moyna Macgill (Anne Hathaway), Mary Rorke (Mrs. Hathaway), and Mary Clare (Mary Fitton), among others.

Flora Robson had a first-act bit as Queen Margaret and doubled in crowd scenes. As quoted by Robson biographer Kenneth Barrow, the renowned actress thought highly of her co-star:

Claude Rains was wonderful as Marlowe. I don't think I ever spoke to him at that time, but I had such admiration for him. He was always good. He began life as Sir Herbert Tree's dresser and had a broad Cockney accent. He would walk round Trafalgar Square, late at night, practicing his 'aitches.[44]

Despite—or, perhaps, because of—the first-rate cast, Aubrey Darlington (chief drama critic for *The Daily Telegraph* [London]) hailed Dane's melange as "The most distinguished failure of its time."

## 1922

The curtain was raised for the first time on Mary Roberts Rinehart and Avery Hopwood's *The Bat* on January 23, at the *St. James Theatre*. Directed by Gilbert Miller, the three-act melodrama offered Rains as Billy (the butler) and starred such august personages as Eva Moore (Miss Cornelia Van Gorder) and Arthur Wontner (Anderson, a Detective).

In December, Rains was seen as La Rubia in the worldwide premiere of *The Rumour* (at the *Globe*). Crafted by C. K. Munro (Charles Kirkpatrick MacMullan), the play attempted to blend the expressionistic patterns made popular by of Karel Capek's *R.U.R.* with English steadfastness; it made a splash, but there were no successful follow-ups.

Caesar (Clifton Boyne) senses something amiss; Marcus Antoninus (Henry Ainley) and Casca (Claude) know it's only a matter of time. *Courtesy Susan Druic*

## 1923

By arrangement with Gilbert Miller (who had bought out Henry Ainley's interest in the St. James Theatre), Rains appeared as Max Quantro—dancing partner of Rozanne Pom Pom—in Seymour Hicks' translation of Louis Verneuil's *The Love Habit*. Pegged "A Piece of Impertinence in Three Acts," the play opened at the *Royalty Theatre* on February 7. Next up was Rains' Louis Dubedat in Shaw's *The Doctor's Dilemma*. Cathleen Nesbitt was Mrs. Dubedat in the five-act work, which Dudley Digges produced for the *Everyman Theatre* in April. Sir John Gielgud vividly recalled that

Rains, as Dubedat in *The Doctor's Dilemma*, was just the romantic boyish figure that I hoped to be, whether in his blue painter's smock sketching the doctors, or in the death scene, when he was wheeled on to the stage wrapped in a purple dressing-jacket with a rug over his knees, and his hands, made-up very white, hanging down over the arms of his chair.[45]

On May 5, Karel and Josef Capek's *The Insect Play* appeared at the *Lyric Theatre*. Nigel Playfair and Clifford Bax provided the translation, and Rains tripled as the Lepidopterist, the Chief Engineer, and the Parasite. Elsa Lanchester had been invited by producer Playfair to enact the "tiny but pivotal part" (Miss Lanchester's phrase) of The Larva in the comic fantasy, which marked

*The Bat:* Billy the Butler (Claude) intrudes on the privacy of Dale Ogden (Nora Swinburne). *Courtesy Susan Druic*

John Gielgud's professional debut (as Felix, a Butterfly), following his participation in a spate of productions at the Royal Academy of Dramatic Art. Angela Baddeley was seen as Mrs. Cricket.

The Czech piece didn't last out the month, and Rains was over at the *Regent Theatre* in time to open (in June) as David Peel in John Drinkwater's chronicle play, *Robert E. Lee*. Also featured in the Nigel Playfair production were John Gielgud, Leo G. Carroll, and Felix Aylmer. Not long thereafter, Rains was seen as Derek Vale (the Earl of Trenton) in Seymour Hicks and Ian Hay's "sporting drama," *Good Luck* (at the *Theatre Royal, Drury Lane*; September 27). Edmund Gwenn and Arthur Treacher could also be found among the cast members.

## 1924

At this point, Rains had been augmenting his income for several years by teaching at the Royal Academy of Dramatic Art. In November of this year, the actor married Beatrix Thompson, one of his students and a competent actress in her own right.

Rains was in repertory at the *Everyman Theatre* from June through December, appearing in a series of George Bernard Shaw offerings. First up was his Napoleon in *The Man of Destiny* with Jeanne de Casalis; per Norman MacDermott, Rains' Little Corporal was "a masterpiece. He wears not only Napoleon's uniform, but his air of vital significance as well."[46] Next in line was his St. John Hotchkiss in *Getting Married*; Edith Evans starred as Mrs. George Collins and Beatrix was Leo in a "disquisitory play" which was both critically and popularly acclaimed. The role of the bully, Pat Donovan, in Ernest George's *Low Tide* interrupted the string of Shavian dramas,[47] but Rains' turns as Richard Dudgeon in *The Devil's Disciple*,[48] and Joey Percival in *Misalliance* (which also featured Alfred Clarke and Dorothy Green) put him back on track. (The actor was a bit disconcerted when, on the morning after *Misalliance* opened, he received a rather wry telegram from GBS himself: "My dear Mr. Rains," wired the playwright, "Must you be so very c-h-a-r-r-m-i-n-g as Joey Percival?")

Rains' final appearance in 1924 was as Leonard Charteris in Shaw's *The Philanderer*, which ran into January of 1925.

## 1925

His repertory contract at the *Everyman* concluded with Rains as Lionel D'Avencourt in MacDermott's translation of an Hungarian play by Ladislas Fodor, which was presented as *Home Affairs* in January. The comedy was a smash, but its aftermath spelled trouble for Rains. One cannot improve on Norman MacDermott's own words:

The notices were almost the best that any Everyman production had: several critics prophesied that it would be transferred quickly to the West End. Enquiries for transfer started within days. Three different theatres were on offer. But each Management wanted to change the player of the leading part from Claude Rains to some matinee idol. When I refused and asked for an explanation they said 75 percent of all audiences were women; Rains was "too short and stocky" and women would not see a lover in him! To us, who knew Rains had only to lift that wicked quizzing eyebrow for every woman present to give an ecstatic sigh, this was at first a joke; then infuriating stupidity. Finally I refused two firm offers in which the change was made a condition. Apart from any reason other, loyalty to Rains who had given so many distinguished performances and given also so generously of spirit left no other decision. His subsequent film career proves how imperceptive conventional theatre managers can be.[49]

At the *Lyric Theatre*, the actor was Faulkland in Sheridan's first play, *The Rivals* (in March). Produced by Nigel Playfair, the three-act comedy included Norman V. Norman (Sir Anthony Absolute); Mr. Playfair (Acres); Miles Malleson (David); Dorothy Green (Mrs. Malaprop); Beatrix Thompson (Julia); and Angela Baddeley (Lucy). What

may or may not have been a trifle awkward was the presence of Rains' first wife, Isabel Jeans, as Lydia Languish. (Per Sir John Gielgud, Rains' second wife, Marie Hemingway, was also in the cast for a number of performances.) In a volume of reminiscences he wrote late in life, author/playwright J. B. Priestley crowed about Rains' turn in the piece:

My sharpest memory of him dates from the middle 1920s when he played Faulkland in The Rivals at *The Lyric*, Hammersmith. As a rule this neurotically jealous character is played as if he were rather a bore, clearly part of a sub-plot, but in this particular production, with Rains playing him, he dominated the piece. The two Absolutes, Bob Acres and the rest, faded away, and you waited with impatience for the return of this half-mad Faulkland.[50]

Thence, on to back-to-back engagements at *Queen's Theatre* (in Paul Armstrong's *Salomy Jane* on June 24 [as Jack Marbury] and in *The Man from Hong Kong* [as Li Tong] on August 3). The *Lyric* was up next (starting on September 17), with Rains as Signor Ponza in Luigi Pirandello's three-act parable, *And That's the Truth (if You Think It Is)*.

On November 30, he opened as Eustace Perrin State in *The Madras House*, a comedy in four acts by Harley Granville-Barker, at *Ambassadors Theatre*. Mr. Granville-Barker produced and directed his comedy, with Aubrey Mather (Henry Huxtable); Frances Ivor (Katherine Huxtable); Nicholas Hannen (Philip Madras); Doris Lytton (Marion Yates), and Cathleen Nesbitt (Jessica Madras), among others.

## 1926–1927

For most of March 1926, Rains was the Bank Cashier in Ashley Dukes' translation of Georg Kaiser's *From Morn to Midnight*; the play was presented at the *Regent Theatre*, in King's Cross.

He then reprised his role as Khlestakov in Gogol's five-act comedy, *The Government Inspector*; the production, which opened for a brief run at the Barnes Theatre (a converted cinema) on April 26, 1926, also marked the stage debut of Charles Laughton, whose admission to the Royal Academy of Dramatic Art had hinged on a successful audition before a panel consisting of Rains, Dorothy Green, and Kenneth Barnes.

On Monday, August 30, Rains and Felix Aylmer opened in Ben Fleet and Clifford Pember's *Before Men's Eyes*; the three-act drama played the *"Q" Theatre* for an extremely limited run—one week. ("What is chiefly memorable about the production is the fine, nervous [sic] acting of Claude Rains as the doctor," clucked an anonymous critic.)

Some sketchy information has the actor next appearing as Martin Walmer in *Made in Heaven* for a short run in October.

Rains then accompanied his wife, Beatrix, to New York, where she was offered the lead in The Theater Guild's production of Basil Dean and Margaret Kennedy's *The Constant Nymph* (*The Selwyn Theater*, December 9); a dutiful husband, Rains assumed the role of Roberto, the butler, under Dean's direction. *The New York Times'* Brooks Atkinson opined that "As Teresa, Miss Thompson gives a notably fine performance," but mentioned her husband not at all. No matter; inside of two months, Rains had jumped ship and was portraying the title character in Henry Stillman's *Lally*.

The latter, a three-act comedy directed by John D. Williams at the *Greenwich Village Theater*, also featured Anne Morrison, Patricia Barclay, and Gerald Hamer. The critics, if not kind, were ineffably understanding:

The title role is portrayed by Claude Rains, a well-known English actor and the husband of Beatrice [sic] Thompson, the Tessa of "The Constant Nymph." As a matter of fact, he quit acting Roberto in that play for the present part. His reasons for doing so are probably to be found in the part itself, for it is a florid, showy impersonation, giving any actor abundant opportunity to create a character that at best is none too credible. In fairness to Mr. Rains it should be said that he has probably done as well with the material given him as any male human could do.

(*The New York Times*, February 9, 1927)

When *Lally* failed to last through the spring, Rains returned to *The Constant Nymph* as Lewis Dodd (the male lead), and played opposite his wife on a tour which lasted from September to the middle of November. The couple appeared together again (he was Arthur Logris) in humorist Don Marquis' *Out of the Sea* on December 5, at the *Eltinge Theater*. "A pompous retelling of the legendary romance of Tristan and Isolde," the play died a good week before the year did. With Mr. Marquis (Donald Robert Perry) at the oars, Rollo Peters, O. P. Heggie, Reginald Barlow, and Lyn Harding were likewise left adrift.

## 1928–1929

In January, Rains took over the role of Samuel Pepys in J. B. Fagan's historical comedy *And So to Bed* at the *Shubert Theater*, and May saw him back in Connecticut (Hartford, this time around) for a couple of months in stock. With Beatrix's acquiescence, Rains signed a three-year contract with The Theatre Guild, to start in the late summer. In July, he relieved Dudley Digges as the title character in Ben Jonson's *Volpone* (adapted by Stefan Zweig for the *Theater Guild*), and found himself on an extended tour as Chu-Yin in Eugene O'Neill's *Marco Millions* as the old year gave way to the new; Rains replaced Digges in that one, too. (About this time, crestfallen at the direction her career was taking, Beatrix Thompson abandoned Rains to his success and returned to the United Kingdom. During the run of *Marco Millions*, the actor met 18-year-old Frances Propper, who had been cast as a Chinese extra. It would take some six years, however, for Rains to clear the way to popping the question.)

On April 29, 1929, Rains opened as Joseph Vilim in Frantisek Langer's three-act comedy, *Camel Through the Needle's Eye* at the *Martin Beck Theater*. The Theatre Guild

**Claude (as Proteus) and Audrey Ridgewell (as Alice, the Princess Royal) in Bernard Shaw's** *The Apple Cart.* *Courtesy Susan Duic*

cast was also graced by Miriam Hopkins, Henry Travers, and Morris Carnovsky. ("Claude Rains makes a capital figure of an irate continental father by the device of playing as if someone had shoved a ramrod down his back." *The New York Times*, April 16, 1929)

Rains went on to appear as the First Prisoner in Leonhard Frank's *Karl and Anna* (October 7, the *Guild Theatre*), with Alice Brady, Otto Kruger, Frank Conroy, Gale Sondergaard, and others. Next, he enacted Lazare Carnot in Romain Rolland's *The Game of Love and Death* for the first time on November 25 (at the *Guild Theatre*). Miss Brady and the Messrs. Conroy and Kruger rejoined forces with Rains, and listed among the play's "Soldiers and Citizens" were Lionel Stander, Frank De Silva, and Henry Fonda, making his Broadway debut. Critics found *Game* "a windy literary play, bordering on closet drama," but decreed that "The most lustrous performance was that of Claude Rains as Carnot." In fact, *The New York Times* was positively effusive:

The play is almost saved by a single performance—the precise dominating acting of Claude Rains, who, as Carnot, contributes magnificently to one scene.

## 1930

From February 4 onward, through a months-long run, Rains was Proteus, the

Claude in *He*, as the elevator operator who fancies himself Napoleon. Edith Meiser has grave doubts. *Courtesy the Wioskowski Collection*

Prime Minister, in Bernard Shaw's *The Apple Cart*. Touted as a "Political Extravaganza in Two Acts and an Interlude," the play—which reunited Rains with Morris Carnovsky—had George Coulouris scurrying around the *Martin Beck Theatre* as assistant stage manager. *The New York Times* critic Richard Watson held that "Mr. Rains' characterization is probably the best piece of acting in 'The Apple Cart'." Joseph Wood Crutch found that "the acting … of Claude Rains (as the Prime Minister) was highly effective." With Tom Powers and Violet Kemble Cooper.

In the summer of 1930, Rains sailed to England for the purpose of securing a quota number so as to return to the United States as an immigrant; he had decided to make that country his permanent home.

## 1931

Rains tripled again in *Miracle at Verdun*, playing Heydner, a Messenger, and Belgian Prime Minister Lamparenne at the *Martin Beck Theatre*, beginning on March 16. Hans Chlumberg's epic drama got the royal treatment from The Theatre Guild; directed by Herbert J. Biberman, the play featured 70 performers and "screen accompaniment"—sound film clips from Universal, Paramount, and Fox studios, projected simultaneously on three screens. Despite such impressive numbers and resources—and a hair-raising scene wherein the dead soldiers rise from the earth, and, bearing the wooden crosses which had marked their graves, stagger homeward—the play was not successful.

> Neither the play nor the production requires much from individual actors, although Claude Rains, as the Prime Minister of Belgium, makes himself heard above the general din and gives a splendid, potent performance.
> (*The New York Times*, March 15, 1931)

In the summer of 1931, upon the expiration of his original contract with The Theatre Guild, Rains signed on for another two years.

Claude Rains, a stripling of 42, in makeup as Georges Clemenceau in *Peace Palace*. *Courtesy Jessica Rains*

On September 21, Rains returned as Napoleon—at least he was in the mind of his onstage character, the Elevator Man—in Alfred Savoir's three-act comedy, *He* (*The Guild Theatre*). Directed by Chester Erskin, the cast included Violet Kemble Cooper and William Gargan. *The New York Times* (on 22 September, 1931), argued that

> "He" is a comedy of singularly flat dialogue; and, at least in performance, it is sluggish and literal… Claude Rains has a vastly enjoyable dignity as the servant who fancies himself Napoleon.

## 1932

The actor appeared in three Theatre Guild productions during 1932. Denis Johnston's

*The Moon in the Yellow River* was the first. Opening at the *Guild Theatre* on February 29, the three-act play featured Henry Hull, Egon Brecher, William Harrigan (who would soon appear with Rains in *The Invisible Man*), and Alma Kruger. Rains enacted the part of Dobelle, and *The New York Times* made a point of mentioning that

Claude Rains and Henry Hull, although inclined to over-elaborate a bit, give excellent performances as the railway engineer and the leader of the revolutionists.

Shaw's *Too True to Be Good* (which debuted on April 4) was next in line, and Rains was seen as the Elder. May 1932 saw Rains move from his midtown Manhattan apartment to a cottage in Middlebush, New Jersey; the daily commute to the *Guild Theatre* didn't bother him at all. In Owen and Donald Davis' *The Good Earth*, Rains topped the bill as Wang Lung. Based on Pearl S. Buck's titular novel, the play—which opened on October 17—saw Sydney Greenstreet in support as Wang Lung's Uncle, and future famed film director, Vincent Sherman— here, in his salad days—doubling as both "A Stranger" and "A Young Speaker." Among others in the acclaimed drama were Henry Travers (as Wang Lung's Father), Donald MacMillan, Geraldine Kay, and Clyde Franklin; Philip Moeller directed. Despite some excellent notices, both Rains and Alla Nazimova (O-Lan) were bypassed by MGM for the 1937 film version.

Among his stops on Broadway, Rains found time (on June 5 and following) to appear in summer stock at the Westchester County Center (in White Plains, New York) in The Theatre Guild's *Peace Palace*. Emil Ludwig's eight-scene play, *Versailles*, had been renamed for the occasion, and Rains, as Georges Clemenceau, headed a cast that included Montagu Love, A. P. Kaye, and Richard Hale. Broadway was the ultimate target, but, despite some positive notices ("[The] cast, on the whole, is sufficiently expert"), the satire closed out of town. Per

Katherine Roberts, "No one thought it would go far and everyone was right about that."

Jean Bart's *The Man Who Reclaimed His Head* opened on September 8 at the *Broadhurst Theater*, and Rains would have the satisfaction of being tapped to record his Paul Verin on film, albeit Universal's adaptation of the less-than-successful drama would forego the character's disfigurements and maladies. Jean Arthur co-starred as Adele Verin, leaving more than one ticket-buyer amazed that so lovely a woman would end up married to an asthmatic, deformed cripple. On the bill were Stuart Casey (as Henri Berthaud); Janet Rathbun (Lulu); Lionel Braham (Baron de Montford); Romaine Callendar (Ferdinand Demoncey), and Richard Barrows (Danglas). Most of the critics conceded that director Herbert Biberman had put on a good show, but felt that showmanship, of itself, was not enough to carry the day. Typical was Brooks Atkinson of *The New York Times*:

A passion for sensational lights and ostentatious scenic effects is an insidious as it may be clever. "The Man Who Reclaimed His Head" succumbs to that sort of display. By the time the third act comes around the succession of group pictures deadens the play. The acting is in the same key. Claude Rains, who is one of the best actors the Theatre Guild ever had, plays Verin in terms of make-up, deformity and asthma.
(September 9, 1932)

The pacifist melodrama, produced by Arthur Hammerstein and L. Lawrence Weber, closed after only 28 performances.

# 1933

Theatrically speaking, this was a lean year for Rains. He was Ezekial Bell in George O'Neil's *American Dream* (February 21), but appeared in only one act (the vignette set in 1849) of the "trilogy." Directed by Philip Moeller, the production also featured Josephine Hull, Douglass Montgomery,

Gale Sondergaard, and Stanley Ridges. In May 1933 Rains vacated his cottage in Middlebush, and bought a house and 58 acres of farmland in Lambertville, New Jersey; real estate seemed the only stable investment possible in those times of worldwide financial chaos. Between the Great Depression and the lock that less-expensive admissions had given the movies, The Theatre Guild disbanded (temporarily), and Rains (and others) had to scramble madly for their living. Fortunately, the call came from James Whale at Universal, and there were new worlds to conquer.

## 1934

Between private donations from philanthropists and a marginal improvement of the economy, the Guild was back in business, and Rains topped the bill as Nathan G. Rubin in *They Shall Not Die*, which opened at the *Royale Theater* on February 21. Directed by Philip Moeller and based on the 1931 Scottsboro Trial in Alabama, John Wexley's courtroom drama electrified audiences for 62 performances. Ruth Gordon played Ruby Bates (re-named Lucy Wells to avoid legal complications), and the large cast included Tom Ewell doubling, the up-and-coming Dean Jagger, and Al Stokes as the black defendant; the perennially pompous Thurston Hall harrumphed as the Judge. Miss Gordon recounted the tension she had felt prior to opening night:

It was my first emotional part, one big scene. Claude Rains had the long part, New York lawyer Samuel Leibowitz, called by another name. In rehearsals, Claude was colorless; it [sic] could sink the play. His seven-page speech, he droned. Everybody worried. He was the pivot of the whole play. Opening night I sat behind the backdrop waiting for the scene to be over. Claude's summation blew the roof off! Even that frosty Guild first-night list had to loosen up and cheer. It's the only time I ever saw an actor wait till opening night to wrap up a show.[51]

Brooks Atkinson said:

Claude Rains does jeopardize his opening scene with histrionic flamboyancy. But in the court-

Deformed, asthmatic, and, for the moment, profoundly disturbed: Claude as Paul Verin in *the Man Who Reclaimed His Head*. This photograph has not been seen for 60 years. *Courtesy Jessica Rains*

room scene, which is the crucial one, the part catches up with him and he plays magnificently.
(*The New York Times*,
February 22, 1934)

## 1948–1949

*A Lincoln Portrait*—Rains was a guest narrator for two performances of Aaron Copland's symphonic work on October 15 and 16, 1948, and again (on April 16 and 18) in 1949, at the Philadelphia Academy of Music. On April 19, 1949, the program was performed at New York's Carnegie Hall.

**A majestic performance in an important play: Claude as Rubashov in Sidney Kingsley's** *Darkness at Noon. Courtesy Theatre Arts Collection, University of Texas at Austin.*

Music critic Irving Kolodin (the *New York Sun*) said that Rains read the lines "as a man convinced of their meaning, rather than as an actor attempting to convince his audience." Rains appeared out of courtesy to Eugene Ormandy and the Philadelphia Orchestra. Sadly, none of the performances was broadcast on radio, nor did Rains ever record the work with the orchestra.

## 1951

Sidney Kingsley's *Darkness at Noon* opened at New York's *Alvin Theater* on January 13, 1951; Rains' Rubashov was acclaimed throughout the theater world, and the actor walked home with all six major drama awards, including the Comedie Matinee Club's Bronze medal, the New York Drama Critics' Annual Best Actor Poll, and

a Tony. (As of 1962, at least, no other actor on the New York stage had equaled that feat.) Sidney Kingsley's play, based upon the novel by Arthur Koestler, would itself win the N.Y. Critics' Circle Award and would feature Kim Hunter (Luba), Philip Coolidge (402); Walter J. Palance (Gletkin); Herbert Ratner (Richard); Alexander Scourby (Ivanoff); Norman Roland (Bogrov); Daniel Polis (Albert); Lois Nettleton (Secretary); and Geoffrey Barr (Andre), among others. Mr. Kingsley directed. After its successful run at the *Alvin*, *Darkness at Noon* moved to the *Royale Theatre* with Harry Worth replacing Philip Coolidge, and several changes among the secondary cast. The title of Koestler's novel was derived from *Job* 5:14— "Darkness comes upon them in the daylight; at noon they grope as in the nighttime." Noteworthy: Walter J. Palance would soon unload his Christian name and curdle the blood as plain old Jack. Noteworthy also is the presence of Maurice Gosfield (whose greatest claim to fame would be as slovenly Private Duane Doberman on Phil Silver's fifties sitcom *You'll Never Get Rich*) as the president.

During the play's run, *The New Yorker* magazine buttonholed Rains for his thoughts on the play:

This Rubashov is the first character I've portrayed on the stage since [**They Shall Not Die**], and I find it quite a job, after seventeen years of murmuring my way through movies, to push out the intensity of the play. The other Russians I've represented were complicated but they weren't in a class with this one. Today I'd probably regard the mad poet in Tolstoy's "The Living Corpse," or Chlestakov, in "The Inspector General," as a fairly light assignment, although when I played them, they seemed formidable…. What a hell of a fine thing to come back to the stage with!
(February 17, 1951)

In a letter (dated September 13, 1996) to JoAnna Wioskowski, Rains' co-star, Kim Hunter, shared her thoughts about the actor and the play:

"Darkness at Noon" was a fascinating play. A number of well known writers had tried to adapt

Gletkin (Walter [later Jack] Palance) has it out with Rubashov (Claude) in *Darkness at Noon*. *Courtesy Theatre Arts Collection, University of Texas at Austin*

it from the novel prior to Sidney Kingsley—but his was by far best and fortunately was also produced—Successfully, thanks to Claude.

Sidney was so frightened that people might think it pro-communist, not *anti*;—because of the times—Joseph McCarthy, HUAC, etc.—that he almost ruined his play in his direction of it—Cutting out all of the "grey," human tones, and trying to make it all black and white—Claude fought him all the way, and managed to bring the necessary humanity to the play—It was pure pleasure working with Claude.

## 1952

On Sunday, March 30, Rains participated

in *Merely Players*, a Gala Performance in aid of Theatrical Charities by The Merely Players Society in London. Held at the *Theatre Royal* in Drury Lane, the benefit consisted of scenes and songs from sundry of the plays, musicals, and reviews made famous by the society's membership. Rains appeared as Casca, and, together with John Gielgud (as Cassius) and gala director Godfrey Tearle (as Brutus), offered Act I, Scene II of Shakespeare's *Julius Caesar*.

Soon after his return to the United States, Rains played Jonah in Owen Davis's *Jezebel's Husband* in summer stock and

Another stage triumph was Claude's turn in T. S. Eliot's *The Confidential Clerk*. Players *(left to right)* are Richard Newton, Joan Greenwood, Ina Claire, and Claude. *Courtesy Photofest*

*Night of the Auk,* and what a cast! *(From left)* Claude, Dick York, Wendell Corey, Christopher Plummer, and Martin Brooks. And still the audiences stayed away in droves. *Courtesy Photofest*

headed back up to Hartford in December for *An Evening with Will Shakespeare,* a prestigious fund-raiser on behalf of *The American Shakespeare Festival,* headquartered (where else?) in Stratford, Connecticut. A half-hearted effort to take the show to the Big Apple was noted by *The New York Times* (December 7, 1952), but nothing came of it. (cf. *Recordings*)

## 1954

Rains next appeared as Sir Claude Mulhammer in T. S. Eliot's *The Confidential Clerk* at New York's *Morosco Theater* (debut on February 11). With Ina Claire (Lady Elisabeth Mulhammer); Joan Greenwood (Lucasta Angel); Richard Newton (B. Kaghan);

Douglas Watson (Colby Simpkins); Aline MacMahon (Mrs. Guzzard); Newton Blick (Eggerson); directed by E. Martin Browne. *Clerk* was previewed for several weeks at Washington D.C.'s National Theatre. (Per notes on the play in *Theatre Arts* magazine [April 1954]:

As portrayed with great sensitivity by Claude Rains, Sir Claude is a man who tries to reconcile the worlds of fact and make-believe, of the real and the ideal; he is a successful financier who has yearned to be an artist, a man who wants "a world where the form is the reality.")

*The New York World-Telegram & Sun* offered an intriguing view of Rains' portrayal, finding it "A sturdy, almost shy performance until despair illuminates the character in the end."

Carnegie Hall, December 7, at 8:30 P. M.

The Collegiate Chorale

*presents*

the World Premiere of

# FOR THE TIME BEING

A Christmas Oratorio

By Marvin David Levy          Text by W. H. Auden

with the distinguished actor

## CLAUDE RAINS

as Narrator

and Lucine Amara, Maureen Forrester, Reri Grist,
Robert Rounseville, Martial Singher, Ezio Flagello

The Collegiate Chorale
The Symphony of the Air

Margaret Hillis, Conductor

Tickets: $4.60, $3.80, $3.00, $2.40, $1.80

MAIL ORDERS WITH SELF-ADDRESSED, STAMPED ENVELOPE TO:
THE COLLEGIATE CHORALE, 130 W. 56th ST., NEW YORK 19

Claude at Carnegie Hall, 1959. *Courtesy Robert G. Dickson*

(February 12, 1954) Brooks Atkinson felt that only Ina Claire's acting was not pedantic, but Walter Kerr had a different opinion:

To Claude Rains falls much of the more sober speculation of the evening, and he makes this rich man's passion for the making of pottery shiningly real.

(*New York Herald Tribune*,
February 12, 1954)

## 1956

Arch Oboler's *The Night of the Auk* opened on December 3 at New York's *Playhouse Theater* and closed eight performances later. Neither critical indifference nor box-office disaster could be staved off by Rains' portrayal of Dr. Bruner. (*The New York Times'* Brooks Atkinson applauded Rains' efforts [sort of]:

As the most experienced actor in the lot, Claude Rains plays the scientist with becoming thought and sobriety, speaking the dialogue as though in a moment everything might come clear.)

(While the play was in previews at Washington D.C.'s *Sam S. Shubert Theater*, critic Richard L. Coe praised the actors, the setting, the production—everything!—except

for what he perceived to be Arch Oboler's far-reaching vituperation. The New York reviewers pinned most of *their* crepe on the convoluted dialogue.) With Wendell Corey (Colonel Tom Russell); Dick York (Lt. Mac Hartman); Christopher Plummer (Lewis Rohnen); Martin Brooks (Lt. Jan Kephart); directed by Sidney Lumet.

## 1959

*For the Time Being*—by Marvin David Levy, with text by W. H. Auden. Rains was narrator for the world premiere of this "Christmas Oratorio" on December 7 at New York's Carnegie Hall. The vocal music was handled by the Collegiate Chorale and an array of stars from the Metropolitan Opera. Margaret Hillis conducted the Symphony of the Air.

## 1961

*Enoch Arden*—a piece for Narrator and Orchestra, with music by Richard Strauss and orchestrations by Lucien Cailliet (on March 20). Rains gave Alfred Lord Tennyson's verses their due, while Eugene Ormandy and the Philadelphia Orchestra took care of the rest. (cf. *Recordings*)

## 1965

Henry Denker's *So Much of Earth, So Much of Heaven* was based on a play by Italian dramatist, Ugo Betti, and its tour of sundry provincial playhouses was to have served as the springboard to Broadway. No such luck. The drama opened to good wishes on August 23 at the *John Drew Theater* in East Hampton (NY), but when it moved on to the *Westport* (CT) *Country Playhouse* for its week-long run, Robin Goodfellow, the theater critic for Westport's local newspaper, *The Town Crier*, bemoaned that

The play is talky, tedious, tiresome, and trite.... The boredom builds up act by act; by the time the audience gets to the few moments of real tension

in act three, they are so embarrassed and be-
numbed that they are hardly in a condition to appreciate it.... Competent professionals like
Claude Rains, Leueen MacGrath and Larry
Gates showed themselves baffled by a pompous
and pretentious script... Direction was at a snail's
pace.

(September 2, 1965)

Five years earlier, an embryonic version of
the drama (entitled *The Burnt Flower Bed*)
had appeared at the Playhouse, where it, too,
had found its forward motion impeded by
the disinterest of both seat holders and reviewers.

The last stop on the tour was at the *Bucks
County* (PA) *Playhouse*, where Bette Davis
caught up with her old friend and mourned
his frailty. Actress Joanna Miles, who played
Rains' character's nurse on the tour, informed the author that Rains had "started to
forget" his lines, but "still held the audiences" for most of the run. "He glowed," recalled Miss Miles, "and he drew the audience
to him." From the *Bucks County Playhouse*,
Rains was taken to the hospital, where he
was diagnosed with internal hemorrhaging;
even had *Earth* won good enough notices to
assure a spot on Broadway, Rains' failing
health would have precluded his joining the
cast in New York.

*So Much of Earth, So Much of Heaven* was
Claude Rains' theatrical swan song.

# Radio

Rains' radio work was as prolific as his stage work, and is infinitely harder to document. The reign of "classic radio" was prodigious—spanning decades—and even the gung-ho efforts of legions of followers and fan organizations haven't yet made a dent in the catalogue of broadcast material. Every day finds "new" transcriptions surfacing somewhere or another, but—with radio (obviously) a totally aural medium—in most cases, very little in the way of credits information is contained therein. Sponsors? Sure. Secondary cast members? In your dreams. Additions to this list would be as welcome as the flowers that bloom in the spring.

When interviewed for a local (West Chester) Pennsylvania newspaper in September 1962, Rains seemed almost to chalk up his broadcast output to serendipity; radio stations just happened to abut his usual stomping grounds:

The NBC Studios in the RCA Building were convenient to the Broadway theatre, where I often appeared—and I relished performing in radio drama as a kind of 'relaxation' from the strain of the stage's continuing demands. The same situation applied in Hollywood, where I'd often commute between movie lots and radio studios.

(Of course, you can't always believe what you read. In a late forties issue of Britain's Film Illustrated Monthly (Vol. 3, #1), Rains admitted to Laurie Henshaw that his "chief hate" was radio, and claimed that he wouldn't have a set in the house.)

## 193?

*They Won't Forget* NBC—as Andy Griffin; with Fay Wray. Adaptation of the award-winning Warner Brothers' motion picture. Possibly an episode of the *Warner Brothers Academy Theater*, broadcast sometime between April 3 and June 26, 1938.

## 1932

*The Good Earth* September 13 on NBC. Rains and his Broadway costar Alla Nazimova returned as Wang Lung and O-Lan in this adaptation of Pearl Buck's Pulitzer Prize-winning novel.

## 1933

*A Bill of Divorcement (The Fleischmann Hour)*; February 2 on NBC. Rains and Janet Beecher shared top honors in this adaptation of Clemence Dane's tearjerker.

## 1934

Appeared on *The Fleischmann Hour* (starring Rudy Vallee); March 17 on NBC.

## 1935

*The Green Goddess (The Lux Radio Theatre)*; January 6 on NBC. Rains filled in for George Arliss as the Rajah of Rukh, and Dorothy Gish replaced Fay Bainter as Lucilla Crespin in an adaptation of the William Archer play which had, by 1935, already been filmed twice.

Appeared in *The Tell-Tale Heart (The Fleischmann Hour)*; April 4, NBC. Rudy Vallee starred, along with Ella Logan and the Stewart Sisters.

*The Last Outpost (Hollywood Hotel)*; July 5 on CBS. With Cary Grant and Gertrude Michael. *Hollywood Hotel* was an eclectic program, featuring adaptations of upcoming motion pictures (usually with the original cast), songs (by Frances Langford), and interviews (by Louella Parsons). Hosts included such luminaries as Frank Parker, Fred MacMurray, Dick Powell, and Ken Murray.

## 1936

*Anthony Adverse (Hollywood Hotel)*; 2 parts—July 17 and 24 on CBS. Rains reprised his role, along with Olivia de Havilland, Donald Woods, and Gale Sondergaard.

*Madame Sans-Gêne (The Lux Radio Theatre)*; December 14 on CBS. Rains was again Napoleon, Jean Harlow was the eponymous heroine, and Robert Taylor joined C. Henry Gordon in topping off a splendid cast in this acclaimed broadcast version of the play by Victorien Sardou and Emile Moreau.

## 1937

Appeared in *The Game of Chess (The Royal Gelatin Hour)*; April 29 on NBC. Star Rudy Vallee and guests Edgar Bergen and Charlie McCarthy visit London and bump into Rains.

*Julius Caesar (1937 Shakespeare Festival)*; one of eight broadcasts (also *Hamlet, Much Ado About Nothing, The Taming of the Shrew, King Lear, As You Like It*, and *Henry IV*) starting on June 26 (Library of Congress materials peg the debut as the *July 26*) on CBS. Rains was Cassius, supported by Walter Abel, Reginald Denny, and Thomas Mitchell, among others. Conway Tearle narrated the Brewster Morgan adaptation. Per information provided by Jonathan Rosenthal of the Museum of Television and Radio, the CBS Shakespeare series was a "pathetic attempt to bring culture to the masses" by entrusting hour-long adaptations of the classic plays to Hollywood's finest:

In a desperate attempt to find something they could use for publicity purposes to promote the

series, CBS network officials decided to conduct live interviews with ordinary people in the street to hear their opinions of the show. The people questioned were screened beforehand to make sure they said positive things about the series. "I think it's wonderful," one man said on a *live* broadcast, but he quickly ad-libbed, "I don't understand a word they're saying, but I think it's wonderful."

Appeared in *The Gift of the Gods (The Royal Gelatin Hour)*; July 1 on NBC. With star Rudy Vallee and Bill "Bojangles" Robinson.

Appeared on Sealtest's *Sunday Night Party*; July 18 on NBC. Rains performed Poe's *The Cask of Amontillado*; hosted by James Melton.

Appeared on *The Kraft Music Hall*; August 12 on NBC.

## 1938

Appeared in an episode of *Park Avenue Penners*, starring comic Joe Penner, with Ozzie Nelson & His Orchestra and vocalist Harriet Hilliard); January 2 on CBS.

Appeared on *The Kraft Music Hall*; June 9 on NBC.

*White Banners (Hollywood Hotel)*; June 10 on CBS. Rains as Paul Ward; with Fay Bainter, Jackie Cooper, Bonita Granville, and the same principals as the Warner Bros. film released several weeks later.

Appeared on *The Kraft Music Hall*; November 3 on NBC.

*Julius Caesar (Great Plays)*; November 20 on NBC Blue. Starred with John Anthony and George Gaul in this adaptation of the William Shakespeare tragedy.

*Confession (The Lux Radio Theatre)*; November 21 on CBS. The broadcast was based on the 1937 Warner Bros. movie of the same name, with Rains taking over Basil Rathbone's part of Michael Michailov. (On September 13, 1943, Rathbone would get his revenge, when he copped the title honors in *Phantom of the Opera. The Lux Radio Theatre* rendition had Susanna Foster, Nelson Eddy, and Edgar Barrier recreate their roles from

Universal's box-office gold mine.) With Richard Greene, Anne Shirley, and Miriam Hopkins.

## 1939

Appeared in *There's Always Joe Winters (The Royal Gelatin Hour)*; January 5 on NBC. With Boris Karloff and star Rudy Vallee.

*The Eigerwund (The Royal Gelatin Hour)*; March 30 on NBC. Rains was pursued by an ogre in this episode of Rudy Vallee's show; Arch Oboler's script was later redone on *Lights Out*.

*Kind Lady (Texaco Star Theatre)*; October 11 on CBS. John (The Great Profile) Barrymore was the master of ceremonies for the hour-long show; the first half was invariably music and comedy from the Coast, while the second half was a drama from New York. Grace George and Alice Marble co-starred with Rains.

Appeared on *The Kraft Music Hall*; December 28 on NBC.

## 1940

*The Story of Benedict Arnold (Cavalcade of America)*; April 2 on NBC.

*The Littlest Rebel (The Lux Radio Theatre)*; October 14 on CBS. Rains(supplanting John Boles as Captain Carey) supported Shirley Temple in her only full-length radio dramatization (taken from her 1935 hit for 20th Century–Fox), concerning a girl's attempts at being reunited with her father, who's about to be hanged as a spy. Cecil B. DeMille hosted the play, which also featured Preston Foster, Bea Benaderet, and Leigh Whipper. Apart from Miss Temple, only Frank McGlynn (as Abraham Lincoln) was held over from the screen version.

## 1941

*As a Man Thinketh (Cavalcade of America)*; January 15 on NBC. Rains headed the cast in Garrett Porter's tale of Thomas

Cooper, the man who was imprisoned for testing John Adams' Sedition Act; with Jeanette Nolan, Agnes Moorehead, William Johnstone, John McIntire.

Appeared on *Lincoln Highway*; February 22 on NBC. *Lincoln Highway*, hosted by John McIntire, was a dramatic anthology which aired on Saturday mornings, of all times. The series entries—most of which featured big names from Hollywood and the Great White Way—supposedly emanated from the eponymous roadway, which stretched from Portland, Oregon, to Philadelphia. Written in tandem by Ed Sherry, Brian Byrne, and Jack Hasty (Theodora Yates usually directed), the show was sponsored by *Shinola* shoe polish. *Highway* lasted two years.

Appeared on *Calling America*; July 11 on the Mutual network. News (read by Drew Pearson) and music (the Erno Rapee Orchestra) highlighted this weekly program.

Guested on *Your Happy Birthday*; July 12 on NBC. This was a short-lived quiz show, hosted by Tiny Ruffner and featuring the Jimmy Dorsey Orchestra.

That same day Rains appeared at NBC in another chapter of *The Lincoln Highway*, entitled *The Hobo with a Harvard Accent*.

Appeared on *Calling America*; July 25 on NBC. On November 23, 1941, the program was rechristened *Listen, America*.

*Blind Alley (Great Moments from Great Plays)*; August 1 on NBC. This was the penultimate episode; with Everett Sloane.

Appeared in *A Man to Remember (The Philip Morris Playhouse)*; September 26 on CBS. Nelson Case was the announcer; Ray Bloch supplied the music.

*The Haunting Face (Inner Sanctum Mysteries)*; September 28 on ABC.

Appeared in *Millions for Defense* on October 14 on CBS. This musical variety series offered stars from all entertainment fields (here, Phil Baker and Kenny Baker), as well as pitches by the Treasury Department.

*Captain Paul (Cavalcade of America)*; October 27, NBC. The biography of John Paul Jones (Rains), as related by playwrights Arthur Miller and John Driscoll; with Gale

Gordon. ("Little-known incidents and people who were merely footnotes in American history were featured each week on the half-hour *Cavalcade of America* series," wrote Ron Lackmann.[52] While relegating Captain Jones, Benedict Arnold, or George Washington [1952] to footnote status may seem a bit harsh, most of the other personalities Rains enacted in the series would have been thrilled to be considered afterthoughts. The long-running show [1935-1953] had started out on CBS, before shifting to NBC in 1939.)

## 1942

*Here Comes Mr. Jordan (The Lux Radio Theatre);* January 26 on NBC. Adaptation of Rains' 1941 Columbia fantasy; he, Evelyn Keyes, and James Gleason repeated their screen roles. With Cary Grant (in Robert Montgomery's shoes), Torey Carlton, Howard McNear, and Bernard Zandell.

Appeared (along with James Stewart and Mary Jane Walsh) in *Keep 'Em Rolling*; February 2 on the Mutual network. George S. Kaufman was M.C. for this episode of the drama/music series in support of the war effort.

Appeared in *Criminal Code (The Philip Morris Playhouse)*; March 20 on CBS. With John Garfield; Carl Frank, announcer.

*You're On Your Own (This Is War)*; March 21 on all four major networks. This propaganda drama, the sixth in a series intended to rouse the passion and raise the spirit of wartime America, also featured Ezra Stone and Everett Sloane; directed by Norman Corwin and produced by H. L. McClinton.

Appeared on *The Lincoln Highway*; March 28 on NBC.

*In This Crisis (Cavalcade of America)*; April 20 on NBC. Rains is patriot Thomas Paine in this historical sketch. With Ray Collins and Gale Gordon.

*Back Where You Came From (Plays for Americans)*; June 7 on NBC. Written by Arch Oboler. (Oboler was a constant presence on radio between 1938 and 1944, and

*Plays for Americans* was one of his showcases. The series lasted only from February to the beginning of July 1942, but—apart from being almost a one-man production on Mr. Oboler's part—it featured such heavy hitters as Bette Davis, James Stewart, and Robert Taylor, in addition to Rains.) *Back Where You Came From* also starred Hans Conreid, Jay Novello, Irene Tedrow, and Frank Graham.

*Soldier of a Free Press (Cavalcade of America)*; September 7 on NBC. The story of Richard Harding Davis, America's first "war correspondent."

Appeared in *Underground (The Philip Morris Playhouse)*; September 18 on CBS. Carl Frank handled the announcing chores.

Performed in *The Man Who Played with Death (Inner Sanctum Mysteries)*; September 27 on ABC. With "Raymond" (Raymond Edward Johnson) as host; Himan Brown directed.

Was in *The King of Darkness (Inner Sanctum Mysteries)*; October 11 on ABC. With "Raymond" as host; directed by Himan Brown.

Guested in *The Missionary and the Gangster (The Radio Reader's Digest)*; October 25 on CBS. Robert Nolan directed.

Appeared in *The Laughing Murderer (Inner Sanctum Mysteries)* November 8 on ABC. With "Raymond" as host; Himan Brown directed.

## 1943

*The French Underground (The Radio Readers Digest)*; January 24 on CBS. Hosted by Conrad Nagel.

*The Texaco Star Theatre* February 7 on CBS. A variety entertainment, featuring sketches with Fred Allen, Portland Hoffa, et al, and Rains and Allen in "The Phantom of Carnegie Hall," a pastiche on Rains' upcoming film, *Phantom of the Opera*.

## 1945

*Philco Radio Hall of Fame* March 18 on NBC Blue. A variety entertainment featuring musical and/or comedy pieces by Chico Marx, Jay C. Flippen, Evelyn Knight, Paul Whiteman and His Orchestra, and others. Rains performed "A Piece of String."

Appeared on *Stage Door Canteen* with Henny Youngman and General Fred L. Walker; March 2 on CBS.

*The Citadel (Theatre of Romance)*; March 20 on CBS. An adaptation of A. J. Cronin's story of an idealistic physician whose marriage and later life fall short of his own expectations. Hosted by Arnold Moss and directed by Marx B. Loeb; with Gertrude Warner.

*President Franklin D. Roosevelt: Death and Funeral (A Legacy for America)*; May 15 on CBS. A special program of poetry and music in tribute to the late president, presented with Rains, Ken Roberts, Leonard Stokes, and Ray Bloch's Orchestra and Chorus. The actor performed dramatic readings from Walt Whitman's poetry.

*Dr. Christian* on CBS. Rains stepped into Jean Hersholt's shoes and headlined as the kindly Dr. Alexander Webb when the Danish actor returned briefly to his homeland on a mission for the National War Fund. Hersholt was heard at the end of the three consecutive broadcasts by short-wave radio.

*Diagnosis After Death*—aired June 6
*Jere to Liebe*—aired June 13
*The Lady and the Wolf*—aired June 20

## 1946

*Murder in the Big Bowl (The Radio Reader's Digest)*; November 7 on CBS. A "Whodunit?" hosted by Richard Kollmer.

Was guest star on *The Fred Allen Show*; December 8 on NBC. With Portland Hoffa, Minerva Pious, Peter Donald, and Parker Fennelly.

## 1947

Appeared in *The Waxwork (Suspense)*; March 20 on CBS. A one-man performance by Rains, in an adaptation of the eponymous 1931 short story by A. M. Burrage. Produced

Rains appeared on *Inner Sanctum Mysteries* four times. This publicity photo was released in conjunction with his performance in "The King of Darkness." *Courtesy Richard Bojarski*

and directed by William Spier, the script was performed again with William Conrad (in 1956) and Herbert Marshall (in 1958).

Appeared on *The Kraft Music Hall*; May 8 on NBC.

*Many Moons (The Radio Reader's Digest)*; May 29 on CBS. A little princess wants the moon and the court jester succeeds in getting it for her. Featured Everett Sloane.

*Freedom Pledge* Rains took part in the live broadcast of a freedom rally, which took place in Philadelphia, Pennsylvania, on September 16. "5000 public and parochial school children, massed in the historical square, repeated after Rains his solemnly intoned 'Freedom Pledge':

I am an American, a free American. Free to speak without fear. Free to worship my own God. Free to stand up for what I think. Free to oppose what

I believe wrong. Free to choose those who govern my country. This heritage of Freedom I pledge to uphold for myself and all mankind."

*A Piece of String (The Radio Reader's Digest)*; October 30 on CBS. This short work by Guy de Maupassant (about the unfair accusations made against a poor Frenchman) would come to be regarded as Rains' radio signature piece. With Alan Hewitt, Tom Shirley, Les Tremayne, and Lyn Murray.

## 1948

*Topaze* (*Studio One*); July 6 on CBS. The previous May, Sebastian Cabot had had the lead in the same play, with the same script, on the same show. Directed by Fletcher Markle; music by Alexander Semmler.

*Valley Forge* (*Theatre Guild on the Air* on The US Steel Hour); 14 November on ABC. Homer Fickett directed the piece by Maxwell Anderson, which also featured June Duprez and George Coulouris.

*The Hands of Mr. Ottormole (Suspense)*; December 2 on CBS. Co-starred with Vincent Price, Verna Felton, Raymond E. Lawrence. Sydney Greenstreet was set to star in this adaptation of Thomas Burke's 1931 short story of the same name, but was unable to do so. It took Rains *and* Price to replace the movies' favorite fat man.

## 1949

*The Game of Love and Death* (*Theatre Guild of the Air* on *The US Steel Hour*); January 2 on ABC. With Katharine Hepburn, Paul Henreid.

*The Jack Benny Program* ("*Jack Has a Music Lesson*"); February 27 on CBS. Rains tries to get out of his *Horn Blows at Midnight* contract.

*The Horn Blows at Midnight (The Ford Theatre)*; March 4 on CBS. Adaptation (by Hugh Wedlock and Howard Snider) of Jack Benny's notorious 1945 Warners' screen fantasy; with Mr. Benny, Mercedes McCambridge, Herb Vigran, Hans Conreid, Byron

Kane, and others. Rains is the Chief of the Small Planets in this entry in Ford Theatre's "Festival of Smiles," which was directed by Fletcher Markle.

Appeared in *Banquo's Chair (The Philip Morris Playhouse)*; March 25, 1949. Directed by William Spier; Art Ballinger, announcer.

*The Goal Is Freedom* April 4 on CBS. Rains stars with then-Senator Lyndon Johnson in a dramatization condemning prejudice in America.

*Experiment in Terror* May 8. Rains starred in this commercial-free melodrama, broadcast via the Armed Forces Radio Network.

*Crime Without Passion (The Ford Theatre)*; May 20 on CBS. More than 15 years after the motion picture made headlines, Margo and Rains were reunited for this radio adaptation.

*Madame Bovary (The Ford Theatre)*; October 8 on CBS. Starred with Marlene Dietrich and Van Heflin in loose adaptation of the classic Flaubert novel.

On November 29, 1949, WCOJ Radio began broadcasting at 1000 watts from 7:30 A.M. to 4:45 P.M., from downtown West Chester, Pennsylvania, and Rains, ever the good neighbor, gave a dramatic reading to initiate WCOJ's first broadcast day. The exact nature or title of the reading is unknown.

## 1950

*Mr. Peale and the Dinosaur (Cavalcade of America)*; March 7 on NBC. Rains is Charles Wilson Peale, who founded Philadelphia's Museum of Natural History. Agnes Moorehead and Parker Fennelly were also heard in this radio play by Arthur Argent.

## 1952

*Midnight Blue (The Big Show)*; January 6 on NBC. Appeared as Mr. Spiers. Radio historian J. Fred MacDonald allowed how *The Big Show* had a big budget—some $35,000

per program—but somehow the 90-minute variety extravaganza "never delivered the anticipated large audience during its two years on radio."[53] Hosted by Tallulah Bankhead; with Herb Shriner, Joan Davis, Vera Lynn, and Meredith Willson and his Orchestra.

*The Catbird Seat (The Big Show)*; February 10 on NBC. Rains was heard as Erwin Martin in this adaptation of the Thurber short story. Also appearing on the program were Tallulah Bankhead, Joan Davis, and Phil Foster.

*Three Words (Cavalcade of America)*; February 19 on NBC. The story of George Washington and "Victory or Death," the American password employed before the Battle of Trenton. Rains as the father of our country, supported by Kermit Murdock and Bill Lipton.

*The Jeffersonian Heritage*: a series of broadcasts on the third president (Rains) and his vision for the country, based on the letters exchanged between Jefferson and John Adams.

*The Living Declaration*, program #1, written by Morton Wishengard.

*Divided We Stand*, program #2, by Mr. Wishengard.

*Light and Liberty*, program #3, written by Milton Geiger.

*The Return of the Patriot*, program #4, by Mr. Geiger.

*The Danger of Freedom*, program #5, by Mr. Wishengard.

*The Experiment of a Free Press*, program #6, written by George Probst.

*The Ground of Justice*, program #7, by Mr. Wishengard.

*Freeing the Land*, program #8, written by Joseph Mindell.

*The University of the United States*, program #9, by Mr. Geiger.

*To Secure These Rights*, program #10, by Mr. Mindell

*Nature's Most Precious Gift*, program #11, by Mr. Probst.

*What the Jeffersonian Heritage Means Today*, program #12.

There may have been 13 episodes to this series, but this cannot be confirmed. This series was first presented in the autumn of 1952 as part of the adult education project of the National Association of Broadcasters.

## 1953

*Our Hidden Wealth (Medicine, USA)*; March 28 on NBC. Rains was Mr. Wheelock, who wondered "What are our resources for leadership?" on this information-oriented program, sponsored by the AMA.

*The Living Declaration (Kaleidoscope)*; July 4 on NBC. Also featured on the program was Fred Waring performing "Songs of America," Margaret Truman and the Robert Shaw Chorale offering "Early American Songs," and Nelson Eddy singing Stephen Foster favorites.

*Philadelphia Orchestra Concert*; December 17 on WFIL (Philadelphia). Cf. *Television*

## 1954

*A Review of the 1953–54 Theatrical Season (Stage Struck)*; May 21 on CBS. Rains was heard (along with Joan Greenwood) in excerpts from *The Confidential Clerk*; all-star cast including Basil Rathbone, Ben Gazzara, Ezio Pinza, Carol Channing, Danny Kaye, Audrey Hepburn, Jack Benny, Rodgers and Hammerstein, Yul Brynner, Shirley Booth, and many more, all doing selections from their own (or others') current theatrical, radio, and television hits. This was the last show of the season.

*The Cross Examination (First Came the Word)*; undated. Rains again was heard as Thomas Jefferson, defending his theory about revolution to a jury of the dead.

## 1955

*Builders of America (Anthology)*; May 26 on NBC. Helen Hayes and Walter Huston did poetry readings, and Rains participated in Harl McDonald's eponymous cantata for mixed voices, based on Washington and Lincoln, for this celebration of Memorial Day.

*Presenting Claude Rains* July 11 to December 9 on NBC.

A narrative program series "presenting Claude Rains" as narrator of strange and unusual stories based on real life and comparatively new to the public—frequently, Mr. Rains mentions that his story is based on a revelatory article appearing very recently in a late issue of some magazine (*Life* magazine often gets a credit acknowledgment [sic] from the narrator). Usually, two stories are used on each broadcast.

> (NBC program cards, courtesy Library of Congress)

As each program was no longer than 10 to 15 minutes in length, those stories, written and/or adapted by Liz Pearce, had to be brief, indeed. Like many of the programs on NBC, this was a "sustaining" program, having no sponsor.

Broadcast from NBC's New York studios, *Presenting Claude Rains* was produced and directed by Kenneth MacGregor. French actor Jean Pierre Aumont filled in for Rains in December.

Aka *Claude Rains and His Stories*.

## 1956

*Titanic* March 28 on NBC. Rains was narrator in this drama of the fate of the "unsinkable" steamship.

# Television

*Many of the sundry appearances Rains made on television in the early fifties were broadcast live and simultaneously recorded in kinescope (a process which offered only rudimentary clarity of image) for delayed transmission. Most of these do not appear to have survived.*

## 1951

*Toast of the Town*; April 8 on CBS. Precursor to *The Ed Sullivan Show*, this variety program was also hosted by the stony-faced Broadway columnist. A portion of this show was given over to John Chapman, president of the N.Y. Drama Critics' Circle, who doled out the Circle's awards to the top plays of the year. Rains enacted a brief scene from *Darkness at Noon* before Sidney Kingsley was handed the trophy for best drama of 1951.

## 1953

*The Bentons at Home (Omnibus)*; January 25 on CBS. *Omnibus* had premiered in 1952 and proved to be a well-received forum for the performance arts, as well as for discussions on folklore, legal issues, and architecture. Along with other segments here, the audience visited with the family of artist, Thomas Hart Benton, and their guests: Rains and folk-singer Susan Reed.

It didn't fully come off due to an obviously "set up" atmosphere. Rains, however, was excellent in his recitation of a long comic poem [by Carl Sandburg].

(*Variety*, January 28, 1953)

**The Man Who Liked Dickens** *(Medallion Theatre)*; August 1 on CBS. *Medallion Theatre* was but one of many sources of live drama which television offered during the fifties. *Dickens* was an adaptation by Robert Tallman of Evelyn Waugh's novel, *Handful of Dust*, and under Ralph Nelson's direction, Rains (James McMaster) wrestled the offbeat story to the ground. Per *Variety* (August 5, 1953):

Rains' portrayal of the jungle recluse who won't even stop at murder if it interferes with the Dickens' readings, managed to capture some of the tenseness and excitement of the Waugh story.

**The Archer Case** *(Medallion Theatre)*; October 3 on CBS. Rains is Sir Edward Carson, a barrister representing a small boy who takes on the entire British Empire in a test case regarding individual rights vs. bureaucratic despotism.

**Philadelphia Orchestra Concert**; December 17 on WFIL-TV (Philadelphia), for the Tasty Baking Company. Rains appeared with Metropolitan Opera mezzo-soprano, Risë Stevens, and the Temple University Chorus. He read Verses 1–20 of Chapter 2 of St. Luke's gospel over the playing of Handel's "Pastoral" Sinfonia from the *Messiah*, and was also the speaker in Thompson's *A Child's Prayer*.

## 1954

*The Confidential Clerk (Omnibus)*; February 14 on CBS. Rains and Douglas Watson appear in a segment from the play, then

233

**Rains as Sir Edward Carson in CBS-TV's "The Archer Case," an installment of** *Medallion Theatre* **broadcast on October 3, 1953.** *The author's collection*

running at New York's *Morosco Theatre* ("This portion was talkily philosophical but Rains' eloquence made it fascinating." Variety; February 17, 1954), while W. H. Auden opines on T. S. Eliot's influence on contemporary poetry, and the play's producer, Henry Sherek, offers some thoughts on Eliot and on the art/science of producing live drama.

## 1956

*And So Died Riabouchinska (Alfred Hitchcock Presents)*; February 12 on CBS. Rains is Fabian the Ventriloquist in this tale of murder and madness. Reggie Lanning photographed Mel Dinelli's teleplay, which was based on a story by Ray Bradbury. With Charles Bronson, Claire Carleton, Charles Cantor, Iris Adrian, Lowell Gilmore, Harry Tyler, Bill Haade, and Virginia Gregg as the voice of Riabouchinska; directed by Robert Stevenson.

...dipped deep into fantasy and intriguing enough to hold the looker despite the strain on credulity.... As the voice diffuser with the 'human' dummy, Claude Rains plays it with poignant restraint.

(*Variety*, February 15, 1956)

*A Night to Remember (Kraft Television Theatre)*; March 28 on NBC. Rains acts as narrator for the teleplay designed by Duane McKinney. According to authors Arthur Shulman and Roger Youman, *Night* was "The most ambitious live drama that had ever been attempted—107 actors, 31 sets, 7 cameras. It was a triumph for its director, George Roy Hill, and was repeated a few weeks later."[54]

*Variety* (April 4, 1956) noted that the production was

a brilliant feat from any angle. As sheer storytelling, its re-creation of the tragic sinking was clearly superior to the several Hollywood film productions framed around the same theme.... Claude Rains was excellent as the narrator, his script [sic] hitting the right tone of questioning and moralizing.

Hill and John Whedon adapted Walter Lord's eponymous book for television. The acclaimed production featured Frederic Tozère, Patrick Macnee, Bradford Dillman, and Clarence Derwent.

*President (The Alcoa Hour)*; May 13 on NBC. Rains plays Paul Westman, a retired Supreme Court justice looking for his party's presidential nomination. Mildred Dunnock costars in David Davidson's live teleplay, which was produced by Herbert Brodkin and directed by Robert Mulligan. *Variety* was effusive in its praise for the actor:

Claude Rains, as the Supreme Court Justice struggling to win the nomination and then the election, held the play firmly together with an excellent performance. His persuasively drawn portrait corrected any tendency of the script to fall into generalizations about the conflict of ambition and idealism. Rains made the abstractions come alive.

(May 16, 1956)

With Everett Sloane, Larry Gates, Fred Clark, Alfred Ryder, David White, and Luis Van Rooten.

*Antigone (Kaiser Aluminum Hour)*; September 11 on NBC: Color. Rains is King Creon and Marisa Pavan has the title role in this modern dress version of Sophocles' classic drama, adapted for TV by Lewis Galantiere. With Alexander Scourby (Greek Chorus), Mildred Natwick (Nurse), Paul Stevens, and Felicia Montealegre. Rains' performance was held to be excellent; "It had authority, sweep and insight." (*Variety*; September 19, 1956).

**Commercial**—*Aim to Live/Headlight Alignment Campaign*, for General Motors.

## 1957

*The Cream of the Jest (Alfred Hitchcock Presents)*; March 10 on CBS. Rains is drunken actor Charles Gresham, whose continual pestering of producer Wayne Campbell (James Gregory) leads to the actor's death at the hands of gangster Nick Roper (Paul Picerni). Directed by Herschel Daugherty and photographed by Reggie Lanning; Joan Harrison was the producer of record. With Joan Banks, Johnny Silver, Don Garret, Carol Shannon, and Tom Martin.

The macabre jest set forth in this Hitchcock episode is rather unremittingly bitter. However, what's even more surprising are the several loose plot ends still dangling untidily at the end of the Sarett Rudley script, from a Fredric Brown original.... Rains handles his assignment with his usual smooth effectiveness.
(*Variety*; March 13, 1957)

*On Borrowed Time (Hallmark Hall of Fame)*; November 17 on NBC: Color.

Rains is Mr. Brink, "A pleasant but businesslike heavenly courier," who comes at various times to summon Gramps (Ed Wynn), Granny (Beulah Bondi), and young Pud (Dennis Kohler) to their eternal reward. Gramps' seeking to foil Mr. Brink's plan forms the basis of this adaptation (by James Costigan) of Paul Osborn's 1938 play. (In the

1939 movie version, Lionel Barrymore tried to outfox Cedric Hardwicke's Angel of Death.)

CAST: Ed Wynn (Gramps); CLAUDE RAINS (Mr. Brink); Beulah Bondi (Granny); Dennis Kohler (Pud); Margaret Hamilton (Aunt Demetria); William Le Massena (Dr. Evans); Larry Gates (Mr. Pilbeam); William A. Lee (Mr. Grimes); Mildred Trares (Marcia); G. Wood (Jim); Dorothy Eaton (Susan)

Live performance, directed by George Schaefer:

I'd much prefer to do a show on film. It's not so much a challenge as live TV. When you get a good, strong yarn though, like "On Borrowed Time," you can't resist. (*TV Guide*; March 22-27, 1958)

The actor's mild caveat about live television may have—in part—be due to the critical perception of his performance in **On Borrowed Time**:

Rains, recreating his old role as Mr. Brink, suffered occasional troubles with his lines, but his overall performance was a fine contribution in perfect counterbalance to [Ed] Wynn's, contrasting calm, wisdom and inevitability with impatience, abruptness and contrariness.
(*Variety*; November 20, 1957)

The "Bible of Show Business," however, found the drama to be "beautiful and touching," despite Rains' occasional hesitation and some last-act camera glitches.

*The Pied Piper of Hamelin* (Color special); November 26 on NBC. The musical retelling of the Germanic fable was later released theatrically by International Film Distributors.

CAST: Van Johnson (Pied Piper/Truson); CLAUDE RAINS (Mayor of Hamelin); Lori Nelson (Mara); Kay Starr (Mother); Jim Backus (King's Emissary); Doodles Weaver (First Councilor); Stanley Adams (Second Councilor); Rene Korper (Paul); Oliver Blake (Leading Citizen)

Producer Hal Stanley collaborated on the book and lyrics with Irving Taylor. All the music was adapted from compositions by Grieg, including the familiar "Peer Gynt Suite." Pete King conducted.

Songs included "How Can I Tell You?"; "Prestige" (sung by Rains, Weaver, and Adams); "Fool's Gold"; "Flim Flam Floo"; "Feats of the Piper"; and "The Lament."

Rains admitted to *TV Guide*:

After the producers sent me the script, they phoned from Hollywood and asked me if I sang. Of course, I answered, "No." Once I got out there, they suggested they just play the music for me, just so I could hear it. Well, as you know, it was based on the 'Peer Gynt Suite' and the melodies are very tenacious. I found myself humming along with the piano and within a week, I was bawling the music as loudly as any of them.
(March 22-28, 1958)

(Per that same *TV Guide*, Rains was to have appeared on March 27, 1957's *Du Pont Show of the Month* as Dr. Manette in *A Tale of Two Cities*, but withdrew.)

*Variety* (December 4, 1957) thought the show

...a physically handsome color film that threatened to be endless, an alleged "adult folk story" that was not only flimsy of yarn but lacked the substance of a mature play besides.... Claude Rains was typecast as the tyrannical mayor and was properly menacing, although he sometimes delivered the verse like Hamlet's King Claudius.

# 1959

*The Diamond Necklace (Alfred Hitchcock Presents)*; February 22 on CBS. Rains plays Andrew Thurgood, longtime manager of Maynard's jewelry store. On the eve of his forced retirement, he is defrauded by a woman who makes off with an expensive necklace. It turns out that the woman is his daughter and that the two are in league together. Joan Harrison and Herschel Daugherty respectively produced and directed the teleplay. Lensed by Lionel Linsdon, the good-natured drama also featured Betsy Von Furstenberg, Alan Hewitt, Stephen Benassy,

Selmer Jackson, Peter Walker, Dorothea Lord, and Norman DuPont.

This Sarett Rudley yarn is good fun, and Rains and Betty Von Furstenberg have themselves a thesping ball enacting it. Rains goes through all the fake misery and repentance in the book with a relish....
(*Variety*, February 24, 1959)

*Judgment at Nuremberg (Playhouse 90)*; April 16 on CBS. Rains is Judge Haywood, presiding justice at the famed trial; also appearing in the highly acclaimed teleplay were Paul Lukas (Nazi Tribunal Leader), Maximilian Schell (Defense Attorney), and Melvyn Douglas (Prosecutor), with Martin Milner, Ludwig Donath, Werner Klemperer, Torbin Meyer, Wendell Holmes, and Oliver McGowan among others in the fine cast. Written by Abby Mann, *Nuremberg* was directed by George Roy Hill, who was applauded for his smooth integration of actual film clips into the tape. Per *Variety* (April 22, 1959):

...a gripping, frequently shocking, semi-documentary reminder of Nazi atrocities and the difficulty in judging those who, as members of the Nazi high tribunal, carried through the inhuman dictates of the Third Reich.... Claude Rains, as the honest, perceptive, but outraged chief justice, created a remarkably incisive study of a man who must make a monumental decision. It was a role that demanded, and got from Rains, the most subtle and significant shadings.

The trade paper also called a particularly petty spade a spade:

That the American Gas Assn. chose to meddle in a work of this stature by blanking out four or five references to Nazi "gas chambers" ranks as an act so childishly outrageous and inconsistent with the high moral tone of this drama as to be worthy of serious public protest. It is ironical that such sound-track snipping occurs in a play that criticizes the immature meddling with men's minds of an infamous era of the past.

*Once Upon a Christmas Time*; December 9 on NBC. This program was a multifaceted (singing, dancing, ice skating) paean to

**Doodles Weaver (left), Claude, and Stanley Adams in "The Table Dance" sequence from NBC-TV's** *The Pied Piper of Hamelin. Courtesy Photofest*

Claude and Betsy von Furstenberg as the Thurgoods, con artists up to no good in the "Diamond Necklace" episode of *Alfred Hitchcock Presents. Courtesy Photofest*

"A judge ... and a drunk." Claude's own caption for this still from "Incident of Judgment" on *Rawhide*. *Courtesy Jessica Rains*

Christmas, unified by a serio-comic narrative. A. J. Russell adapted an original story by Paul Gallico, and Rains (doubling both as John the Woodcutter and Santa Claus) was supported by Charles Ruggles, Margaret Hamilton, Pat Henning, Patty Duke, and others. Most television critics found the narrative framework tedious and overblown, much preferring the music (including a resounding rendition of "Christmas Spirit" by Kate Smith), the hoofing, and the blade work. Leon Leonidoff produced and Kirk Browning directed.

## 1960

*To Walk in Silence (Naked City)*; September 11 on ABC. Rains plays John Weston, a financial expert-cum-horseplayer, who's shot accidentally while visiting his bookie; concerned about the publicity, he opts not to have the bullet removed. When the series had premiered in 1958, John McIntire and James Franciscus had headlined some of those "8 million stories." The 1960 season saw the cast change to star those actors (Paul Burke as Flint, Horace McMahon as Parker,

Claude as the unbending desert officer who makes life miserable for young lieutenant Keir Dullea. Richard Conte *(background)* checks the terrain. From "The Outpost," telecast on the *DuPont Show of the Week. Courtesy Photofest*

and Harry Bellaver as Arcaro) usually associated with the program almost four decades later. Guest Star: Telly Savalas (Gabe Hody).

*Shangri-La (Hallmark Hall of Fame)*; October 24 on NBC. Rains is the High Lama in this version of James Hilton's novel, *Lost Horizon*, adapted for the small screen by actor James Valentine and Hilton himself. Critics regarded the pretentious effort as "another elaborate failure on TV." Rains ("...succeeded in giving a persuasively pro performance...." *Variety*; October 26, 1960) and John Abbott (as Chang) were almost universally excepted from the scathing reviews, which focused more on the poor quality of Harry Warren, Jerome Lawrence, and

Robert E. Lee's songs and the dismal vocalizing of them by such nonwarblers as Marisa Pavan (as Lo-Tsen) and Richard Basehart (Conway) than on the familiar plot itself. With Gene Nelson (Robert), Helen Gallagher (Lise), Alice Ghostley (Miss Brinklow), Chris Gampel (The Doctor), and Mr. Valentine (Mallinson). George Schaefer may not have wanted to own up to producing and directing the musical extravaganza after the notices came out.

## 1961

*The Horseplayer (Alfred Hitchcock Presents)*; 14 March on NBC. Besides hosting this installment (as he always did), Hitch was the director. Rains is Father Amion, whose worries about the church roof may or may not be assuaged by his new parishioner, Charley Sheridan (Ed Gardner, late of *Duffy's Tavern*), who gets the priest to combine betting at the track with supplicating on his knees. Henry Slesar crafted the teleplay from his own story, and John L. Russell was the cinematographer. With Percy Helton, Mike Ragan, William Newall, David Carle, Ada Murphy, and Kenneth McKenna.

## 1962

*The Door Without a Key (Alfred Hitchcock Presents)*; January 16 on NBC. Rains plays Leonard Eldridge, an amnesiac who befriends (and, at the urging of Police Captain Shaw [John Larch], ultimately agrees to adopt) Mickey (Billy Mumy), a young boy he has met in a police station. Irving Elman wrote the teleplay, based on a story by Norman Daniels. Joan Harrison and Herschel Daugherty did the producing and directing honors; Dale Deverman was the director of photography. With Connie Gilchrist, David Fresco, Sam Gilman, Andy Romano, Jimmy Hawkins, and Jeff Parker.

*Incident of Judgment Day (Rawhide)*; February 8 on CBS. Rains is Alexander Langford in an interesting installment of the popular Western, wherein Rowdy is brought to trial in a ghost town by some of his old Confederate Army buddies, who are angry with him for having revealed their escape plans from a Union prison camp. Featuring series regulars Clint Eastwood (Rowdy Yates), Eric Fleming (Gil Favor), Paul Brinegar (Wishbone), and Steve Raines (Quince); with guest stars John Dehner (Captain Francis Cabot) and John Kellogg (Leslie Bellamy).

*The Daniel Clay Story (Wagon Train)*; February 21 on NBC. Rains is Daniel Clay, a judge known for harsh sentences, and this doesn't win him any friends as he and his family move west with Hale and the wagon train. Featuring series regulars John McIntire (Hale), Frank McGrath (Wooster),

Terry Wilson (Hawks), and Scott Miller (Duke); with guests Fred Beir (John Cole), Maggie Pierce (Frances Cole), Peter Helm (Ethan Clay), Frances Reid (Margaret Clay), and Jack Mather (Frank Lathrop).

*The Outpost (DuPont Show of the Week)*; September 16 on NBC. Teleplay by Roger O. Hirson. Rains plays the commandant of a desert outpost who accuses a young lieutenant (Keir Dullea) of having hallucinations when the latter reports enemy troop movements. Featuring Richard Conte (the Captain), Neville Brand (the Sergeant), and Everett Sloane (the Private). Taped at NBC-TV's Brooklyn color studios, *Outpost* was the first of seven live-on-tape dramas from the Producers Company, a short-term creative partnership between (producer/director) Fiedler Cook and Franklin Schaffner. Critics felt the drama augured well for DuPont's upcoming season.

Around the time of the broadcast, the network alerted the media that *The Outpost* marked Rains' 30th-anniversary year as a performer for NBC. Tapped for reminiscences during the taping at the Brooklyn studios, Rains offered:

> Broadcasting is the real miracle of entertainment. The theatre hasn't substantially changed in 400 years. Movies have progressed from silents to talkies to wide-screen epics. But against this, broadcasting has in less than four decades grown from local radio broadcasts to network television—and now Telstar....

*Nor Practice Makes Perfect (Sam Benedict)*; September 29 on NBC. Rains is Thomas Jundelin, an attorney about to be disbarred, who is defended by Benedict (Edmond O'Brien). With regular cast members Richard Rust (Hank) and Joan Tompkins (Trudy), and guest stars Linda Watkins (Emma Horngrath), Narda Onyx (Vicki Anneau), and Frank Puglia (Ricco); written and produced by William Froug.

## 1963

**Something About Lee Wiley** *(The Bob Hope Chrysler Theatre)*; October 11 on NBC.

Piper Laurie plays Miss Wiley, a noted jazz singer from an earlier era. (*Variety* [October 16, 1963] cracked that the actress played the thrush with "true soap opera flavor," adding that "Her hair was authentic, though.") Rains(as Mr. Faird) can't save the dreary teleplay; neither can Steven Hill nor Alfred Ryder. *Variety* didn't find the lip-synching much good, either.

**The Takers** *(DuPont Show of the Week)*; October 13 on NBC. Rains is Baron Van der Zost in Jacques Gillies' drama of grand theft at the Caesar Hotel. With Walter Matthau (Harley Downing) and Shirley Knight (Charmian Scott)

### 1964

**Why Won't Anybody Listen?** *(Dr. Kildare)*; February 27 on NBC. Rains is Edward Fredericks, who accuses Drs. Gillespie (Raymond Massey) and Kildare (Richard Chamberlain) and the entire Blair hospital staff of insensitivity when he hears laughter in the corridors. Assembling a time bomb, Fredericks hides it in Gillespie's office, and then makes an appointment to speak with the doctor. Gillespie explains to the distraught man that laughter among doctors and nurses is frequently a release from their daily pressures and that no disrespect was intended. With regular cast member Steven Bell (Lowry), and guests Susan Brown (Ann Fredericks), Walter Brooke (William Fredericks), William

Demarest (Aimes), and Bert Mustin (Franklin).

**A Time To Be Silent** *(The Reporter)*; December 4 on CBS. Series regulars included Harry Guardino (as Danny Taylor, hardworking New York reporter), Gary Merrill (his no-nonsense editor, Lou Sheldon), George O'Hanlon (Artie Burns), and Remo Pisani (Ike Dawson). Rains is knee-deep in big-name guest stars in this episode, rubbing shoulders with Eddie Albert, Sidney Blackmer, Mildred Dunnock, Pippa Scott, Michael Conrad, and Lee Philips.

### 1965

**Cops and Robbers** *(The Bob Hope Chrysler Theatre)*; February 19 on NBC.

At an Italian hotel for retired gentlemen, there's an air of excitement due to the arrival of a former safe-cracker named Cesare. The elderly rascals at the hotel have decided to use Cesare's criminal knowledge to plan a bank heist—just for the fun of it.

(*TV Guide*)

Bert Lahr (Cesare), **Rains** (Valentino); with Ken Murray (Vicenzo), Billy de Wolfe (Inspector), Eduardo Cianelli (Captain Margo), Cyril Delevanti, and John Qualen in a story by Eric Bercovici and Jud Taylor. Bob Hope hosted and starred in some episodes of this hour-long anthology program, which ran from 1963 through 1967. This was Rains' last television appearance.

# Recordings

Tracking down Rains' sundry recordings has been nightmarish, as cross-checking (for verification) titles found in catalogues published over the decades is near impossible. The author welcomes information on additions to this section (or any other), so that they might be included in future editions of this book.

## 1940s

*The Christmas Tree* Mercury Childcraft Records (78 rpm) with the Hugo Peretti Orchestra and Chorus. Read by Rains

## 1948

*Bible Stories for Children* Capitol Records: DBS-92 (78 rpm). Joseph and His Coat of Many Colors; David and Goliath. Adaptations by Axel Gruenberg; Music by Nathaniel Shilkret. Read by Rains

*Bible Stories for Children* Capitol Records: DBS-94 (78 rpm). Moses in the Bulrushes; Noah and the Ark. Adaptations by Axel Gruenberg; Music by Nathaniel Shilkret. Read by Rains.

## 1949

*Valley Forge* In 1949, the Fort Orange Radio Distributing Company released a 60-minute sound cassette of the 1948 radio broadcast of Maxwell Anderson's historical drama. With Rains, June Duprez, George Coulouris, and Dean Jagger.

## 1952

*An Evening with Will Shakespeare* Theatre Masterworks; 4 sides, 2 LPs. Scenes from *Richard II*; *Macbeth*; *Twelfth Night*; *Merchant of Venice*; *Henry V.* Selected Shakespearean Songs (Richard Dyer-Bennet). Recording of gala fund-raiser for American Shakespeare Festival with Rains, Arnold Moss, Eve La Gallienne, Nina Foch, others.

## 1953

*Literary Readings in the Coolidge Auditorium* The Archive of Recorded Poetry and Literature. Contents—*Ballade in D Minor* by Johannes Brahms; *Enoch Arden* by Alfred, Lord Tennyson; *The Canterbury Tales* (excerpts) by Geoffrey Chaucer; *Journey of the Magi* by T. S. Eliot; *Richard II* (scene) and *Julius Caesar* (scene) by William Shakespeare; *Builders of America* (Washington and Lincoln) by Edward Shenton. Featuring Rains, with Jack Maxim at the piano.

This recording (LC#93-842939 R) was made during a live poetry reading (October 12) at the Coolidge Auditorium (at the Library of Congress, Washington, D.C.), sponsored by the Library of Congress and the Gertrude Clarke Whittall Poetry and Literary Fund. While not released commercially, copies may be obtained through the Library of Congress.

## 1957

*The Song of Songs and the Letters of Héloïse and Abelard* Caedmon Records (England):

TC 1085. Read by Rains, Claire Bloom, Nancy Wickwire. Directed by Howard O. Sackler.

## 1959

*Builders of America (Washington and Lincoln): A Cantata for Mixed Voices* Music by Harl McDonald, text by Edward Shenton. Columbia Masterworks: ML 2220. Read by Rains; with the Columbia Chamber Orchestra and Chorus, Harl McDonald, conductor. Also included the composer's *Children's Symphony*.

## 1960

*Remember the Alamo* Noble Records. Narrated by Rains; music by Tony Mottola.

From the album notes: "Claude Rains brings to this reading of 'Remember the Alamo' the great gifts of a true artist—a magnificent voice, an outstanding interpretive ability, stirring dramatic power, an unequalled [sic] warmth and reverence."—1970 (approximate).

*The Jeffersonian Heritage* National Association of Educational Broadcasters. Rains as Thomas Jefferson. 7 12" monaural discs.

This was the archival recording of the 1952 12-episode radio series, with the addition of a thirteenth episode (*The Democrat and the Commissar*), which was inserted into the proceedings as Chapter 2. 1989 (approximate).

*The Jeffersonian Heritage* Audio Services (Kalamazoo, MI). Rains as Thomas Jefferson. Six sound cassettes. A reissue of the original 1952 broadcasts (without *The Democrat and the Commissar*).

## 1992

*Selections by Richard Strauss* Sony Classical: SM2K-52657—SM2K-52658. *Ophelia-Lieder*, op. 67: three songs after Shakespeare; *Enoch Arden*, op. 38: a melodrama for piano after Tennyson; *Piano Sonata in B minor*, op. 5. *Five Piano Pieces*, op. 3 with Rains, speaker; Glenn Gould, piano; Elizabeth

Schwarzkopf, soprano—reissued as part of **The Glenn Gould Edition.**

Author Otto Friedrich recounts:

Gould happened to be in the office of Schuyler Chapin, then the head of Columbia Masterworks, when Chapin got a telephone call from Eugene Ormandy about Strauss's musical setting to Alfred Lord Tennyson's *Enoch Arden.*...

"Ormandy wanted to do it," Chapin recalls. "He'd just had Claude Rains as a guest doing an orchestral version in Philadelphia, and they wanted to record it.... Glenn was in my office, and he heard the conversation and he said, '*Enoch Arden*—it's really a lot of fun. I'd love to do it.' So this was the moment. Claude Rains had just finished it. Why not? ... So then I got hold of Rains, and he was a great admirer of Gould's, so all this was tickety-boo. Until we came to Mrs. Claude Rains.

"Mrs. Rains was quick to imagine slights to her husband and right away she picked up the idea that the atmosphere was not right, "Chapin wrote in his memoirs, *Musical Chairs*. To keep the two collaborators separated, each was surrounded by a series of screens. "They could look over at each other but pursue their individual parts without distraction.... " Chapin recalled. "They set to work with mutual suspicion. Gould would romp through florid piano parts while Rains rolled out the language with suppressed chokes and sobs that were so much a part of nineteenth-century declamation. Mrs. Rains was constantly furious and the conversations between the artists were peppered with her comments.... But they did finish it and at the end stiffly acknowledged that they had both done some service to Tennyson and Strauss."[55]

*Enoch Arden* was originally issued by CBS Records in 1961 and by Columbia Records in 1962. It was reissued on disc several times by those companies in the intervening decades.

Within the last 20 years or so, companies specializing in preserving classic radio have issued—on record, tape, and CD—countless broadcasts for the amusement and edification of aficionados. While these items cannot be legitimately considered as "recordings," they are, of course, of interest to the Rains completist. The following short list isn't even remotely comprehensive, and there may well be numerous other companies offering each/all of these titles:

*Here Comes Mr. Jordan:* Center for Cassette Studies

*The Littlest Rebel:* Center for Cassette Studies

*Now, Voyager:* Quality Sound

*Suspense:* Radio Memories

*The Phantom of the Opera:* Sountrak

*The Horn Blows at Midnight*: National Recording Company

# Afterthoughts

**Vincent Sherman:**

I first met Claude Rains back in 1928, when I was an understudy (making $16 a week) in both *Volpone* and *Marco Millions*, two of the Theatre Guild's offerings that year. We all noticed that Claude was very quiet—he usually kept to himself—and did his work seriously; he examined every line, word, and gesture. He was there to replace Dudley Digges in *Volpone* (as he would later in *Marco Millions*, as well), and I thought he'd never get the part right. He seemed so very slow in building his own characterization. Of course, he was a hit, giving a different performance than Digges, with more of an evil, sly-fox quality.

Over the course of the next few years, we talked a bit—always about the theater, for Claude was a very private person—and just as I became the [Actors'] Equity deputy, Claude was called to Hollywood for what would turn out to be his role in *The Invisible Man*. I said goodbye to him, never expecting to see him again. Nine months later, *I* was called to Hollywood and stopped at the Chateau d'Elysee, the posh and beautiful hotel where Claude was staying (I believe it's now the headquarters for the Church of Scientology). Claude had just bought himself a little Ford roadster with red wire wheels, so he took me out for dinner at Musso and Frank's, and then showed me the Pacific Ocean. I saw him once or twice afterwards—I was working with John Barrymore on *Counselor at Law*—before I returned to New York. In 1937 I was back in Hollywood, under contract to Warner Bothers, and my friendship with Claude was renewed.

Claude was my only choice for the part of Anne Shirley's father [in *Saturday's Children*], and I was nervous (at first) giving him direction. I mean, he was much older than I was and had been a star when I had still been playing bits at $40 a week. He was marvelous, though, and we began to see each other socially.

The original [*Mr.*] *Skeffington* script had been written by John Huston, and I didn't like it. When the twins [Julius J. and Philip G. Epstein] wrote a new script, Bette Davis and I both wanted Claude for the title role. The studio tested John Loder first, however—and others, I think—as they seemed to want the character to be more of a conventional romantic lead. It took some doing, but I convinced them that Claude was just perfect for the part and, of course, he was.

Claude was such a wonderful man to work with; he was one of the easiest actors to work with. He was very impatient with "unprofessionalism," with people who didn't study their work, or give the proper thought to their character's attitude, or relationship with others, or the point of a scene. He had inner poise and security; he'd stand still and only move when he had a reason to move.

Claude was a solid, simple guy. I poured out my heart to him once, telling him that, as badly as we wanted a child, my wife couldn't manage to get pregnant. I hadn't even finished speaking when he began pointing to himself while laughing hysterically. As a friend, he was wonderful.

247

**Sir John Gielgud:**

In a way, Claude Rains was my first inspiration in the professional theatre. I'd had one job before I met him, in a provincial tour of a West End play... and during that tour an actor of the company said to me, "I don't think you're much good; you ought to have another year's training." I then applied for a scholarship to the Royal Academy of Dramatic Arts, and they gave me a scholarship, and Rains was my principal and most inspiring teacher.

He was very attractive—rather stocky; brown hair, sort of combed over one eye; very smart double-breasted dark suits and large knotted ties; and beautiful linen—and he was very agreeable and enthusiastic, not at all bullying. I became extremely attached to him because he seemed to give me a lot of chances.... I felt he was rather interested in my work and was willing to help me all he could.

[After a while,] I was offered my first London professional engagement, which was in a play called *The Insect Play*, by the brothers Capek, which was done under Nigel Playfair's management at the *Regent Theatre*. I played a small part in the first act and I think I understudied Rains, who played three parts in different parts of the play and was wonderful in all of them. Anyhow, my scenes were rather a failure and I was very much aware that I didn't know how to act at all and he used to give me hints. In the next play that was done there after *The Insect Play*, *Robert E. Lee* by Drinkwater, he also played one of the leading parts, and I understudied him. I went on for him on two or three occasions and did rather well, and he was very sweet about it and very encouraging.

All the girls were mad about him in the class at RADA. We used to make jokes about the two who were Honorables, and we called them "the duchesses" or something. But he didn't, so far as I remember, pick me out or favor me, but he did give me some good chances and through those two jobs, I did become extremely fond of him and ex-

tremely aware of his talent. I saw him in a number of plays, including *The Doctor's Dilemma* at the *Everyman Theatre,* in which he was wonderful. I was very envious because, in the last act—the 4th act, I think it is—he comes on dying in a wheelchair, and Claude was there in this beautiful dressing gown, white hands over the edge of the chair, dying, and I thought, "This is marvelous." It was a pity he didn't play some Shakespeare, because he would have been a marvelous Tybalt, and perhaps Macbeth. Some of the great classical parts should have been in his repertoire.

He had a very twinkling eye and a very good sense of humor. He didn't take himself too seriously, which I think is such a frightfully good thing for an actor. Claude didn't give one the impression of being madly self-centered, even, but he obviously was enormously hard working and practical, and gathered strength from the people 'round him.... I know when he wasn't busy being married, he was busy perfecting his own art and he perhaps learned more about his own acting from his teaching.

Claude became an enormous success in films and was splendid in all of them; he was Bette Davis's favorite partner. I remember going to see an evening she gave in New York—at one of the theaters—in which she appeared and spoke about all her work (and very well, too). But when Claude Rains's name came up at the first frame of her recital, there was an *enormous* round of applause, which I thought would have pleased him inasmuch as he was dead by then.

I always had a great attraction for Claude's virtuosity and timing and attack and personality, and he had very strong personality. [He had] a beautiful voice and spoke beautifully. I do remember that in *Reparation*, that Tolstoy play which I saw him in, he played a sort of mad genius in one scene, and, the moment he came on, he lit up the stage very much.

One couldn't forget him.

**Kim Hunter:**

It was a great pleasure working with Claude Rains. All *my* scenes, basically, were with him. But I think the entire company of *Darkness at Noon* felt the same way. Such a dear man, as well as an extraordinarily good actor.

Claude had known [playwright] Sydney Kingsley for a number of years before we began rehearsing, but that didn't make it any easier, his working with him. They disagreed about many things, particularly in relation as to *how* Claude should deal with his character. But Claude wouldn't let these arguments affect the rest of the company. He'd always put Sydney off, insisting that they discuss the point, or points, *after* rehearsal. Which they did, so we were spared their "fights." Only once did Claude tell us a story that clued us in to their off-stage relationship… and that was *after* we'd opened in New York.

Claude had gotten the brilliant reviews he'd deserved, but Sydney still wasn't satisfied. He came to every performance and gave us *all* notes after each one, until one matinee performance, a couple of weeks after we'd opened.

Claude's story: Sydney came backstage to his dressing room after the final curtain and said, "What happened, Claude? You were quite good this afternoon?" Claude looked at him, and then said, "Well, I just went on-stage and said to myself, 'Fuck Sydney Kingsley'."

That was the last time Sydney came backstage … to talk to *any* of us.

# Endnotes

1. Gielgud, *Distinguished Company*, 142.
2. Davis, *The Lonely Life*, 229.
3. Harmetz, *Round Up the Usual Suspects*, 332.
4. Bansak, *Fearing the Dark*, 470–71.
5. *AFI Catalog, 1931–1940*, 1034.
6. Curtis, *James Whale*, 106.
7. Higham, *Hollywood Cameramen*. Although, in an interview given for this book, cinematographer Lee Garmes claimed, "I directed about 60–70 percent of the picture; we'd start at nine a.m. And some days Hecht was there, some days MacArthur; they'd start working on the picture at eleven a.m.! So they relied on me. They set the style of how they wanted the dialogue done, and I would direct the whole physical side of it."
8. For years only Vogue Picture Corporation's truncated reissue, *The Evil Mind*, was available; this public-domain offering is missing some nine minutes, and opens with Maximum and Rene's appearance in the music hall. In keeping with the trend toward cherishing potentially lucrative examples of the various niches of cinematic history, the original-release print debuted early in 1997, courtesy of the Rank Organisation.
9. Freedland, *The Warner Brothers*.
10. Michael B. Druxman, *Basil Rathbone: His Life and His Films*, 166.
11. Behlmer, *Inside Warner Bros. (1935–1951)*, 82.
12. Robertson, *The Casablanca Man*, 48.
13. Quirk, *Fasten Your Seat Belts*, 189.
14. Sherman, *Close-Ups*.
15. Robertson, *The Casablanca Man*, 53.
16. Sennett, *Great Movie Directors*, 34.
17. Beaver, *John Garfield: His Life and Films*, 25.
18. Higham, *Hollywood Cameramen*, 101.
19. Wallis, *Starmaker*, 101.
20. Rainsberger, *James Wong Howe*, 91.
21. Stine, *Mother Goddam*, 165.
22. Davis, *The Lonely Life*, 260.
23. Wallis, *Starmaker*, 105–6.
24. Brunas, *Universal Horrors*, 361.
25. Freedland, *The Warner Brothers*, 163.
26. Behlmer, *Inside Warner Bros.*, 239.
27. Sherman, *Close-Ups*, 344.
28. Dukore, *The Collected Screenplays of Bernard Shaw*, 137.
29. Dukore, 141.
30. Truffaut, *Hitchcock*, 124.
31. Harris, *The Films of Alfred Hitchcock*, 126; other sources are not as generous.
32. Higham, *Bette: The Life of Bette Davis*, 204–5.
33. Stine, *Mother Goddam*, 226.
34. Sherman, *Close-Ups*, "Claude Rains," 130.
35. Robertson, *The Casablanca Man*, 98–99.
36. Todd, *The Eighth Veil*. In Miss Todd's autobiography, something of a snoozer in its own right, *The Passionate Friends* merits scant mention except in conjunction with that fateful introduction to Lean. Todd's book refers to the film as *One Woman's Story*, which is the title of the original U.S.-release version.
37. Brownlow, *Davis Lean*, 258.
38. Milland, *Wide-Eyed in Babylon*, 246–51.
39. Letter dated February 13, 1957; collection of Susan Duic.
40. Hardy, *The Encyclopedia of Science Fiction Movies*, 211.
41. Kael, *Kiss Kiss Bang Bang*, 133.
42. Silverman, *David Lean*, 151.
43. MacQueen-Pope, *Carriages at Eleven*, 41–42.
44. Barrow, *Flora*, 18.
45. Gielgud, *Distinguished Company*, 140–41.
46. MacDermott, Everymania, 63.
47. MacDermott, 64. "...Not an inch that was not acting, from the muscles of his neck to the jut of his thigh."
48. MacDermott, 66. Rains' portrayal was lauded as "far more robust in his devil-may-careness" than earlier interpreters Sir Johnston Forbes-Robertson, or Rains mentor, Granville-Barker.

49. MacDermott, 70–71.
50. Priestley, *Particular Pleasures*, 137.
51. Gordon, *My Side*, 298.
52. Lackmann, *Same Time ... Same Station*, 60.

53. MacDonald, *Don't Touch That Dial*, 82.
54. Shulman, *How Sweet It Was*, 203.
55. Friedrich, *Glenn Gould*, 236–37.

# Bibliography

Acland, Rodney, and Elspeth Grant. *The Celluloid Mistress, or, The Custard Pie of Dr. Caligari*. Allan Wingate, London, 1954.

*AFI Catalog of Feature Films, 1931–1940*. University of California Press; Berkeley (CA), 1993.

Bansak, Edmund G. *Fearing the Dark: The Val Lewton Career*. McFarland & Company, Jefferson (NC), 1995.

Barrow, Kenneth. *Flora: An Appreciation of the Life and Work of Dame Flora Robson*. Heinemann, London, 1981.

Beaver, James N., Jr. *John Garfield: His Life and Films*. A.S. Barnes and Company, New York, 1978.

Behlmer, Rudy, ed. *Inside Warner Bros. (1935–1951)*. Viking, New York, 1985.

Billips, Connie, and Arthur Pierce. *Lux Presents Hollywood: A Show-by-Show History of the Lux Radio Theatre and the Lux Video Theatre, 1934–1957*. McFarland & Company, Jefferson (NC), 1995.

Bogart, Stephen Humphrey, with Gary Provost. *Bogart: In Search of My Father*. Plume, New York, 1996.

Booth, Michael R. *Victorian Spectacular Theatre: 1850–1910*. Routledge & Kegan Paul, Boston, 1981.

Brownlow, Kevin. *David Lean: A Biography*. Richard Cohen Books, London, 1996.

Brunas, John, Michael Brunas and Tom Weaver. *Universal Horrors*. McFarland & Company, Jefferson (NC), 1990.

Curtis, James. *James Whale*. The Scarecrow Press, Inc., Metuchen (NJ), 1982.

_____. *James Whale: A New World of Gods and Monsters*. Faber and Faber, Boston, 1998.

Davis, Bette. *The Lonely Life: An Autobiography*. G.P. Putnam's Sons, New York, 1962.

Deschner, Donald. *The Films of Cary Grant*. The Citadel Press, Secaucus (NJ), 1973.

Dick, Bernard F. *City of Dreams: The Making and Remaking of Universal Pictures*. The University Press of Kentucky, Lexington, 1997.

Dukore, Bernard F., ed. *The Collected Screenplays of Bernard Shaw*. The University of Georgia Press, Athens (GA), 1980.

Dunning, John. *Tune In Yesterday: The Ultimate Encyclopedia of Old-Time Radio: 1925–1976*. Prentice-Hall, Inc., Englewood Cliffs (NJ), 1976.

Eames, John Douglas. *The Paramount Story*. Crown Publishers, Inc., New York, 1985.

Etheridge, Anne. "Bette Davis and Claude Rains; Two Opposites That Attracted" in *American Classic Screen* (magazine), Volume 5, No. 2, pp. 9–13.

Everson, William K. *The Bad Guys: A Pictorial History of the Movie Villain*. The Citadel Press, New York, 1964.

Freedland, Michael. *The Warner Brothers*. St. Michael's Press, New York, 1983.

Friedrich, Otto. *Glenn Gould: A Life and Variations*. Lime Tree, London, 1990.

Gielgud, John. *Distinguished Company*. Doubleday & Company, Inc., Garden City (NY), 1973.

_____. *Early Stages: 1921–1936*. Taplinger Publishing Company, New York, 1976.

Gifford, Denis. *The British Film Catalogue 1895–1985*. Facts on File Publications, New York, 1986.

Gordon, Ruth. *My Side: The Autobiography of Ruth Gordon*. Harper & Row, New York, 1976

Guiles, Fred Lawrence. *Marion Davies*. McGraw-Hill Book Company, New York, 1972.

Halliwell, Leslie. *Halliwell's Harvest: A Further Choice of Entertainment Movies from the Golden Age*. Charles Scribner's Sons, New York, 1986.

Hardy, Phil. *The Encyclopedia of Science Fiction Movies*. Woodbury Press, Minneapolis (MN), 1986.

Harmetz, Aljean. *Round Up the Usual Suspects: The Making of Casablanca—Bogart, Bergman, and World War II*. Hyperion, New York, 1992.

Harris, Robert A., and Michael S. Lasky. *The Films of Alfred Hitchcock*. The Citadel Press, Secaucus (NJ), 1976.

Hartnoll, Phyllis, ed. *The Oxford Companion to the Theatre*. Oxford University Press, London, 1967.

Henreid, Paul (with Julius Fast). *Ladies Man*. St. Martin's Press, New York, 1984.

Higham, Charles. *Bette: The Life of Bette Davis*. Macmillan Publishing Company, New York, 1981.

_____. *Hollywood Cameramen: Sources of Light*. Garland Publishing, Inc., New York, 1986.

Hirschhorn, Clive. *The Warner Bros. Story*. Crown Publishers, Inc., New York, 1979.

_____. *The Universal Story*. Crown Publishers, Inc., New York, 1983.

Hobson, Harold. *Verdict at Midnight: Sixty Years of Dramatic Criticism*; Longmans Green, London, 1952.

Jerome, Stuart. *Those Crazy Wonderful Years We Ran Warner Bros*. Lyle Stuart Inc., Secaucus (NJ), 1983.

Juran, Robert A. *Old Familiar Faces: The Great Character Actors and Actresses of Hollywood's Golden Era*. Movie Memories Publishing, Sarasota (FL), 1995.

Kael, Pauline. *Kiss Kiss Bang Bang*. Little, Brown and Company, Boston, 1968.

Konigsberg, Ira. *The Complete Film Dictionary*. Penguin Reference, New York, 1997.

Lackmann, Ron. *Same Time ... Same Station: An A–Z Guide to Radio from Jack Benny to Howard Stern*. Facts On File, Inc., New York, 1996.

Lanchester, Elsa. *By Herself*. St. Martin's Press, New York, 1983.

Loder, John (and Audrey Henderson, ed.). *Hollywood Hussar*. Howard Baker, London, 1977.

Lodge, Jack, John Russell Taylor, Adrian Turner, et al. *1930–1990; Hollywood: Sixty Great Years*. Prion, London, 1992.

MacDonald, J. Fred. *Don't Touch That Dial: Radio Programming in American Life from 1920–1960*. Nelson-Hall, Chicago, 1979.

MacDermott, Norman. *Everymania: The History of the Everyman Theatre—Hampstead—1920–1926*. The Society for Theatre Research, London, 1975.

MacQueen-Pope, Walter. *Carriages at Eleven: An Account of the Theatre from 1897–1914*. Hutchinson & Co. Ltd., London, 1947.

_____. *The Curtain Rises: A Story of the Theatre*. T. Nelson, Edinburgh, 1961.

McGill, Raymond, ed. *Notable Names in the American Theatre*. James T. White & Company, Clifton (NJ), 1976.

Milland, Ray. *Wide-Eyed in Babylon: An Autobiography*. William Morrow & Company, Inc., New York, 1974.

Museum of Television and Radio. *Jack Benny: The Radio and Television Work*. HarperPerennial, New York, 1991.

Nash, Jay Robert, and Stanley Ralph Ross. *Motion Picture Guide*. Cinebooks, Inc., Chicago, 1986.

Nicoll, Allardyce. *World Drama: From Aeschylus to Anouilh*. Harcourt, Brace & World, Inc., New York. Undated.

Priestley, J.B. *Particular Pleasures: Being a Personal Record of Some Varied Arts and Many Different Artists*. Stein and Day, New York, 1975.

Quinn, Arthur Hobson. *A History of the American Drama; from the Civil War to the Present Day*. Appleton-Century-Crofts, New York, 1936.

Quirk, Lawrence J. *Fasten Your Seat Belts: The Passionate Life of Bette Davis*. W. Morrow, New York, 1991.

Rainsberger, Todd. *James Wong Howe: Cinematographer*. A.S. Barnes & Co., Inc., San Diego (CA), 1981.

Richards, Jeffrey. "In Praise of Claude Rains" in *Films and Filming* (magazine), February 1982 (pp. 12–17) and March 1982 (pp. 8-14).

Robertson, James C. *The Casablanca Man: The Cinema of Michael Curtiz*. Routledge, London, 1993.

Sennett, Ted. *Great Movie Directors*. Harry N. Abrams, Inc., New York, 1986.

Sherman, Vincent. "Claude Rains: Astute Craftsman" in *Close-Ups: The Movie Star Book*, edited by Danny Peary. Workman Publishing Company, Inc., New York, 1978.

Shulman, Arthur, and Roger Youman. *How Sweet It Was; Television: A Pictorial Commentary on Its Golden Age*. Bonanza Books, New York, 1966.

Silverman, Steven M. *David Lean*. Abrams, New York. 1989.

Simenon, Georges. *The Man Who Watched the Trains Go By*. Reynal and Hitchcock, New York, 1946.

Singer, Kurt. *The Laughton Story*. The John C. Winston Company, Philadelphia, 1954.

Spoto, Donald. *The Dark Side of Genius: The Life of Alfred Hitchcock*. Little, Brown & Company, Boston, 1983.

Stein, Jeanne. "Claude Rains" in *Films in Review* (magazine), November 1963; pp. 513–528.

Stine, Whitney. *Mother Goddam: The Story of the Career of Bette Davis*. Hawthorne Books, Inc., New York, 1974.

Summers, Harrison B., ed. *History of Broadcasting: Radio to Television*. Arno Press/The New York Times, New York, 1971.

Thomas, Tony; Rudy Behlmer and Clifford McCarty. *The Films of Errol Flynn*. The Citadel Press, Secaucus (NJ), 1969.

Todd, Ann. *The Eighth Veil*. G.P. Putnam's Sons, New York, 1981.

Truffaut, Francois (with the collaboration of Helen G. Scott). *Hitchcock*. Simon & Schuster, New York, 1966.

Vinson, James, ed. *International Dictionary of Films and Filmmakers, Volume III—Actors and Actresses*. St. James Press, Chicago, 1986.

Wallis, Hal, and Charles Higham. *Starmaker: The Autobiography of Hal Wallis*. Macmillan Publishing Co., Inc., New York, 1980.

Wearing, J. P. *The London Stage, 1900-1909: A Calendar of Plays and Players*. Scarecrow Press, Metuchen (NJ), 1981.

_____. *The London Stage, 1910-1919: A Calendar of Plays and Players*. Scarecrow Press, Metuchen (NJ), 1982.

Zettl, Herbert. *Television Production Handbook* (Second Edition). Wadsworth Publishing Company, Inc., Belmont (CA), 1961.

# Index

Page numbers in **bold type** indicate photographs.